JOHN McGRATH –
PLAYS FOR ENGLAND

This is an edition of nine of McGrath's plays both for the English 7:84 Theatre Company and outside it. It covers McGrath's work spanning four decades, from the 1960s through to the 1990s. The book has a substantial contextualising introduction and commentary on the plays by Nadine Holdsworth, one of the leading specialists in the work of John McGrath, set alongside supporting documents such as programme notes, reviews and letters.

Also published by University of Exeter Press: *Freedom's Pioneer: John McGrath's Work in Theatre, Film and Television* edited by David Bradby and Susanna Capon.

Nadine Holdsworth is Senior Lecturer in Theatre Studies at University of Warwick and editor of John McGrath's *Naked Thoughts that Roam About: Reflections on Theatre* (Nick Hern Books, 2002).

Cover image: Johnny Mulcahy as Alf Chancer, Pauline Melville as Mrs Chancer and Tim Munro as Joe in *The Life and Times of Joe of England*. Photo by Bob van Dantzig, from the 7:84 England Archive, Cambridge University Library; reproduced courtesy of the Syndics of Cambridge University Library.

Exeter Performance Studies

Exeter Performance Studies aims to publish the best new scholarship from a variety of sources, presenting established authors alongside innovative work from new scholars. The list explores critically the relationship between theatre and history, relating performance studies to broader political, social and cultural contexts. It also includes titles which offer access to previously unavailable material.

Series editors: Peter Thomson, Professor of Drama at the University of Exeter; Graham Ley, Reader in Drama and Theory at the University of Exeter; Steve Nicholson, Reader in Twentieth-Century Drama at the University of Sheffield.

Also published by University of Exeter Press

JOHN McGRATH –
PLAYS FOR ENGLAND

selected and introduced by

Nadine Holdsworth

UNIVERSITY
of
EXETER
PRESS

First published in 2005 by
University of Exeter Press
Reed Hall, Streatham Drive
Exeter, Devon EX4 4QR
UK
www.exeterpress.co.uk

British Library Cataloguing in Publication Data
A catalogue record of this book is available
from the British Library

ISBN 0 85989 718 4

Typeset in Sabon 10/12 pt by
Exe Valley Dataset Ltd, Exeter

Printed in Great Britain
by Antony Rowe Ltd, Chippenham

Contents

Illustrations

Figure 1 courtesy of Liverpool Everyman Archive, Liverpool John Moores University; Figures 2, 3, 4, 5, 6, 15 and 16 from the collection of Elizabeth MacLennan; Figures 7, 8, 9, 10, 11, 12, 13, 14 and the cover image from the 7:84 England Archive, Cambridge University Library, courtesy of the Syndics of Cambridge University Library.

Acknowledgements

I would like to thank the following for their help and support during the process of bringing this collection to publication: Ros Merkin, Richard Perkins and staff in the manuscripts department of Cambridge University Library for helping me to access sources; staff at University of Exeter Press, especially Simon Baker, Anna Henderson, Peter Thomson and Rachel Rogers, for their enthusiasm and attention to detail, and Emily Harding for her initial copy-typing of scripts.

I especially want to acknowledge the debt I owe to Elizabeth MacLennan for asking me to take on this project following John's death in January 2002 and for all her encouragement, practical advice and willingness to find and lend precious illustrative material during the process of putting the book together.

As always, Geoff Willcocks has offered invaluable laughter, care and support—thank you.

Foreword
by Michael Billington
Drama Critic of *The Guardian*

I can't pretend to write objectively about John McGrath. I first met him when I got to Oxford in 1958. I still felt like a raw schoolboy. John, having done National Service, was not only older but seemed infinitely better-read and more theatrically knowledgeable. Despite my naivety, he cast me as a priest in a terrific production of Aristophanes' *The Birds* which he staged in Christchurch gardens in the summer of 1959. And although he gave me one devastating note—'you sound as if you're speaking with one lung'—I was dazzled by his charm, skill and ability to ransack the time-honoured devices of music-hall, silent movies and popular theatre.

Over the years I came to review John's plays—including many of those in the present volume—and to engage with him in friendly debate. We had one particularly lively encounter at the Cheltenham Literary Festival. From my implacably bourgeois, soft-left standpoint, I argued for the need for writers to infiltrate big institutions like the National and the RSC and even to penetrate the bastions of commercial theatre. John, unsurprisingly, attacked what he elsewhere termed the 'close-carpeted blandness' of the national companies and argued for the importance of creating a radical, popular theatre capable of playing to new audiences. Even though we disagreed, my admiration for John was constant. He pursued his own vision, and through the creation of 7:84, in both its English and Scottish manifestations, helped to change the theatrical landscape. In that sense he belonged to the pioneering tradition of Joan Littlewood and Theatre Workshop in its peripatetic 1940s heyday.

What has got overlooked, however, is John's skill as a writer. Given his vast output, his work is inevitably uneven. But, looking back over his career, two things instantly strike me. One is his prophetic ability to write about the really big issues: the tentacular nature of the multi-nationals and the giant corporations, the power of the mass-media to shape our lives and create a permanent mental musak, the resilience of individuals in confronting the power of state capitalism. All these are ideas which still animate political theatre. But, as a writer, John also showed how popular forms could be adapted to socialist causes. In *A Good Night Out* he writes about the importance of comedy, music, emotion and directness in addressing working-class audiences; and it is this that differentiates him from the bulk of his contemporaries.

Political theatre in Britain is shaped by many things: public events, theatrical economics, social context. But it is also determined by the temperament and background of the individual writer. John, saturated in popular culture from panto and stand-up to the ceilidh and the rock concert, believed that drama should have a similar communicable *élan*. That is why his form of theatre is totally different from that of David Edgar, who believes in the power of rigorous dialectical debate, or David Hare, who has injected political argument into existing bourgeois forms such as the hard-boiled thriller (*Knuckle*) or the Chekhovian family-play (*Amy's View*). It would be fruitless to argue about who is right or wrong. The point is that John, with his detestation of institutions and faith in working-class audiences, wrote in the only way he knew how.

Along with a belief in popular forms, John's work is also characterised by a fascination with women. Where many of his radical colleagues—Trevor Griffiths and David Edgar most especially—deal almost exclusively with male protagonists, John constantly creates female characters to express the contradictions of capitalist society or to act as agents of change. In an early work like *Angel of the Morning*, the eponymous heroine is a young, anarchic political activist who invades the home of a computer technician. In *Plugged in to History* the character of Kay, the schizophrenic inhabitant of a high-rise block, speaks in newspaper headlines as if her personality has been appropriated by the mass media: a brilliant anticipation of the 24-hour news era. And, even though *Trees in the Wind* shows a male working-class figure invading a middle-class female world, it is the three women who most powerfully embody radical hopes and dreams.

The latest work included in this volume, *Watching for Dolphins*, written in 1991, takes John's preoccupation with women to its logical conclusion. It is a one-woman play, initially performed by John's wife and creative partner, Elizabeth MacLennan. And the play deals with the experiences of a 52-year-old socialist about to open a B&B in North

Wales. As she looks back over a life spent selling the Daily Worker to Cowley factory-hands, joining the International Socialists and teaching Marx, Engels and the Koran to primary-school students, she wonders whether it was all worth it and whether her political views were the projection of a psychic need. But, at the point of disillusion, she takes comfort from the fact that throughout Eastern Europe 'people have stood up together and won'.

This was certainly not John's last word for the theatre. His final play, *HyperLynx*, was seen in Edinburgh and London in 2002 and was performed by his wife and directed by his daughter, Kate. It was John's 9/11 play and showed a senior MI5 operative confronting the realities of that hideous day and vowing to do her best to stop either Islamic fundamentalists or global corporations turning the whole world into a battleground between the clever rich and the desperate poor. She was under no illusions about her power. But, as she said, 'the worst crime of all is not seeing, not trying to understand, of blinding yourself with your own lies'.

That might well stand as John McGrath's final testament. His whole career as a dramatist was bent on making audiences see and understand and on acknowledging the need for radical change while recognising the idealist's capacity for self-delusion. He was a good man writing in harsh times; and the plays in this volume are proof of his ability to, in the words of Sir Philip Sidney, 'instruct through delight'.

Introduction
by Nadine Holdwsorth

Theatre is by its nature a political forum, or a politicising medium, rather than a place to experience a rarefied artistic sensibility in an aesthetic void. Theatre launches even the most private thought into a public world, and gives it social, historical meaning and context as it passes through the eyes and minds of the audience. It is a place of recognition, of evaluation, of judgement. It shows the interaction of human beings and social forces. How could it remove itself from the other public acts of recognition, evaluation and judgement known as politics? How could it ignore the study of past interaction of human beings and social forces known as history? Of course, try as it may, it cannot.[1]

This quotation from John McGrath's *A Good Night Out* (1981) is vital to an understanding of the plays contained in this collection. Written by McGrath between 1960 and 1992, each play illustrates McGrath's responsiveness to changing political circumstances. In differing ways, each play also provides evidence of McGrath's experiments with theatrical form, language, music and multiple performance strategies. When approaching these plays it is crucial to bear in mind McGrath's assessment of 'theatre as an event, with a complex language involving many aspects of that event beyond the verbal construct as recorded on the page'.[2] These plays cannot be divorced from their immediate socio-political context, the companies they were created for, the venues they played in, the marketing that promoted them, the programmes that framed them and, above all, the audiences they reached in community centres, work-based clubs, colleges and arts centres across England, Wales, Scotland and Ireland. This introduction aims to bring some of that context alive by including references to other voices—company documents, letters and reviews—in order to illuminate the production histories of plays that not only say something about the time they were written, but also remain topical and provocative at the beginning of the twenty-first century.

John McGrath's early career: 1958–70

McGrath had already been writing stories and poems whilst studying English Literature at Oxford, when Collette King approached him to write a play. The result, *A Man Has Two Fathers,* was 'constructed like a poem with about five or six levels of meaning running through it. It was really, on different levels, about the struggle between America and Russia, between two kinds of imperialism'.[3] In contrast to John Russell Taylor's assessment of the play as 'an awkward and immature allegory',[4] Kenneth Tynan pronounced it 'an undergraduate play of extraordinary quality'.[5] This was an accolade that caught the attention of George Devine, who promptly invited McGrath to work on a project at the Royal Court with the director, Anthony Page. McGrath recalled:

> Anthony Page had been working in America with a guy called Sanford Meisner, and Meisner had a specific rehearsal technique which was to do with working on an astringently truthful form of improvised relationship with actors. Which was to be used outside the text completely. But in order to create the right feel, to give the actor the right feel for a relationship within a text. Now, what they wanted was not to improvise a play, but for me to get to know the actors and to write a text which they could use as a basis for working in this way.[6]

With this brief, McGrath wrote *The Tent* and *Tell Me, Tell Me.* Whereas *The Tent* is primarily naturalistic, *Tell Me, Tell Me* is stylised and suggests the influence of early Eugene Ionesco as Mrs A and Mrs B debate the relative merits of various foodstuffs in curt dialogue that emphasises shifting rhythms, repetitions and linguistic play. McGrath continued to experiment in this mode with two short plays, *Take It* and *They've Got Out,* which toured with Michael Horowitz's *Live New Departures* initiative during 1961 and 1962. In tune with the growing influence of the American Beat movement, Horowitz launched *Live New Departures* to present jazz and poetry concerts. As Robert Hewison notes, '. . . these anarchic but essentially celebratory affairs were important forerunners of the conferences, teach-ins and demonstrations of the later sixties'.[7] Alongside jazz and poetry, Horowitz intermittently programmed short theatre pieces by European innovators such as Samuel Beckett and Ionesco. *They've Got Out* presents the communication failure between Mr and Mrs A as they contradict, refute and antagonise each other. A study in sexual frustration, *Take It* has a playful, circular structure in which a couple refuse to leave each other for the night and their minimal language descends into non-verbal communication as they cry, laugh, click their tongues and hoot like owls.

After returning to Oxford in autumn 1958, McGrath directed productions of James Joyce's *Ulysses*, when he first cast his future partner and creative collaborator, Elizabeth MacLennan, and Aristophanes' *The Birds*. The latter was performed in modern dress in a garden in Christ Church College with design by Sean Kenny and music by Dudley Moore. The cast was equally impressive: Jonathan Cecil played Euripides, Giles Havergal was Epops, Michael Billington played a priest, Ken Loach was the Inspector, David Rudkin was Second Messenger and Peter Snow, the future broadcaster, played the Triballian God.[8] McGrath followed this show by writing *Why the Chicken?*, a play about a middle-class social worker's relationship with a group of working-class teenagers who hang around a derelict barn on the edge of a new town.

> In spite of the plot's dependence on an offstage climbing incident (in which she causes the death of a boy who has tried to rape her), the action effectively penetrates the girl's almost loving involvement with a class that must ultimately reject her, however bravely she commits herself, however close she comes to winning the love of the ringleader.[9]

Devine encouraged McGrath to develop the script and Michael Codron and Lionel Bart, who were keen to promote new writers in the West End, picked it up. At this point, McGrath became disillusioned with theatre as he encountered the creative and ideological compromises required for West End success, a realisation that prompted his retreat from the theatre and move into film and television.

McGrath returned to theatre with *Events While Guarding the Bofors Gun*, which Ronald Eyre directed at Hampstead Theatre in 1966. Centring on seven men, a combination of regular soldiers and those doing their National Service, stationed in Germany during a bitterly cold winter in 1954, the play explores their various motivations, ambitions and the consequences of their actions and inactions during one night in February. A tense atmosphere prevails, due not only to the destabilising presence of Gunner O'Rourke, but also to the freezing, claustrophobic conditions as the men guard obsolete weapons. 'Superficially it invites comparison with *Chips with Everything*, but McGrath has more to say than Wesker about human beings and has produced a finished, properly constructed piece of work instead of an open-ended tract.'[10] Eighteen-year-old Lance-Bombardier Evans is in charge of the men and hopes for an uneventful night for his first stint as Guard Commander. Nervous and inexperienced, working-class Evans makes an unconvincing leader, but hopes to return to England the following day to face Officer selection. McGrath linked Evan's ambition with homesickness, 'an overwhelming, over-powering emotion' that compels him to reject his working-class roots in order to manage 'his disorientation, his feeling of exile'.[11] McGrath reveals Evan's simultaneous desire for and ambivalence towards home during a conversation with Flynn:

> I dream all day about home, but the laugh is, when I'm there I can't stand the place. I don't know what I'm doing here, nor why, nor who for, not even where I am on the map all that accurately. All I know is that I have to go home. I will even offer myself as a jumped-up eighteen-year-old joke of a Second Lieutenant for just one chance to get home.[12]

For McGrath who, during National Service, 'each night crossed off another day on the calendar nailed to [his] tent post (beneath a bat's nest) . . . "120 days till Oxford, 119 days till Oxford"',[13] this feeling of exile must have been all too familiar. Having been selected for Oxford, the army pigeonholed McGrath as officer material, a route he chose because 'At that time my main objective was to get out of Germany'.[14] In an illuminating chapter on *Bofors Gun*, Peter Thomson highlights the similarities between McGrath and Evans, suggesting that he 'has set his eighteen-year-old dead self a dilemma, more extreme than, but not different from, dilemmas faced by the living self a dozen years earlier'.[15] During National Service, McGrath encountered class privilege and later acknowledged that 'The real conflict in *Bofors Gun* was between the way I felt then, in 1966, and the way I felt when I was in Germany, in the army in 1953 or 1954.'[16] Hence, *Bofors Gun* provides a telling study of one man's struggle to negotiate loyalty to his roots with his ambition to experience another reality, whether that be the Officers' mess or Oxbridge, and how his failure to make a decision either way proves his undoing.

Evans experiences resentment from the men who all realise his inade-quacies. O'Rourke, a bitter, heavy drinker with a volatile temper and propensity for self-destruction, particularly undermines Evans. O'Rourke represents 'the other, the root-consciousness of the oppressed, who are driven to futile, alienated work, and who react quite understandably, with a kind of passionate abandon, abandonment of purpose, and fall back on to immediate, slightly irrational and self-destructive emotions'.[17] After viciously exposing and mocking Evans' limitations and contradictions, O'Rourke tests Evans' leadership by abandoning his duties to get drunk. By failing to put O'Rourke on a charge, Evans confirms his weakness in the eyes of the men and ends up ruining his chances to return home after

O'Rourke kills himself with a bayonet. After seeing *Bofors Gun*, McGrath's agent Peggy Ramsay sent him a novel, *The Danish Gambit* by William Butler. Attracted by the way Butler's novel continued debates in *Bofors Gun*, McGrath completed an adaptation for the stage, renamed *Bakke's Night of Fame*. Through interactions between Bakke, a murderer waiting execution on death row and a priest, warders and his executioner, the play explores the distinction between murder and capital punishment and notions of the self, truth and reality.

Elizabeth MacLennan refers to McGrath's next play *Random Happenings in the Hebrides* (1970) as 'a bridge between the kind of writing in *The Bofors Gun* and the later McGrath 7:84 plays'.[18] Directed by Richard Eyre for the Edinburgh Lyceum, *Random Happenings* contains the traces of its long gestation period and the socio-political environment of the late 1960s. A new generation was intent on challenging the world bequeathed to them by their elders—Vietnam, the Apartheid regime, Prague Spring, the class system, racial and gender inequality—and a global movement against capitalism; social injustice and American imperialism emerged. Like many Left-leaning artists of his generation, this climate of revolt energised McGrath. Shortly after beginning *Random Happenings*, he went to Paris in May 1968 'as a representative of British writers and artists to express solidarity with the occupants of the Ecole des Beaux-Arts. Together with his friend Jean-Jacques Lebel, McGrath became involved in a revolutionary arts committee constituted by anarchists, Trotskyists, and Maoists.'[19] Completed late in 1969, *Random Happenings* is revealing about McGrath's transition to a revolutionary socialist stance during this period.

Rather than the condensed time frame of plays such as *Bofors Gun* and *Bakke's Night of Fame*, *Random Happenings* presents events between 1964 and 1970, allowing McGrath to explore changing political circumstances. The play is infused with the revolutionary hopes of 1968 and the crushing disappointment of Harold Wilson's failure to carry through a radical socialist agenda whilst in government. Despite progressive bills on social issues such as homosexuality, divorce, abortion and theatre censorship, 'on the economic and industrial front Labour was forced to take decisions which were deeply unpopular with the unions, the militant left, and, increasingly, the general public'.[20] As Wilson's capitulation to international capitalism and American foreign policy became more and more evident, those hoping for radical social change became increasingly disillusioned with political processes and angry at the government failures that enabled the Conservatives to sweep to power in 1970.

Thematically, complex personal relationships remain paramount in *Random Happenings*: John James and Catriona's incestuous relationship, the strained relations between McPhee and John James and the

uneasy union between Jimmy and Catriona. The audience become
intimately acquainted with McPhee's descent into alcoholism, Jimmy's
promiscuity and the psychological damage inflicted on Catriona and
John James by their relationship. However, interwoven with these strands,
McGrath develops a narrative centred on Jimmy and his changing
political consciousness. A rootless character, Jimmy romanticises the
island and its people as he pursues his personal ambitions elsewhere.
Continually drawn back to the island, he struggles with the knowledge
that '*this* is where socialism has to start, here, where the people live and
work'.[21] Through the mid-1960s, Jimmy attempts to unionise the
fishermen, to encourage the political ambitions of McPhee and to
represent the island himself as a local MP. By 1968, Jimmy's personal
and political compromises have left him riddled with guilt. He is in a
loveless, opportunistic marriage and he allows organised party politics to
defuse his socialist ideals. As the play closes, a Tory government has
been re-elected, the unions are facing unprecedented pressures and
Fergusons are rationalising the fishing fleet. A battle commences for the
heart and the head of Jimmy. His wife Rachel insists he can only hope to
acquiesce to the power of international capital and try to reach the most
fruitful compromise with it. Alternatively, Catriona romantically appeals
to his radical political instinct and his desire to nurture the island
environment. Jimmy's decision to abandon the large political stage to
pursue his heart and community-based politics echoed the journey
McGrath was taking from mainstream theatre to a politicised theatre
that placed communication with local and working-class communities at
the top of its agenda.

The Liverpool Everyman: 1971–72

In autumn 1969, McGrath returned to his hometown Birkenhead and
during his visit attended a production of the musical documentary *The
Braddock's Time* by Stephen Fagan at the Liverpool Everyman. Directed
by the newly appointed Alan Dossor, the play told the story of the local
Labour MP, Bessie Braddock. McGrath appreciated the localism of the
material and Dossor's ambitious project to develop a regional theatre
practice that took notice of the surrounding working-class community, its
cultural traditions and entertainment values. Inspired by Dossor's
approach, McGrath started writing material that drew on his knowledge
of the local community. *Unruly Elements,* a series of five short pieces
entitled *My First Interview, They're Knocking Down the Pie Shop, Angel
of the Morning, Out of Sight* and *Plugged in to History*, received its first
performance at the Everyman in March 1971. The stage directions

depict the increasing encroachment of commerce and consumption that provides a central theme throughout the plays. Each piece involves emotionally and politically charged conversations between characters with radically different experiences, attitudes or responses to gender relations, sexual politics, class-based activism and capitalism. During these exchanges, McGrath became very interested in Beckett's use of language, particularly in novels such as *Molloy*, and this influence is discernible in McGrath's highly inventive and penetrating use of language that shifts between the naturalistic, poetic, lyrical, visceral and oblique. Moreover, McGrath frames each piece with semi-comprehensible prologues delivered by 'myopic little men in the Liverpool street, mouthing opinion research clichés in that curious new Scouse talk which merges Irish, Polish, West Indian and Pakistani out of Joyce and Lennon'.[22] Invited in the stage directions to address performers and audience, these figures provide aggressive attacks on 'da stayta da cuntry' and advocate violent repression of 'da irking clas', 'unksters' and 'whyves of da big men'. Deeply reactionary, these narrators set an antagonistic tone for the various episodes that unfold, goading the audience to find their own way through material where solutions and authorial signposts are hard to find.

> Da pig-men make-a da piles a doe. Dey buyum up da man-shuns, dey buyum da carpets, dey buyum da boos, dey buyum da fur-knickers, dey buyum da wooms, ta me-and-her about in: Wha' more good a gurl arsefor? An do dey play ball? Do dey luv up da fella, keep da home cuddly and sty for da pig-man? Ook up a din-dins, scoff for da trough, huggim and fuggim an drop a few piglets? Doe doe doe. Ear me doe. Wha' do dey do? Dey go sky-so-free-nik. I ony go one ques-chun: (*Shouts*) Whadafugginells-damarrawidum?[23]

This verbal assault frames *Plugged in to History* and relates to Kay, a disturbed young middle-aged, middle-class mum who is married to a Managing Director. In Kay, McGrath created one of his most interesting and complicated female characters. Owing to her gender, Kay has been told to hide her fascination with abuse and sado-masochistic practices: 'sit on it, sit on it, don't open your box, keep the lid on it, suffocate it—be what we want you to be, little girls aren't supposed to do *that*'.[24] She consciously retreats into insanity and manically communicates through the language of newspaper headlines. Tales of planes crashing, collapsed mines, environmental damage, terrorism, human rights abuses and struggles against American imperialism and white supremacists, engulf her conscious thought and spill from her mouth in a torrent of mediatised jargon.

Figure 1   Elizabeth MacLennan as Kay and Robert Hamilton as Derek in
Plugged in to History.
(*Photo:* Julian Sheppard)

Repeated metaphors of occupation, defilement and obliteration suggest the trauma Kay experiences and her fractured, out-of-control language reveals an inability to contain and make sense of this trauma. Themes of abuse, gender relations and a refusal to conform to societal roles continue when Derek joins Kay. Derek, representing the hippy generation, has dropped out from his destiny as a minor cog in the capitalist economy. Instead, he does 'one week out of three, or two out of six, something like that, reasonable, enough to keep me alive—I mean, I'm not all that *interested,* do you see what I mean, in work *as such'.*[25] A romantic dreamer, he thinks people should be free to travel, read and philosophise. Despite his progressive thinking, the revelation that he physically assaulted his girlfriend and is relentlessly pursuing her, corresponds with Kay's experience of female annihilation, 'to love honour and obey you till death, death of something, death of you, death of your life, death of your spirit, do you part'.[26] When Derek leaves, the final image is of Kay. A lasting, unsettling image of a woman who is at once profoundly connected to the abusive histories she reads about and increasingly alienated from her own reality.

Conflict between generations and political activism are at the heart of *Angel of the Morning* and *They're Knocking Down the Pie Shop*. In *They're Knocking Down the Pie Shop*, a family debates the closure of their local pie shop and its replacement by an American inter-continental hotel: an event Mr Walden, an old school socialist, explains as the all-pervasive influence of American-dominated monopoly capitalism. A weary and disillusioned ex-advocate of political activism, Mr Walden now predicts an inevitable, working class defeat. In contrast, his idealist daughter, Jenny, rejects abstract intellectualising in favour of direct action, whilst satirising the fractured state of Left politics, 'the Maoists seemed to go all out for burning the hotel down, the Anarchists wanted to burn the pie-shop down, and the Spartacus League wanted to burn them both down'.[27] A beneficiary of the hopes instilled by the events of 1968, Jenny seizes the opportunity to galvanise the local community and urges her father not to turn his back on thirty years of activism. Yet, Mr Walden knows that for every political activist like Jenny, there is an increasing number of young people like his son Neil, who accept the logic of aggressive entrepreneurial capitalism and the value of individual material gain: a pessimistic viewpoint consolidated at the end of the play when Mrs Walden enters brandishing the last of Pelissier's pork pies and hopes for a job in the new hotel.

In *Angel of the Morning*, Mr Lodwick, a repressed suburbanite, waits up for his rebellious teenage daughter Barby. During this vigil, his daughter's friend, Tralee Clausewitz, interrupts and distracts him whilst members of their 'urban guerrilla' group tie up his wife and rob him of his savings. Through their intimate and sexually charged conversation, McGrath reveals Lodwick's inability to cope with his daughter's blatant flouting of his parental and patriarcal authority or with her enthusiastic participation in the sexual revolution. However, McGrath lends this simple inter-generational conflict a much darker edge by the contradictions in Lodwick's position. Not only does he fantasise about Tralee, he also displays incestuous, masochistic undertones when imagining restraining his daughter:

I'll pin you down on that bed like an Amazonian Purple Moth, pinned to a spread of black velvet. I'll tie you, tie you down my beauty, so you won't be able to move a finger to resist me, and *then* we'll see where your crane-drivers are, what good your bloody giant navvies are going to do you . . . Hah! You won't move for a week when I've finished with you.[28]

Whilst Lodwick denounces sexual liberation, he has been completely seduced by management speak that endorses aggressive market forces to liberate the power of the consumer. By utilising technological advances to create new and more efficient ways to encourage and facilitate consumption, Lodwick aims to dispense with shops and shop assistants by producing 'a bloody great hall of selling-machines, effortlessly replenished morning, noon and night, the flow of supply and demand electronically regulated, computerised forecasts, totally flexible programming, consumer-regulated markets':[29] a vision he thinks will be welcomed by a new go-getting generation who know what they want and how to get it. The appeal of this motivated and energised generation, epitomised by Tralee, temporarily leads Lodwick to reassess his stifling existence and complacent acceptance of an unhappy and sexually unfulfilling relationship. Following the revelation of Barby's betrayal and the ensuing robbery, Lodwick manically weighs up his options and fantasises about escaping to the hot sun of Australia. Despite impassioned rhetoric, he does nothing and relinquishes responsibility to others; just as, faced with the possibility of change, he responds with fear and apathy.

No disrespect is intended to John McGrath in describing this sharp-witted set of short plays as British to the core.

There are five pieces, each one concentrating on characters who are reaching a turning point in life. Excepting the final sketch (of which more later) the figures are pretty familiar: and the general purpose is to show such stock emblems of traditional Britain colliding with members of the alternative society.

In one, a frustrated husband awaiting his daughter's late-night return is visited instead by a Liverpool girl guerrilla who tries to liberate him while her comrades are looting his life's savings. Another Liverpool piece shows an old Socialist acting as umpire between his Maoist daughter and a son savagely pledged to the profit motive, and finally confessing his own political bankruptcy. Attached to an outside event (the demolition of a pie shop to make way for a luxury hotel) this is the best made and most resonant piece of the group.

Interestingly, it is also the only one in which a character does change his position. Otherwise Mr. McGrath's worms fail to turn. As the moment of decision approaches they flunk it and revert to their old ways. And theatrically this produces the depressing effect of a series of derailed climaxes.

It is here that nationality comes in. Whether he is writing about a former account executive turned aging hippy or a suburban prisoner dreaming of escape to Australia. Mr McGrath repeatedly falls into the posture of British impotence. He tries to plug into the violent forces of the modern world, but in the end the waters of insular conformity close over his head. Evidently he is all too aware of the blockage, and the plays amount to a repeated attempt to break it.

The passages of strenuous over-writing in which the plays abound show him trying to use sheer verbal style to penetrate alien areas of experience.

He makes a partial escape at the end in a park bench encounter between two strangers: a working-class boy who has beaten up his girl, and a fur-coated wife who wants to be beaten. The woman is schizophrenically possessed by newsflashes of world disasters with which she punctuates the dialogue: the point being that only by masochism can she establish any connection between her own life and the outer world: a new and persuasive gloss on *le vice anglais*.

Alan Dossor's production is played on a snappy pop art set by a quick change company led by Gavin Richards and Gillian Hanna who couple their roles in the sketches with moral backlash interludes in Joycean newspeak.

Irving Wardle[30]

Doreen Tanner praised these 'distinct, sharply-packaged small plays', arguing that 'They have a real power and originality that continually gets below the surface of things to produce their alarms and ironies',[31] and Jonathan Hammond declared 'the plays were remarkable for the ways in which they integrated political themes into subtle, complex studies of the people in the situations'.[32] Despite critical acclaim, Dossor's commitment to new work was a risky strategy and, by May 1971, he conceded that audiences were reaching a dangerously low level. The same month Dossor produced the outcome of his invitation to six writers, McGrath, Fagan, John Arden, John Hale, Charles Wood and Roy Minton, to provide a contemporary response to Brecht's *The Private Life of the Master Race*. Taking the primary theme of the unions' fight to secure decent pays rises and the government's fight to stabilise an economy racked with high inflation, McGrath wrote *Hover through the Fog*. McGrath's biting comedy centres on Mrs Reece, a woman appointed by the government as an independent, academic expert on an arbitration panel on pay negotiations. Mrs Reece's failure to establish her own opinion results in much of the comedy as she confidently spouts the opinions of the last person she encountered. The evening was given a mixed reception, but McGrath found it a useful experiment as he 'could see what was working with the audience and guess why'.[33] Increasingly, he was convinced that a concentration on popular forms of entertainment and, in particular, a strong musical component was vital to secure large working-class audiences at the Everyman, and his next piece, *Soft or a Girl?*, proved his point.

I want to tell you about SOFT OR A GIRL. Why? Because SOFT OR A GIRL is about our city now. It's funny, sharp, extravagant, satirical, compassionate. The play is by John McGrath—you'll know him for his T.V. work on 'Z Cars' and plays which include 'Bofors Gun' and 'Unruly Elements'. SOFT OR A GIRL is a rock-comedy with music written and played by PETTICOAT AND VINE the famous local folk and rock band. SOFT OR A GIRL provides astounding revelations of SEX ON THE WIRRAL and will expose the secret life of the arty set in Speke.

Why not bring your local councillor? The chances are he thinks you're SOFT OR A GIRL anyway. Introduce him to the delights of catching a bus in Liverpool, and then walk to the EVERYMAN THEATRE in Hope Street . . . I can promise you the best night out you've had at the theatre in a long time. We'll take you from the Liverpool Blitz of 1941 straight into the astounding scenes of 1971, and the 1st LIVE appearance of the Liverpool Echo. If you join us for SOFT OR A GIRL I can promise you'll not regret it. [34]

Soft or a Girl?, a rock musical, opened at the Everyman on 24 November 1971. In the play, two home guard officers from diametrically opposed backgrounds and political camps, Mr Hurley and Mr Martin, reach a degree of wartime comradeship as firewatchers stationed at the top of St George's Tower during the Blitz. After sharing their hopes and dreams for the future, McGrath transports his characters to 1971 to watch and comment on the activities of their grown-up children. Mick, Mr Hurley's son, is involved with Ella, Mr Martin's daughter, and Jenny, a firebrand involved in feminist and class-based politics. As Mick and Ella unsuccessfully attempt to establish their relationship and Mr Hurley and Mr Martin are reunited, Jenny shatters the polite veneer and reminds everybody that there is a class war. She tells Mr Hurley: 'You are owned by them . . . so how can you have them indoors, and drink with them and make polite small talk? No wonder nothing changes.'[35] The thematic territory is familiar: inter-generational conflict, sexual politics and changing conceptions of working-class identification and activism, but the 'scouse-salty explosion of wildly mixed styles, held together by the Merseyside theme'[36] marked a radical shift in McGrath's practice. The combination of high comedy, coruscating political commentary, direct address, numerous local references, Flanagan and

Allen inspired music-hall numbers and music by local group Petticoat and Vine, led Tanner to record that 'the Everyman has never been quite the same since. Even on the first night there was a perceptible charge of excitement linking audience to actors in an unbroken electrical circuit of genuine theatrical magic. This was the thrill of communication, the quality only live theatre can provide. Merseyside recognised it, and rushed to enjoy it.'[37] Audiences 'doubled to a miraculous 93 percent average', prompting Dossor to bring the show back for a second three-week run in January 1972, by the end of which 'it had been seen by more than 11,000 people'.[38]

Throughout 1972, McGrath built on the localism of *Soft or a Girl?* in adaptations of Brecht's *The Caucasian Chalk Circle* and Peter Terson's *Prisoners of the War* for the Everyman. His next full-length original play for the Everyman, *Fish in the Sea*, appeared in December 1972 with Alison Steadman, Jonathan Pryce and Anthony Sher in the cast. 'The title is taken from Mao's analogy of the Party or Front as the head and body of the fish, and the population as the water through which it moves.'[39] In his preface to the play McGrath discusses how this term had been appropriated by Brigadier Frank Kitson, the British Army's counter-insurgency expert, in his book *Low-Intensity Operations: Subversions, Insurgency and Peace-Keeping* (1971). McGrath quotes Kitson's claim that:

> If the fish has got to be destroyed, it can be attacked directly by rod or net . . . But if rod and net cannot succeed by themselves, it may be necessary to do something with the water which will force the fish into a position where it can be caught. Conceivably it might be necessary to kill the fish by polluting the water . . . The first aim of those involved in counter-subversion is to gain control of the people, because in most cases this is a necessary prelude to destroying enemy's forces—and in any case it is the ultimate reason for doing so.[40]

In *Fish in the Sea*, McGrath provides a microcosm of society through the Maconochie family and addresses the various factors contributing to the pollution of the water and hence the failure of revolutionary forces to mobilise the general population. Despite the underlying seriousness of the material, critics were impressed, once again, by the combination of political commentary, emotive drama and romantic comedy laced together with music from Petticoat and Vine. Stanley Reynolds, in a typical review, found the play 'largely very enjoyable, cracking with McGrath's usual wit and way with funny lines, and positively steaming with up to the minute social and economic messages'.[41] The messages revolve around familiar McGrath territory: the need for collective opposition to class-based oppression, the impact of industrial militancy, the role of women in society and the consequences of disruptive elements for individuals and the family unit. As McGrath illuminates:

> Into the complicated texture of the family life of the Maconochies, two powerful forces erupt. One is the occupation of the factory where Mr Maconochie earns his living: a determined, patient, organised working-class action against the ruthless rationalisation of a multi-national corporation. The other is the arrival of Andy, a Glaswegian wild man—anarchist, individualist, articulate—who recognises in Mary, one of the daughters, a kindred spirit.[42]

Worker occupations occurred across Britain during the 'politics of confrontation' era of Edward Heath's Conservative government: a mode of political action encouraged by the success of the Upper Clyde Ship-builders who responded to the Government's decision to close the shipyards in 1971 with a work-in that resulted in a change of management and increased Labour Movement support. McGrath's familiarity with worker occupations came from covering several as a journalist for the socialist magazine 7-Days, 'notably at Mold in Flintshire and Fisher-Bendix in Kirby. 7:84 had also taken a show to an occupied engineering factory in Glasgow. It was this Glasgow occupation which most related to the occupation in the play, re-set fictionally in Liverpool'.[43] With these real-life events as his immediate backdrop, McGrath creates a political narrative around the decision by Mr Maconochie, and his son-in-law Willy, to participate in strike action and an occupation for better pay and conditions at Robertson's factory. By presenting the Maconochie family living, working and facing the consequences of industrial action together, McGrath explores the different practical, familial and political factors that surface and the potential reasons for failure. McGrath implicates the desire for self rather than collective advancement, the lure of commodity culture, diversions into other political activity and the loss of determination. In terms of explicit political commentary, McGrath also criticises the increas-ing trend for non-confrontational conflict management and conciliation by trade unions and the Labour Party to settle disputes without addressing the core problem of exploitative working practices. The end of the play renders the settlement reached between union leaders and bosses useless because it coincides with a government-ordered wage freeze. In addition, because the unions fail to negotiate long-term workers' rights, Mr Maconochie and Willy face redundancy and operations are set to move to Germany, a move that indicates the increasing threat posed to workers by multi-national corporations and a globalisation of the market place.

Alongside the political narrative, McGrath presents a bustling drama of everyday family life that involves the complex inter-relationship of cramped living conditions, sibling rivalry, gender divisions, marriage plans, unrequited love, fights, reconciliation and psychological difficulties. Setting out his multi-faceted aims in the preface to the published edition, McGrath claims:

> The main elements I wanted to set in some form of dialectical motion were—the need for militant organisation by the working class; the anarchistic, anti-organisational violence of the frustrated working-class individual in search of self-fulfilment here and now; the backwardness of some elements of working-class living: attitudes to women, to socialist theory, to sexual oppression, poetry, myth, etc.; the connections between this backwardness and Christianity; the shallow optimism of the demagogic left, self-appointed leaders of the working class; and the intimate realities of growing up and living in a working-class home on Merseyside.[44]

Mr Maconochie is an old-style socialist who rails against the police and media as mechanisms of the state, whereas Mrs Maconochie gets on with domestic chores and nurtures her family with freshly ironed clothes and regular meals. Through their four children, McGrath explores the concerns and attitudes of the next generation. Derek provides ample evidence for his father's loss of faith in an apathetic, commodity-seduced culture. Dismissing his father's working-class identification, Derek opposes trade unionism and epitomises the rejection of his father's belief systems by joining the police cadets and compliantly accepting his deferential worker role. Generational shifts and the increasing presence of feminist modes of thinking are also evident through the Maconochies' three daughters, who recoil from their mother's domestic drudgery as they search for independence and varying degrees of sexual liberation. Whilst Fiona focuses on her schoolwork and playing the field, Sandra embarks on a romantic courtship with her future husband and Mary begins a damaging relationship with Andy, an intense, psychologically complex and unstable character, who recognises something of his tortured psyche in Mary. However, whereas Mary dreams of 'old women hammering nails into their eyes, children peeling open like bananas, empty drums dropping from the sky',[45] Andy is on a self-destruct mission of heavy drinking, fights, football hooliganism and paramilitary activity in the Ulster Defence Association. McGrath generates a sense of lament around Andy, a fascinating character, as he channels his considerable energies away from class politics into anarchic nihilism and macho posturing.

Emerging from a sheltered upbringing, Yorry, who is also in love with Mary, embodies McGrath's concern with 'the political education and growing to socialist consciousness of the individual'.[46] Initially McGrath parodies Yorry's enthusiastic rhetoric on the theoretical tracts of Marx, Luxemburg and Gramsci. However, McGrath demonstrates Yorry's capacity to learn and be useful to the revolutionary cause when he relinquishes his university career and gets involved in industrial action alongside Willy and Mr Maconochie. Proposing 'how the intelligentsia can be of actual practical use in political struggle',[47] Yorry ends up creating a daily newsletter for the workers and community, in which he includes individual worker profiles, a signal of his growing appreciation of the relationship between lived experience and political action. As the play closes, Yorry decides to relinquish ownership of his dead father's house to live communally with Sandra, Willy and their baby. As Janelle Reinelt concludes: 'the sense of extended family, of communal struggle, is what the strike action produces. It unites the two families—one could even say across class lines—and provides a way of living, if not tidy closure'.[48] This vision of solidarity crystallises McGrath's central concern in *Fish in the Sea*—the triumph of a common socialist cause over diverse needs, upbringings and perspectives.

Inevitably, I suppose, because he is in the world of gunmen on the run from Ireland, John McGrath's new play for the Liverpool Everyman descends into melodrama. One could of course say the same thing for O'Casey, but McGrath, although he is striving for it and sometimes succeeds here and there in a speech or two, does not have that magic ability to make his prose sing like O'Casey did. I shouldn't make too much of this however. This is a long play and largely very enjoyable, cracking with McGrath's usual wit and way with funny lines, and positively steaming with up to the minute social and economic messages. It also has songs by Petticoat and Vine with lyrics by McGrath and music by Norman Smeddles, the lead guitarist. This is the same combination which brought record houses to the Everyman in November 1971 and again in January 1972 with McGrath's play, 'Soft or a Girl?'

In 'The Fish in the Sea', McGrath once again deals with a family in working class Liverpool. The father and son-in-law (Brian Young and Terence Durrant) get involved in a factory sit-in. Antony Sher plays Yorry, the Marxist son of a Welsh Presbyterian manse, who has designs on the daughter, Mary (Angela Phillips), who is also pursued by Andy (Jonathan Pryce), a mad Glasgow-Scot who is wanted by the police for bombing in Belfast. When I tell you that Mary's brother is a policeman set on the trail of Andy it may perhaps seem like too much. And it is. But there are some really fine moments like Yorry, the long-haired student, delivering this wild parody of a revolutionary speech: 'The Don Quixote of capitalism would long ago have been impaled on the windmills of working-class militancy were it not for the Sancho Panza of reformism.'

The songs show a good range too, from the lovely little ballad sung by the three sisters:

> Drifting, drifting, anyway the wind blows
> Anyway the tied flows

To the hard-driving rock title song which contained the play's revolutionary message:

> We move left, we move right
> Fish in the sea.
> Bigger sharks in the night
> Swallow up with one big bite
> Little sharks in the sea
> That live off fish like you and me.

There is a lot to look at and listen to in this new play and it should prove successful as McGrath's other work for director Alan Dossor.

Stanley Reynolds[49]

In the stage directions, McGrath describes the style of the play as 'neither "epic" nor naturalistic' and stresses that the performers must sustain 'throughout the play a relationship between their characters and the audience by way of their own personal stage personae'.[50] McGrath facilitates this relationship through direct address, which at the beginning of the play establishes that the events of the play have already taken place. The actors playing Willy, Yorry and Mr Maconochie invite the audience to make sense of what they see and, in Brechtian terms, to make maps that suggest alternative routes and endings. Direct address continually disrupts the naturalistic exchanges throughout *Fish in the Sea*, a performance strategy that reveals specific motivations and information to frame events as they unfold. McGrath also continues his experiments with music and song to drive the narrative forward, inject potent shifts of energy and rhythm and evoke humour and pathos. The variety of effects is central to the success of *Fish in the Sea* as high-energy songs, love-struck poems, quick-fire comedy, farcical exchanges, emotive scenes, political speeches and revelatory monologues bombard the audience. McGrath had found the fast-paced variety format that became a staple of 7:84's theatrical output in the following years.

7:84 Theatre Company: 1971–73

During his association with the Everyman, McGrath established the policies and practices that fuelled the 7:84 Theatre Company he formed with Elizabeth MacLennan and David MacLennan in 1971. Politically, McGrath signalled the orientation of the company by adopting a name taken from a statistic that appeared in *The Economist,* which revealed 7% of the population of Britain owned 84% of the nation's wealth. Alongside other left-wing theatre groups that emerged during the late 1960s and early 1970s, such as Red Ladder, General Will and Portable, 7:84 wanted to echo the Workers' Theatre Movement of the 1920s and 1930s to create a revolutionary theatre practice that used 'theatre as a weapon': a weapon that, by debating society and presenting oppositional agendas, could contribute to the broader climate of collective protest rooted in industrial action, class-based activism, the student movement and campaigns centred on identity politics such as civil rights, the Women's Movement and gay liberation.

7:84's first play, *Trees in the Wind,* written and rehearsed in six weeks, premiered at the Edinburgh Fringe Festival in 1971 and toured to a newly emerging small-scale touring circuit of studio theatres and arts centres. The title of the play echoes a quotation by Mao—'wind will not cease even if trees want to rest'—associated with the Chinese Cultural Revolution (1966–76), whose ideological principles and contradictions inform the play's subject matter. For many during the late 1960s and early 1970s, Mao's aim to restructure Chinese society, culture and ways of living offered a beacon of progressive thinking. However, the results and aftermath of the Cultural Revolution revealed deep contradictions in Mao's position. Hopes for a democratic political structure and the end to bureaucratic tyranny and oppression turned into the consolidation of a one-party state, the subordination of the people to the will of the dictatorship and the strengthening of bureaucratic state apparatus. Instead of a popular democracy, the Chinese people encountered a brutal regime in which dissenters faced execution, persecution and exile to labour camps. Rather than increased political conviction, many withdrew into political passivity and the young became known as the 'lost generation' because of their cynicism about political processes. As Maurice Meisner states, 'Few episodes in modern history are filled with so many ironies and paradoxes, plagued by such deep incongruities between means and ends,

INTRODUCTION BY NADINE HOLDSWORTH   19

and marred by so large a gulf between intentions and results.'[51] Deeply disturbed by events in China, McGrath reflects his disillusionment through the characters in *Trees in the Winds* who simultaneously 'lament . . . the failure of radical forces to unite and rescue the world from complacency'[52] and embody the very contradictions and acts of betrayal that lead to this failure.

The play revolves around three female characters, Aurelia, Belle and Carlyle, who share a flat and provide 'a study of three modes of feminist practice'.[53] Belle, a psychiatric social worker dealing with the aftermath of an unsuccessful relationship, is a bourgeois feminist whose knowledge and experience of an unjust social system fails to galvanise her to political action. Carlyle, a socialist feminist, is membership secretary of the local PRP and educating herself in theoretical Marxist-Leninism. Aurelia, who rages against man's relentlessly destructive force, takes up the radical feminist line. Into their lives and space bursts Joe, a part written for Victor Henry, who uncovers their contradictions by questioning their motives and actions. He arrives to resign from the PRP, a 'betrayal of the cause [that] mirrors what is seen as the Chinese betrayal of all European Maoists',[54] and to justify his actions to Carlyle, whom he hopes to seduce in the process. McGrath pits Joe's intention to manipulate capitalist structures to make an immediate material difference for himself and his friends, against Carlyle's wider political idealism. Echoing the unease of many political activists of the time, Carlyle's growing awareness of the brutal suppressions occurring throughout the world in the name of socialism, destabilises her political conviction. Nonetheless, she desperately clings to her belief in the theoretical principles of socialist reorganisation and, through Carlyle, McGrath asserts his central message—do not throw the baby out with the bathwater. Despite evidence of humankind's ability to belittle, oppress, torture and kill in the name of political progress, McGrath urges the audience not to capitulate as Joe threatens, or to retreat 'from direct action to formulate theories on why the world is bad'[55] as Aurelia has, or to ignore systemic problems as Belle does.

McGrath employs a dialectical structure in *Trees in the Wind* to reveal the often contradictory relationship between political theory and lived experience as his characters debate the tensions between collectivism and individual ambition, gender politics and sexual desire and revolutionary goals and the failures of the left. Influenced by 'Stockhausen pieces . . . where you have four or six loudspeakers in a hall, each one carrying a different message, each one doing a different thing, but all of them related to each other',[56] McGrath ruptures the initial naturalistic framework to introduce a complex musical structure. Different realms of looking at and perceiving various opinions are emphasised by moments of harmony and counterpoint through interwoven monologues, cross-cutting dialogue, changes in energy and direct address to the audience. The second Act becomes even more fractured as McGrath introduces Brechtian-style songs: 'The Song of Driving Mad', 'The Song of Knives at Throats' and 'The Song of Why They'll Never Know'. McGrath's experimental staging proved integral to the play's articulation of concepts, relationships between characters and the audience's role. For instance, McGrath surrounded the audience with three sharply defined playing areas that represent each female character's personal space, whilst simultaneously highlighting their isolation and interconnectivity. Interestingly, Carlyle's bedroom doubles as the shared living space, a visual signifier that her position could provide the point of intersection for all three women. As McGrath claimed, in order to suggest a more 'exciting future' he had to 'break down the convention of the three girls being in three rooms, in cells, so that the space, physical and imaginative, was reconstituted'.[57]

In the production, Aurelia's space was filled with contemporaneous images of British soldiers in Northern Ireland, Vietnam, space exploration, political disorder and the tapes on which she obsessively records

Figure 2   Elizabeth MacLennan as Aurelia in *Trees in the Wind*.

personal testimonies of sick, violated, burnt and mutilated bodies that bear the wounds of war, torture, pollution and political persecution. By placing this material on tape, Aurelia creates a permanent evidential record of humanity's degradation. Aurelia's radical feminist stance inverts traditional hierarchical gender relationships by proposing that men are the source of all societal ills because of their incessant pursuit of power and that women should be valued for their roles as nurturers and custodians of society:

> Women move among the realities: hunger, shelter, clothing, love, birth, death, children, shit, pain, anger, beauty. Men inhabit a world of destructive fantasy: wars, torture, cruelty, rat-races, boots in faces, stabs in the back, control, domination, rape, self-adoration . . .[58]

Joe echoes contemporaneous debates between those advocating radical feminism versus those pursuing class-based activism when he proposes that her position provides a diversion from the 'real' enemy:

> Your vision—your feminist utopia: how, er—how are you going to get it together? I mean, between you, now, and that happy land, somewhere in the future, there stands something called western civilisation, and something else called the capitalist state, and something else called American Imperialism with the most advanced methods of physical control and psychic repression ever known in the history of the world—I, er, just wanted to ask you, really, what you intend to do about them?[59]

Aurelia responds that she will 'cut them up' and underlines her point with the razor blades she wields: a particularly potent theatrical image given the heavily publicised Society for Cutting Up Men (SCUM), whose founder Valerie Solanas provided the inspiration for Aurelia.[60]

The influence and consequence of feminism and increasing sexual liberation is central to *Trees in the Wind*. On the one hand, the audience encounters independent, confident, liberated women who extol the virtues of the pill and their sexual freedom, but McGrath fractures this representation with Aurelia's tales of violent misogyny, Joe's admission of his sister's prostitution and Belle's negative body image. The dismissive response Belle receives from Denton also highlights the sexual double standard that men want sexually liberated but fundamentally undemanding women who still conform to feminine ideals of passivity and dutiful subservience. Equally, Aurelia addresses women's complicity in their own subordination by accusing them of internalising the perfor-

Figure 3   Victor Henry as Joe and Elizabeth MacLennan as Aurelia in *Trees in the Wind*.

mance of gender required of them by patriarchy: 'Nice, passive, accepting, "cultivated", polite, dignified, subdued, dependent, scared, mindless, insecure, approval-seeking women—who can't cope with the unknown, who want to feel safe with the apes, who want a Big Daddy in the background . . . .'[61]

A dominant theme in the play is how failure to resist equals compliance with exploitation: a factor powerfully explored in a scene between Joe and Belle, when Joe jumps into a spotlight to proclaim himself 'The Demon King', a provocateur who will challenge complacency. Turning to the audience, he asks 'Why don't we shoot all killer dogs?',[62] and then answers his own question by implicating the failure of political conviction, will and aggression. In 'The Song of Driving Mad', Aurelia and Carlyle join Joe to illustrate how he will exploit women, workers and tenants and drive them to insanity as he climbs the social ladder. Yet, when Joe hands Belle a knife and urges her to use it on his bare chest, she refuses. At this point, McGrath counterpoints Belle's failure to act with Aurelia and Carlyle recalling 'revolutionary moments' when knives were drawn and retracted: the end of the First World War, Spain 1937, Greece 1944, Paris 1968 and Glasgow 1971. McGrath concludes with a poetic reprise of factors that should compel the population to revolution and the women unite in hope that:

CARLYLE: cries mount up, like sand below the sea, a ridge,
AURELIA: A bar,
BELLE: A barrier.
CARLYLE: A mountain
AURELIA: Throwing up a ripple.
BELLE: Then a wave.
CARLYLE: Then a whole incredible tide
    Of breakers racing steaming for the shore
    The crack and spit as they bellow at the land
    And leap and whirl and spire and jet
    With energy, energy, energy bounding
    And the shore awaits.[63]

Probably the most impressive new play to come out of the 1971 Fringe was John McGrath's *Trees in the Wind,* presented by an ad hoc professional group, the 7:84 Theatre Company. Almost solely on the Fringe it ensured audience absorption in a drama of ideas by actually establishing character with compelling, intelligent dialogue and a remarkable realism of setting—well *before* making people spout their personal hedonism, Maoism or Women's Liberation. Done on three small connecting stages, an apron around the audience, it took the lives and attitudes of three flat-sharing girls challenged in their personal philosophies by one demonic man embodying the evil inversion of all their hopes. At one moment the three chat, or slang, or console each other, in and between the three rooms (utterly, touchingly authentic, and achieved with a beautiful sense of the rhythm of living in this way); the next moment they slip easily into convincing monologue in their own rooms; the next again, they are joined in speeches, songs or fantasy mime which advances the political argument of the play.

Mixed with this are readings from newspapers, political texts, and medical case histories—and against most of the rules, largely because of the sheer verve, fluency and compassion of the writing, this technique works. Mr McGrath's naturalistic dialogue renders the cadences of current speech with enormous precision and understanding; his satirical invective is coldly powerful and wonderfully funny by turns. The four parts in *Trees in the Wind* were taken by Elizabeth MacLennan, Deborah Norton, Gillian Hanna and Victor Henry. And if new drama *should* be moving the way this year's Fringe suggests, with playwrights going for texts to Marx, Marcuse, Mao and Millett, it could learn how not to bore too profoundly—not to bore at all—by taking in something of Mr McGrath's vibrant and moving play on the way.[64]

Following *Trees in the Wind*, 7:84 used project funding from the Arts Council and money earned by McGrath's work in film and television to tour productions of *Occupations* by Trevor Griffiths and McGrath's plays *Out of Sight, Underneath* and *Unruly Elements*, renamed *Plugged in to History*. During 1972, McGrath also began reformulating the company's organisational structure to incorporate greater democracy and collective working methods. The rationale behind 7:84 was documented in a programme note for its next production, an 'updated version' of John Arden's political parable *Serjeant Musgrave's Dance*, which toured from August to November 1972 with a new play by Arden and Margaretta D'Arcy, *The Ballygombeen Bequest*:

> Till now it has been impossible for the Company to be more than semi-permanent, but from this point on it will have a strong nucleus of actors, writers, directors, and stage management to run the Company as a collective undertaking. They are united by their attitude to society, and to the role of theatre in society, an attitude informed by a socialist awareness. They have no desire to be demagogic, or simplistically 'agitational'. They see their role as trying to raise consciousness. Primarily of the working class and its potential allies. Consciousness of what? Firstly what is actually happening to human life, in all its complexity. Secondly the kind of society we have created. And thirdly the relationship between the two. This relationship is political in the deepest sense, and theatrical in the deepest sense. They do not feel they are as yet fulfilling this role totally; nor do they see themselves as more than part of a large movement towards raising consciousness in this direction. They also want to present work which is good theatre, and to give people a few laughs.[65]

Engagement with contemporary social realities was at the forefront of Arden's request that McGrath re-work *Serjeant Musgrave's Dance*. A programme note states,

> Arden has always had a nagging suspicion that the urgent contemporary relevance of his play has been glossed over. Set in 1880, clothed in Red coats and Victorian costumes, spoken in Arden's own language—a mixture of the modern and the languages of the ballads and some nineteenth-century idiom—the play was too easily seen as a thing of the past, an 'art-work'—in spite of its sub-title 'An Unhistorical Parable'.[66]

Arden presented McGrath with an image of Musgrave as a para sergeant returning from Northern Ireland rather than some remote

Victorian colonial war and McGrath took this image a stage further by having Musgrave and his soldiers returning from Derry after the events of Bloody Sunday to another politically charged arena: a Yorkshire mining village during the 1972 Miners' Strike. John Bull argues that McGrath connects the use of repressive forces in Northern Ireland to the strike narrative to question whether the government could deploy British troops to quash industrial action in the same way.[67] This connection certainly chimed with concerns over Edward Heath's use of repressive tactics when tackling opposition. Immediately after his election, Heath introduced an Industrial Relations Bill to curb the power of the unions 'which made collective industrial bargains enforceable at law and established the National Industrial Relations Court to enforce them'.[68] Unions called a series of one-day stoppages in protest against the act, a mood of defiance that came to a head in 1972 when Britain's 280,000 miners came out on strike for more pay, supported by railway workers who refused to move coal trains. After the resolution of this conflict, dockworkers caused another strain on the Industrial Relations Bill. 'In June three dockers who had been picketing a container depot refused to appear before the newly created National Industrial Relations Court and their arrest for contempt was ordered.'[69] This heavy-handed action led to 30,000 dockers withdrawing their labour in sympathy for the jailed dockers. The government was defeated in both instances and this climate permeated the mood and production of *Serjeant Musgrave Dances On*.

The production, directed by Richard Eyre, employed various agit-prop techniques such as audience plants and direct address. As McGrath acknowledged, 'The opening up of the third act of that adaptation, when the audience is very intimately involved in what is going on, was probably a stage further in the development of our relationships with and direct political challenge to the audience'.[70] However, it was the decision to re-situate the action in Northern Ireland that caused diffi-culties. Relations between Britain and Ireland were particularly volatile given the imposition of direct rule in March 1972, an increased armed presence, the continuing policy of internment and accusations of brutality towards detainees. In a substantially rewritten third Act, Hurst and Attercliffe recall torture in internment camps, violent raids on IRA sus-pects and their involvement in the Bloody Sunday massacre in January 1972. McGrath's adaptation played alongside Arden and D'Arcy's *The Ballygombeen Bequest*, which offers a wider attack on the role of capitalism and British imperialism in subjugating Ireland. According to a programme note:

Britain's economic stranglehold on the land of Ireland is the target for the hurling of abuse, gunfire, songs, jokes, boots and custard

pies even. A turmoil of theatrical styles blitz against our un-
conscious ignorance of Ireland and the Irish provoking us through
laughter and merriment emerging into horror and outrage to a
deeper understanding of the conflicts which have daily become part
of our lives.[71]

Both productions offered an unflinching account of contemporary
Anglo-Irish relations and caused political and legal controversy.
Arden and D'Arcy faced accusations of slander and 7:84 took *The
Ballygombeen Bequest* off in the middle of its final week of a thirteen-
week tour at the Bush Theatre in London to avoid prosecution. The Arts
Council received letters of complaint about the representation of the British
army, with one arriving from General Tuzo, the British Commander-in-
Chief in Northern Ireland. Railing against the representation of British
soldiers 'as obscene, near-bestial and moronic', Tuzo concludes his letter
by expressing his doubts as to whether *The Ballygombeen Bequest*
'would be considered by any reasonable cross-section of the public to be
a proper object for their financial support'.[72] Tuzo touched a nerve
about public money supporting work that was critical of government
policy and the Arts Council consequently withdrew its intimation of
annual subsidy for 7:84.

7:84 England Theatre Company: 1973–75

Forced to remain on project funding, discussions took place about the
company's future and various radical decisions took place. Gavin Richards
left 7:84 to form Belt and Braces Theatre Company and remaining
personnel divided into separate English and Scottish branches, with
McGrath remaining Artistic Director of both. 7:84 Scotland's first
production, *The Cheviot, the Stag and the Black, Black Oil* (1973)
developed ideas on the intersection between capitalism and imperialism
through an exploration of the history of the Highlands from the
clearances to the discovery of North Sea Oil. The production was a
massive success and widely credited with redefining the nature of Scottish
theatre's subject matter, aesthetics, context of production and modes of
reception. This production marked the beginning of a long relationship
between McGrath and Scottish audiences, a relationship often accused
of detracting from his work in England.

As 7:84 Scotland emerged during 1973, 7:84 England toured Adrian
Mitchell's *Man Friday* and an adaptation of Robert Tressell's novel *The
Ragged Trousered Philanthropist* in a co-production with Belt and
Braces. The company did not produce any work in 1974, but re-emerged

in 1975 with an annual subsidy from the Arts Council and as a permanent company. Performers including Harriet Walter, Colum Meaney and Hilton McRae, and Chrissie Cotterill joined; McGrath began a long-standing collaboration with the musical director Mark Brown and the musicians, Chas Ambler, Mike Barton and Mike O'Neill, and Sandy Craig came back to administrate the company. From this point, 7:84 England began prioritising the establishment of a credible working-class audience for their particular brand of socialist entertainment and, throughout 1975, McGrath and Craig worked tirelessly to promote the company with alternative venues, funding bodies, trades unions, Trades Councils, Labour Movement activists and audiences.[73] The company also began to step up 'flying pickets', a few performers taking a sketch or some songs to perform at local factories in support of a particular strike or dispute.[74] The first show produced by the re-formed 7:84 England, a large-scale revival of a slightly rewritten version of *Fish in the Sea*, directed by Pam Brighton, marked a significant development in 7:84 England's campaign to reach non-theatre going audiences. Specifically, Craig successfully lobbied Merseyside Arts to subsidise a five-night mini-tour of Liverpool venues including Titchfield Street Community Centre, Tate and Lyle Social Club, Kirby Labour Club and the Fisher-Bendix factory. The Fisher-Bendix date was particularly relevant given the on-going work-in at International Property Development (formerly Fisher-Bendix).

Increasing industrial unrest and incidences of factory occupations in the years between *Fish in the Sea*'s first production at the Everyman and 7:84 England's revival, ensured the piece's continued relevance. As the programme for the show documents, 'There have been at least 22 wholly or partially successful factory occupants [sic] in England, Scotland and Wales since Upper Clyde Shipbuilders . . . All were effective to some degree in preventing redundancies.'[75] In November 1973, the National Union of Mineworkers banned overtime and weekend working in support of a pay claim defiantly above a Government-imposed threshold. In the aftermath of the 1973 Arab-Israeli War and the resulting oil crisis, the miners' action put immense pressure on energy supplies, prompting the Government to declare a state of emergency and a three-day week. Following the failure of pay negotiations, the miners called an all-out strike from 9 February 1974, which ultimately brought down the government as Heath was forced to announce the general election that saw Labour's Harold Wilson reinstated as Prime Minister. The new government and TUC immediately agreed a Social Contract, which promised a repeal of the 1972 Industrial Relations Act in exchange for voluntary wage restraint to curb inflation, that by 1974–75 was running at 24.1%. However, by 1975, it was clear that the Social Contract was

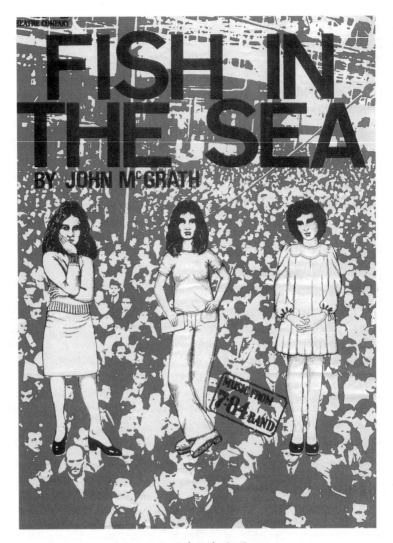

Figure 4   Fish in the Sea Poster.

failing as some wage settlements reached 30%, leading the government to impose the type of wage freeze that renders the settlement in *Fish in the Sea* useless. *Fish in the Sea's* pungent critique of government policy and the Labour Movement's increasing use of conciliation tactics during industrial disputes remained highly topical, particularly as the 1975 Employment Protection Act provided statutory recognition to the Advisory, Conciliation and Arbitration Service. Nonetheless, McGrath

Figure 5   The Maconochie family visit the youth club summer camp in 7:84 England's
production of *Fish in the Sea*.

re-wrote small sections to reflect his optimism at the level of industrial
action evident across Britain. Firstly, McGrath adds an extended direct
address to the audience by Mr Maconochie, who admits he was feeling
'old, and tired, and cynical. . . . Then bugger me: *this* happened. Action.
Determination. At last. Young Willy—a new generation—getting stuck
in there like a good 'un. Even Yorry, for all he's a bit damp behind the
ears—everybody was alive, and having a go. It's got to work'.[76] A sense
of renewed optimism also permeates the final lines of the play when Mr
Maconochie responds 'yes' to Mrs Maconochie's rhetorical '. . . it's time
you started winning, isn't it'.[77] A marked shift in tone from the
uncertainty of the original ending when Mr Maconochie asks: 'Can we
let them get away with it? Life and exploring goes on. How to make
sense of it. How to save anything useful from it, that's what we want to
know'.[78] At the end of *Fish in the Sea*, Yorry asks: 'Capitalism was
changing: the question was: were we going to change with it—fast
enough, big enough and well enough organised to catch up with it?'[79] In
his remarkably prescient play *Lay Off*, McGrath responds to Yorry's
concern with globalisation and the shift in power from the politics of the
nation state to multinational corporations.

Occupations are becoming an increasingly popular form of industrial action in this country; and it is not difficult to see why. When, say, an American-owned company wishes to close down its British subsidiary, because it believes greater profits can be made in Spain, Sicily or wherever the working class is weak and disorganised, the work-force in the subsidiary has two basic choices. One is to accept the closure and the redundancy money that goes with it; and the other is to fight to save the jobs at risk. In an inflation-ridden economy, where unemployment is rising and jobs of almost any kind are progressively harder to come by, more and more workers are choosing the second alternative. A strike is worse than useless in a situation of this sort, as the employers can then go ahead with the task of dismantling the factory's machinery and shipping it overseas, without fear of interruption. So the only thing the workers can do is occupy the factory and prevent the owners from carrying out their plans.

John McGrath's *Fish in the Sea,* which deals tangentially with an occupation and draws on the 1972 Fisher-Bendix sit-in for some of its source material, explores areas highly appropriate for a socialist company like 7:84 to work on. It has much of the dramatic skill, powers of invention and insight into character for which McGrath is justly renowned. The play, interlaced with music, revolves around a Liverpool family, the Maconochies, with three daughters and a son. Of the daughters, Sandra is wooed by Willy, a happy-go-lucky character working in the same factory as Mr Maconochie; Mary by Andy, a Scots anarchist on the run from the British Army in Ireland with a feeling for the mad poetry of life; and by Yorry, a university student with pretensions to Marxism, whose idealised image of the working-class in no way corresponds to the reality. The son, Derek, becomes a policeman, with all the reactionary prejudices that that job entails. (Shades of the Tory son, anxious to advance himself at any cost, in McGrath's *Angel in the Morning*) Yorry and his kindly, ironically self-deprecating uncle Dafydd live with Yorry's father (never seen), a pastor in a Welsh 'chapel', and provide an amusing sub-plot, full of beautiful social observation.

The characterisations and relationships are superbly drawn. The Maconochie family are entirely believable, both individually and collectively. So are the other characters, in the psychological and social relationships; and there are many beautifully funny, sad and memorable scenes. Ones that stand out are where Yorry sends up his Marxist pretensions; where Andy, on the run, tries to convince Mary of the validity of his anarchism, reflecting as it does in one way the underlying madness of our society; and where the three girls, early on, sing a song

Drifting, which expresses their adolescent aimlessness at that point in the play. Here are many lovely, subtle moments which could only arise out of a deep understanding of the characters and their situation on the part of the author. On the level of creating a modern-day working-class family saga, McGrath has been completely successful.

Where he has been much less successful, it seems to me, is in his depiction of the occupation that takes place at the factory where Maconochie and Willy work, its political implications, the psychological strains it imposes and the ways that these relate to the characters' quality of life, in particular the subtle changes it brings about. In stark contrast to the care and sensitivity with which McGrath has built up the characters and their relationships in the family context, the actual occupation is displayed in perfunctory, almost comic-strip terms. Surprisingly little feeling of the occupation's social realities and their effect on the characters is communicated. For instance, the scene where the three squabbling MPs come to investigate the occupation is amusing, but in a flip and superficial way, playing for easy laughs; and this approach tends to rub off on the rest of the occupation sequence. Consequently, the relationship between the overt politics of the situation, which is never properly established, and the everyday life of the characters is not explored in the depth in which it should be. This fundamental imbalance is faithfully reflected in Pam Brighton's production, which is strong where the author is strong, in the scenes of family life, and less assured in the occupation scenes. About the acting, however, there can be nothing but praise. John Judd is splendid as Willy, as is Will Knightley as the disturbed Andy. Shane Connaughton as Yorry and Howell Evans as Dafydd make the most of their characters' individual quirks; while Shay Gorman is a tower of strength as Maconochie.

Jonathan Hammond[80]

Stylistically, *Lay Off* retained the on-stage band, rousing songs and direct address to the audience of *Fish in the Sea*. However, whereas *Fish in the Sea* primarily conveys political messages through the naturalistic depiction of events affecting a fictional family, *Lay Off* interrogates topical political events through a variety format of sketches interspersed with songs, comic interludes, first-person narratives, captions and research materials. Variously described in reviews as a 'didactic cabaret' and a 'vaudeville revue', the playing style is all 'out front' and demands pantomimic engagement with song-sheets and captions. Commenting on this shift, Beata Lipman's review in the *Sunday Times* suggests that

McGrath feels that the grain of his radicalism is to some extent hidden by the details of the fascinating family that he created in the recent, highly successful 'Fish in the Sea'. People can no longer embody ideas; they may even mask them, and for this reason, he personally much prefers Brecht's archetypal 'Arturo Ui', for example, to his more naturalistic 'Mother Courage'.[81]

Figure 6   John McGrath outside the Mickery Theatre, Amsterdam.

The stress on socialist ideas and the conveyance of information in an entertaining and accessible way is central to *Lay Off* as the Monopolies Top Twenty, delivered *Top of the Pops* style, demonstrates. The way McGrath generated material echoes the devising and writing processes undertaken on *The Cheviot, the Stag and the Black, Black Oil*, as McGrath prepared new sections after researching, discussing and rehearsing with the company all day.

In the first Act, *Lay Off* provides a fast-paced exploration of factors influencing the latest phase of capitalism. The first section deals with the post-war consumer boom illustrated by the over-sized consumer items that provide the backdrop to a sketch depicting a couple so seduced by their desire for and consumption of goods that they ignore the diaristic accounts of unemployment, poverty, malnourished children and premature deaths that enable their affordable coffee, television and car.

The material stresses the mechanisms capitalism employs to maximise efficiency and profit, such as the wholesale adoption of Fred W. Taylor's scientific management theories and Henry Ford's production line. In a sketch between Brassneck, an old-school boss, and a new-style labour-relations expert, McGrath highlights the manipulative tactics employed to manage the labour force, increase productivity and reduce militancy.

Figure 7   Dennis Charles and Chrissie Cotterill surrounded by consumer goods
in *Lay Off*.

Despite a defiant song that includes the chorus: 'Oh they're not going to win / No we'll never give in / For we stand side by side together',[82] the mood at the end of Act 1 is increasingly downcast as McGrath examines the impact of growing numbers of company take-overs, buy-outs and mergers. The audience is faced with the statistic that, 'In two years, 1967 and 1968, 5,000 British firms were taken over or eaten alive by the bigger fish.'[83] The 'bigger fish' refers to the multinational corporations that were coming under increasing scrutiny during the volatile economic climate of the mid-1970s because of their power over exports, the importance of their corporate taxes and their ability to influence inflation and deflation by moving profits from one country to another.

In Act 2 McGrath explores how multinationals exert political influence, a concern that makes *Lay Off* extremely topical in the present climate of anti-globalisation commentary and activism. 'Certainly, nearly thirty years after *Lay Off* was written, McGrath's recognition of the erosion of national borders as capitalism's ultimate utopia appears alarmingly prophetic in the context of a world dominated more and more by American economic interest and the World Trade Organization.'[84] In particular, McGrath turns his attention to ITT, its founder Sosthenes Benn and his successor Harold Sydney Geneen. Hammond found that, 'A nicely sardonic touch is provided by a reading from Anthony Sampson's book on multi-nationals, describing a social jamboree where ITT middle-management executives of many different European nationalities display identical behaviour patterns and mannerisms and are sickeningly sycophantic towards their American boss.'[85] In a more serious scene that anticipates recent discussions on the sale of arms prior to the 1992 and 2003 Gulf Wars, McGrath highlights contradictions that emerge when multinationals chase profit over and above any ideological concerns or national interest:

COLIN: Well he [Sosthenes Benn] made so much money in Germany he had to invest in something. And Hitler was being nice to ITT, so he was nice to Hitler: he invested in Fokke-Wulf bombers. And sold equipment to German submarines.

DENNIS: But he was an American.

COLIN: Oh sure, a patriotic one too. He didn't neglect America— why he sold High Frequency Direction Finders to American destroyers so they could knock out the German submarines who were attacking convoys crossing the Atlantic full of ITT radio equipment for our boys in Europe. But he wasn't biased. He also ran the telephone system that connected Argentina to Berlin along which German spies told the German bombers and submarines when the American convoys left to cross the Atlantic.[86]

Lay Off also chillingly addresses the ITT's role in the brutal events following Salvador Allende's election as the socialist President of Chile in 1970, after he promised to confront Chile's economic, technological, cultural and political dependence. McGrath implicates the forces of industrial capitalism in Allende's murder by directly referring to reports into how American business interests, particularly those of ITT, led Richard Nixon and Henry Kissinger to exert pressure on Allende by withdrawing aid and using CIA agents to incite the right-wing insurrection that fostered the military coup under General Pinochet in 1973. In performance, this section was interspersed with songs by Victor Jara, the Chilean folk singer clubbed to death after Pinochet deposed Allende. In the British context, McGrath explores Harold Wilson's blatant capitulation to the multinationals when he revoked his 1974 pre-election pledge to oppose the excessive profits multinationals were raising from North Sea oil, and instead levied a 45 per cent petroleum revenue tax, which sustained a 20 per cent profit margin for oil companies.

The conclusion to *Lay Off* becomes increasingly didactic as performers urge the audience to fight for socialism and to recognise that '... the one great service the multi-nationals have performed for humanity, is that they have made the fight for socialism truly international, on a practical, day-to-day level. The workers of the world will

Figure 8   The Four Strikes of *Lay Off*.

have to unite'.[87] McGrath illustrates this point by documenting four strikes at Standard Telephones and Cables, a subsidiary of ITT, which took place between 1961 and February 1975. McGrath reveals how union activists in East Kilbride made unofficial links with ITT workers across Europe so that when the workers were striking over a pay dispute in 1975, they were able to call on other factories to 'black' parts made in other plants so that ITT's previous trick of moving production to another country became ineffective. The immediacy of this event, which took place a few of months before *Lay Off* started touring, and the topical nature of the issues explored in the piece, proved crucial to its impact and appeal for promoters and trade union activists. For example, the company received a request from Roger Hands from Dudley who wrote: 'On behalf of the Cannon Industries Shop Stewards Committees (AUEW & TASS) I would like to enquire about the possibility of booking your theatre group for a union concert. I feel that the play *Lay Off* is of particular relevance to us working in the GEC frontline.'[88]

Lay Off toured to university theatres, small arts centres and clubs such as the People's Centre in Liverpool and the Robin Hood Club in Stourbridge and received overwhelmingly positive reviews. Coveney found it 'expertly constructed and argued and charmingly performed by a young company whom only the most cynically inclined could accuse of righteousness or complacency'.[89] Reviewing the show at Cardiff Arts Centre, Beata Lipman confirms, 'I was informed, stimulated and vastly entertained'[90] and *Time Out* reviewer Anne McFerran reports a performance at Ruskin College, Oxford when 7:84 England met demands for an encore by giving a second outing to songs from the show.[91] Composed by Brown, with lyrics by McGrath, songs were a vital component of *Lay Off* as they contributed to the variety format, conveyed information and kept the show lively and entertaining. Indeed, the music was so popular that 7:84 England released an LP of songs from *Lay Off*.

When the 7:84 performed their new show 'Lay Off' at Ruskin College, Oxford, the audience enjoyed themselves so much they wouldn't go home. 'More, more,' they cried, though it was past closing time and we'd been there since 7:30.

'But he hasn't written any more!' retorted one of the actors pointing at an exhausted John McGrath sitting in the audience. So we sang the songs from the show again.

'Lay Off' is about the biggest of big business, the multi-nationals; why they started, how they operate, where they could lead. 7:84 have taken what seems to be a complex world of high politics and sophisticated economics and shredded it into music, song and sketch with a stunning result of a show that literally dances rings around its subject.

Avoiding nobody's corns, the sketches range from the outrageously funny—Old-fashioned Bossman Brassneck being cajoled by his new-fangled Labour Relations Expert to 'avoid confrontation with the workers and take the problems to our more amenable National Union Leaders'—to the moving election speech of the late President Allende.

Mark Brown's music, which deserves its own LP, incorporates the sour muzak of commercialieze ('Science is a wonder, sha-na-na'), Gilbert and Sullivan type ditties, a Multi-Nationals Top Twenty and many songs rooted firmly in rock.

Similar in style to the twice televised 'Cheviot, Stag and Black, Black Oil', the idea for this musical documentary was dreamed up by Writer/Director John McGrath just a few months ago. For two weeks the company read, talked and researched, a vigorous process which brought them mentally and physically together. Then for three weeks they rehearsed during the day and McGrath wrote the necessary dialogue and lyrics in the evening. Although this is the reverse process of 'normal' plays with previously written scripts and subsequent rehearsal, Administrator Sandy Craig is quick to point out that 'Too many people have an ultra-romantic picture of 7:84. They think that everybody does everything. Although we work communally, finally everybody has their own job. We hope that this way of working does, however, demystify the function of the writer.'

Demystified McGrath may be, but his talents as a writer and director cannot be debunked. This is a stomping show which could simply *make* pub theatre. It's difficult to single out any of the actors for particular merit but I'm glad that Hamish McCrae (sic) hasn't signed up with the R.Stones. The inevitable path to socialism should be paved with such moments of optimism.

Anne McFerran[92]

Acknowledging the impact of the women's liberation movement and internal pressure within 7:84 England for the company to address 'complaints that in *Lay Off* the women hadn't had enough to do',[93] McGrath turned his attention to women's rights in the next 7:84 England show. *Yobbo Nowt* toured arts centres, trade union organis-ations, working men's clubs and Miners' Institutes during a year when women's inequality came under increasing scrutiny. 1975 was not only International Women's Year, but also the year when the government planned to implement fully the 1970 Equal Pay Act, passed the Sex

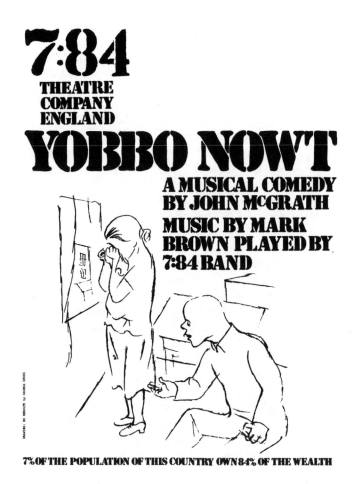

Figure 9   *Yobbo Nowt* programme.

Discrimination Act, established the Equal Opportunities Commission and when the TUC adopted the Working Women's Charter. The play also coincided with a concerted campaign by the Labour Movement to confront the male bias of trade union activity and discourse.

Taking Brecht's adaptation of Gorki's *The Mother* as a structural and thematic model, McGrath traces a working-class woman's journey into feminist and class-consciousness in England during the 1970s. Moreover, with references to domestic violence, the sexual division of domestic labour, equal pay, single-parent families, payment for housework, sexual objectification, contraception, sexual fulfilment and societal pressure on women to define themselves in relation to men, *Yobbo Nowt* is firmly located within contemporaneous campaigns for women's liberation. In particular, McGrath offers a searing socialist feminist analysis of the interconnection between patriarchy and capitalism as Marie, *Yobbo Nowt's* central character, tackles her subordinate position within the classic nuclear family, struggles to gain autonomy from an abusive husband and fights for financial independence as a single parent with two teenage children. Marie soon learns that patriarchal structures stretch beyond the domestic environment. Without a man to support her she is reliant on social security or part-time, low-paid jobs tied to the domestic realm: cleaning, laundry or school meal service. After Marie secures a job in an electronics factory on piecework, McGrath shifts his focus to women's subjugation within the workplace and as workers within capitalism. He also tackles gender politics in union organisation and activity through George, Marie's union representative. Instead of negotiating a settlement on a guaranteed wage, he concentrates on jokes and sexual innuendo, highlighting how the primacy of sexual oppression could circumvent legislation such as the Equal Pay Act.

Michelene Wandor accused McGrath of subordinating gender issues to a male-defined, traditional economic class struggle and argued that Marie discovers nothing about sexism, feminism or sexuality.[94] Other critics recognised Marie's dual questioning both in the domestic space as she develops an understanding of the feminist rallying cry 'the personal is political', and in work-based arenas. Importantly, she is seen in a process of transition, as McGrath acknowledges: 'Marie . . . is shown in the oppressed, passive state of many women. She is then shown in the process of self-assertion, self-realisation, active participation in life and articulate, positive militancy.'[95] To close the play, McGrath stresses Marie's autonomy and feminist consciousness when she rejects her husband, claiming, 'things have changed—attitudes, ways of looking at things',[96] and her son Stephen provides proof of this development by rejecting his father's chauvinistic stance to contribute to the home environment.

Once again, McGrath did not allow his social agenda to overshadow his desire to experiment with theatrical form. In the programme accompanying *Yobbo Nowt*, he writes:

> In our productions we have used many styles and techniques, from highly verbal confrontation, to variety and ceilidh forms, from fantastical parable to stark realism, from family drama to review-cum-rally, from knockabout comedy to personal narrative. Common to all is the attempt to express something of the complexity of being alive today in a way that working-class audiences will recognise and enjoy. *Yobbo Nowt* is another tentative step in this direction.[97]

Intended as a contrast to the didacticism of *Lay Off*, McGrath wanted *Yobbo Nowt* to 'explore several ways of relating music to speech and story-telling: the sung narrative, straightforward character- and situation-songs, plus scenes in which the characters cut from speech to song, and scenes completely set to music'.[98] McGrath amalgamated an extensive and varied use of music and song with a domestic comic drama, direct address to the audience and Brechtian-style narrators: a combination which led Billington to enthuse, 'this exuberant musical nails the old myth that left-wing theatre must necessarily be grey as a plate of cold porridge and just about as digestible . . . this is political theatre with guts and gaiety'.[99] Similarly, Desmond Pratt of the *Yorkshire Post* called it, 'a remarkable production, full of rhythm, humour and pathos, all revealing the human condition'.[100]

Dear Sir,

We are two students who saw 'Yobbo Nowt' and 'Lay Off' as performed by the 7:84 Theatre Company (England) while on a rare visit to Glasgow.

We were impressed by the music and songs sung in the plays, especially 'Lay Off', and we would be interested to know if there are any means of obtaining copies of the words sung in the plays. We are also interested to know if there are any 7:84 Theatre Company (England) posters, t-shirts, badges, etc. available for purchase.

We have become interested in socialism and its aims through the company and if you feel there is any way in which we could be of any service to the company, we would be pleased to do so.

Yours faithfully

Lucy O'Reilly and Morag MacDougall

P.S. Not financial help (we gave all we could to the Right to Work Campaign . . . so . . . we are skint!)[101]

7:84 England Theatre Company in decline: 1976–79

After a year's constant touring, 7:84 England fell into sharp decline due to exhaustion, a lack of clear direction and a period of producing work that failed to achieve the high standards of the company's earlier work. After a lacklustre production of Shane Connaughton's *Relegated* was taken off halfway through its tour and replaced with *Yobbo Nowt* and *Lay Off* in repertoire, McGrath wrote and directed *The Rat Trap* for a *Morning*

Star rally. A short comedy about inflation based on a classic whodunit formula, *The Rat Trap* is set in a country residence, where guests Herr Cashminder, Lady Watch it Grow, Plain Mr Fuckitup, Mrs Dodgeabout and Sheik Gotya by the Short and Oilies, are accused of killing the Very Reverend Sickly Pound by contributing to rising inflation. By 1975 'Average weekly earnings had risen by 27 per cent. Whilst productivity had fallen and prices had risen by 24 per cent',[102] so a play about inflation was certainly topical. However, in comparison with other agit-prop style pieces such as *Lay Off*, *Rat Trap's* analysis is slight and unsubtle. McGrath blamed the company: 'it should have been a tremendous hit and they killed it. They killed it stone dead, by just not being alive enough, not responding to it'.[103] Frustrated by 7:84 England's rapid disintegration, McGrath withdrew his labour:

> I just said, 'Right, I'm not actually going to direct this lot. I'm going and I won't be back,' because I couldn't bear it any longer. That's the way I remember that year, as a kind of decline: people getting more tired, pale, sickly looking, lethargic and lazy.[104]

Looking at the touring schedule for the first four months of 1976, it is no wonder that company members were exhausted. In March, 7:84 England played twenty-five dates in ten separate venues with performances of *Lay Off, Yobbo Nowt, The Rat Trap and Relegated*.

During this period and over the next few years, there were many difficulties associated with collective working and 7:84 England's attempt to establish a democratic management structure. A 'collective management', consisting of long-standing associates and current members of the company who held full contracts, held decision-making authority. Those employed on a task-basis, for example as actors, writers, directors or designers, did not automatically qualify for a place on the collective, but participated in company meetings that reported to the collective. Minutes documenting company meetings during the mid to late 1970s reveal a high level of dissatisfaction, antagonism and confusion over the theatrical and political objectives of 7:84 England. Issues arise relating to personality clashes, different levels of political commitment and the relationship between the collective, the company and McGrath. As Eugene van Erven highlighted, '7:84 is more or less collectively organized, but its very existence, perpetuation, and artistic style depend on the initiative and creativity of a single person.'[105] This was a difficult power structure to negotiate and many writers, directors and performers were uneasy with it. The situation came to a head during 1976 after several pivotal members left the company. A new company was established and immediately destabilised by the collective's decision to pull *Relegated*, by Dave Bradford's withdrawal from directing Steve Gooch's *Our Land, Our Lives* and by the collective's decision to cancel several performances of *Our Land, Our Lives*. In an illuminating letter, Craig tries to clarify some of the reasons for Bradford's decision:

> He feels that any group through touring tends to develop a strong individual identity and style of work. Thus they present an entity which he can approach as an outsider and work with. However, given that (1) [the] company [is] going through a number of personnel changes; and (2) the company's relationship to John McGrath who gives identity to the company—it is very difficult for an outside director to assume responsibility for [a] show. In other words, there are a huge number of problems. Who is leaving and why? Who is staying and why? . . . Is 7:84 there to perform John's work, or is it something else as well or something including that? Where does the real power within 7:84 lie? He feels that it is part of a director's job to confront and tackle all these kinds of relationship problems. . . . However, there is a contradiction here—he must take up these problems, but as an outside director he is hired and hired for one show only so in what sense can he take up these responsibilities?[106]

7:84 England's next show, David Edgar's *Wreckers*, eased tensions in the company and according to Edgar initiated a degree of 'euphoria'. Edgar explained:

> 7:84 England has not done a successful show (successful defined as not being taken off) by any writer other than John McGrath since 1973. A succession of extra-marital droops is a powerful argument for monogamy. The company rather courageously decided to have another go . . . I think the feeling of euphoria resulted from the success of that limited project.[107]

Unfortunately, McGrath's return to 7:84 England did not continue the company's upward trajectory.

McGrath returned in 1977 with *Trembling Giant*, a pantomime with over twenty songs, which Jim Sheridan directed. As with *The Rat Trap*, McGrath retreated from recognisable, topical characters in favour of fantasy figures who trace the development of capitalism through the allegory of a dwarf who turns into a giant because peasants succumb to his every whim. *Trembling Giant* was not a great success and McGrath admitted '. . . there's something about allegorical plays and working-class audiences that doesn't quite fit'.[108] 7:84 England followed *Trembling Giant* with *The Life and Times of Joe of England*, written and directed by McGrath. Richard Beacham offers a useful synopsis:

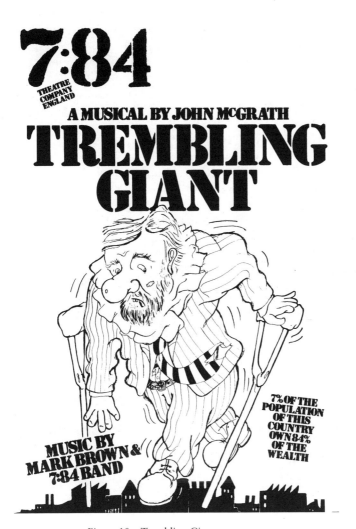

Figure 10   Trembling Giant programme.

The Life and Times of Joe of England, a musical which McGrath wrote with Mark Brown, tells the story of an innocent eighteen-year old from Sheffield who goes to London in the best Dick Whittington tradition to make his fortune through hard and honest work. He finds a hostile city of leeches and greedy money-makers, a place of "ducking and diving" where his dreams of productive work founder among a corrupt and bewildering system in which fortunes are made by "shifting things around". As he realizes the true nature of the society he had entered, Joe no longer wide-eyed, becomes involved in a shady world of capitalist high finance and wheeling and dealing in a city where nobody actually works to create anything real, and trade union leaders are as debased as their capitalist bosses.[109]

McGrath planned to target Jim Callaghan's Labour administration and 'the nihilistic feeling one got at the time that politics was becoming pointless on a parliamentary level'.[110] Labour were in trouble and Callaghan was widely viewed as a weak leader with a poor sense of judgement. By January 1977, the Government's overall majority had fallen to one and by March, Callaghan implemented a pact with the Liberals to ensure the government's survival. 7:84 England were experiencing a similar decline. After a series of under-par shows, the company found it hard to secure dates and *Joe of England* toured to a few unfamiliar venues including Wickford Community Centre and Portsmouth Poly-technic, before embarking on an extensive tour of Holland and Belgium. It was clear that this show was not going to mark 7:84 England's revival as, 'on the whole it felt flimsy'.[111] In 1978, 7:84 England toured a revival of McGrath's *Underneath* and *Vandaleur's Folly* by Arden and D'Arcy. Despite difficulties, evidence suggests that the company were still managing to reach an unusual proportion of traditionally non-theatre-going audiences. During 1978, the Arts Council approached Mass Observation Ltd. to conduct market research into audiences attending performances by 7:84 England, Triple Action and Monstrous Regiment.

> Of the three groups, 7:84 attracted the greatest representation from that section of the population normally severely under-represented in theatre and other arts performances. At Clay Cross 67 per cent of the audience was drawn from a manual worker background (C2, D, E) and 70 per cent finished their formal education at eighteen or earlier.[112]

McGrath followed his 1979 production of *Big Square Fields*, about the beginning of the Industrial Revolution and the Enclosures Act, with *Bitter Apples*, a large-scale musical co-produced with the Nottingham Playhouse, with Dossor directing. With *Bitter Apples*, 7:84 England hoped to attract a new audience into more traditional middle-scale venues and appealed for broad support from the Labour Movement:

> . . . for 7:84, no strangers to the larger theatres, this tour is an exciting challenge in their aim to prove that a much wider audience can be attracted to the larger theatres—when shows of interest to the broader mass of the population are presented.

It is important, if this new development in political entertainment is to be successful, that it is supported by trade unionists, community groups, tenants groups and all other action groups who aim for a more socially just future. Large audiences turning out to support and enjoy this venture will greatly strengthen the growth of this type of entertainment and, as a result, strengthen the Labour Movement itself.[113]

Through *Bitter Apples,* McGrath attempted to recapture earlier successes with family-based sagas set in Liverpool, but unfortunately, *Bitter Apples* lacked the thematic and theatrical clarity of his work at the Everyman and received a mixed critical reception. Set in 1968, Act One pits one set of values against another when a collective of poets, painters and musicians squat in a flat opposite the Leitrim family. The squatters are part of a 'hippy' sub-culture associated with dropping out, getting stoned and free love; whereas the Leitrims are presented as working-class conformists who prize a strong work ethic and social respectability. The two worlds collide through a burgeoning relationship between musician Theo and Mary, the Leitrims' sixteen-year old daughter. With the aim of exploring hegemonic processes and the failures of 1968, McGrath charts his characters as they become embroiled in dominant social structures. Despite her rebellious spirit, Mary becomes a packer where her dad works, and Theo's band, Liverpool Liberation Army, carefully dressed to look like rebel poets, sing about revolutionary action to make money for media corporations. McGrath intersperses this narrative with short dramatised extracts depicting wider political attempts at liberation such as Paris 1968 and Che Guevara' s guerrilla warfare in Bolivia. In a letter written after attending *Bitter Apples*, Philip Hedley, Artistic Director of the Theatre Royal, Stratford East, expressed his unease with these didactic interludes:

I think it is that I over-react against being informed directly in any play. I've so often been bored by instructive Everymans or Common Mans or Disguised Lecturers, I am obsessive about this, consequently being 'informed' by the Paris letter, or the statement on the '68 revolution *feels* like didacticism. This would not be so much so if the *whole* play's tone was more documentary but the family scenes are so vital and alive the contrast makes the poet appear didactic.[114]

Despite an indication that McGrath intended to develop references to political events in Act Two, these do not materialise. Alternatively, the second half of the play tackles apathy, selling out and reactionary ideology as 'the great leap of liberation in '68 has turned into a hard, rather more pedestrian struggle'.[115] The band has dissolved; Mrs Leitrim is on tranquillisers; Mr Leitrim is a xenophobic member of the long-term unemployed and the spectre of a Tory government looms.

During 1979, McGrath also produced *If You Want to Know the Time*, a short play for the Blair Peach benefit concert held at the Royal Court on 16 July 1979. Blair Peach, a young New Zealand teacher, died on 23 April 1979 after being hit over the head by a police officer whilst he demonstrated against the National Front holding an election meeting in Southall. *If You Want to Know the Time* 'was really about the creeping advance of a pre-fascist mentality in England. The most ominous character had analysed the "anarchy" of the young, and had come to the conclusion that the only way to bring discipline back to the streets was physical violence':[116] a horribly prescient vision of the urban unrest and increasing police powers, which characterised the early years of the Thatcher administration.

Responding to Thatcherism: 1980–85

The socio-political context of the early 1980s brought devastating consequences for the alternative theatre movement that flourished throughout the 1970s. 'Ideological repression and fiscal misery combined to change the geography of the arts'[117] and by the end of the decade many companies, including 7:84 England, Joint Stock, Foco Novo and CAST, had their funding withdrawn. By 1980, the ethics of free market enterprise were steadily seeping into cultural practice and placing projects like 7:84 England in jeopardy. The Arts Council withdrew funding from forty companies in 1980 and in the aftermath of this unprecedented cull, selected 7:84 England for an extensive review, citing concerns with high administration costs, too few performances and low audience figures. In response, 7:84 England launched a new touring policy designed to establish a regular network of forty small-scale theatres and non-traditional venues such as Corby Trades and Labour Club, Cotgrave Miners Welfare Club and Kinsley Working Men's Club, near Pontefract. Alan Tweedie also worked hard to establish new contacts and to nurture ongoing relationships with venues and local Labour Movement activists as Promotions and Liaison Officer for the company.

During the 1980–81 season, 7:84 England produced Barrie Keefe's *Sus* and *One Big Blow* by John Burrows. The latter earned the company rave reviews, a Fringe First Award at the Edinburgh Festival and toured for a year to over fifty venues.

Dear Mr McGrath

I write as Assistant Secretary of the Rushcliffe Constituency Labour Party. Over the last two years we have acted as promoters of three shows performed by the 7:84 Theatre Company and we are now one of your regular venues in the East Midlands. It was, therefore, with some horror that I learnt that your grant was under threat from the Arts Council. The plays that we have seen have all been of a high standard with 'One Big Blow' being generally regarded as outstanding. We use a large mining community, Cotgrave, as our venue: this is a place which is not visited by other more traditional groups although "Red Ladder" have played there twice. We are attempting to build up audiences there and it is noteworthy that the average size has increased from about 100 two years ago to over 300 when you last came. This in itself is a measure of your success at attracting audiences. I am sure that many who came would not have gone to plays put on in Nottingham. I do hope that the Arts Council will continue your funding as the service you, and other groups provide, is one which is vital if 'theatre', in its widest sense, is to reach ordinary working people.

Roger Milyard[118]

McGrath returned in 1981 to write and direct *Nightclass,* a 'musical extravaganza' with music by Rick Lloyd, who had been in *One Big Blow* and went on to chart success with The Flying Pickets. *Nightclass* presents an evening class on the British constitution and attempts by a cynical lecturer Keith Nuttall, played by Alfred Molina, to investigate mechanisms of power and democracy in the British state. Theatrically, it utilises numerous songs in which Nuttall 'becomes Dandini and W.C. Fields combined, a glamorous, grotesque monster'[119] to enliven long speeches about the commodification of knowledge, the monarchy and parliamentary democracy.

After the originality and theatrical flair of *One Big Blow,* reviewers of *Nightclass* were disappointed with a competent and serviceable production. The Arts Council, still closely monitoring the company, gathered several reports on the show. One adviser found '7:84 were doing their thing rather more than competently, the overall effect was perfectly acceptable . . . And that's the problem. We certainly weren't into new areas of experience or theatrical language. But we were in Clock Face, and that's a tiny town that doesn't often, I guess, see theatre. And that's the boon.'[120] Another, less sympathetic reviewer wrote: 'The

Figure 11   David Straun, Diane Adderley, Alfred Molina, Alan Hulse and
Dona Croll in *Nightclass*.

problem is the usual John McGrath one: a very intelligent, shrewd and witty man trying to write political theatre for the working classes and producing simplistic slogans. No doubt I'm being elitist when I say this strikes me as a prostitution of his talents.'[121] The struggle to appreciate McGrath's performance aesthetic and 7:84 England's efforts to reach a traditionally non-theatre going working-class audience, typify many Arts Council reports.

Following a production of Claire Luckham's *Trafford Tanzi,* directed by Pam Brighton, 7:84 England staged *Rejoice!,* written and directed by McGrath. Created in the immediate aftermath of the Falklands War, the play takes its title and inspiration from Thatcher's triumphant cry, 'Rejoice', after the re-taking of South Georgia. Employing the title ironically, McGrath uses it to frame his scathing attack on Thatcherite policies that saw no contradiction in spending huge amounts of money on war, whilst unprecedented cuts in public spending, rapidly rising unemployment and large-scale inner city protests and race riots wreaked havoc across England and Wales. *Rejoice!* provides a theatrical response to the Thatcherite 'survival of the fittest' mentality and 'delivers its punches with deftness, music and humour'.[122]

Set in Liverpool, the musical comedy has four characters: Molly, a social worker; Joyce, Molly's partner; Leon, a black youth with a crush

Figure 12   Flyer image of *Rejoice!*

Figure 13   Bridget Thornborrow, Nick Stringer and Angela Bruce in *Rejoice!*
(*Photo:* David Ellis)

on Molly; and Jack Browning, a local Conservative councillor and Joyce's boss at Brownings Tea and Coffee Merchants. When local authority funding cuts threaten Molly's centre for alcoholics, she asks Browning to donate money from his recently acquired inheritance. Browning offers to establish a rural retreat for addicts if he can successfully conduct a social experiment with Leon. Described by McGrath as his 'answer to *My Fair Lady*',[123] Browning wants to prove that if Leon, who was involved in the Toxteth Riots, comes to live with him for four weeks, he can turn him into a credible young Tory to parade at a forthcoming Conservative garden party. Through this narrative, McGrath generates a comic exploration of the culture of individualism promoted by Thatcherism and there ensues a humorous take on social Darwinism as Browning teaches Leon values of self-interest and self-assertion. Nonetheless, Leon has the last laugh as he manipulates the situation for his own political and financial advantage by providing a marketable image of a non-threatening, apolitical, enterprising young black man that the media queues up to interview. However, during interviews Leon mercilessly mocks race relations during the early 1980s. He is recorded saying: 'Instead of hanging round the streets, we could be making things to sell, say leather belts, or beads or wooden animals for the tourists, raffia mats, painted CS canisters—we must get our aggression channelled into business'.[124] Ultimately, Leon and Molly stick to their principles, but McGrath is aware of a rapidly changing environment and ends on a pessimistic note as Joyce tries to secure her job against redundancy, regardless of her fellow workers, and Browning concludes 'We're winning'.

Fringe audiences at the Edinburgh Festival are a wonderfully motley bunch. They range from the small groups of theatrical connoisseurs and international talent spotters who might turn up at 10 o'clock in the morning to see an interesting new piece by a professional company, to the solid phalanxes of respectable Edinburgh citizens who come out year after year to support local amateur groups like the Jerwood Players or the Davidson's Mains Dramatic Club.

But anyone who has taken a close look at the assembled crowds of students, tourists, and Edinburgh theatre buffs, is bound to admit that only a very small proportion of the Fringe audience could be described as working class.

That fact alone makes it unfathomable exactly why John McGrath, director of the radical 7:84 theatre companies in England and Scotland, so often chooses to open his new productions in Edinburgh.

McGrath has always argued that working-class audiences need and demand a completely different style of theatre from the normal middle-class public.

His latest play 'Rejoice!'—a charming, mellow little musical about political attitudes in Margaret Thatcher's England, which has been playing to packed houses at the Circuit this week—certainly has some delightful and refreshing qualities.

It's colourful, direct, emotionally open and politically unambiguous. But is also astonishingly—and it seems quite deliberately—amateurish and naïve in its standards of singing, dancing, acting and design.

Of the four actors, only Nick Stringer as the lovable rogue of a capitalist gives anything like a fully professional performance, with the disconcerting result that the whole play is far more memorable for his affectionate jibes at welfare state socialism than for its basic stand against Toryism.

I was left wondering once again why John McGrath should assume that the way to appeal to modern, sophisticated working-class people is to present them with simple, pop-up book socialism, performed with a kind of inexpert charm which is bound to remind any self-respecting audience of an end-of-term school play rather than a serious professional theatre production.

Joyce McMillan[125]

Rejoice!, premiered at the Herriot Watt Theatre Upstairs during the 1982 Edinburgh Festival. It received a mixed critical reception with some critics scathing of contrived plotlines, under-developed characterisation and 'pop-up book socialism'. However, Ned Chaillet in *The Times*, noted 'new life in Mr McGrath's writing' and acknowledged: 'Part of the pleasure of the play, and there are many pleasant surprises, is the way in which he gives all the best lines to a Liverpool capitalist. By treating his enemy with respect his own ideas on social justice shine forth and allow Nick Stringer to click his heels in a delightful performance.'[126] Whilst McGrath concentrated his efforts in Scotland with the Clydebuilt Series and the ill-fated General Gathering initiative, 7:84 England produced *V-Signs*, a double bill of topical one-act plays by Peter Cox: *Jimmy Riddle and Tickertape and V-Signs* about unemployment and a young black man fighting for his country in the Falklands. Next came *Spike in the First World War*, a play based on *The Good Soldier Švejk* by Jaroslav Hašek, written and directed by Jim Sheridan, who transported Švejk from Czechoslovakia to Ireland at the beginning of the twentieth century. During the tour of *School for Emigrants*, a devised piece directed by Paul Thompson, 7:84 England learnt it faced closure as part of the 1984 *Glory of the Garden* initiative launched by William Rees-Mogg. According to the Arts Council, the *Glory of the Garden* strategy was to channel resources to key 'centres of excellence' and to decentralise funding to regional arts associations. The decision to cut 7:84 England was controversial because it revealed many inconsistencies in the Arts Council's position. For example, if the strategy was to redirect resources to the regions then 7:84 England already embarked on extensive tours across the country and in many non-traditional venues. Accusations of political censorship were commonplace and featured heavily in 7:84 England's appeal document which contained numerous letters from prominent members of the Labour Movement and the arts such as David Edgar, Ian MacKellen and Arnold Wesker, alongside a petition signed by thousands of theatre-goers. The Arts Council declined to reconsider its decision.

Dear Luke Rittner

I understand that is the intention of the Arts Council to cut the grant to 7:84 Theatre Company England next year. It seems to me a savage and inexplicable step to withdraw funds from a company that has for many years provided work that is vigorous, witty, entertaining and stimulating often to audiences who have not experienced drama outside television, or in communities that have no theatres within accessible distance.

I urge you to reconsider your decision. British theatre needs *variety* of artistic policy if it is to retain its much vaunted claim of excellence.

Richard Eyre[127]

McGrath responded to the 'Tory cultural assassination squads'[128] by adapting *Six Men of Dorset*. Commissioned by the TUC, Miles Malleson and Harry Brooks wrote *Six Men of Dorset* to celebrate the centenary year of the Tolpuddle Martyrs in 1934. Combining documentary material within a modern morality play structure, it received an amateur premiere at the Dorchester Corn Exchange in 1934 and its first professional production in 1937 with Lewis Casson and Sybil Thorndike heading the cast. McGrath's adaptation marked the 150th anniversary of the Tolpuddle Martyrs and gained massive multi-union support from the Labour Movement. Trade Union money accounted for £45,000 of the £90,000 production budget and the programme for the show acknowledges support from twenty-five different unions and councils. Norman

Willis, the TUC General Secretary and Neil Kinnock, a 7:84 England Board member, launched the show at the House of Commons. Kinnock also provided a statement for the programme and a flyer declaring: 'If the Arts Council effectively abandons enterprises like 7:84 it will have abandoned its central purpose. In the process it will encourage the idea that "culture" is an exotic island that can only be inhabited by the affluent and the elevated.'[129]

In the wake of legislation to limit the power of the trade union movement and with the Miners' Strike raging in the background, the fight against injustice and the power of collective resistance represented in *Six Men of Dorset* remained alarmingly relevant. Kinnock found that: 'The struggle, in essence, has not changed since 1834. Under the Thatcher Government the Judiciary has again been thrust into the front line of trade union repression. The events of 1984 are proving a grim echo of the past'.[130] The connections were not lost on the audience. Joan Bakewell attended a performance at the Crucible Theatre, Sheffield, to record an item for BBC2's *Newsnight*. She documents, 'Four hundred miners—the men on strike have been invited free. They are deeply moved by the performance. "I've been out for 24 weeks and this tells me nothing's changed, we're still under attack".'[131] McGrath's adaptation highlighted contemporary resonances and 'transformed Malleson's deeply felt piece of 1930s social realism into stinging Brechtian agit-prop, heavily cut and studded with short, rousing songs of defiance'.[132] This praise was echoed by Robin Thorber who encountered 'a brilliantly clear, strong, and vital revival of a text that could easily have seemed stilted and dustily out of date'.[133] The success of the production is largely attributed to Pam Brighton's direction, 'the hard-edged energy of the company', Geoff Rose's 'economically fluid set' and the addition of 'male voice Methodist harmonies by John Tams', which for Sandra Bisp offered 'a stirring lament and battle cry'.[134]

The show toured to large-scale venues in Sheffield, Liverpool, Norwich, Ipswich, Newcastle, Weymouth, London and Cheltenham and ignited intense media coverage. The vast majority of reviews link the play's events with contemporary threats to the Labour Movement, but also highlight the intersection between 7:84 England's plight and the ideological repression faced by the Tolpuddle Martyrs. Michael Ratcliffe suggests Rees-Mogg and Luke Rittner 'have boxed themselves into a daft ideological corner'[135] and Benedict Nightingale's review is highly revealing:

> I can remember its name coming up again and again at the Drama Panel when this or that crusading tribe presented itself for assessment. 'Very interesting' people would say of Clenched Fist or Blood-Stained Banner or whatever, 'but not quite 7:84, don't you agree?'

Or, more positively: 'Quite promising—maybe one day we'll be able to mention it in the same breath as 7:84.' The company was what we kept in our mental pockets, ready to be whipped out and used to measure the quality of others; it was also, of course, clinching counter-evidence whenever anyone attacked the Council for funding combative or proselytising work. Yes, politically radical aims and high artistic standards could be reconciled. 7:84 proved it.[136]

After producing *The Garden of England,* a play by Peter Cox addressing the impact the Miners' Strike was having on individuals, families and communities, 7:84 England produced its final show, *All the*

Figure 14   All the Fun of the Fair flyer.

Fun of the Fair, in April 1986. After a complicated and controversial inception, which is documented at length in *The Bone Won't Break, All the Fun of the Fair* was finally produced at the Half Moon Theatre in London with a cast including Meera Syal, Peter Capaldi and Eve Bland and directed by Chris Bond. Experimenting with carnivalesque forms, McGrath created a promenade performance with contributions from Farrukh Dhondy, Chris Bond, David Anderson and David MacLennan. Originally conceived for a big top, McGrath maintained his vision of a funfair of booths, stalls and sideshows at the Half Moon Theatre. Hot-dog stands, loud music and brightly coloured booths daubed with famous right-wing statements such as 'On Yer Bike' and 'Rejoice!' greeted the audience as an M.C. figure guided them to various warped scenes of popular entertainment. A Punch and Judy show on the state of the NHS; 'Matcho Murdoch's Hall of Mirrors' offering a 'Wapping Wonderland' of media distortion and Farrukh Dhondy's possessed Bibi talking in tongues to provide ambiguous commentary on British colonial rule, anti-immigration legislation and contemporary race relations.

McGrath's 'Strip, Strip, Strip' scene presented the most disturbing section as Britt Aniella appears, 'the body of our voluptuous British state, unadorned by a single scrap of Public Relations, a single tissue of cosmetic mythology'.[137] As Herbert, a military-style pimp, introduces her, he strips the model revealing disease, deformity and decay. After uncovering her legs, Herbert explains:

> Oh heaven forfend—her legs deformed!
> The State must totter, come to harm—
> Oh why is this, what can it mean?
> This one so gross, and this so lean?
> This wasting limb, with due respects,
> Is those our state now quite rejects,
> The old, the young, the unemployed
> The sick whose lives are just a void,
> The ones whose welfare was our pride
> Until our state their worth denied—
> And now for all their welfare stamps
> Their sole supports are iron clamps.
>
> And this the gross and pampered leg
> The enterprising few who beg
> For more and more to fill their sacks
> Whose flab demands less Income Tax
> With one so gross and one so small,
> Will Britt Aniella walk at all?[138]

Unfortunately, *All the Fun of the Fair* 'suffered from its painful gestation: it should have been a thing of great joy: it became bitty and bitter'[139] and it received mixed critical reception. Typical is Lyn Gardner's review: 'John McGrath's intention to use the funfair as a deeply ironic metaphor for the unfunny realities of inner city life is a great idea which, although strongly atmospheric and performed with gusto, is negated by a wildly unfocused and frequently banal script'.[140]

Watching for Dolphins in the 1990s

After a five-year absence, McGrath returned to the English stage with *The Wicked Old Man,* directed by Jude Kelly at the West Yorkshire Playhouse in July 1992. He explained: 'I was becoming increasingly obsessed with the personal values of the beneficiaries of the Thatcherite free-market policies, of the people who kept voting her back in. I had conceived, and worked very hard on, a Molière-esque story of the way I saw these people's values: as a conflict between lust and greed.'[141] The multi-level staging, designed by Pamela Howard, represented key sites where the rich play out games of power and intrigue: a London embankment penthouse flat, a Tuscan villa, a Manhattan loft apartment and a country house in Sussex. A world founded on an underclass that services the rich whilst living amongst 'the condoms, the turds and the corpses: all golden, glowing in the light from the Western sky'.[142] A two-tier world based on a supply and demand ethos in which everything has become a tradable commodity. A classic whodunit narrative evolves as McGrath traces the various motivations for killing anarchic Harry Trowbridge, *The Wicked Old Man* of the title. After being widowed, seventy-two-year-old Harry decides to spend what time he has left trading his expensively acquired *objets d'art* for sex with young black men, in particular Sugar, a West Indian, heroin-addicted rent-boy. Harry's family find his actions financially, rather than morally, reprehensible as he threatens their plans to pay off debt or float on the stock market. 'McGrath's cold-eyed view of both the avaricious moneyed class and the desperate, drug-dealing underclass is bleak—this is what the ditching of altruism in the eighties has done to us all.'[143] McGrath never reveals the truth about Harry's death; instead, he exposes a morally bankrupt world governed by personal ambition, lust and greed.

A vision of society dictated by the power of market forces resides at the heart of *Watching for Dolphins,* a one-woman play written for Elizabeth MacLennan and 'in many ways co-created by her'.[144] McGrath and MacLennan gave a work-in-progress rehearsed reading of the play

Figure 15   Watching for Dolphins flyer.

at the Assembly Rooms during the 1991 Edinburgh Festival. Hastily staged and revised to respond to the momentous events in the Soviet Union when army tanks rolled into Estonia, Latvia and Georgia, the play spoke passionately of a crisis in socialism and the emergence of a new world order. Writing in the *Scotsman*, Colin Donald found the play marked 'an exciting new era' for McGrath's writing 'in the very best traditions of immediate, reactive, vital theatre'.[145]

Variously described as an elegy and lament for the Left, *Watching for Dolphins* concerns Reynalda, a rebellious socialist and feminist who participated in the struggles for liberation in the 1960s and 1970s, maintained an oppositional voice in the increasingly reactionary climate of the 1980s and finds her political beliefs discredited and marginalised in the 1990s. Reynalda is an intelligent, warm and creative character who intermittently plays Beethoven, Bartok and Scott Joplin on the piano and takes the audience into her confidence about her memories, hopes and fears. The play opens as Reynalda prepares to open a Bed and Breakfast in the mountains of North Wales by arranging food, fresh linen and decorative plants for her veranda. Reynalda is reluctantly commodifying the only resources she has, herself, her home and her heritage, for global tourists seeking Welsh charm and quaintness. Mocking heritage tourist brochures, she lapses into Dylan Thomasese as she imagines receiving her first guests:

> Come in, come in, here you will find a house proud hausfrau, with dinky cakelets on the doyley and winking Welsh warmth (*She winks warmly*)—not to mention crisp Welsh-laundered linen laden with lavender on the lay-awake beds, dream sweet, sweet dreams ... oh boyo—here is the nooky nook to ingle in, the olde-worlde oakie-beamies to Tudor under, the kiss-me-quick canopied beds to four-poster in.[146]

As in earlier plays, McGrath exhibits a deft command of language as his monologue shifts between intimate confessional, impassioned speeches, comical parody and ironic commentary. Through these multiple voices, McGrath achieves an intimate portrait of a disillusioned activist and an epic political survey of the last forty years. Reynalda explains how encountering patriarchal structures, colonial oppression, class-based exploitation, American imperialism and the demonisation of socialism ignited her political consciousness. She articulates her faith in and contribution to revolutionary causes and confesses to active participation in 'Demonstrations, rallies, meetings, car-stealing, border-hops, failed kidnappings, graffiti campaigns'.[147] Nonetheless, McGrath also presents the Left as a flawed and contra-dictory project given to compromise at best and violent suppression at its worst. The protests against political repression and corruption in Communist countries across Eastern Europe in the early 1990s are set against earlier historical events such as the Hungarian Uprising in 1956 and Prague Spring in 1968. Given the evidence around her, Reynalda has to reconcile herself to the triumph of capitalist forces throughout the world and to the fact that 'the very word socialism has become a foul word, anathema, another scar on history, like Nazism and the holocaust. We have become, in the eyes of the world, the very horror that we had set out to drive off the face of the earth'.[148] Hence

Figure 16   Elizabeth MacLennan as Reynalda Ripley in *Watching for Dolphins*.

Reynalda, who has dedicated her life to promoting the cause of socialism, faces a shocking and disorientating world in which political apathy reigns, the cult of celebrity rules and Francis Fukayama pronounces the 'end of history'.

McGrath also attempts to engage with the cultural condition described by postmodernity, in particular its defining characteristics of commodification and mediatisation. At an early point in the play, the intimate narrative is disrupted by Reynalda reconstructing her life as a cheap 'made for television' movie, followed by a Channel Four documentary charting her trajectory from progressive primary school teacher to blacklisted employee. As she enacts a producer demanding she repeat to camera: 'No, I can't get teaching work anywhere', McGrath signals his concern with this 'most important cultural nexus in our society'.[149] As Olga Taxidou observes, McGrath's 'optimism about the emancipatory and critical potential of television folds over in this play into the narcissism and indulgence of postmodernism'.[150]

Despite the political and cultural environment depicted in *Watching for Dolphins*, Reynalda continues to look for new signs of activism, the dolphins of the title. She scans the audience for evidence and admits: 'Every night I read the newspapers, watch my telly, phone my friends— "just to keep in touch". But I stand here now, at the rail, at 52, watching for dolphins. I scan the sea, but it's polluted, empty. But they are there. They will come'.[151] Giving in would leave her 'living with an incapacitating guilt, a sense of disgusting complicity'[1521] and the play ends with an ambiguous twist as she imagines greeting her first guests, Judge and Frau Schenker and Vice-President and Mrs Offaly. The Judge presided over the Bader Meinhof trials and Joe Offaly is 'in charge of buying bits of central America, Latin America, South-East Asia on the cheap,—oh and labour—even cheaper, I suppose'.[153] They represent everything Reynalda despises and as the doorbell rings, she contemplates an act of political terrorism:

> Judge and Frau Schenker
> Vice President and Mrs Offaly
> I am your servant.
> I am you assassin . . .?[154]

McGrath and MacLennan toured *Watching for Dolphins* to various venues including the Tricycle Theatre in London, a festival of women's theatre in Turin, the Glasgow Citizens' Theatre and the Theatre Workshop in Edinburgh. Overall, critics responded warmly to the piece and MacLennan's portrayal. Billington found it 'essential viewing both for its painful honesty and for its unquenchable belief in a more just and humane society'[155] and, despite reservations, Joyce MacMillan found that 'as a portrait of grief, the [play] is finally, almost in spite of itself, utterly convincing. Reynalda is widowed, bereft, lost and just often enough both the text and the performance find the courage to look straight into that emptiness'.[156]

How does the left deal with the collapse of state socialism in Eastern Europe? On Newsnight recently I saw a British communist official bobbing and weaving in front of just such a question from Jeremy Paxman. But John McGrath addresses the issue head-on in a fascinating one-woman play, Watching for Dolphins, playing late-nights at the Tricycle in Kilburn.

Elizabeth MacLennan plays a lifelong 52-year-old socialist preparing to open a B and B in North Wales and reminiscing about a life of political activism. She sold the Daily Worker to Cowley factory-hands as a student, joined the International Socialists, was in Paris for May 1968, was part of a women's group in the seventies and got sacked from a primary school in the eighties for teaching Marx, Engels and the Koran. Now she confronts the fact that socialism is a 'hate-word' akin to Nazism.

What is instantly striking about this play is its soul-baring honesty. Mr McGrath's heroine wonders whether confrontations with the state were purely ritualistic, whether her political views were the projection of a psychic need and whether faith overtook the reality 'We are defeated and it's better to admit it,' she says. But she takes comfort from the fact that throughout Eastern Europe 'people have stood up together and won' and contents herself with fantasising about wiping out corporatist German, American and Japanese guests at her B and B.

She is, however, endowed by Ms MacLennan with a remarkable fragility and the play itself is essential viewing both for its painful honesty and for its unquenchable belief in a more just and humane society.

Michael Billington[157]

Throughout the 1990s, McGrath worked primarily in Scotland. He continued to write one-person plays for MacLennan such as *Reading Rigoberta* (1994) about the life of Rigoberta Menchu and human rights abuses in Guatemala and *The Last of the MacEachans* (1996) about identity, migration and displacement in the Highlands. He created three plays for schools, *Media Star* (1996), *Worksong* (1997) and *The Road to Mandalay* (2000). With the political journalist Richard Norton-Taylor, he co-wrote *Half the Picture* (1994), a documentary account of the 'Arms to Iraq' Inquiry, which 'reduc [ed] 80 to 90 hours of evidence into one evening's "infotainment"'.[158] Between witness statements by Margaret Thatcher, John Major and Alan Clarke, McGrath inserted monologues recording the marginalized voices of those affected by the government's duplicitous actions: 'To this end, a Kurd victim of British arms, a Matrix Churchill worker, and a Palestinian supporter of Saddam all make an appearance.'[159] The result was an explosive piece of documentary theatre staged at the Tricycle Theatre, London in July 1994, and subsequently broadcast on BBC2. It is also notable for being the first play ever to be performed at the House of Commons and for sparking off a tradition of ground-breaking tribunal plays at the Tricycle Theatre that includes *Srebrenica*, *The Colour of Justice* and a forthcoming piece on the Hutton Inquiry.

Throughout the 1990s, there was increasing evidence of a new generation of political activism. Widely referred to as an 'anti-globalisation' movement, this term encompasses a multitude of interconnecting concerns with, amongst other things, the power of multinational corporations, American imperialism, environmental damage and third-world debt. A worldwide popular resistance movement has emerged and made its presence felt at large-scale public demonstrations against the World Trade Organisation, World Bank and the International Monetary Fund in cities across the world including Seattle, Prague and Genoa. McGrath's last play, *HyperLynx* (2001), began as an engagement with this political climate and cites many of its sources in the published edition of the play: STOPESSO and Christian Aid websites, George Monbiot's *Captive State: The Corporate Takeover of Britain* (2000), John Humphrey's *The Great Food Gamble* (2001) and Naomi Klein's *No Logo* (2000). During the writing process, and following a rehearsed reading at the Edinburgh Festival in 2001, the devastating events of 11 September 2001 intervened and McGrath embarked on radical revisions to incorporate a second Act that provides commentary on Palestine, Islamic fundamentalism and the threat of war in Afghanistan.

A one-person play, written for MacLennan to perform, *HyperLynx* received its first production after McGrath's death in January 2002. Directed by Kate McGrath for Floodtide Theatre Company, *HyperLynx* appeared at the Citizens' Theatre, Glasgow, the Edinburgh Festival and the Tricycle Theatre in London between May and September 2002. The play explores the moral dilemma faced by Heather Smithson, an MI5 agent with responsibility for Iran and Afghanistan, when her superiors ask her to infiltrate the anti-globalisation movement. Spending the morning of 11 September 2001 on a park bench, Smithson contemplates globalisation, government compliance with multinational corporations and the role she is being asked to play: 'I sense barbed wire, razor wire, land mines, new borders, new police: am I about to become a border guard for the new global empire?'[160] It transpires that Smithson has her own reservations, not only about government policy in the Middle East, but about the workings of global capital: its brutal suppression tactics, crippling drugs policies and the toxic chemicals employed to increase yields in food production. By Act Two, Smithson has witnessed the world change as hijacked aeroplanes exploded into the ultimate symbols of 'American commercial power, and American military might'[161] and McGrath connects the conditions that lead to this appalling act of terrorism with the conditions that fuel the anti-globalisation movement. According to Robert Dawson Scott, 'McGrath sign [ed] off his theatrical account with the anger, the commitment, not to mention the technique, undimmed.'[162]

The preceding account of McGrath's work in England, and the history of 7:84 England, provide a context for the plays that follow. It is hoped that by situating these plays within a wider body of work, readers will be able to identify the stages in McGrath's career that they represent and their connections with, and points of departure from, earlier and later plays. They are very different pieces, but each, in their own way charts McGrath's consistent faith in a theatre which explores and debates the nature of human agency, politics, historical processes and society.

Notes

[1] McGrath (1981c), p. 83.

[2] ibid., p. 81.

[3] McGrath (1975b), p. 41.

[4] Taylor (1979), p. 210.

[5] Cited in Carpenter (1985), p. 181.

[6] McGrath (1975b), pp. 41–2.

[7] Hewison (1986), p. 96.

[8] Carpenter (1985), p. 183.

[9] Hayman (1979), p. 88.

[10] Jeremy Rundall, 'First Nights: Events While Guarding the Bofors Gun', *Plays and Players* (June 1966), p. 48.

[11] McGrath (1975b), p. 44.

[12] McGrath (1966), p. 37.

[13] Bob Finch, Letter to *The Times*, 31 January 2002, p. 19.

[14] McGrath (1975b), pp. 39–40.

[15] Peter Thomson, 'Get Out and Get On: Events While Guarding the Bofors Gun', in Bradby and Capon (2005), p. 17.

[16] McGrath (1975b), p. 44.

[17] ibid.

[18] MacLennan (1990), p. 11.

[19] Van Erven (1988), p. 88.

[20] Kershaw (1992), p. 123.

[21] McGrath (1972), p. 17.

[22] Robin Thornber, 'Liverpool', *Plays and Players*, Vol. 18, No. 8 (May 1971), pp. 57 and 62.

[23] See below *Plugged in to History*, p. 92.

[24] ibid., p. 92.

[25] ibid., p. 92.

[26] ibid., p. 92.

[27] See below *They're Knocking Down the Pie Shop*, p. 104.

[28] See below *Angel of the Morning*, p. 77.

[29] ibid., p. 77.

[30] Irving Wardle, 'Unruly Elements', *The Times*, 11 March 1971, p. 13.

[31] Doreen Tanner, 'Everyman Puts on Sparkling Play Package', *Daily Post*, 23 March 1971, p. 6.

[32] Jonathan Hammond, 'Fringe', *Plays and Players*, Vol. 20, No. 1 (October 1972), p. 49.

[33] McGrath (1981), p. 52.

34 Alan Dossor, promotional poster for *Soft or a Girl?*, Elizabeth MacLennan's personal collection.

35 Cited in Itzin (1980), p. 125.

36 Tanner (1974), no page number.

37 ibid.

38 ibid.

39 McGrath (1977b), preface.

40 ibid.

41 Stanley Reynolds, 'The Fish in the Sea in Liverpool', *Guardian*, 30 December 1972, p. 12.

42 McGrath (1977b), back cover.

43 ibid., preface.

44 ibid.

45 See below *Fish in the Sea*, p. 156.

46 Craig (1980), p. 45.

47 Reinelt (1994), p. 192.

48 ibid., p. 193.

49 Stanley Reynolds, 'The Fish in the Sea in Liverpool', *Guardian*, 30 December 1972, p. 12.

50 See below *Fish in the Sea*, p. 156.

51 Maurice Meisner, *Mao's China and After: A History of the People's Republic* (New York: Free Press, 1999), p. 293.

52 Allen Wright, 'Suffering Play by Writer of Great Ability', *The Scotsman*, 28 August 1971, p. 6.

53 MacLennan (1990), p. 42.

54 Nicholas De Jongh, 'Fringe Benefits', *Guardian*, 31 August 1971, p. 12.

55 Itzin (1980), p. 121.

56 McGrath (2002b), p. 51.

57 McGrath (1971), p. 14.

58 See below *Trees in the Wind*, p. 114.

59 ibid., p. 114.

60 MacLennan (1990), p. 20.

61 See below *Trees in the Wind*, p. 114.

62 ibid., p. 114.

63 ibid., p. 114.

64 Anonymous, 'Commentary', *Times Literary Supplement*, 17 September 1971, p. 116.

65 Programme note, *Serjeant Musgrave Dances On*, Cambridge University Library, 7:84 England Theatre Company Archive, Box 5/28.

66 ibid.

67 John Bull, 'Serjeant Musgrave Dances to a Different Tune: John McGrath's Adaptation of John Arden's Serjeant Musgrave's Dance' in Bradby and Capon (2005), p. 39.

68 Alan Sked and Chris Cook, *Post-War Britain: A Political History*, 2nd edn (Harmondsworth: Penguin, 1984).

69 ibid., p. 262.

70 McGrath (2002b), p. 53.

71 Programme note, 7:84 England Archive, Box 5/28.

72 McGrath (2002b), p. 58.

73 Nadine Holdsworth, 'Finding the Right Places, Finding the Right Audiences: Topicality and Entertainment in the Work of 7:84 England' in Bradby and Capon (2005), p. 55.

74 Sandy Craig, in conversation with the author, 25 February 2003.

75 Programme note, 7:84 England Archive, Box 5/28.

76 See below *Fish in the Sea*, p. 156.

[77] ibid., p. 156.

[78] *Fish in the Sea* manuscript, Liverpool Everyman Archive, Liverpool John Moore's University, p. 88.

[79] See below *Fish in the Sea*, p. 156.

[80] Jonathon Hammond, 'Fringe', *Plays and Players*, Vol. 22, No. 12 (April 1975), pp. 27–8.

[81] Beata Lipman, 'Cardiff', *The Sunday Times*, 15 June 1975, p. 33.

[82] See below *Lay Off*, p. 236.

[83] ibid., p. 236.

[84] Nadine Holdsworth, 'Finding the Right Places, Finding the Right Audiences: Topicality and Entertainment in the Work of 7:84 England' in Bradby and Capon (2005), p. 55.

[85] Jonathon Hammond, 'Lay Off', *Plays and Players*, Vol. 22, No. 12 (September 1975), p. 35.

[86] See below *Lay Off*, p. 236.

[87] ibid., p. 236.

[88] Letter dated 28 June 1975, 7:84 England Archive, Box 5/28.

[89] Michael Coveney, 'Lay Off', *Financial Times*, 1 September 1975, p. 12.

[90] Beata Lipman, 'Cardiff', *The Sunday Times*, 15 June 1975, p. 33.

[91] Anne McFerran, 'Monopoly Bop', *Time Out*, 11–17 July 1975, p. 7.

[92] ibid.

[93] McGrath (2002b), p. 91.

[94] Michelene Wandor, *Carry On, Understudies: Theatre and Sexual Politics* (London: Routledge, 1986), p. 152.

[95] John McGrath, 'Letters', *Time Out*, 29 April–5 May 1977, p. 3.

[96] McGrath (1978), p. 61.

[97] Programme note, *Yobbo Nowt*, 7:84 England Archive, Box 5/28.

[98] McGrath (1978), preface.

[99] Michael Billington, 'Yobbo Nowt', *Guardian*, 10 December 1975, p. 10.

[100] Desmond Pratt, 'Theatres', *Yorkshire Post*, 7 November 1975, p. 8.

[101] Letter dated 3 May 1976, 7:84 England Archive, Box 5/28.

[102] Alan Sked and Chris Cook, *Post-War Britain: A Political History*, 2nd edn (Harmondsworth: Penguin, 1984).

[103] Interview with Colin Mortimer, 27 March 1980, 7:84 England Archive, Box 10/28.

[104] McGrath (2002b), p. 92.

[105] Van Erven (1988), p. 88.

[106] Letter dated 10 May 1976, 7:84 England Archive, Box 10/28.

[107] David Edgar, 'Wreckers—Thoughts on the Project', undated manuscript, 7:84 England Archive, Box 10/28.

[108] McGrath (2002b), p. 106.

[109] Beacham (1979b), p. 50.

[110] McGrath (2002), p. 107.

[111] ibid.

[112] Mass Observation Ltd, 'Report of the Survey of Small-scale Drama Groups' Audiences', Arts Council Library, Market Research Collection (1978), p. 9.

[113] *Bitter Apples* press release, 7:84 England Archive, Box 6/28.

[114] Undated letter, 7:84 England Archive, Box 6/28.

[115] Bitter Apples press release, 7:84 England Archive, Box 6/28.

[116] MacLennan (1990), p. 86.

[117] McGrath (1990), preface.

[118] Letter dated 29 October 1981, 7:84 England Archive, Box 7/28.

[119] Unpublished manuscript, p. 8, 7:84 England Archive, Box 2/28.

120 Arts Council of England, 7:84 England Company file.
121 ibid.
122 Walter Huntley, 'Looking at a Tory Life with Humour', *Liverpool Echo*, 8 September 1982.
123 McGrath (1990), p. 29.
124 See below *Rejoice!*, p. 284.
125 Joyce MacMillan, 'Affectionate Jibes from a Rejoicing McGrath', *Sunday Standard*, 29 August 1982, p. 20.
126 Ned Chaillet, '. . . and Authentic Revelations on the Fringe Too', *The Times,* 30 August 1982, p. 9.
127 Letter dated 14 May 1984 contained in 'Reasons for Not Terminating the Active Life of 7:84 Theatre Company England', 7:84 England Archive, Box 11/28.
128 Programme note for *Six Men of Dorset,* 7:84 England Archive, Box 8/28.
129 Publicity flyer for *Six Men of Dorset,* 7:84 England Archive, Box 8/28.
130 Programme note for *Six Men of Dorset,* 7:84 England Archive, Box 8/28.
131 Joan Bakewell, 'Death Threat to a Company', *The Listener,* 20 September 1984, p. 15.
132 John Peter, 'This Side of Revolution', *The Sunday Times*, 14 October 1984, p. 41.
133 Robin Thornber, 'Six Men of Dorset', *Guardian*, 5 September 1984.
134 Sandra Bisp, 'Powerful Drama of Truth', *Gloucestershire Echo,* 16 October 1984.
135 Michael Ratcliffe, 'Theatre', *Observer*, 14 October 1984, p. 14.
136 Benedict Nightingale, 'Standing Together', *New Statesman*, 19 October 1984, p. 35.
137 Unpublished manuscript, p. 19.
138 ibid.
139 McGrath (1990), p. 50.
140 Lyn Gardner, 'All the Fun of the Fair', *City Limits,* 10 April 1986.
141 McGrath (2002b), p. 197.
142 Unpublished manuscript, p. 24.
143 Robin Thornber, 'The Wicked Old Man', *Guardian*, 4 July 1992, p. 30.
144 Olga Taxidou, 'Three One-Woman Epics' in Bradby and Capon (2005), p. 156.
145 Colin Donald, 'Watching for Dolphins', *The Scotsman*, 27 August 1991, p. 9.
146 See below *Watching for Dolphins*, p. 325.
147 ibid., p. 325.
148 ibid., p. 325.
149 McGrath (1990), p. 146.
150 Olga Taxidou, 'Three One-Woman Epics' in Bradby and Capon (2005), p. 156.
151 See below *Watching for Dolphins*, p. 00.
152 ibid., p. 325.
153 ibid., p. 325.
154 ibid., p. 325.
155 Michael Billington, 'Watching for Dolphins', *Guardian*, 16 November 1991, p. 22.
156 Joyce Macmillan, 'Watching for Dolphins', *Guardian*, 2 June 1992, p. 34.
157 Michael Billington, 'Watching for Dolphins', *Guardian*, 16 November 1991, p. 26.
158 Aleks Sierz, 'Armed with the Truth', Red Pepper, July 1994, p. 41.
159 ibid.
160 McGrath (2002a) p. 11.
161 ibid., p. 35.
162 Robert Dawson Scott, 'HyperLynx/Wild Raspberries', *The Times*, 1 June 2002, p. 25.

Bibliography and Further Reading

Published Plays

Arden, John and Margaretta D'Arcy, 'The Ballygombeen Bequest' in *Scripts 9: The Irish Troubles,* Vol. 1, No. 9 (September 1972), pp. 4–50

Arden, John and Margaretta D'Arcy, *Vandaleur's Folly* (London: Methuen, 1981).

Edgar, David, *Wreckers* (London: Methuen, 1977).

Griffiths, Trevor, *Occupations,* (London: Calder and Boyers, 1972; revised ed. Faber and Faber, 1980).

Keefe, Barrie, *Sus* (London: Methuen, 1979)

Luckham, Claire, 'Trafford Tanzi', in Michelene Wandor (ed.) *Plays by Women: Volume Two* (London: Methuen, 1983).

Malleson, Miles and Harry Brooks, *Six Men of Dorset* (London: Victor Gollancz, 1934).

McGrath, John, *Events While Guarding the Bofors Gun* (London: Methuen, 1966).

McGrath, John, *Random Happenings in the Hebrides or The Social Democrat and the Stormy Sea* (London: Davis-Poynter, 1972).

McGrath, John, *Bakke's Night of Fame* (London: Davis-Poynter, 1973).

McGrath, John, *The Game's a Bogey* (Edinburgh: EUSPB, 1975a).

McGrath, John, *Little Red Hen* (London: Pluto Press, 1977a).

McGrath, John, *Fish in the Sea* (London: Pluto Press, 1977b).

McGrath, John, *Yobbo Nowt* (London: Pluto Press, 1978).

McGrath, John, *Joe's Drum* (Aberdeen: 7:84 Publications and Aberdeen People's Press, 1979a).

McGrath, John, *The Cheviot, the Stag and the Black, Black Oil* (London: Methuen, 1981a).

McGrath, John, *Two Plays for the Eighties: Blood Red Roses and Swings and Roundabouts* (Aberdeen: 7:84 Publications and Aberdeen People's Press, 1981b).

McGrath, John, *HyperLynx* (London: Oberon Books, 2002a).

Secondary Material

Beacham, Richard, 'Political Satire in Britain: The 7:84 Company', Theater, Vol. 10, (1979) pp. 49–53.

Bradby, David and Susanna Capon (eds) *Freedom's Pioneer: John McGrath's Work in Theatre, Film and Television* (Exeter: University of Exeter Press, 2005).

Bull, John, *New British Political Dramatists* (Basingstoke and London: Macmillan, 1984).

Carpenter, Humphrey, *OUDS: A Centenary History of the Oxford University Dramatic Society 1885–1985* (Oxford: Oxford University Press, 1985).

Cherns, Penny and Paddy Broughton, 'John McGrath's "Trees in the Wind" at the Northcott Theatre, Exeter', *Theatre Quarterly*, Vol. 5, No. 19 (September, 1975) pp. 89–100.

Craig, Sandy (ed.), *Dreams and Deconstructions: Alternative Theatre in Britain* (Ambergate: Amber Lane Press, 1980).

DiCenzo, Maria, *The Politics of Alternative Theatre in Britain 1968–1990: The Case of 7:84* (Cambridge: Cambridge University Press, 1996).

Gooch, Steve, *All Together Now: An Alternative View of Theatre and the Community* (London: Methuen, 1984).

Hayman, Ronald, *British Theatre since 1955: A Reassessment* (Oxford: Oxford University Press, 1979).

Hewison, Robert, *Too Much: Art and Society in the Sixties* (London: Methuen, 1986).

Holdsworth, Nadine, 'Good Nights Out: Activating the Audience with 7:84 (England)', *New Theatre Quarterly*, Vol. 13, No. 49 (February, 1997), pp. 29–40.

Itzin, Catherine, *Stages in the Revolution: Political Theatre in Britain since 1968* (London: Methuen, 1980).

Kershaw, Baz, *The Politics of Performance: Radical Theatre as Cultural Intervention* (London: Routledge, 1992).

McGrath, John, 'Power to the Imagination: Conversations with John McGrath about Theatre and the State', *Scottish International* (October 1971), pp. 10–15.

McGrath, John, 'Better a Bad Night in Bootle . . .', *Theatre Quarterly*, Vol. 5, No.19, (September, 1975b), pp. 39–54.

McGrath, John, 'The Theory and Practice of Political Theatre', *Theatre Quarterly*, Vol. 9, No. 35, (September, 1979b), pp. 43–54.

McGrath, John, *A Good Night Out*, (London: Methuen, 1981c).

McGrath, John, 'Popular Theatre and the Changing Perspective of the Eighties', *New Theatre Quarterly*, Vol. 1, No. 4 (November, 1985), pp. 390–99.

McGrath, John, *The Bone Won't Break* (London: Methuen, 1990).

McGrath, John, *Naked Thoughts That Roam About*, ed. by Nadine Holdsworth (London: Nick Hern Books, 2002b).

MacLennan, Elizabeth, *The Moon Belongs to Everyone: Making Theatre with 7:84* (London: Methuen, 1990).

Peacock, Keith D., *Thatcher's Theatre: British Theatre and Drama in the Eighties* (Westport and London: Greenwood Press, 1999).

Poggi, Valentina and Margaret Rose (eds), *A Theatre That Matters: Twentieth-Century Scottish Drama and Theatre* (Milan: Edizioni Unicopli, 2000).

Rawlence, Chris, 'Political Theatre and the Working Class', in *Media, Politics and Culture* ed. Carl Gardner (Basingstoke: Macmillan, 1979), pp. 61–70.

Reinelt, Janelle, *After Brecht: British Epic Theater* (Michigan: University of Michigan Press, 1994).

Stevenson, Randall and Gavin Wallace (eds), *Scottish Theatre Since the Seventies* (Edinburgh: Edinburgh University Press, 1996).

Taylor, John Russell, *Anger and After: A Guide to New British Drama*, 2nd edn (London: Methuen, 1979).

Tanner, Doreen, *Everyman: The First Ten Years* (Liverpool: The Merseyside Everyman Theatre Company, 1974).

Taxidou, Olga, 'Where Exactly is Scotland?: Local Cultures, Popular Theatre and National Television', in Jeremy Ridgman (ed.), *Boxed Sets: Television Representations of Theatre* (Arts Council of England, John Libbey Media and the University of Luton, 1998), pp. 89–105.

Theatre Quarterly Symposium, 'Playwriting for the Seventies: Old Theatres, New Audiences, and the Politics of Revolution', *Theatre Quarterly*, Vol. 6, no. 24 (November 1976), pp. 35–78.

Trussler, Simon (ed.), *New Theatre Voices of the Seventies* (London: Methuen, 1981).

Van Erven, Eugene, '7:84 in 1985: 14 Years of Radical Popular Theater in Great Britain', *Minnesota Review*, Vol. 27, (Autumn 1986), pp. 103–16.

Van Erven, Eugene, *Radical People's Theatre* (Indiana: Indiana University Press, 1988).

There are extensive archive collections on John McGrath and the 7:84 Theatre Companies held at the Manuscripts Department, Cambridge University Library, and the National Library of Scotland in Edinburgh.

The Plays

THEY'VE GOT OUT

Mrs A
Mr A

A small living-room. MR A *fiddling with something.*
Enter MRS A *from street.*

MRS A: *They've got out.*
MR A: Oh. Oh.
MRS A: I have telephoned the police.
MR A: Mm—Mmm.
MRS A: There was no reply.
MR A: Hold that.
MRS A: Why do you think that was?
MR A: Probably all pissed as farts.
MRS A: Probably all out looking for them.
MR A: Flicking snot at the sergeants, puking all over the inspectors—I've
seen a coppers' outing, in my time.
MRS A: The coppers are all out hunting them down.
MR A: Hold that . . . Who said they got out?
MRS A: I had the wireless on.
MR A: The wireless's closed down.
MRS A: Yes, but I had it on, and out of the crackling comes a call, and a
girl laughing, and then that man said 'This is the Angel Gabriel
speaking—they've got out'.
MR A: Then it went dead again.
MRS A: Bit more trumpets. When you're asleep, they come round gluing
your eyes together.
MR A: Ha—who told you that?
MRS A: I seen it—on the pictures: look at life.
MR A: They *showed* you?
MRS A: No—they mentioned it. Araldite.
MR A: Ha Ha. What about your lips.
MRS A: What about my lips?
MR A: Hm—I suppose they stitch them together.
MRS A: Stitch?
MR A: Concrete the nostrils . . .
MRS A: What are you talking about?
MR A: Plug up your earholes . . .
MRS A: I shall in a minute—

MR A: Bung up your bum . . . That's what they do, I suppose.

MRS A: (*Peeved*) No—it's just the eyes. Whoever said anything about all
           that other?

MR A: Ha—ha . . . you're outmanoeuvred
           (*Pause*)
           Hold this.

MRS A: They *are* said to be beautiful.

MR A: I suppose they come on singing the Eriscay Love Lilt.

MRS A: I don't know what makes you think they're all Scottish—

MR A: Beautiful. Tt. Stinking.

MRS A: I believe in the resurrection of the body. You've said that—you'll
           say it again.

MR A: I doubt it. Not after this episode.

MRS A: Oh yes you will.

MR A: I believe in the resurrection of the body beautiful—that's what
           you're saying. Mr A and Mr A's Universe only need answer the
           trump . . . that's not what it says.

MRS A: All bodies are beautiful.

MR A: Yes, and all you need is love: you do talk a load of old cobblers.

MRS A: Why are you so *sour*?

MR A: Sour?

MRS A: You're insanely jealous.

MR A: Jealous?

MRS A: You don't want to know about their transcendental
           mellifluousness . . .

MR A: Transcendental mellifluousness?—Rubbish.

MRS A: That'll be what it is.

MR A: Oh will it?

MRS A: If not that—what?

MR A: You don't know the half.

MRS A: What?

MR A: You're under-informed, and not sensitive to my moods.

MRS A: What?

MR A: You go on as if you wish me to strike you.

MRS A: Tell me then. What don't I know the half of?

MR A: That's better. You see it's nicer when you're reasonable.

MRS A: Mm. (*Pause*) What?

MR A: Well just think about it.

MRS A: I have done.

MR A: And?

MRS A: And what?

MR A: Didn't it occur to you what a terrible shambles, what a shameful,
           disgraceful, an unbearable indignity, what an unbearable balls-up
           it would be?

MRS A: No.

MR A: What? You'd be the first to complain: to start with three-quarters
           of them would be foreigners, bleeding Romans, Angles, Saxons,
           Jutes, them conquerors, Normans, Vikings, Danes, great hairy-
           assed Finns lusting for a good rape after all that time in the

ground—how far back do you go anyway, bleedin' little stone-age twits grunting about the place. Neanderthals, cannibals—how far back do you go?

MRS A: I hadn't thought of that . . .

MR A: No—you don't think, woman—And just remember how many of them there's going to be—hullyballooing around, all chatting in bloody Latin, and Norse, and Goidelic, and horrible grunts: nobody'll understand a blind bloody word anyone says: it'll be pandemonium.

MRS A: Oh it won't be like that at all.

MR A: All those centuries, you see, they were very clever—inventing the wheel, and the hammer, and illuminated manuscripts and beautiful poetry and suchlike—but they just didn't know how to behave. Hold that.

MRS A: Oo look—the crazy paving's started to heave.
         (*They both go over to the window.*)

THE END

UNRULY ELEMENTS/PLUGGED IN

These three plays were originally presented at the Everyman Theatre, Liverpool in 1971 as part of a series with *Out of Sight* and *My First Interview* called *Unruly Elements*. These three plays were subsequently performed, together with *Hover Through the Fog*, as *Plugged In* by the 7:84 England Company in 1972. These productions involved the following casts:

Angel of the Morning

Mr Lodwick:	Roger Sloman/Anthony Haygarth
Tralee:	Gillian Hanna

Plugged in to History

Kay:	Angela Philips/Elizabeth MacLennan
Derek:	Robert Hamilton

Knocking Down the Pie Shop

Neil:	Dermot Hennelly/Clifford Cocker
Malden:	Gavin Richards/Anthony Haygarth
Jenny:	Angela Philips/Vari Sylvester
Mrs Malden:	Gillian Hanna

These plays take place in an acting area cleared between piles of furniture, grotesquely inflated objects (e.g. six-foot toothbrush, ten-foot coke bottle, giant detergent packet, etc.) and against a background of the geometric patterns of contemporary life in bright colours. A couple of freestanding doors and a window frame will help. The sets are changed at the end of each play and the characters beginning the next play are in position before and during the introductory pieces. These pieces are spoken by one or several of the company but dressed in the same minimal drab uniform. It is important that these pieces are spoken as if they make complete sense to the character speaking them. They can move around the set and even address the waiting characters in the plays as well as the audience.

Introduction to *Angel of the Morning*

Enter a middle-aged JERRY BUILDER. *He speaks to the audience, grinning confidentially.*

JERRY BUILDER: Yobble de hoo. Dare we mar again. Uvly new ousses dey bilt or lover de swamp ere. (*Sniffs*)
   Sniffa da chemiculls—norrabadtin, cumtatinkofit: wurd we all be, mittout da plastix? Uvly ousses—
   Da trouble is da unksters. All dose young leople hoppin all over da flower-debs. Im dey Tum, whisk end dey do. Piserable ungsters, danksters dey are—no luv. Luv mean bugrall. An whaffor? Luv is a pleny-wendored wing, o-o, yes an dey no onting off it. Dey'm flooming tikiotic. Dem make murk along. Brawdnig—broom, broom, broom, broom, ikey-botors, broom broom unt smash, squash, alldabuddy nie long.
   Ya see, we'm da buzzy biddies: edifying monstructions, oobling up mouses—oo tlive in, ook, ook, nike people, ook at de mouses we oobled por dem. Und loaf we have por dem, oops and oops of loaf por dem, too much loaf praps, bu wegorri—funnything, mennything, rennything dey grab we got we give. Oops of loaf. Dem esposed dig us like crazy. Do dey? Do dey duck—egg your margin, imsis, egg your margin, urse, itch get otched off away, noo noo. (*Sighs*) Dem unksters.
   Ta debing vit: we'm da kiddies vot blooed it all up! All dat russhib. Blooed it all pie-sigh. Agos twas robble: horrible. Oo many ouses, oo many leople—not enug spatse. Bu *ve* dign leebensroom shout—oh doe, ear me dow doe. Agos Tiggler shotted dat und boom boom tvas drabstruction. Vem da kiddies vot bilt up da nooo ickle cuddly ickle mousing ersties: da hairy noo sububs, down by da swamp, lika dis won ere (*Sniffs*). Por da ickle kiddies ta fill der lungs an grow up wrong an wealthy. Da old tizzy dwellins, da bax to bak, da tennymens was robble, horroble—now dey rubble, hurruble, an auf auf auf of dem ole tummunities, into da noo wins—it was a try-umph.
   Bu da bruttle is dis—da unksters. Dey'm dinjusted mitta noo vons. Dey wun marred. Ich bin bruttly mangry mittum. Ve'm all be bruttly mangry, agos dey doan per-reesee—hate it. Dey'm dingrateful. Ug Bruttle Tebbruttle Ich bin trebly mangry, agos dey give da mousing er-sties a stinkin rotten re puke-ation, an down goes da pwices. An dey hop all over da flower-debs. Lak a sed. Ich doan diggus, no'a'or: ich undiggum.

ANGEL OF THE MORNING

A few props to indicate a suburban living-room. MR LODWICK, *43-year-old Dad, sits ulcerously hunched over his stomach pretending to read a volume of the Encyclopaedia Britannica. It is 2.30 in the morning.*

MR LODWICK: Any minute now she'll be fitting the key into the lock.
Inserting it.
Turning it, slowly but firmly,
rolling the tumblers,
easing the tongue,
withdrawing the blade
slipping it back, ever so quietly—
and tip-toeing in through that there front door.
Then what? Huh.
Tippy-toe,
shoes off,
stocking feet
over the hall carpet and up them creaky old stairs.
Every sodding night since she was fifteen—
five years.
And do you think she won't know I'm here? Of course she
will—hah. She'll have seen the light on, chinks in the curtains,
crack under the door, SHE CAN SMELL ME HERE.

Anyway, I'm always up waiting for her, two o'clock, three
o'clock, one bloody Bank Holiday half past four—tried to kid
me on she'd been to a folk-club in Rochdale. 'And who was
plucking his old guitar?' I asked her. Usual answer. Sniffs her
nose up another half-an-inch higher, and stalks off to bed.
Hussy. Do you know what's the first thing she does, the minute
she gets in her pink little Boudoir?
Strips off. The lot.
So's I can't get in and give her what for. But I will. One
night I will. I'll really make her pink little arse tingle. Except
for her, her up there, snoring. Her with the bingo-card where
her brain ought to be. Old cut-price. My cut-price wife. Do
you know, she brought home six dozen tins of dog-food, cut-
price: a sin to miss it, she said. Now she's keeping her eye
open for a cut-price dog to eat the bloody stuff. She wouldn't
like it if I tanned the arse of our Barby: leave her, she says,
don't know why you wait up, she says, why can't you come
up to bed, she says—doesn't know the meaning of
responsibility.
It's beginning to affect my work, actually. Four years, no,
nearly five—and I've got to be up by quarter to seven, I've got
a long way to go—it's hitting me, I'm getting prematurely old,
it'll be the death of me.
Sh!
Aha—this'll be her now.
Listen: key in key-hole
(Sings) Bend it, bend it, just a little bit and—
take it easy now you're liking it—
Sh!
Now she'll be creeping across the hall, sneaking up the stairs.

NOT SO FAST YOUNG LADY!
(*Bounds across room. Door opens in his face. Enter a young girl of eighteen*—TRALEE CLAUSEWITZ)

TRALEE: Hello—

MR LODWICK: You're not our Barby—

TRALEE: Aren't I?

MR LODWICK: Is she out there?

TRALEE: Who?

MR LODWICK: I thought I heard—

TRALEE: Your Barby's not out there. She's in the back of an old Ford Prefect with a fellow drives a floating crane.

MR LODWICK: She's never—where is it—just let me get my hands on her.

TRALEE: They wanted to come in here, but—

MR LODWICK: *In*? In here? *They*? *Wanted*? Bloody hell.

TRALEE: Well a Ford Prefect's a very small car, and he is a very big fella. She'll be getting crushed to death. Probably won't mind though.

MR LODWICK: I'll give her a Ford Prefect. I'll give her Mister bloody Floating bloody Crane. I'll let her in alright—in for the biggest bloody seeing-to she's ever had in her life—

TRALEE: Mm—she'll be getting that, alright.

MR LODWICK: Aa? What?—who *are* you?

TRALEE: Barby's friend. She gave me the key. She said you'd be waiting up.

MR LODWICK: And—?

TRALEE: Well, here I am . . . You see, Barby thinks you're being unreasonable. We all do.

MR LODWICK: All?

TRALEE: Me and Barby and Janet and Alice. I mean, staying up. Why can't you go to bed?

MR LODWICK: And let her sneak in here with crane-drivers? Not on your— Under my roof?

TRALEE: (*Angry*) Well just think how bloody uncomfortable your daughter is in the back of that tin Lizzie. Dangerous, too.

MR LODWICK: What do you mean—?

TRALEE: Some of these fellas can turn a bit nasty, you know. Well, I mean, it's one thing in your own sitting-room; it's something else again in some rotten field off the East Lancs Road. There's that, too.

MR LODWICK: What?

TRALEE: Peeping Toms. Creeping about in the shadows. Peering in. Getting worked up, carried away. Trying the door, waving a knife at you. Wanting God knows what. That's happened to me you know. And the scuffs. The police is worse than what they're protecting you from. Driving up with no lights on, then FLASH and running out to have a good look, make you open the door and get out in the cold, then they've got the bloody nerve to give you a little sermon: and if you speak up—that's it. Kiss in the car case, all over again—do you remember that case?

MR LODWICK: Mm. Disgusting.

TRALEE: Well how'd you like your Barby to have her good name
dragged through the courts of the land, just because you're too
mean to go to bed early? We think it's because you don't fancy
your old lady.

MR LODWICK: Now listen young woman—

TRALEE: Can I sit down a minute?

MR LODWICK: Help yourself—but I'll want to know, you know, just exactly
where this car is . . .

TRALEE: Oh, I couldn't say—I really don't know.

MR LODWICK: East Lancs Road, you said.

TRALEE: Well there's hundreds of fields off it, aren't there, and for all I
know they've slipped up the motorway: you can be in the Lake
District in an hour or so, you know. Scuffers are nicer up there,
and you get a better view. *Do* you fancy your old lady?

MR LODWICK: In some *field*? In the *Lake District*? With an enormous *crane-
driver*? You just wait till you get home, my little chicken, just
you wait. I'll teach you. I'll make your arse tingle so much you
won't want to sit down for a fortnight. I'll shake you and
shake you till your teeth are rattling in the back of your head.
(*Smacks hands together*) And you won't get out again so easy.
Oh, you can fight and bite and struggle, but you won't get the
better of *me*. You've bitten me before, haven't you, my pretty
one? (*Pulls up sleeve*) Look, look at that. But you never got the
better of me, did you? Did you? No. I'll pin you down, on that
bed like an Amazonian Purple Moth, pinned to a spread of
black velvet. I'll tie you, tie you down my beauty, so you won't
be able to move a finger to resist me, and then we'll see where
your crane-drivers are, what good your bloody giant navvies
are going to do you . . . Ha! You won't move for a week when
I've finished with you. (*Pause*) What are you doing?

TRALEE: Taking my coat off. Do you mind?

MR LODWICK: Help yourself.

TRALEE: Can I have a drink?

MR LODWICK: Oh, I'm sorry—over there love. Good of you to bother to come
and tell me, really—I'm very grateful.

TRALEE: Anything for you?

MR LODWICK: Oh—I don't, no. Very rarely touch it. Very, very rarely.

TRALEE: Go on. Have a little whisky. Steadies the nerves.

MR LODWICK: Oh my nerves are steady enough—

TRALEE: Hold out your hand.

MR LODWICK: What?

(*She takes his hand and holds it out. It trembles.*)
Haha. Trembling. (*Looks at her*) Alright then, better have a
little whisky. Oo, not too much. Ta.

TRALEE: Here's to your continuing vitality, Mr Lodwick.

MR LODWICK: Cheers. Here's to yours, er—

TRALEE: Tralee.

MR LODWICK: Tralee?

TRALEE: My grandmother comes from there.
MR LODWICK: I see.
TRALEE: Just as well it wasn't the other one—she came from Cracow; but she's Polish and altogether too bloody healthy.
MR LODWICK: Well—Good health, Tralee.
TRALEE: Cheerihoh, Mr Lodwick.
              (*They drink. A silence. Noise from upstairs*)
MR LODWICK: What's that?
TRALEE: Could be Mrs Lodwick—
MR LODWICK: Sh!
              (*They both stand, arms stretched out. She takes his hand, for protection*)
TRALEE: Can't have been anything. These old houses.
MR LODWICK: It's a new house.
TRALEE: Settling down, probably. These new houses.
MR LODWICK: Do you live round here? I can't remember seeing you around the place?
TRALEE: Willowbank Glebe—you know, through Poinsettia Walk. They all look the same anyway. Our house is identical with this one really. Stuck in a different field—thrown up by a different bunch of crooks. What beats me is how they think of the names: what's yours called—Laudatory Manor Parkway—can't you just see some old jerry-builder, and a couple of thuggy money-men and a bent accountant putting their heads together. 'Ere, Sir Jack, what we gonna call dis heap of breeze-block and chip-board we got goin' up in da' marshy bog on de edge of de chemical works?' 'Warrabow Effluent Alley' 'Warrabow Hum Corner' 'Warrabow Slag Meadow'—'Getting Warm'—Now what I want to know is—which one of them thought of Laudatory Manor Parkway?
MR LODWICK: Don't you like the name? Mm? My wife—Mrs Lodwick—that was why we moved here in the first place. It was the name—caught her eye.
              (*Silence*)
TRALEE: Mr Lodwick.
MR LODWICK: Yes?
TRALEE: Do you fancy Mrs Lodwick?
MR LODWICK: Er—haha. Haha. (*Shifts about*) Funny you should ask that.
TRALEE: Why are you shifting about?
MR LODWICK: Am I?
TRALEE: You know what you need, don't you?
MR LODWICK: Me? Need? What? No. I mean. Haha.
TRALEE: You need a—
MR LODWICK: (*Puts hand up*) No no, let me guess. Don't tell me, don't tell me. Er—maybe it had better come as a surprise, when it happens—
TRALEE: What do you do, Mr Lodwick?
MR LODWICK: Ah. Very dull, very dull. Not the sort of thing I'd want to chat to a young lady like yourself about:

TRALEE: Oh? What, then?

MR LODWICK: Well now, er—er—

TRALEE: Tralee—

MR LODWICK: Yes, Tralee—humm—well, I work in: we used to make
              chocolate machines, those old red iron jobs, tanner in the slot,
              pull out the little drawer—bar of chocolate. You remember.
              Don't get much call for that sort of thing these days. Cigarette
              machines. Food machines. Shoe polishers. Chemist's products.
              Systems, you see. There's a lot of American money in it now, of
              course, wholly-owned subsidiary: so we don't think machines
              anymore, we, er, think systems. Look, I'm very upset about my
              daughter. I mean, you young people treat all this sort of thing
              as a bit of a laugh, but I'm afraid I can't.

TRALEE: There's nothing for you to worry about, Mr Lodwick.

MR LODWICK: Hm. Glad you think so.

TRALEE: Well is there?

MR LODWICK: Only the obvious.

TRALEE: What?

MR LODWICK: You know. One in the oven. Mrs Lodwick, she'd die. And for
              me. The shame of it. I'm not a prude, but—

TRALEE: (Laughing) Barby? Get pregnant?

MR LODWICK: I can't see it as a joke. I love my daughter, I don't want her to
              go through that suffering—

TRALEE: But she's been on the pill since she was fourteen. We all have—

MR LODWICK: What, you as well?—Barby, my little girl, on the pill, giving
              herself blood-clots, risking death—

TRALEE: But you must have known. You must have thought about it at
              the very least.

MR LODWICK: Must I? I suppose I must have forced those speculations out of
              my head. Ostrich, eh?

TRALEE: Don't be upset about Barby, Mr Lodwick. She's alright.
              Probably never been happier in her life than she is right now.

MR LODWICK: Do you think? I'm not sure that makes me feel any better.
              (Pause)

TRALEE: Tell me about these systems.

MR LODWICK: Systems? Oh, nothing really. They don't concern me. I'm only a
              Supervisor—checker really—I insert the first sixpence in to the
              virgin fruit-machines, watch them disintegrate, send them back.
              You see, we don't sell machines any more—we sell ways of
              marketing goods, and services, without shop-assistants. Why
              have shops? Miserable bloody places, aren't they? Who'd want
              to be selling things all day long, exposed to the terroristic
              activities of the general public? Anyway, who needs to stand in
              rotten queues, even in supermarkets, listening to jingles on the
              loudspeaker, getting rammed into by hundreds of other weary
              shoppers? We don't need that. What we need is a bloody great
              hall of selling-machines, effortlessly replenished morning, noon
              and night, the flow of supply and demand electronically
              regulated, computerised forecasts, totally flexible programming,
              consumer-regulated markets—

TRALEE: It's the vision of the future, Mr Lodwick.
MR LODWICK: Don't you see the possibilities?
TRALEE: Well—er—it's a bit impersonal—1984–ish.
MR LODWICK: Nonsense. Nonsense. I've read 1984. I've seen it on television—
               before your time I expect—funny that, to think of something
               on TV being before anybody's time. No, George Orwell got it
               all wrong. Because he didn't think systems.
                   You see, what is the beauty of systems? It's this: they're not
               impersonal. Why? Because when you stop thinking PRODUCT,
               you start thinking of a SATISFY-NEED SYSTEM, and when
               you stop thinking MACHINE you start thinking GET-JOB-
               DONE-SYSTEM, and when you stop thinking BUSES, you
               start thinking PEOPLE FROM A to B SYSTEM—And don't
               you see—it's asking the right questions: not—what can the
               factory make, but what do the people need, not "how many
               slaves to run this mill to make the cotton", but what do people
               want to wear, not how many more buses can we cram onto the
               streets, but how can we get people from where they are to
               where they want to be. You see, that's the beauty of systems:
               they always come down to the *people*: what do they want?
               How can we organise it best, cheapest, and with the fewest
               people slaving away. It's not *im*personal—it's setting persons
               free, liberating them, personally—people won't have to stand
               behind counters all day, collect bus-fares—they'll have to share
               the work-load—of the systems, I mean, help the factory-men,
               the maintenance-men, the creators themselves—BUT *nobody'll*
               need to do more than two hours a day—provided it's all co-
               ordinated by a proper master-system, not a mob of bloody
               money-men carving each other up and everybody else too, like
               in America—thoroughly inefficient, wasteful, deleterious way of
               going on that—no—a government system, a flexible,
               responsive, obedient system, protecting, not attacking people,
               doing what *we* want—expressing *us*, the will of the liberated
               people made flesh—what about that?
TRALEE: But—I'm not sure people would ever know what they really
               want, if you see what I mean—that's the one thing people
               really don't want: having to decide—having to choose: because
               most people don't know; deep down they're covering up an
               awful monster that devours everything, feeds on what they
               think, gobbles up every idea, crams every experience into its big
               fat mouth; the terrible monster called Don't Know, lurking
               somewhere between your stomach and your back-side,
               growling at everything.
MR LODWICK: No. I can't believe you. Are you like that?
TRALEE: I'm not. I know what I want. But my mother can never decide,
               nor my father—and I bet Mrs Lodwick—

MR LODWICK: Yes, I suppose you're right: she does have a certain gnawing lack
               of decision not very far below the surface. But, you know, when
               I see this world in my head, I see it full of young people—nice,

intelligent, well-educated, people—trying to live out their own lives in ways that they might have read about or dreamed about, pushing onwards to something better, always better, for more and more people. I see people like you, Tralee—that's what I see: you.

TRALEE: Have you ever told this to anybody?

MR LODWICK: No.

TRALEE: It's quite touching, really. Is that what you sit here thinking about night after night?

MR LODWICK: (*Wearily*) No.

TRALEE: You do love her, don't you?

MR LODWICK: Well—I *am* her father . . .

TRALEE: But you *know* she's alright, and happy—

MR LODWICK: Do I?

TRALEE: Yes, you do know that: don't you want her to be?

MR LODWICK: Well—does she have to—?

TRALEE: Yes: everything in her own way.

MR LODWICK: Then—
(*Pause*)

TRALEE: What is it you want her to do for you, Mr Lodwick?
(*Pause*)

MR LODWICK: I keep hoping she might save me. Did *I* say that? I've never seen you around these parts, Tralee, you've not been in to call for Barby, have you?

TRALEE: Oh yes. I've seen you going down the station, too, very early in the morning, about a quarter past seven. You always look grey, and ill, but springy—bouncing over it all, hup into the morning—am I right? I'm always getting up at quarter past seven, and I like to sit on the bed and stare out of the window: and there you are.

MR LODWICK: Just call me Angel of the Morning, as the song goes.
(*Pause. They hear a noise upstairs*)
What—? There is somebody up there, going through the drawers—

TRALEE: Oh, don't be silly. Who's somebody? Here—do you know why you keep hearing things upstairs?

MR LODWICK: Why?

TRALEE: Guilty conscience . . .

MR LODWICK: Guilty? What of?

TRALEE: Me. You know, talking to, having a laugh with—fancying, a little bit—? Don't you?

MR LODWICK: Fancying? Ha. Haha. I'm old enough to be your father—not that you're not, well, you know, quite comely.

TRALEE: Comely?

MR LODWICK: Attractive.

TRALEE: Really?

MR LODWICK: Well, yes, not that—well, you *are*. A young woman, full of beans, vitality, big eyes, mouth, smile—

TRALEE: Yes?

MR LODWICK: Oh yes. You seem a very forthcoming person, a girl one could become—deeply-attracted to.

TRALEE: I'm on the pill, too . . .

MR LODWICK: What?

TRALEE: You're on the whole an extremely sensual man, I'd say. Well, I mean, I can tell. If I was lying in front of you smiling at you with nothing on except my vitality—you *do know*, now, what you'd want to do with me, don't you?

MR LODWICK: Wh—do I?

TRALEE: Mmm. You've worked it all out, haven't you?

MR LODWICK: But no such thoughts ever crossed my mind—

TRALEE: Haha—they may not have crossed, but they crept in and circled around a bit, didn't they?

MR LODWICK: Tralee: don't mock me. I'm old—

TRALEE: No you're not, you're . . . forty-one.

MR LODWICK: Forty-three.

TRALEE: D'you call that *old*? Listen, I heard a poet who's seventy-*seven*, lecturing in this teachers' training college; they say he's after every bit of knicker in the campus—getting them off too. Don't get down-hearted: you've got thirty-four years of rich sexual experience ahead of you—at least.

MR LODWICK: That's more than I've got behind me—put that way, life becomes quite sprightly. What do you propose?
(*She goes over and sits on the arm of his chair*)

TRALEE: It doesn't have to be me, you know.

MR LODWICK: No, but—

TRALEE: Any girl, young girl, would do, I imagine—just to start you off.

MR LODWICK: Why—*any*?

TRALEE: You have been thinking about me, haven't you? Have you? Having fantasies?

MR LODWICK: You have—er—given me cause—to wonder if—

TRALEE: Oh, stop it, you're making yourself all old again: you were just getting a bit of a glisten in your eye, a bit of a nervous thing in you, that thing that strikes when you might be going to get it, but you're not sure—the elixir of life, the great rejuvenator— then you lost it. If it should come back—don't lose it again.

MR LODWICK: Why?

TRALEE: I liked it.

MR LODWICK: Oh. I think it's coming back alright—

TRALEE: Have you been faithful to her?

MR LODWICK: Yes. In my own way. It's been difficult, but—I managed. I succeeded.

TRALEE: Why?

MR LODWICK: She's my wife. She does the breakfast—cleans the house, does the shopping—we have our daughter, Barby—

TRALEE: Who's big enough to look after herself. Listen—any man that kips with me cooks his own bloody breakfast—mine too: what's so special about cooking breakfast and cleaning a rotten house—? Is she so fantastic you couldn't think of any woman in the world? Does she ennoble you, sexually, to a pinnacle of passion from which you choose not to descend?

MR LODWICK: When we—you know—she never moves. I feel like the white
              woman's burden.
TRALEE: Then what are you wasting your life on her for?
MR LODWICK: I don't know.
TRALEE: Sixteen thousand cooked breakfasts? A clean house to hate
              each other in?
MR LODWICK: She's my wife.
TRALEE: You keep saying that as if you're in some sort of mystic
              trance—
MR LODWICK: I need her—marriage is more than just—that.
TRALEE: Aha!
              What, more?
              How *much* more?
              Tell me, mister man, then, what *else* you extract from your
              woman?
MR LODWICK: Well, I don't know—
TRALEE: Security, is it? A nice, motherly old bum to rub up against in
              the dark, when the fears of dying are upon you? Is that it?
MR LODWICK: Not with my wife, no hope—
TRALEE: Sympathy, is it? Somebody you can tell your failures to, and
              turn them into triumphs? Somebody to hold your hand as you
              vomit up your misery? Someone who's there, no matter what?
              Is that it?
MR LODWICK: Ha—sympathy—Fat lot of that *I* get.
TRALEE: Or is it just owning somebody? Isn't that what *really* makes
              you swing—knowing she's *always* there, always always
              always—makes you feel a bit more permanent yourself—
              doesn't it? Having somebody under your thumb—for ever.
MR LODWICK: I'm not a domineering husband—
TRALEE: No, but you won't *go*, will you? Because if *you* go—*she goes*.
              Goes her own way. And if you haven't *got* her—not for ever—
              not even for now, you're knackered, aren't you? But if you turn
              her into an object, you can *own* her for ever—
MR LODWICK: But she's not an object—she's a person . . .
TRALEE: Better and better.
MR LODWICK: And I don't *own* her . . .
TRALEE: Yes, you bloody do. If you didn't, there'd be no sad little line
              laid down between you and yourself, no mirror to bounce
              reality off, no slave-woman to hide you from everything. You'd
              have no excuse for wasting the best days of your life in
              misery—no excuse for getting old and grey-faced twenty years
              too early, no excuse for all that bitterness and self-torturing
              you're enjoying so much; you'd have to stop having sneaky
              little fantasies about me, Mr Lodwick, and *do* something.
MR LODWICK: Did Barby want you to say all this?
TRALEE: We talked about you, a bit. But she thought you were a
              hopeless case, gone past all redemption. She likes you though—
MR LODWICK: Does she?
TRALEE: Yes.

MR LODWICK: Then why does she—?

TRALEE: What? Live?

MR LODWICK: Torment me? Sometimes I think she's going to drive me quite mad, clean round the bend. Harpic—

TRALEE: What?

MR LODWICK: Mad.

TRALEE: What is it drives you mad about her?

MR LODWICK: Oh—it's just the way she—

TRALEE: Her body? She's not all that fantastically well set up, your Barby—I mean, I'm not much to write home about myself, but *her*—

MR LODWICK: She's not ugly.

TRALEE: She's just plain bloody sexy. Is that what gets you?

MR LODWICK: She *is* my daughter.

TRALEE: And the other one '*is*' your wife—it seems to me you're in a bit of a mess, Mr Lodwick: a wife you don't fancy and won't leave, and a daughter you do fancy and can't have. What are you going to do about it?

MR LODWICK: Think systems, I suppose. Will you come off with me, then?

TRALEE: Come off? Where to? Living tally down the 'pool?

MR LODWICK: I've always wanted to move nearer my place of work.
(*Pause*)

TRALEE: Barby's right. You are bloody hopeless. Couldn't manage across the street on your own. Do you know what's going on?

MR LODWICK: Ah—I thought something might be 'going on'—what?

TRALEE: (*Angry*) Look at you—happy at the idea, are you? Pleased as Punch now you've spotted something to be miserable about— where's your five-minute-old liberation, where's your prodigious sexual athletic freedom?—

MR LODWICK: Do you mind telling me what is going on in this house? Quite frankly, young lady, I don't like the way you keep covering up. There's somebody else in this house, isn't there—(*Bullying*) Come on now, isn't there?

TRALEE: You really are—

MR LODWICK: Who is it?

TRALEE: Right. I'll tell you. Two fellas. One's called Vernon and he works a pneumatic drill only he's fed up with working a pneumatic drill and he wants to be a director of I.C.I., and the other one's my current bash, Ernesto, who's about as subtle and intelligent as a steam-driven pile-driver.

MR LODWICK: What, if I might ask, are they doing?

TRALEE: Ernesto's probably gagging and trussing up your old lady, while Vernon goes through the drawers for your money. Don't worry, *she'll* be alright.

MR LODWICK: I see. (*Gets up*)

TRALEE: I wouldn't go up there if I were you—

MR LODWICK: I thought I'd call the police, actually—

TRALEE: No. They wouldn't like you to do that. They'd have to stop you, and Ernesto's not so considerate with men as he is with women.

MR LODWICK: Perhaps they wouldn't know I'd gone, until it was too late.

TRALEE: Oh yes. You see, I'd leap across the room onto your back, bring you down, heave at your hair and bite you until they came down.

MR LODWICK: You'd do that, would you?

TRALEE: I don't like people who call the police. They're only looking for money. Don't say you haven't got any up there—we happen to know you have—*and* how much: thirteen hundred pounds, in fivers.

MR LODWICK: Barby.

TRALEE: You won't miss your rotten money—you weren't using it, anyway. So sit down.

MR LODWICK: How could she do this?—I've always looked after her . . . my little girl.

TRALEE: Oh stop talking like a silent film—

MR LODWICK: You lot—I couldn't care less about you lot—parasites, the lot of you, give you half an inch, next thing you're holding the country up to ransom—who are these hoodlums bashing old women over the head—they're free milk—free-meals—free-expression—free-love—free-assistance-money kids, you read about them day in day out on the back page of the *Echo*, seven, ten, twelve, every night, molesting old age pensioners for three and sixpence, harassing bus-conductors on late-night buses, kicking each other's heads in, knifing, knuckle dusters, bicycle chains, acid-guns, sawn-off shotguns, air-pistols, Lugers—it's like Chicago—Liverpool, the Windy City of England—it's that lot I pay taxes for, to make sure they've got enough calcium in their bones, enough spending-money in their pockets, enough hospitals to be carted off to—*you lot*.

TRALEE: Mm. Just as well we're not living tally down the 'pool then.

MR LODWICK: Me?

TRALEE: Yes—you and me. Mister Sensuality.
(*Pause*)

MR LODWICK: Who *are* you?

TRALEE: Tralee Clausewitz. Second commando, Fazackerley Tupamaros—urban liberators. The men upstairs are Ernesto Mathews, and Vernon Broadstreet, full-time activists. You can tell the press if you like, we've decided it's time to publicise ourselves a bit. We've been doing banks, wage-snatches, hold-ups: now we reckon we're strong enough to step out. For a moment, just a marvellous moment back there, when you were talking about your systems—I had a feeling for you. I had a feeling you were not only with us, but years ahead of us. It was beautiful, what you said, about people, choosing everything, and warming and opening up, and that lovely, willowy graceful master-system, the will of the liberated people made flesh, you said: and then you started letting go, really letting go, sensuality, sex, fire, desire, lust, I thought you were going through into wonderland—you were heroic, magnificent, hup into the morning, into the future, into something we'd never dreamt of. Then you sank back, you

got all mean and miserable, and old and ugly again—WHAT DID YOU DO IT FOR? WHAT ARE YOU AFRAID OF? WHY DIDN'T YOU STAY YOUNG AND SEXY?
(*Pause*)

MR LODWICK: Is—Barby—is *she* in all this?

TRALEE: We've both been activists since we were in first-year sixth. She's done seven banks, has Barby: one of our strongest cadres.

MR LODWICK: Banks?

TRALEE: Mm. Like the Tupamaros in South America—urban guerrillas. Listen, I think I've said enough . . .

MR LODWICK: But what do you do with the money?

TRALEE: Invest in ICI. When objective conditions are right to mobilise: we've got finance; we've got organisations; and we know what we want. Now, that's enough.

MR LODWICK: But listen—I'm very interested . . .

TRALEE: Are you? In getting yourself shot? You can't even leave your wife, can't even let your daughter enjoy herself, can't even tell yourself why, either—how are you going to face up to the combined armies and police-forces of Western capitalism? What have you got to offer the working-class of England?— Wet strength?
(*Pause. Then a knock on the door*)
They're through. I'm off.

MR LODWICK: Will—will Barby be coming back, do you think, tonight?

TRALEE: She wants you to promise you'll keep quiet.

MR LODWICK: About that money? About being *robbed*?

TRALEE: She'll want to know what you care more about—her—or thirteen hundred pounds.
(*Pause. She shrugs and goes to the door.*)

MR LODWICK: No. No—you know, don't you: I love little Barby.

TRALEE: Little?

MR LODWICK: Keep that money. Spend it. Invest it. Store it up for the revolution. I don't care. If I can have Barby—back. As she was.

TRALEE: She'll never be as she was, Mr Lodwick. Not now. If you can make your peace with that, you'll probably be alright. If you can't—you'll just have to join forces with all the other little Hitlers and exterminate us. And her. I *must* go.

MR LODWICK: Tralee. I—of course, of course. I've enjoyed meeting you, in some way.

TRALEE: Do you still fancy me?

MR LODWICK: Well—yes, in a way.

TRALEE: (*Laughs*) Good. Cheerio.
(*She goes. Voices off, door slams. A crucial moment for* MR LODWICK. *He laughs, amused at his problem.*)

MR LODWICK: What I've always wanted to do, is work on construction. I've got the qualifications.
    In Australia. See the country. Come face to face with nature in the raw. The hot sun, the arid desert, the punishing terrain. I'd like that sort of life. Restore the balances, a bit.

I've always hankered to apply the systems approach to some really untouched part of the world. Abandon roads, invest in hover-car construction. Set up a proper navigational grid like aeroplanes have, and never get lost: travel the beam, never mind about tarmac. Move the up-beams and the down-beams half a mile apart, eliminate crashes. Cut out bull-dozers: how does nature bull-doze?—extremes of heat and cold, they crumble the rock—then floods wash it away, that's how nature works: very well, high and low temperature physicists and hydrodynamic engineers must meet, and get to work. Bridges. I must think about bridges.

(*Pause*)

She's right, that little girl. If I don't get out, I'm done for.

(*Pause. Suddenly starts*)

Sh! Is that Barby?

(*Concentrates. Shakes his head*)

I'm hearing things.

Any minute now, though, she'll be back: fitting the key into the lock.

Inserting it. Tip-toeing in. Taking her shoes off.

(*Stops himself*)

No. I mustn't I mustn't think about her. Her and the— floating crane merchant. Robbing banks. Driving up lonely lanes in Cumberland. Stopping. Having a cigarette. Swallowing a pill. Men.

How *many* men? Great God, it's making me shake—look at that, look at my hands, my hair, my hair's standing on end, I can feel it, all from there and up there and right over, crawling up on end.

Do you know: I *think* I've never been more afraid in my life. I'm terrified. Intruders, in *my* house. Bandits. That vulgar, guttersnipe of a girl, just chatting me up while her accomplices robbed and looted. And what about Mrs Lodwick—what *will* they have done to her? And my daughter—what have they been doing to my daughter? *Using* her, as a hostage, threatening to distrain her affections, raping her, in fields.

They can't do this to normal, civilised people!

My family demands the full protection of the law!

They ought to stop these things before they begin, grapple with them before they gnaw away at the very foundations of our society!

Bandits—Roaming the streets. Wild, lascivious, free-love-making hooligans, South Americans, coloureds, licentious white women, moving gangs defying the laws of decency and morality and the laws of the land. And the police—what are they doing? Namby-pamby, if-you-please tactics—that'll get them nowhere. A strong hand! Attack Attack Attack! These wild, unfettered imps of darkness on the rampage through the night must be given a good seeing-to, hammered, smashed, wiped out, removed, *exterminated* from England's green and pleasant land.

Yes, exterminated. *Exterminated*!
(*A door-noise, off.* MR LODWICK *stops, electrified.*)
Barby!
(*He aims himself at the door, but is paralysed. Sound of Barby going upstairs. Closing her door. He unsticks himself. He is in a panic. Doesn't know where to turn. He becomes hang-dog, drops.*)
My wife. I must know what they did to my wife. And my money. Thirteen hundred. Worked for. Every penny ground out of me. My life savings, money saved, life lost. Money lost, life saved. Yes, Australia. (*Shrugs*) I suppose I ought to call the police. Spew up the whole sordid episode. Protect other people. Get them put away for a good stretch . . . Barby too. She deserves it.

The only thing is, I couldn't do it. I wonder how this is going to turn out?
(*He sits and stares, torn apart. MUSIC: 'Angel of the Morning'*)

Slow BLACKOUT

THE END

Introduction to *Plugged in to History*

Enter the middle-aged PARK-KEEPER *who talks to audience.*

PARK-KEEPER: Oh. Oh. Oh. Fie on dem. Fie. Da ungsters bin dingrateful, lackased. Bud I godda shock for ya. Am gonna stunnya. Een in a duplex pent-up houses, high, scraping da sky, een in da man-shuns, een in da man-gin erectors bell-ordered homes, der bin un-ruly elemens. Der bin utters, utter been in da nut-ouses, der been Sigh Gothics, an you-rotics, an Care-a-noids, an, wuss of da lot, der been sky-so-free-nicks. Da sky-so-free-nicks been dingrateful, lacka ungsters—dey been wuss, agos da man-gin erectors an da duplex men and da-shock-exchangers been noodle has-bands, tieing dem up, givum da doe, bash on demand, bash on delivery, and is da dingrateful spouces da been sky-so-free-nik: whoffor? Ah doan no whoffor. Dey muss be utters, daffy and palmy, whyves of da big men, da pig-men da runna cuntry.

Wassamarrawidum?

Da pig-men make-a da piles a doe. Dey buyum up da man-shuns, dey buyum da car-pets, dey buyum da boos, dey buyum da fur-knickers, dey buyum da wooms, ta me-and-her about in; Wha' more good a gurl arsefor? An do dey play ball? Do dey luv up da fella, keep da home cuddly and sty for da pig-man? Ook up a din-dins, scoff for da trough, huggim and fuggim an drop a few piglets? Doe doe doe. Ear me doe. Wha' do dey do? Dey go sky-so-free-nik. I ony go' om ques-chun: (*Shouts*)

Whadafugginellsdamarrawidum?

PLUGGED IN TO HISTORY

Noise of fairly bustly street. Shadows of passersby. Feet. KAY, *a young middle-aged mum, pretty, frayed, but well looked-after: loud middle-class voice. A few newspapers under her arm. Sits wearily on a bench on the pavement.*

KAY: Oh dear. I'm so tired. Worn out. Oh dear, oh dear.
(*Looks at imaginary passers by, anxiously*)
I say—do you mind? Do you think—nobody would *object* would they, I mean, if I sit here?
(*Laughs, self-deprecatingly. Hums a tune brightly. Suddenly:*)
Liner, luxury cruise liner beached. Many—many—feared lost. Luxury cruise liner Princess Annabel ran aground near volcanic island of Malevolente late last night. Stop. Passengers in their nightdresses were flung into the ocean, seething with sharks and one thousand varieties of predatory fish. Stop. Ship's doctor strangled. In amazing horror accident the only doctor on board, Doctor Pry, was choked to death by his stethoscope which caught on a knob or protuberance as he was flung

forward when the boat struck the island. Stop. Distress signals many—many—distress signals from the wrecked vessel were sighted in all parts of the South Atlantic, Indian Ocean, China Seas and South Pacific. Their colours were blue, red, green, mauve, yellow, pink, scarlet, blue, terra-cotta, purple, emerald, white, white, blue, terra-cotta, green, pillar-box red, blue terra, blue terra Stop An intensive search is being carried out for survivors.

(Opens handbag, gets out mirror, does her face. Puts away make-up, smiles at imaginary passers by. Chattily.)

Hear about the mining disaster? Wellbourne Mining Horror Tunnel Collapse. Late last night the main tunnel and several minor tubes at Wellbourne Dorset colliery collapsed crushing many. Stop. Rescue work continues hampered by lack of correct equipment. Stop. Coal Board officials are being accused of lack of interest which they strenuously deny. Stop. See page 8, can anything be done to save crushed people?

(Gets up, walks round bench twiddling her fingers violently, sits again, calm)

Awful, actually. Frightful. Ghastly. Dreadful.

(Opens one pink paper)

'Financial Times'. Good old FT. A good read. Juicy. A bit hard to follow, one must admit. Yes. Hard. Hard and juicy, the old FT.

(She puts it down, having glared at it avidly for a few moments, but scarcely having read it. Sighs)

Events do catch up with one so. My husband—oh, it doesn't matter. Seize the Time. Black militants from all over Africa assembled overnight here in Uppsala for the first Congress of ARM, the African Resistance Movement. Mr Terry Koheer—

(She stands on bench, gives Panther salute)

seen here in his native Chad—

(She gets down, continues)

Mr Terry Koheer has called for a more integrated and efficient deployment of the resistance-fighters' forces in order to achieve maximum impact on 'those parts of our struggling continent still in the clutches of Imperialism'. He called for help from all civilised countries in their struggle against white supremacists. They are big and bad and strong, he said, we need help.

(During this last speech, DEREK, a young man, has come in. He stands looking at her, amused, excited, anticipating. She has taken out her handbag again and dabbed at her face, looking searchingly in her mirror. He goes and sits beside her. She is not surprised or alarmed.)

I know one shouldn't, I know it's awfully low-class of me to *do* this at table. But you don't mind do you? Oh you really are a sweetie.

DEREK: What were you saying, just then?

KAY: Isn't it nice just to sit here and watch all these people scurrying by? Like silly squirrels rushing about with nuts in autumn—hurrying with nuts to nut-holes, popping them in for winter—Awful squirrels, they work *so* hard racing up and down popping nuts away—but when winter comes they forget which houses they popped the nuts in and just leave them there. Sometimes they starve to death, you know, out of pure forgetfulness. Not much comfort to the acorns, though. After all, *they* might have grown into *huge* trees.

DEREK: Perhaps they might still grow, in their nut-houses . . .

KAY: Oh, no, oh dear no.
(*Silence*)
Talks Deadlock Paris Wednesday Talks between Madame Ngu Chock of the Oppressed People of Vietnam and American chief negotiator Arthur Swine have reached an quote impasse unquote. Whither now, asks UN observer Digby Pruri, my guess is only time can tell.
(*Silence.* DEREK *makes several attempts at starting a conversation, but can never break into words.*)

KAY: (*Sadly*) Actress Melissa Voke is selling her Sussex home. Formerly the residence of Sir Alexander Carter, City Whip tycoon, this languid sixteenth century small manor-house in almost perfect condition can be purchased for something in the region of £28,000. Miss Voke is moving back home to South Africa. 'The veldt calls me' she told me, 'I shall go as soon as my house is taken.' The house is, at the moment, vacant.
(DEREK *nods*)

DEREK: Do you—Do you know this part of the world? Do you come from here?

KAY: Oh no of *course* not, can't you tell from the way I talk? (*Does an exaggeration of her own already exaggerated voice*) I am a lady, young man, from a widely respected and occasionally knighted family whose *bases* are, very firmly, in the Home Counties. Don't you know.

DEREK: No—I mean, do you live here? Have you been living here long?

KAY: God. Yes. Centuries. Seven, eight light-years.
(*She starts to cry*)

DEREK: I'm sorry. Have I upset you?

KAY: (*Shakes her head*) I was brought here. You know. Marriage. Starfighter. Bonn Friday. West German Luftwaffe's seventy-ninth Starfighter crashed early this morning, right in the centre of a fashionable suburb of Cologne. Miraculously avoiding all human habitation, it buried its nose deep in the centre of a decorative grass roundabout. No-one was hurt except the heroic pilot, who was killed outright. UPIA, UPIO.

DEREK: Do you know if there's any hotels round here—digs, lodgings, rooming houses for a couple of nights? I'm sorry to bother you. I can see you're upset. But I'm afraid I've got problems, too, and if you want me to help you by listening to your problems, I'll do that, but I'd like you to help me with mine as well.

KAY: Earth shifting. From our Science Correspondent. Sir David Goliath announced this afternoon that the earth was moving nearer to the sun at the rate of one and a quarter inches per week. This process, he warned, was gradually accelerating as it continued: the nearer we move to the sun, the stronger the effects of its gravitational pull, the quicker the pace of the earth's ultimate doom, and the total conflagration of the solar system. Sir David said he did not wish to sound like a prophet of doom, however, as this process could take an incalculable number of years.

(*Pause*)

I don't know any hotels or rooming houses or empty rooms. Everywhere seems full to me—look at all the people in the world, they don't seem to me to be able to all fit on together, hectoring and jostling each other. I prefer to sit and watch.

DEREK: I really am pushed. I've been living with this girl, you see, over in Leeds: at college, she was.

(*He shrugs his shoulders, gets into a brood. She waits, then*)

KAY: Well?

DEREK: Oh, you're listening are you? I was pretty confident you were going to sit there ignoring me, just chatting like a newspaper, until I moved away . . .

KAY: Franco's Bullies Beat Schoolboy to Death: Sixteen-year-old Pedro Arunez of Barcelona Academy was discharged from Madrid's Central Prison Hospital today in a sealed coffin. His family will not be allowed to open the coffin to see the dead boy for the last time. An armed guard accompanies it wherever it goes, until it is buried. Arunez is believed to have some connection with a non-aligned group of admirers of Mao Tse-Tung, who call themselves the Disasters of War, after the sequence of Goya drawings . . .

DEREK: Alright, alright, I'm sorry.

(*Pause*)

Well, I *wasn't* a student. I was what for lack of a better word can only be called a working-class layabout. I had a trade: switchgear I suppose was my line of business. But I spent a lot of my time walking along canals—running my eager hand up the inside of low bridges, tight-roping across lock-gates, waving cheerily to bargee's wives and families as they chugged past me, touching those beautiful smooth edging-stones, spitting into the water, avoiding the rotten mattresses everybody thinks ought to be dragged along to decorate the tow-path, hitting myself over the head for the sheer bloody joy of a sunny day, reading poems in moody sheds while it pissed down with rain. I preferred that to the manufacture of switchgear. I preferred that to almost everything until I met Natasha. I thought at first she was some incredible Russian heroine, the kind you see in the pictures belting down the cobbled streets of St Petersburg waving a pennant in the revolutionary dawn. But no—she was a cookery student from Liverpool, and she rode a moped. The moped almost ruined our relationship right at the start. I met her at a Save the Children Fund dance in a church hall. I arrived pissed, and danced with her till I could hardly stand up. We laughed like little boys peeing up a wall, we fell about all over the Save the Children Fund Raffle Prizes, we were hysterical with the excitement of meeting each other. But when I offered to walk her home, there was this moped—either she went home on her own, on it, or I pushed it. If we'd gone *straight* to her place, we'd have been alright—but footless-drunk moped-pushing and moonlit romance have an evil effect on each other . . . (*laughs, then looks crestfallen*) Perhaps if I hadn't treated her so bad—I really did, unforgivable she said it was, and it was too. She was right, I've *got* to tell her, though, I've *got* to.

KAY: Thin skeins of mist hauntingly encircle the peaks of the ever-majestic Andes.

DEREK: Thank you.

KAY: Bracket Bolivotours three hundred pounds. Tourist class flight by recognised airline, best hotels available end bracket.

DEREK: That's why I want a room.

KAY: Why? Does she live here?

DEREK: Yes, Northampton Terrace, just round the corner. She won't see me at the moment: can't say as I blame her. So I've got to stay on—to convince her that I mean it.

KAY: Do you?

DEREK: Yes, I do. I couldn't go back without her, not to bloody Leeds. I hit her, you see.
(*Pause*)

KAY: Statues Threatened. A new wave of terror bombings has broken out in Portsmouth. Another four statues of eminent men have been totally or partially demolished in the city, bringing the total to twenty-seven. The dynamitings, which are said to be 'very professional', appear to be the work of a multi-racial woman's rights organisation flourishing among naval families in the town. Police are investigating the as yet undisclosed purpose behind this outbreak of violence.

DEREK: It's not as if she's smaller than I am. I wasn't bullying her. It's just that I wouldn't let anybody, *anybody*, say some of the things she said to me, not even if they were seven foot tall world heavyweight all-in wrestling champions.

KAY: What on *earth* did she say?

DEREK: She patronised me. After we'd been living together for a few months, she'd keep trying to get me to go to work *every day*. Well, normally, I'd do one week out of three, or two out of six, something like that, reasonable, enough to keep me alive—I mean, I'm not all that *interested*, do you see what I mean, in work *as such*.

KAY: My husband goes to work every day.

DEREK: Yes, but he's probably an important man, wielding power, dominating an office, HE dictates, SHE types, HE inspects, THEY modify. Personal involvement, I would say is not so difficult for a man of your husband's calibre in your husband's position. He probably *lives* his work—am I right?

KAY: Thailand Secures Itself Bangkok Monday. High Thai Military men revealed late last night that in 'soft' areas in Northern Thailand vulnerable to Red Infiltration, American Pacification experts had already taken over the administration of villages and communities. 'We intend to re-organise these people', said an anonymous American peace leader, 'in such a way as to facilitate their total retention of the democratic freedoms without the external interference in their affairs.' Asked to comment on why America was spending so much money in these areas, he said: 'With us, it is an act of love.'—Reuter, UPIA, UPIO.

DEREK: With me, it's not so easy. I lose enthusiasm for work after four hours. I think people shouldn't have to do it. I think all our brilliant technology should be *concentrated* on eliminating work. I think that as soon as a man is made redundant by a machine, he shouldn't have his wages stopped—no, on the contrary, he should be offered either a world cruise, three years—all found for him and his family—at a special Adult University, or leisurely re-training in some higher and brighter skills, like aircraft navigation, or marine biology. Or a special Nature Group could be set up, to ramble the world in search of its beauties, crossing all frontiers by inalienable right.

KAY: Did you tell her that?

DEREK: She said work was a man's duty, his pleasure and her right. Every man has a right to work, and you can never take that away from him, she said, so get off your arse and get yourself a job.

KAY: But surely you can't *hit* somebody, just for saying that?

DEREK: No, it wasn't so much that. It was what she implied. She tried to tell me that I only thought of my philosophy to give me an excuse for being bone-idle. Well, in a sense, that is true. Certainly if I hadn't been bone-idle I would never have thought of such a philosophy at all. It was something that grew, most definitely, along the canal banks. Famous composers, too, you know, flourish in idleness. But I wasn't making up any excuses I didn't need. It's obvious to anybody who's taken a quiet walk by some water, and who's also spent a week operating a Heineken lathe, which is better for you. I didn't mind her calling me a layabout, but her letting on I was lying about it got up my nose. Then when she said anyway I wasn't bloody intelligent enough to be allowed to do sod-all, I whacked her.

KAY: Where?

DEREK: On the face, on the arse, and a right stinger across the back of the legs.

KAY: Did you *really* hurt her?

DEREK: No—not at all—it was just a warm-up.

KAY: Didn't she like it? It sounds fun to me. Didn't she try to hurt you back?

DEREK: Did she buggery—she got all up-tight and rushed off into the night. Came back the next morning for her belongings. I gave her a right bloody ear-full. Usual drama. Tears. Showed me the weals on her arse. She was lucky I didn't fill in the gaps for her. I chucked her gear down the stairs, told her she was a stuck-up, servile get, and she wasn't as bright as she reckoned she was— that did it. The last bit. Bloody hell. Touched her on her raw nerve: she smashed the place up—cost me fifteen quid in compensation to the landlady. I had to work for six and a half days over the odds. She knew how to get her revenge alright. As she went down the stairs I tried to kick her arse for her, but I missed and fractured her elbow. She wouldn't see me after that.

KAY: I'm not surprised . . .

DEREK: I *told* her it was an *accident*—listen, don't you start giving me stick about it, Mrs, I've had just about enough—

KAY: Yes, but I mean it's one thing to smack somebody's bottom, that can even be quite enjoyable—but breaking their *elbow* . . .

DEREK: Listen, I've *suffered* for that.

KAY: I imagine she did too—

DEREK: (*Angry*) You can't *say* that, you can't—I want you to understand that, yes, breaking your elbow is painful: of course: you can do it any minute of any day, walking down the road, slip, wham, elbow busted. Coming downstairs too fast, running for a bus, falling off a ladder—

KAY: Getting kicked?

DEREK: *YES. IF THE KICK WAS AIMED SOMEWHERE ELSE AND MISSED, IT WAS AN ACCIDENT*—You don't seem to know your arse from your elbow. Anatomically speaking, as receivers of boots, they're totally different. Oh, what I'm getting at is, she, accidentally, had to put up with a certain quality of pain: with the help of modern drugs and the comfort of her ever-loving father who only turns out to be a dentist—ugh—I always knew she had some funny blood in her . . .

KAY: Dentists can be quite charming people—

DEREK: You haven't seen her father.

KAY: Have you?

DEREK: Yes. But what I'm saying is—my *suffering* was *no accident*. I brought it on myself. Can you see that? It wasn't a matter of a weighable, measurable amount of pain in the elbow, it was endless, measureless, it was forever: it wasn't a thing that was there and would go away—it was a thing that had gone away and would never come back. From the minute she said she wouldn't see me in that rotten hospital, I knew I loved her. Passionately. I've suffered without her now for five weeks. I kept waiting for it to go away, the agony I mean, but no. I used to hang around outside the lecture-halls in case I could see her, but I never knew which ones she went to. I did see her once, but she had her arm in plaster, and I couldn't bring myself to— anyway, she was with a fellow, with blond hair. Then they all left Leeds, the students, for the holidays—

KAY: You're too moony—that's your trouble. When you said you'd hit her, I thought you were going to be something big, something tangible—but you just moped and moaned around the place for five weeks and then you let her go away. Conference in New Delhi, Secretary-General Predisch, said: Prosperity tends to form an attitude of detachment if not indifference to the well-being of others.

DEREK: Why do you keep saying those things?

KAY: Because I'm going mad. I say those things to prove it.

DEREK: Why?

KAY: Otherwise I wouldn't believe it, and that would be really frightening. (*Puts her hand up*) Don't. No more. Mrs Emily Griffiths of Nuneaton was 107 late last night. Harry Parry, Wales's leading goal-scorer of 1949, died suddenly in Llandudno aged 52. The RSPCA is prosecuting a woman who fed her 17 cats on live mice she bred in her kitchen. They are prosecuting her for cruelty to the mice.

DEREK: Shall I talk about Natasha?

KAY: Yes. Don't talk about me. Patience (*Suddenly*) WHY DO YOU WANT TO KNOW?

DEREK: I like you. You're like a green pool with bubbles in it.
          (*Pause*)

KAY: (*Sharply*) Don't be so moony.
          (*Pause*)

DEREK: That's why I came here. I had to see her. She came to the door, just now. I said: I want you to come back and live with me in Leeds, in the boarding-house. She was trembling: I don't know what with, but she was shaking like an injected rabbit. Because I love you, I said, an octave lower. Her dad came to the door, boggling at me, heaving on her poor arm that was still in plaster—Do you see that, he said, as he dislocated her shoulder, you should be in prison for that. I don't need your advice, I said, I need your daughter. That was it. SLAM. So I shouted my ultimatum through the letter-box. I shall not leave this borough without my true love comes with me. I can wait. I have no plans for any future without her. I can wait forever.
          (*Pause*)
          As I walked off backwards up the path, Natasha's face appeared, tear-stained, fleetingly at the window. 'I know you'll come back—I LOVE YOU', I shouted so all the neighbours

could hear, 'AND YOU LOVE ME'. (*sniffs*) I reckon that should do it, don't you?

KAY: Poor Natasha. You're obviously quite wrong for her.

DEREK: Wh—Wha—a—at?

KAY: Don't sound so outraged. You don't imagine you're right for *everybody*, do you?

DEREK: What's this 'right for' got to do with it? I love her.

KAY: Yes. If your man's not right for you, *he's* OK—oh yes, of course, Mister Grand Vizier is all hunky-dory. But *you're* not. It happens to women all the time. Natasha. Poor Natasha.

DEREK: I intend to pursue her vigorously—

KAY: Oh yes. No doubt. And get her. And win her, body, soul, heart, throbbing old feelings, take her, to have and to hold, to love, honour and obey you till death, death of something, death of you, death of your life, death of your spirit, do you part.

DEREK: But I'm not like *that*. I'm no monster, I'm not a crusher—

KAY: Men are all crushers. What men are not?

DEREK: Listen: until we had that barney, she was nuts about me. I was her fella. She loved my rough, guttersnipe fingers on her protected pink skin, my harsh grating sounds enchanted her molly-coddled ears, my rough ways she had to have, my every belch went right into the fat face of that cosy father, every fart polluted the sweet-scented atmosphere of her dental home. That's what she picked me for—that's what she got. And it worked. It gave her confidence. So much confidence that she went too far.

KAY: Britain's Trade Booms. Britain's trade with the rest of the world had a champagne sparkle in December and we ended up—

DEREK: Oh stop that, it's a very irritating habit you've got, that.

KAY: (*Fiercely*) Don't you dare come between me and my illness. My sanity depends on it.

DEREK: Alright, alright—say what you were going to say—

KAY: How can I, *now*?
(*Pause*)

DEREK: No, no—listen.

KAY: You see, my husband is the managing director of a large firm, and I'm not used to speaking to underlings. I couldn't sleep with my chauffeur, no more that I could with my children's nanny.

DEREK: Who said anything about sleeping—

KAY: You did. You asked me for a room, didn't you? You know perfectly well I'm not a rooming-house keeper, so if you want a room from me you've jolly well got to pay for it, and quite frankly your currency is counterfeit, your coins bend.
(*He goes and sits on the bench.*)

DEREK: (*Thoughtfully*) Would you like me to belt you one?

KAY: Where?

DEREK: Across the back of the legs?

KAY: Oh. (*She looks at him, afraid, excited.*)

DEREK: (*Amazed*) You would—wouldn't you? You're a bloody Fascist's moll.
        (*She walks back to him, and, ignoring the last remark, kneels and says*)

KAY: When I read my papers, I feel plugged in to history. I feel the course of events coursing through my veins. I feel taken over, crushed, by many many men. I feel occupied, a house, squatted in, defiled. I feel like a deserted ball-room being defecated in by a halted army. I feel like South America after the Yankees have finished with it, like Dresden after the bombing. I feel like a shed full of cats. I feel like a midnight zoo. I feel like a clump of trees outside a barracks, full of soldiers in rough khaki having under-age village tarts. I feel like Pompeii the next morning. I become a human news-tape, mile after mile of me, torn out, pecked at by destiny's square lettering, ripped off, abandoned. Do you know why? Do you begin to? It's because I feel everything, all the way through me.

DEREK: I—I'm sorry.

KAY: I need pain. It stops me suffering.
        (*Pause*)
        That's funny. The newsflashes seem to have stopped, for the minute.
        (*She closes her eyes, smiling, relaxed but almost immediately is overcome with the horrors again.*)
        No. It's no good. You're cheating. (*Full of manic scorn, disgust*) You can't help me. You'll never do anybody any good. You're *disgusting*. Eugh!
        (*Makes horrific animal disgust noises, over and over again, getting herself into a kind of frenzy of disgust, with him, with herself and with life. He watches, anxious, uncertain. She suddenly stops.*)
        See—you didn't know what to do, you hadn't got the first clue, you just stood there, twiddling your fingers; *pathetic*!

DEREK: You—you're right.

KAY: You don't believe it, do you? (*Laughs*) You look like the first man walking into Belsen—or perhaps you never heard about Belsen, you and your moony love-people, you and your pathetic flower-powers.

DEREK: (*A little primly*) I did hear about Belsen, actually—

KAY: Yes, Belsen *over there*, *then*, you may have. But you've never seen the skeletons crawling along inside your own tunnels, have you, mounds of tortured flesh rotting in your own skull, have you? Have you?

DEREK: Why should I? I like canals, and the countryside, no—

KAY: You walk along your tow-path and listen to water quietly lapping against the bank—

DEREK: Yes. What do you want me to listen to?

KAY: You don't hear the deafening crunch of millions of small animals, eating each other, you don't hear the thundering echoes of the women's tears, the scream of kittens, silently drowning, the groans of flesh collapsed by the years, the whisper of disintegrating bodies, shrieking against every second that ticks by.

DEREK: I think you ought to stop—

KAY: No, no. You've opened the box, it's jumped out now, it's handkerchiefs out of a conjurer's hat all over the room, you can't stop it now you've taken the lid off: that's what you want me to do, isn't it, that's what *he* wants me to do, they all, always, have wanted me to do—sit on it, sit on it, don't open your box, keep the lid on it, suffocate it—be what we want you to be, little girls aren't supposed to do *that*, take your hand out of your knickers, smile, sweet smile, shall I smack you, yes please, don't be a silly girl, girls don't like being smacked, why did you prick me, take *that*. *CLOSE YOUR BOX TO BOYS*, never show them that they're frightening you, don't scare them or they won't marry you. You saw what happened to that nice Arnold, he seemed very keen, until he aroused you that night and you carried on in that alarming manner, screaming and biting and begging him to punish you—now where is he? Now where is he? You see, once you open the lid the tiniest bit, even just to peep in, all those screams and festering horrors jack-in-the-box out. SO KEEP IT CLOSED, MEN DON'T LIKE THAT SORT OF THING. Hubby won't like it, oh dear no. Men are the only ones allowed *that* kind of wallowing. Women comply. How to keep your man. (*Pause*) When he eats, his large teeth tear like tigers' claws at innocent flesh. But at night, he drinks cocoa.

(*Long silence*)

DEREK: I don't know what to say. We don't seem to meet, at any edge. I don't even read the same newspapers.

KAY: No. (*Looks furiously thoughtful*) But I *have* enjoyed talking to you.

DEREK: Once upon a time, I was travelling at seventy miles an hour along the motorway: I'd hitched an MGB, driven by a business-woman, and the bit we were going along was raised above some houses, on stilts, with concrete walls so you couldn't get on, or off. Suddenly, all the cars in front of us started breaking, and swerving, missing each other by inches, practically turning over. There, right in front of us, blundering about in front of the unstoppable traffic, were two little month-old kittens. Do you see, somebody, some unspeakable murderer, must have chucked them out to get run over. We couldn't stop. She literally put the car on two wheels and drove under the front wheels of a continental container-lorry, trying not to hit them, but she might as well not have bothered. They couldn't get off. They could hardly walk. They had to get hit, by something. One of them by a long-distance bus. The other by a Rolls-Royce. Or a mini. My driver stopped whenever she could, and got out to be sick. I began to learn a bit about hating people. Just a little bit. I see those little cats every night before I go to sleep. And I try to imagine the fella that chucked them out.

KAY: Can you?

DEREK: Dimly. He gets to look more and more—ordinary, really, the more I think about him. A bit more like me, in many ways.

KAY: Paris. A girl student who prefers to remain anonymous, testified on oath, after her release from Beaujon prison yesterday, that she had seen a young boy student after he had been tortured by the French CRS. He was running screaming up and down the corridor between the cells, she claimed, urinating uncontrollably, his penis beaten to a pulp by police batons. Beaujon prison authorities questioned the authenticity of the report, saying they had not received any complaints from the boy.
(*Pause*)

DEREK: I'll go then, on my merry way. I'm not going to leave the borough without her, whatever you say. I hope you find some happiness.

KAY: Thank you. And you too.

DEREK: Good-bye.

KAY: Good-bye.
(*He goes. She stares out. The noise comes up, the shadows pass over her, the feet on the pavement trot by. She picks up a paper, and still looking out, opens it, dream-like. When it is open, she shivers at what she has thought, and, with a sickening compulsive gulp looks, almost bites, down at the paper in front of her, plugging herself in to history.*)

THE END

Introduction to *They're Knocking Down the Pie Shop*

Enter another or the same PARK-KEEPER, *who speaks to the audience.*

PARK-KEEPER: Slaveys an pent-up men—Ah'm be dis-turbed—Ah'm be dis-turbed by da stayta da cuntry. In da dole days, when a good dole King George da vee an da good dun King George da sick was raining, da commun people wass in a sty of pigality. Dey digged what dey was tolled an dey obeyed when dey was paid. Dey had luvly ickle ousses, an dey keptum goddan clean. Dey was nice, da common people, dey noed der stay-shun, and der dey shunnted, steaming an glad, gladda da hand-out, so sweet an so neat.

But now mit da lady King, she can getta grip of um. Dey come-on people, come-on gimme dis, come-on gimme dat, sod Vinten Church-hall, da scar-smoking warrier, sod Missus Carr's-hole, da union's friend. Da hole trouble wit da cuntry, it's da irking class. Dey doan do ennuff irk. Dey'm in da under-land, da fun-to-see-land, dey'm truly unreally, dey'm really unruly.

An what shud we givum. Da big stick. Da real stick. Dey muss be real-i-stick, so showum da pig-stick—Das wha'ah'm'sane. Ah'm sane whackum—Ah'm sane cudgellum—Ah'm sane—eat up da carrot an hit wit da stick. Ah'm sane: Ah'm sane. Das what ah'm sane.

An da wiggle-pool irkers bin wuss dan da Squirminghams, and wuss dan da Blunduners, and ean dan da Glassvegetables. Dey'm shockin, da wiggle-pudlians. Agos why? Agos o de mix. Dey'm mixers. An de Taffs, dey'm taft. An da buddy Bessie Bradox an da people shud no better. Dey'm wildcats an strikin and 'sputin' an spoutin and marchin and soutin more dan dey irkin. Agos why? For da money? Dey doan need mush money to live in dem stinkin flats, in dem pokey houses. (*Points to set*) See? Dirty bob a week, robbin landlord. Whoffor da money? For da boos an da clubs: pissartists, all ovum. An sum ov da ungsters bin wuss dan da irkers: sturrin it up, ageetaters—das buddy political. Whoffer dey do da? Dey'm really unruly. You seeum: das wass wrong mit da nay'shun. Shuck'em in clink: da hole lot ovum. Goo-night, slaveys, goo-night pent-up men.

THEY'RE KNOCKING DOWN THE PIE SHOP

MR MALDEN *in the armchair reading the Echo, his son* NEIL, *20-year-old go getter, at the table studying (he is at University, living at home).* JENNY, *17-year-old schoolgirl daughter comes in very late from school. She expects a reaction when she comes in but apart from* NEIL *looking ostentatiously at his watch, there is none.*

JENNY:	Hey dad.
MR MALDEN:	What?
JENNY:	They're knocking down the pie shop.
MR MALDEN:	Uh.
JENNY:	You don't seem very upset—
MR MALDEN:	Oh? Don't I?
JENNY:	I thought they were your favourites, Pelissier's Pies.
MR MALDEN:	Ever since I could afford them.
NEIL:	Here he goes.
MR MALDEN:	Shut up you. Smart-arse.
NEIL:	Where's she been, anyway? It's half past six. Two and a half hours to walk home from school?
JENNY:	(*Evasively*) Netball practice.
NEIL:	Oh yeah.
JENNY:	Oh shurrup, will you. You're worse than me ma: 'Where've you been till this hour'. God!
MR MALDEN:	It's the relentless advance of Monopoly Capitalism.
NEIL:	(*Sings the Red Flag satirically*)
JENNY:	What is?
MR MALDEN:	Pelissier's Pork Pie Shop had to be destroyed in accordance with the growth of larger and larger businesses, as foreseen by Marx in the 1850s. What he could not foresee, poor bugger, was the intransigence of the petty bourgeoisie. He thought all the small business-men would be forced to join the ranks of the workers, thus making the proletariat more powerful. Unfortunately, Mr Pelissier, dispossessed proprietor of Pelissier's Pie shop, will not be turning into a leading luminary of the revolution after all: nor will Mrs Pelissier. If I know anything they'll invest the proceeds of selling up the shop in shares in a Supermarket, retire on the income to a plastic bungalow defiling some otherwise beautiful part of North Wales, and grow their own vegetables. Their managers and van drivers will just manage and van drive for somebody else, and their pimply bloody son will end up as a Tory MP.
NEIL:	He'll be lucky.
MR MALDEN:	Not so bloody fast as *you* will, I agree. But then you're just a living exemplar of parallel but uneven development.
JENNY:	He's a backsliding rat.
	(*She slams her case on the table opposite him and puts out her books.*)
MR MALDEN:	Not eating?
JENNY:	(*Mutters darkly, incomprehensible, meaning no.*)
NEIL:	She's been down the Golden Glory-hole.
JENNY:	(*Looks at him for the first time*) Do you know, you're a real bloody copper's nark, you are—a born informer.
NEIL:	See—I was right. Red Mole Kiddies Tea Party was it? Or just heavy petting to heavy rock?
JENNY:	Like the minutes, would you—to sell to the Special Branch?
NEIL:	They should cocoa. Five infant pinkos staring at pictures of Mao Tse-Tung or Tariq Ali or Vic Feather or somebody.

JENNY: Vic Feather? Bloody Hell.

NEIL: Special Branch . . . don't you lot think you're so rotten
             important.

JENNY: Arthur's phone's tapped.

NEIL: Not the only thing that's tapped in the house. His ma's round
             the bend and poor Arthur's fair bit doodle-alley himself you
             know—

JENNY: It's blatant intrusion on his privacy—

NEIL: Bugger all to what you lot'd do if you got in.

JENNY: Off with your head for a start you treacherous scab.

NEIL: Got a list have you, down the Glory-hole?

JENNY: Yes, and you're top of the pops, next to Selwyn Lloyd.

MR MALDEN: Will you two shut up and stuff some knowledge into your
             empty heads. If you spent less time shouting the odds and more
             reading your books one day you might come out with
             something useful.
             (They read a bit.)

JENNY: Where's ma?

NEIL: Gone out.

JENNY: Gerraway . . .
             (She reads a bit more then laughter.) Do you know what? Our
             trendy little English teacher started us off reading this play by
             John Arden to show us how with-it she was—you know, the
             old con:—I'll pretend to be groovy if you'll swallow this load
             of rubbish I'm giving you—without any awkward questions.
             (Laughs again) Well, last night she saw him on the telly being
             arrested on that demonstration. Do you know what she's done?

NEIL: Shot herself.

JENNY: She's cut five scenes out of his play and told us not to read
             them. She must have been up half the night, terrified.

NEIL: Quite bloody right. What would the parents say? Wasting their
             kids' time reading a Commie hooligan's rant?
             (Silence as she looks at him, fierce and dangerous)
             (The father looks over at her, NEIL looks down at his book. She
             drops it as he hasn't taken up her challenge, and they all get
             back to reading again.)

MR MALDEN: Hey—they are knocking down the pie shop—

JENNY: I told you that—don't you believe a word I say?

MR MALDEN: Yes, but—it's in the Echo. (Quite upset) Photos too. Landmark
             to go. Familiar to many generations of Liverpudlians, Pelissier's
             Pork Pies delivered their last batch today. Mr A. Pelissier,
             whose great grandfather founded the firm over one hundred
             and seven years ago, said: 'Our own shop and bakery in
             Alvanley Road has to come down to make way for a new
             twenty storey hotel to be put up by Inter-Continental Hotels'—
             bloody Yankee Imperialism again. 'We are sad to leave our
             friends but we do realise that more hotel-space is needed in the
             city'—Bugger's obviously got shares in it—'Besides, he added,
             we haven't been showing a profit on our bakery for four years

now—and we simply couldn't compete with the big boys at their process without total loss of quality. Mr Pelissier, 57, is to retire to Llandudno, where, he says, he can pursue his hobby of dinghy sailing without interruption. His son, Mr Andrew Pelissier, who is a local councillor, pointed out that the hotel would certainly bring a lot of business to the area, as well as being an imposing sight in itself.'

That's it then, the son fixed the planning permission. That's how it goes. Monopoly capitalism drives out the small man, Imperialism the highest form of Capitalism steps in, bribes the bureaucrats, and cleans up what's left; the poor victim, far from complaining, goes off to sail his rotten dinghy like an aspiring Edward Heath.

NEIL: I hope they widen the road while they're at it.

MR MALDEN: (*Gives him a contemptuous sniff, and a glance at* JENNY) I liked those pies. Always have. Even during the war, they managed to make something eatable.

NEIL: That was where they went wrong, wasn't it? Buy donkey gristle at one tenth of the price, invest the rest in advertising and planned expansion and Pelissier's could be as big as Walls— they could be diversifying into cat-food, dog-food, pre-wrapped bacon, sausages, battery hens, broiler chickens, ready-cooked do-it-yourself, Rotisso-mats, machine tools, precision engineering, subbing to the aircraft industry, catering, to airlines, to weddings in their own hotels, to film companies— they could buy film companies—broaden to one-hour cleaners, launderettes, TV hire, motorway cafes, then it's no distance to North Sea Oil, tankers. Listen, old Pelissier could have been as big as—well, you name it—

MR MALDEN: Rolls-Royce?

NEIL: Instead—what does he do. Makes the best meat pies in Liverpool, charges twice as much for them, and *still* doesn't make a profit. It makes you weep. It's criminal, the way that man threw it all away—he could have been a one-man conglomerate but he's retiring at 57 to mess about in small boats for the rest of his pathetic life.

MR MALDEN: And what are you going to do with the rest of your *admirable* existence?

NEIL: Make money. Alright, so I'm starting in civil engineering, and fairly low down the ladder. Even once I've got this stupid degree I'll still be earning less than a bloody navvy, but in five years I'm going to be right up on top and out the other side. There's a lot to be made in civil engineering, but it's all sewn up, it's all too beautifully tied in bundles. I've got a few other ideas, for later on. Fresh fields and pastures new.

JENNY: You should go to America really: they need your sort over there.

NEIL: Wrong: in America they're *all* like that, they're *all* smart—but *here*: most of them are helpless. That's why so many smart

Americans come over here—I tell you, it's going to like robbing a blind man.

(*A silence.* JENNY *and* MR MALDEN *stare, flushed with anger, at the ground, too embarrassed to speak*)

NEIL: Oh hell, look at you. Have I farted in your chapel?

MR MALDEN: You'd better get back to your books. Read up a thing or two.

NEIL: Oh look Dad—I know it was hard for you—didn't have the opportunities we have, school, university—I'm not blaming you—you mustn't blame yourself.

MR MALDEN: For what?

NEIL: Well—for not . . .

JENNY: Not making it? Is that what you're saying—he mustn't blame himself for not making it . . . Sweet Jesus Christ, if I don't strangle you slowly to death—

MR MALDEN: (Loud) Now then, Jenny. (Quieter) God, Neil, I think maybe you had better read a few books, lad. Not Dale Carnegie either. (*He turns away, puts up the Echo as a barrier, the other two turn back to their books. But after a second we see that he can't be reading as his hands are shaking. He puts the paper down, very near to tears.* NEIL *doesn't notice this, but* JENNY *can see him. She watches a moment.*)

JENNY: Dad—ignore him. Pay him no attention. (NEIL *turns round at this.*) He's dirt. He's not fit to lick your boots.

NEIL: I'm sorry if I've upset you, Dad—

JENNY: *Upset* him?

MR MALDEN: No no, that's alright, you're perfectly entitled to your attitude to life, whatever that may be. I was never such a foolish father as to reckon my son would turn out anything but the split opposite of everything I wanted. I've always known that. I've felt you were going to come out with something like that for a year or two: ever since you got into that jumped-up technical college. Never mind—I'm sure you're not the only one. At least we know where we stand.

(NEIL *has somehow got himself into a towering anger, born of guilt and probably jealousy. He stands up and yells.*)

NEIL: Yes we do, don't we? As a matter of fact we have for quite some time: we're just not interested in each other, are we? You couldn't care less about how I get on. You never have been and you're never going to be the slightest bit of help, you just about spew up every time I come in the room and if you want to know, so do I when you do. You've never given me a penny-piece since I was fifteen, not one rotten penny, are you saving it all up to give me a start in life, when I need it, when I leave university? No. You certainly are not. Right, then—I'll find my own way, thank you. I can't even afford to leave this house, not for another six months, but I don't have to stop in and listen to you all night.

MR MALDEN: Sit down lad, sit down.

NEIL: (*Sits*) I can always eat in the canteen, work in the library.

MR MALDEN: Yes, and sleep in the waiting room on Lime Street station: don't be ridiculous, Neil. We've managed so far, we can all manage a bit longer. Now we know where we stand, we know what subjects to avoid don't we?

JENNY: Do you mean to say you're going to let him get away with that? Are you going to sit there and let him insult you and talk like a bloody gangster, and not pitch him head-first under the next bus?

MR MALDEN: You've displeased me in your time, Jenny. So far I've not shown you the door. I could have, once or twice.

JENNY: So far I've not called you a failure and promised to exploit the last penny out of you and your kind, have I? He talked to you like the managing director patronising the night watchman. I'm amazed he didn't slip you a few new pence.

NEIL: Jenny, I think Dad and I can understand each other better without your help—

JENNY: Understand each other? You won't begin to understand him to the day you die.

NEIL: Listen, you boring little moraliser, why don't you go and shake your tambourine somewhere else, because I'm *not* washed in the blood of Joe Stalin. Or Mao Tse-Tung come to that—or Fidel Castro.

MR MALDEN: Right, that'll do: if you're going to live in this house, Neil, you'll have to watch your tongue.

JENNY: How can you take it, Dad—you, your last thirty years have been one long pitched battle against morons like him, you've spent your life trying to annihilate them: now you find you've bred one, you just sit there like a bloody umpire, calling out the score.

MR MALDEN: Read your books, Jenny. You'll have a lot of work to do. And you *are* a bit late home from School.

JENNY: I'm late because I've been doing important work. Against lizards like him. There's going to be a lot of feeling against him. There's going to be a lot of feeling against that hotel. Arthur's organising a campaign against it.

MR MALDEN: Oh yes?

JENNY: We had a meeting with the Community Action people about it, but they don't understand a word you say to them: they don't really believe in politics, they think it's like magic, the way everything happens to us and all we have to do is activate our communities: whatever that means. Arthur told them if we're going to beat Intercontinental Hotels of America we're going to need politics, and they all smiled with that coy hippy sweetness, as if somebody's cat had been on the table. So we're on our own.

MR MALDEN: And what's your angle?

JENNY: Well a revisionist move to make the slogan: Save Our Pie Shop, was instantly crushed. The Maoists seemed to go all out for burning the hotel down, and the Spartacus League wanted to

burn them both down. The SLL walked out at this point,
leaving the young Communists, me and Arthur. The Young
Communists suggested an orderly protest march to City Hall,
led by Old Age Pensioners in Wheelchairs, then I made a
speech. I said whatever we did, we weren't going to win, and
the best way we could use the situation was as a graphic
illustration to the people living around here of the way
capitalism works. We don't want a twenty-storey hotel, we
want Pelissier's pies, I said—but who consulted us on the
subject—did *you* vote for it, did *you*? You see what their so-
called democracy means—big business first, people nowhere.
Get the message over—you're all under the thumb, the lot of
you, but then once they realise that, get them working against
it: organise, organise, organise. Arthur said: Comrades, we've
got two slogans—People Before Business, and Houses not
Hotels. We'll have no protest marches, but we *will* have two
street meetings in *every* street within half a mile of the site: one
now, another in six months time. The Anarchists and the
Spartacus League stormed off in different directions, one lot
looking for bombs, the others for newspaper reporters,
everybody else agreed, so that's what we're doing—What do
you think?

MR MALDEN: It's a bit populist, if you're asking me—practically Narodinik.
Sounds like hard work too. But I don't see what else—

JENNY: It's the only way: go and talk to people.

MR MALDEN: Yes, but you see, love, it's not going to work.

JENNY: Oh, come on, dad, don't *you* start talking like that. We know
we're not going to change the hotel—but the hotel might just
change the people. It'll be the biggest anti-capitalist symbol in
Liverpool after Forte's toadstool. For years, people will be
gazing on it and saying: look at it: symbol of exploitation. And
when the time comes, they'll trust us. Join us. Guide us. Help
us.

MR MALDEN: It might happen in your lifetime, love, I don't see it in mine.

JENNY: (*Angry, upset at the idea of him dying*) Oh yes it will—it
must.

MR MALDEN: Objective conditions, Jenny. Objective conditions.

JENNY: For God's sake, dad—they're only the background to action—
when have objective conditions *ever* looked right at the time?
In Cuba when eighty men set off from Mexico on a leaky boat
to start their revolution? Seventy of them got shot within a
week of landing. And *still* they made it.

MR MALDEN: Because they had the right conditions for it, very, very different
from here.

JENNY: But who *knew* they had the right conditions?

MR MALDEN: They just *were*: otherwise they wouldn't have won, would
they?

JENNY: Oh, Dad—you're being infuriating. Anyway, if you're not
interested, you're not interested, and you can sit and watch and

be theoretically correct, and say I told you so every time events coincide with your mournful prophecies. But we're going to act. Intervention: ever heard of it?

MR MALDEN: Listen, I'm feeling old and tired, and you make me feel older and more tired with every word you say.

JENNY: Oh come on, Dad, you sound like an ex-Secretary of the TUC, what's the matter with you?

MR MALDEN: Listen, we've just taken on a new feller at work. Can-lad, makes tea, runs to buy packets of ciggies, general gofer: gofer this, gofer that. He seemed older than usual, nice feller, so I had a chat with him. Turns out he's very bright, very bright indeed. I asked him how he came to be a can-lad. He told me. He was a top technical boy on the new Mersey Tunnel—fantastic qualifications, University, everything, just like our Neil, in some ways. Anyway, it turned out that the actual labourers down the tunnel, and the fellers operating the mole, the engineers, were getting the bends through being down too long, under the river. They were pushing them, you see, to save the hire-charges on the mole, and there were penalty-clauses for not completing on time. So they came out on strike—for decent breaks, up on the surface. They didn't get far, till this lad at work, and the other top lads, came out in sympathy. That did it. Everything stopped when they stopped, even the approach roads. In a couple of days, the men got an agreed one hour on the surface out of every four on the job. So back they went. And back went the technical boys, or so they thought: but no: they were suddenly redundant—laid off—sacked. They couldn't do anything about it, they all had contracts, they'd broken them, and there were twenty applicants for every job. They picketed the site for a month or two—got nowhere. Then they tried to get jobs somewhere else. Only nobody else would touch them: trouble-makers, shit-stirrers, disloyal employees, traitors to their new class. This bloke's got two kids and a mortgage: his union wouldn't help—the strike was unofficial, wildcat. He sold his house, moved in with her mother. After eighteen months on the dole, he considers himself lucky to be a can-lad to a bunch of welders.

JENNY: Disgusting. Victimisation run riot.

MR MALDEN: But that's not the end. He swears it's a fact that within a month all those underground mob were working exactly the same hours, if not longer: things being what they were, it was worth the sub-contractors time to drop them a secret cheque for £20 a week extra to keep the machine turning. How's that for solidarity. . . ?

JENNY: What's that meant to prove?

MR MALDEN: We just can't win. As a matter of fact, I'm beginning to wonder if we *should*.

JENNY: You don't mean that?

MR MALDEN: I'm afraid I do.

JENNY: Listen, all that story proves is what a lot of rats run the unions: they should have called half of Merseyside out if necessary, until they got those fellers their jobs back. That's all it proves.

MR MALDEN: But they didn't, did they? And the other blokes, down the tunnel: nothing. Never even had a whip-round. It means something. And it didn't just not happen.

JENNY: But there are *always* set-backs.

MR MALDEN: Exactly.

JENNY: We've just got to will ourselves to overcome them.

MR MALDEN: I don't know how much your will or my will or anybody's will has got to do with it. (*She goes to reply*) I know all the text-book answers, so don't bother—I taught them to you, if you remember—(*Silence*) I thought this moment would never come.

JENNY: What are you saying, Dad?

MR MALDEN: I'm packing it all in. Getting an allotment for the long evenings. Letting history take its course—it's not paid much attention to my exertions so far, anyway: why should it ever?

JENNY: You can't just give up, like that. Thirty years effort. And sacrifice. And solidarity. All for a mix-up on the Tunnel. Listen, the buggers who are knocking down that pie-shop are burning whole villages in Cambodia, napalming children in Laos, cutting Vietnamese women in half because they look like enemy. The men who build twenty-storey hotels in Liverpool are building rocket-silos in Greenland, to protect themselves, and dropping bombs on Asian villages, to secure their interests. How can you just *give* up? There's a war on.

NEIL: Leave him alone, can't you? You go on about me upsetting him. Ha.

JENNY: Keep out of this, Neil, you don't know what you're walking into. You're one of the Killers, remember? You're one of the people he's conceding defeat to: God help us. Well, I'm not.

MR MALDEN: Jenny, you're a good girl, you've learnt all your lessons well, and everything you say is true: but you're too young to really understand—

JENNY: (*Blazing angry*) Now don't give me that terrible old line: if I'm too young, explain. If I'm not, don't patronise me. You're covering up your own miserable cowardice, that's all, your own miserable cringing defeatism.

MR MALDEN: (*Loud*) That will *do*, Jenny.

JENNY: (*Loud*) No it won't. If you're going to rat on the whole movement, betray the people you've worked with and taught and inspired for thirty years, I'm not staying in this house.

MR MALDEN: Sit down.

JENNY: No, I won't.

MR MALDEN: Alright, stand then.

(*He again puts up the Echo as a barrier. She stands quivering in front of it, not knowing whether to go, or to drag him out again. She again sees his hands quivering and she turns away. The door opens, and* MRS MALDEN *comes in, a fairly miserable, depressed-looking woman. She's carrying a paper-bag, which she puts on the table.*)

MRS MALDEN: (*to* JENNY) Oh, you're back then.

JENNY: (*Mumbles*) Netball practice.

MRS MALDEN: Hear they're knocking down the pie-shop.

(NEIL *groans.* MR MALDEN *puts down his paper.*)

MR MALDEN: Yes, dear. It's in the Echo.

MRS MALDEN: They're going to build a big posh hotel.

MR MALDEN: American money.

MRS MALDEN: That'll be something. I thought I might come in for a soft job there—they always need help. It'll be handy, a bit extra. I'm fed up with this house all day. What do you think?

MR MALDEN: What's that? (*Nods to paper bag*)

MRS MALDEN: It's the last of the Pelissier's pork pies: (*She rips the bag open to reveal a non-factory family-sized pork pie.*) Anybody fancy a slice? Mm? Mm?

THE END

TREES IN THE WIND

Presented by the 7:84 England Company in 1971 and 1979 with the following casts:

Aurelia:	Elizabeth MacLennan	Tina Marian
Belle:	Gillian Hanna	Cecily Hobbs
Carlyle:	Deborah Norton	Annie Hayes
Joe:	Victor Henry	Philip Donaghy

ACT 1

Three stages surround the audience, or three acting areas, sharply defined. To the audience left, AURELIA'S room—a bed, walls covered in newspaper cuttings and photos, a few books and a small cupidon. In the centre, CARLYLE'S room, also the living room—a sofa bed, work and dining table, a good hi-fi, a few more chairs and a large cushion on the floor below the bed, bookshelves. On the right, BELLE'S room—bed, dressing table, small TV, chest of drawers, hanging cupboard—cosies, more 'feminine'.

For ten minutes before the play begins, AURELIA has been reading in her room, and CARLYLE is at the table making notes from The Poverty of Philosophy *in hers. As house lights go down, AURELIA goes into CARLYLE'S room, picks up the* Guardian, *reads it to herself.*

AURELIA: Ransacked bodies.

CARLYLE: 'Application of the Law of Proportionality of Value.'

AURELIA: Looted wombs.

CARLYLE: 'Gold and silver were the first commodities to have their value constituted.' Good.

AURELIA: The usual symptoms of cholera are first vomiting and diarrhoea, followed by agonising cramps in the limbs and lower abdomen. After death, the cramps continue to wrack the body for several hours.

CARLYLE: 'However gold and silver are of all commodities the only ones *not* determined by their cost of production, and this is so true that in circulation they can be replaced by paper.' (*Clutches brow*) Oh God.

AURELIA: Taste of bile. Fear in the lower spine.

(*The outside door closes. A clatter in the hallway. Enter* BELLE. *She clutches a heavy briefcase and is looking at a couple of letters she's just picked up. As she passes* AURELIA *she absent-mindedly drops the Evening Standard.*)

BELLE: There you are, news-bilge. (*She goes over and sits on the bed, still working out who the letters might be from.*) I've got such a headache—my headache runs all the way from my arse to my eyebrows. (*She rips open one of the letters, an airmail from the USA. She looks at it as a visual object, turns it around, smells it, looks at it again.*) Aurelia . . .

AURELIA: Mmm?

BELLE: What do you make of that? (*She holds the letter up like a painting.*)

AURELIA: (*After studying it*) Oh dear.

CARLYLE: You can't tell when they go to America—

BELLE: You don't know him.

CARLYLE: Aurelia does.

BELLE: Yes. That was why I asked her.

CARLYLE: Sorry.
(*Pause*)

AURELIA: What's the word from the Pentagon?

BELLE: I haven't read it yet.

CARLYLE: It's true though.

AURELIA: Is it the one you've been waiting for?

CARLYLE: Anything can happen to a person who goes to America: if I had a man I wouldn't let him go to America. Particularly not working for our Ministry of Defence in their Washington—

BELLE: *That* is supposed to be secret.

CARLYLE: And *that* only makes it worse.
(*Pause*)

AURELIA: Belle—

BELLE: Yes.

AURELIA: Shall I read it first . . . see if it's alright?

BELLE: Er—no, I'll manage. (*Gets up, sweeps together her stuff, stands encumbered*)

CARLYLE: David's coming round tonight. (AURELIA *yawns.* BELLE *groans.*) At least I've got an excuse for staying on the pill.

BELLE: You don't have to have a reason for it, do you?

AURELIA: Of course not.

BELLE: Pill for pill's sake, that's how it is with me, mate. It sets me up. Makes me feel like a free woman. Gives me a feeling of— impregnability.

AURELIA: (*Groans, then*) Belle—

BELLE: Yes—

AURELIA: Give it to me.
(BELLE *looks at* AURELIA, *gives her the letter, and stomps off to her room. She dumps her stuff, takes off her jacket and sits on the bed chewing her nails while* AURELIA *reads the letter.* CARLYLE *watches* AURELIA *read. When she finishes* AURELIA *looks at* CARLYLE *ruefully.*) You were right. She shouldn't have let him go.

(CARLYLE *drops needle on to record. Loud music.* AURELIA *walks through to* BELLE'S *room, gives her the thumbs down, sadly hands her the letter, waits, sympathetically, while* BELLE *reads it.* BELLE *finishes it, sniffs, looks at her, shrugs.* AURELIA *goes to the bathroom, comes back with a bottle of aspirins and some water for* BELLE, *gives them to her. As she crosses* CARLYLE'S *room, the phone rings.* CARLYLE *answers the phone.* AURELIA *waits to see who it is, turns music down, then goes to her own room*)

CARLYLE: Hello . . . Hello, David . . . Are you saying you'd like the meeting to be in my place, then? . . . Don't be so bloody middle-class—I'd tell you if it wasn't, wouldn't I? . . . I see, and you want me to ring everybody to tell them . . . of course I mind, it's a drag, but I'll do it . . . Listen don't *thank* me, I'm not doing it for *your* sake—No, this is my room, I kip in it, the others will just have to crawl off to their own . . . Alright. I'll ring everybody—Oh, wait—how can I get hold of Joe? . . . I'll ask the others . . . Look—are you saying—you're not coming round tonight? . . . Well why didn't you just say it. Goodbye. (*She puts on another, very quiet, record, lights a cigarette, starts organising a list of phone numbers.* BELLE *gets up, paces around the room, looks at its dimensions.*)

BELLE: This is my room. My living space. My personal cube, part of a nest of cubes, set in amongst other nests of cubes, cubes above me, cubes below me, cubes left, cubes right, cubes converted from huge Victorian maxi-living-cells, diminished to family-size flats, partitioned off to three girl share-a-flats. Divided finally to this, solitary one-person mini-cube, mine, me in it, alone, nobody else allowed, Western civilisation's answer to the collective farm. Chokey. (*Looks at letter briefly*) You shit. You could have got me out of this. Still, I'm free, aren't I, free? Free to come and go, outside working hours, do what I like in here, take all my clothes off. Get pissed, shoot heroin, masturbate, have fellas in, yeah, fellas, great lusting hairy-arsed fellas, one after the other, banging away till the poor little cell's awash with sex—what more could a girl ask for? (*Looks at letter again*) You rotten stoat. I could have girls. (*Thinks*) Oh, it would be much easier if I fancied girls. (*Thinks*) No, I don't suppose it would. (*Looks at letter*). 'She is a Senator's daughter— Republican I'm afraid, you won't have heard of him, he hasn't distinguished himself by half-witted attacks on America's Far Eastern policy, nor has he been extravagantly hawkish—more your silent majority type of Senator . . .' (*She sits, puts letter down, closes her eyes. In her room,* AURELIA *picks up a tape-recorder microphone, switches it on, dictates from the book she is reading.*)

AURELIA: Testimony of Hoang Tan Hung. "I am 45 years old, and I am a native of the village of Tan My, in South Vietnam. I am a rice-grower and merchant. On 10th May 1965, I was on my way to buy goods in the village. A wave of American jets appeared,

and began to drop bombs and fire rockets. I heard a
tremendous explosion behind me and was immediately covered
with flames. The heat was unbearable. I ran around screaming.
Houses caught fire, and the village was hidden by clouds of
smoke. Women and children were screaming. I managed to run
a little, then I slumped to the ground and lost consciousness".
(*Switches off tape*) This is my room. I sit in my room and read
about such things, occasionally I record them. If ever I have a
grandson, he might be interested. I shan't bother my own
children.

(CARLYLE *has begun to dial.* AURELIA *goes back to reading.* BELLE
is lost in thought.)

CARLYLE: Hello, Marianne? Hello—look, it's Carlyle, about the meeting.
It's the Poverty of Philosophy, the revolution will be all over,
and we still won't have found out why exactly.

AURELIA: (*Into microphone*) 'When I recovered my wounds were
bandaged. I was in a state of semi-consciousness. When the
bandages were changed, I saw that my flesh was burned and
there was a yellowish puss oozing from the wounds. I could
scarcely see with my left eye. My left eardrum was burned and
mutilated'.

BELLE: (*Reading letter again*) 'We have known a lot of love together'—so
that's what all that groping and fumbling was supposed to be—
'and I want to thank you for it'—receipt enclosed, please find—
'and to tell you that I shall never forget it'—Oh I wish you
would—I can't bear the thought of some horrible male fantasy
image of myself lurking around his squalid little imagination—me
naked on the frilly sheets, smiling adoringly up at him,—that's
what he'll want to bloody-well remember: well he can forget me
NOW. I won't have him going through his inept sexual
gymnastics of frustration with some forthright Senator's daughter,
and consoling himself for the calamity he always induces, with
fantasy memories of a non-existent me. No. Forget me. Please. I'll
manage. (*She feels like crying, but reads on to cover up.*) 'You
will never forgive me, I know, for this betrayal; believe me, our
love *was* overwhelming, but this new love is completely
unstoppable.' Oh for God's sake, lad—(*She throws it away.*) I'd
rather be told I'm inadequate than read *that* load of clap-trap.

CARLYLE: (*simultaneously with* AURELIA. *On phone*) How about Engels on
the Irish then, all that about how dirty they were, as if they
were a disease the capitalists had infected the noble English
working-class with.

AURELIA: (*Simultaneously with* CARLYLE) 'An hour later, white smoke,
like burning tobacco, was still rising from the burns on the
nape of my neck and on my back. I was in agonizing pain. Ten
days later I was transferred from the village to a provincial
hospital. The road was long, the means of transport precarious,
it was raining, and my wounds became infected with insect
larvae.' (*Switches off*)

CARLYLE: (*Into phone*) Marianne, I must phone all the others—let's talk about it on Thursday. Bye, see you then. (*Hangs up, dials again*) How anybody's supposed to contact Joe is beyond me.

AURELIA: (*Switches on, reads*) 'After six weeks of hospital treatment I was still in terrible pain. I had fever and could not sleep. Often, when my wounds were being dressed, my flesh would come off in pieces, giving off an unpleasant odour.' (*Stops*)

CARLYLE: Hello, Beryl—it's Carlyle here, Carlyle Reed . . . yes, that's right, it's about the classes actually . . . well, I've been struggling with it, and I'm no wiser either, so you don't have to worry . . . well, so long as your eyes have travelled up and down the pages, at reading pace, my dear, you've read it—the rest is up to David, isn't it, he's the guru, or whatever the Marxist for guru is. Yes, now, Beryl, all I want to tell you is that the meeting is at my place, third floor, 97 Richmond Terrace, at the same time on the same day—OK? . . . Yes, see you then. Bye . . . what? Great Portland Street, it's in the A to Z. Bye. (*Hangs up, dials again*) How some people can expect to overthrow the capitalist state in its entirety and many dimensions, and still not find Great Portland Street is one of the mysteries of contemporary life. (*Into phone*) Jill, Thursday's meeting—same time, but here, my place, OK? Now how the hell can I contact Joe—have you got any ideas?
At *that moment a figure appears in a doorway in a horrible mac, his hands upheld like John the Baptist, his spectacles luminous with diabolical energy, his trousers ragged, his shirt grotty but noble, his self-congratulation ironic but astounding. He listens, mock-sweetly, to the next bit of* CARLYLE's *phone conversation.*)
I can't think why he wants to come to Marxism for beginners anyway, he goes on as if he *was* Karly bloody Marx, *and* Engels, *and* Lenin . . . (*Sighs*), yes, well you're right, but a pain in the arse is a pain in the arse, darling, and some things I'll do for the cause and others I won't, . . . *did* you? *Well.* (*Laughs*) Anyway, if you should receive *another* visitation, would you tell your left-wing Lochinvar where the next meeting is? Lovely. Bye. (*Hangs up, starts to dial again, sniffs, sniffs again, turns and sees* JOE *in the doorway sweetly smiling*)
Joe!—

JOE: I came to see you. I've decided to retire from the working-class, I can't afford it. (*She lets the dial go and stares at him. He comes in and sits down, making himself comfortable amongst her confusion.*)

AURELIA: (*In her room, quietly*) 'Most of my wounds healed after six months of treatment, but the whole of my left arm remains attached to my body, keloid scars have appeared on my skin, even after two years, the wounds on the back of my neck have not yet completely healed.'

CARLYLE: Do you want a cup of coffee?

JOE: No, thank you.

AURELIA: 'My name is Hoang Tan Hung, of Tan My, in the commune of Pho Minh, in the province of Quang Ngai.' (*She turns off the tape, and puts the book on the shelf then goes through to* CARLYLE'S *room.*)

CARLYLE: (*Points to phone*) That was Jill.

JOE: Mm?

CARLYLE: I was talking to Jill Feather—

JOE: Yes. About me.

CARLYLE: Yes.

JOE: Did I get a good report?

CARLYLE: Top of the class.

JOE: Good. (*Walks across the room*) Is that *your* bed?
           (*Pause.* AURELIA *comes in, in a bit of a daze.* JOE *leaps up and pumps her hand, smiling into her face*)
           Hello, I'm so pleased to meet you, delighted, absolutely delighted, my name's Joe Stanion. What's yours?

AURELIA: (*Still dazed*) Aurelia Simpson. I didn't hear the bell—sorry, excuse me—

CARLYLE: No, don't be silly. It *is* your sitting-room—

JOE: Is it?—(*To* CARLYLE) and your bedroom?

CARLYLE: Yes, why do you ask?

JOE: Seems a bit of a constricting arrangement, that.

CARLYLE: I pay less than they do; I'm a student, penniless . . .

JOE: I thought you were an actress—

CARLYLE: I was, but now I'm a student. I read the same books now for six quid a week that I used to read for nothing. Sit down, Aurelia, he's quite tame.

JOE: (*Offended*) How do you know? Cheeky cow. (*Turns to* AURELIA) So you exploit her because she hasn't got any money, do you?

AURELIA: I—? Exploit—? I don't know what language you're talking.

CARLYLE: They don't have to *have* me in their sitting room—they *could* manage—

JOE: No but you *are* in their sitting room, aren't you? Ha, ha, yes. Wriggle your way out of that one—

CARLYLE: How did you get in here?

JOE: No—won't wash, not good enough. (BELLE *comes in, bright and determined*)

BELLE: Mind if I use the phone?

JOE: No, go ahead, it's only her bedroom and her sitting room, it might as well be your kiosk—is she paying some of *your* rent for the privilege as well?

BELLE: Who the hell are you?

JOE: (*Gets up*) Oh sorry, Joe Stanion (*Shakes her hand vigorously*)— who the hell are you?

BELLE: (*to* CARLYLE) Is this one of yours? I never heard the bell.

JOE: One of my many accomplishments is that I am an expert, un-apprehended cat burglar. I prefer to enter unannounced.

BELLE: Bullshit.

JOE: I came in through the kitchen window.

BELLE: Ha—it's three floors up—

JOE: Exactly. Actually, I gave up cat burgling for personal gain four years ago. I used to make my living at it, you see. Then I became a member of the PRP—you'll have heard of that I suppose, from Carlyle here no doubt—and joined the working-class—not only in their ideological struggle, but in their daily toil. To my delight, I found you get paid for it. I no longer needed my hard-won expertise with drainpipe and window-latch. I kept my hand in, of course—whenever the Party needed some money, I'd nip off and do a few jobs of an evening, send in the proceeds, anonymous, of course, just to keep the struggle going forwards. I've enjoyed the last four years. (*Sighs*)

CARLYLE: (*Slowly*) Joe—what exactly are you planning to do?

JOE: (*Suddenly becomes all fumbles*) Well—er—you see, it's this bloke—he's a friend of my brother's actually. Put me on to a good thing. (*Pause*) I find it very difficult to explain this, you see, because it's so very trivial, probably, to you. I don't see how you can take it as seriously as I do. It's absolutely nothing really.

(*Pause*)

BELLE: You've at the very least joined the Metropolitan Police.

CARLYLE: Sounds more like the Green Berets to me—come on, cough it up.

JOE: Well, for the last two years I've been in the building trade, conning my way round as a bit of a chippy—done the odd bit of plastering, brick-laying, on the side, you know, little jobs come up, no tax—roped a few of the lads in, did the arguing for them, split the price between us, always, fair shares. I was losing money on that, forty, sixty quid a deal. I didn't mind that, of course, being a fellow-worker—but now what's happened? You see, I'm such a lousy chippy, and such a powerful negotiator, the lads absolutely *insist* that I start my own firm—stop working myself, go after work for them, line up the contracts and hire my own mates. Next step, of course, is buy a few acres of land, pull a few strings for the planning permission, and contract my own firm for a housing development—you can get government grants for that. In a year or two, I shall be a property tycoon. Of course, I'll need to run the business efficiently to keep my men employed, so I shall have to make suitable contacts in the city, change my image to one that will inspire those city financiers with confidence, I shall have to progress to a suitable life-style and a suitable home to practise it in. I shall be called upon to produce a wife at trade dinners in the West End, at dinner-parties in Tring, at Boat-Race luncheon parties by the Thames, at bridge-opening ceremonies and who knows, she might even have to launch the odd boat, at Yarrow. (*Looks up*) I have not come to ask you to perform that role in my life, Comrade Read, not only because you would remain ideologically opposed to it, but also because you would be very bad at it. No. I come to ask you your opinion. Do you mind?

CARLYLE: What do you want me to say?

JOE: Well—I'm jacking in the Party, aren't I?

CARLYLE: Are you?

JOE: I'm serious about that, you know. I've come to you, as Membership Secretary, to tender my resignation. (*Silence*)

CARLYLE: And you've come to ask my *opinion*?

JOE: I've jacked in the job—Go ahead.

BELLE: (*Dialling*) I mean, you won't want my opinion, will you, so I'll get out—(*Listens*) if he's in . . . He's not. Damn. (*Hangs up, turns to* JOE *cheerfully*) Perhaps you ought to be able to feel what you feel, and believe what you believe, however you earn your living.

CARLYLE: Oh yes, you can. But our Party is about *doing*, not feeling and believing. We're a group of activists, militants: a revolutionary organisation, not a love-in.

BELLE: Oh you are, are you?

CARLYLE: That's just what they *want* you to think politics is all about: feeling and believing. Never about changing, and destroying, and building new structures that they can't get their greedy hands on . . .

AURELIA: (*To* JOE) Why do you think you're going to be so successful?

JOE: Oh, but I am. I just *am*. Because I know the way it all works. Four years rigorous Marxist training and you should be able to play the Stock Exchange like Ludo with loaded dice. And I'm not the first—look at them all, the House of Lords is full of them.

AURELIA: Then why are you doing it?

JOE: Because I've got to.

CARLYLE: Then why have you bothered to come and see me?

JOE: Three things really. One is to discuss my resignation. The second was because I fancy you, and I thought I'd try my luck before my defection to the boss-class disqualified me forever. And the third was I've paid up for these next ten classes and, if I resign, I'm due a six-weeks refund.
    (AURELIA *and* BELLE *look at each other, and leave for their separate rooms;* BELLE *to watch her* TV, AURELIA *to listen to the radio.* CARLYLE *advances on* JOE *and hits him hard across the face. He stands up and pushes her back on to a chair. He walks towards her, holding his cheek. He checks, and sits, instead.*)
    You don't seem to believe in reality.

CARLYLE: Oh yes, I do—

JOE: Well you can't be said to have a very firm grip on it, Comrade. You can't be said to apprehend its workings or comprehend its logic, or even to have grasped its contradictions.

CARLYLE: Until five minutes ago I thought we were both trying to *change* the world, not comprehend its logic.

JOE: Yes, but the difference between us is this: you're not part of it, are you? *You're* on the rails, shouting the odds, tic-tacking to your academic friends at the top of the grandstand, giving the odd cheer. But me, I'm in the bloody race, mate, riding the three-legged carthorse, trying to keep up with the field, giving it the big stick.

CARLYLE: So that's where you are, is it?

JOE: You don't know anything about me, do you?

CARLYLE: I don't know much about your past, but I can see quite a long way into your future.

JOE: (*Controlling himself*) Don't sneer at me—

CARLYLE: Why not? It's what you've come for, isn't it?

JOE: I said don't sneer at me—I might just lose my temper, do you understand, I might just flare up—

CARLYLE: Why don't you just go away—here (*Looking in her handbag for money*)—I'll give you your refund: why don't you invest it in Dow Chemicals.

JOE: (*Jumping up*) Listen, Joan of Arc, you just stuff your money, stuff it, do you hear me—

CARLYLE: That's the other thing you came for, isn't it?

JOE: I mentioned three things: the second is the one I really wanted.

CARLYLE: Meaning me?

JOE: Yes.

CARLYLE: Why?

JOE: (*He looks at her.*) You don't know what it's like to be poor in England, do you? You've never slept five in a bed, have you, or had nothing but bread and marge and school milk to fill you from one Sunday to the next, have you? You think there's just a heroic soul called 'the working class', don't you? It never occurred to you there might be a rich working-class, a poor working-class and a nothing-at-all working-class like the mob I was emptied into, did it? You never had to stop at home from school because your trousers wouldn't stitch together any more, did you?

CARLYLE: No. So what are you trying to tell me?

JOE: You don't *know* anything, do you?

CARLYLE: Are you speaking now as a future member of the House of Lords or an ex-member of the working-class?

JOE: Both. At once. And *that* is one thing you really don't know, Comrade Read.

CARLYLE: (*Going over to him*) Will you go now?
(*She walks out in disgust. He takes his mac off and looks through her records. In her room,* BELLE *decides to act. She gets up, starts to pace around, then gets out a tape measure and starts to measure her room, length, breadth and height, in a very determined way. She puts the figures down on a piece of paper as she gets to them, muttering them to herself. When she's got them all, she multiplies them out loud until she arrives at the exact cubic capacity of the room.*)

BELLE: Seven hundred and sixty-eight cubic feet . . . I suppose I could fill it with hens.
(*In* her *room,* AURELIA *throws down the paper onto a pile of papers, rubs her eyes.*)

AURELIA: Near Stevenage a seven-year-old boy got his arm stuck on a level crossing between a rail and a sleeper. A woman who tried to free him couldn't bring herself to break his arm off, so he was run over by the Aberdeen-Kings Cross express. In the papers they try to make it all connect, like a nineteenth-century novel, like endless Tolstoy. But it doesn't. I know it doesn't. There are not so many connections as we think there are. It's impossible for me to believe in history: it's all a fiction, invented by men. They need something to console them, something complete-looking, logical-looking, powerful-looking. Because they can't feel anything, I suppose. They can't feel being alive, they can't feel their feet on the world turning, they can't feel trees, and weather, and other people. So they invented history. Tamburlaine the Great.
   Is it not brave to be a king, Techelles,
   Usumcasane and Theridamas,
   Is it not passing brave to be a king,
   And ride in triumph through Persepolis?
I can't believe in that. I'm coming to hate men. (*Looks at paper*) But: 'Car Plunges Over Beachy Head Three Dead', I can believe. I can see that. (*Reads*)
(*Back in* CARLYLE'S *room,* JOE *has been looking through her records. He picks one out. She comes back in.*)

JOE: Can I put this on?

CARLYLE: You haven't gone then?

JOE: What would I want to go for? I haven't got my refund yet, have I? (*She goes and sits*)
What's the matter with you?

CARLYLE: You do know what's going on in the world, don't you? It happened to the Russians—now it's happening to the Chinese—our guides and teachers.

JOE: I've been observing it, quietly.

CARLYLE: Is *that* why you're resigning—

JOE: No.

CARLYLE: Listen: (*Grabs book, reads*) . . . This is what they did it for— 'I was born in Hunan Province, in 1901. My father was a tenant farmer. He had a small farm of two and a half acres. I was the sixth of eight children.
   Our local General forced my father to pay so many taxes he could no longer feed all of his children, although he worked very hard.
   One day, in the winter of 1913, he went to find beech leaves. My mother used to boil them for us to eat. He did not come home. My mother and my sister found him by the side of the road. He had died of hunger.

I was twelve years old, so I was able to leave home to find work. I went to Shanghai, and secured work as a servant on the railway trains. When I was thirteen or fourteen, I was promoted to switching rails—which I still do.

We work eighteen hours a day, seven days a week. If we complain, a Russian foreman beats us. If we complain about this, we are sacked. If we try to form a Union, we are shot. My closest friend could no longer bear this kind of life. He killed himself. When his wife found his body, she beat it and kicked it with fury for leaving her and their children alone in such a world.'

JOE: Don't give me the starving hordes of bloody Asia—*here*, it happens too—things *do* happen here, you know—it's not just a double-glazed observation post on the universe, contrary to what you might think—China . . . For about fourteen years, I thought that the world was just like that—so I took it—had a few laughs and robbed a few shops and smashed in a few faces just to keep me going. Then I discovered I'd got a cock, and it did things to girls, made them wilt a bit, and they wanted it—I actually had something somebody wanted—You've *always* had something somebody wanted, haven't you? Well, suddenly I had that. Of course at school they said it was dirty—not to be handled, and some of the girls used to lower themselves into the sexual act as if it was a tub of reptiles—
(AURELIA *crosses* CARLYLE'S *room on her way to get the paper back from* BELLE. *They continue talking*)
—till they got comfortable in it. Slowly, through the eye of my cock, I began to perceive a different world—of pleasure, and satisfaction, and joy—and power over people. I began to understand: there was a war on, and we were all in it, members of the war: at first it was me, all on my own, against them—the world, then there was us, me, and my mates, and a few birds, against them,
(AURELIA *passes back with the paper, trying not to be there.*)
the dirt brigade, telling us fucking was sinful. Then we realised they weren't just sitting on our sexual joys, they were sitting like toads, fat-assed warty toads, on everything: and not just on me and my mates, but on all our lot—all of the kids and all of the grown-ups too. We were living in Manchester, underneath Strangeways Prison: suddenly we realised who was inside it: we were. They had us by the short and curlies. And nobody seemed to be doing anything about it. I spent twenty-five of the best years of my life in that rotten city, the last ten of them doing rubbishy jobs for no money, wondering how I could get out. Then I realised. All you needed was money. And there was a lot of it lying around—for the picking up.

CARLYLE: Shanghai, 1927. Chiang Kai-Chek was advancing on the city. Stalin decided he was our ally, so he told the Chinese comrades to rise up, take the City, and hand it over to Chiang Kai-Chek as a present. So they did. Then Chiang said could he have our guns, as well, so Stalin said yes, of course; so when he'd got all of our guns, he organised a couple of gangs of criminals; with the aid of the Americans and the British—to take all the comrades out, one by one, and shoot them. Except for the leaders. They were shoved, alive, into the furnaces of locomotives: just for kicks. Chou-En-Lai was one of the leaders. As he was being led to the slaughter, by some extraordinary stroke of luck, he escaped: he went up into the hills.

JOE: I became a cat burglar. Part-time, of course. I used to practise on our house. In case I got caught. That was how I discovered my own kid sister had gone on the game: she was bringing fellows home from the clubs in the evenings for a quick bash before closing time—thirty-five bob. Not even two quid. You should have seen her face when I came in through the window that first time. You should have seen this poor sod. Shot off like shite from a shovel, never even waited for his change. During the day, I got a soft job doing deliveries: that way I could check up on the likely areas—you know, the rich suburbs. By night—in. I wasn't a shitter. No. There's some who can't leave a drum without shitting—here, there and everywhere on the carpet, rub it on the walls, chuck it at the pictures. I can't say I never felt an overwhelming desire to—I did. The richer the house, the stronger the desire. But it also struck me as undignified—childish. I just used to take money. Never touched anything else—it got to be a superstition—just money. (*In her room,* BELLE *gets up, goes over to* CARLYLE'S *room, knocks; goes in, says 'excuse me', unplugs the phone, and carries it through to her own room, where she plugs it back in and dials.*) I made so much I couldn't spend it in Manchester—they'd have sussed me out. So I came to London.

CARLYLE: And now Chou-En-Lai is the Prime Minister of All China.

JOE: That's what I'm saying—you know *nothing*.
(CARLYLE *goes and gets book,* BELLE *gets through on phone*)

BELLE: (*On phone*) Hello—Denton? . . . Remember you asked me to dinner last week and I wriggled out of it . . . oh of course I was lying, don't be stupid, I never go anywhere, let alone Covent Garden alright, alright, don't get all upset, it happens all the time, it wasn't that I didn't fancy you, it was just, well, I was saving myself . . . (*Louder to stop him*) Yes, well the point is I've changed my mind—if you still want me to, I mean . . .
(AURELIA *throws her paper down and starts pounding on the arms of her chair. She gets up and jumps on the paper, frenziedly ripping it with her feet.*)

AURELIA: Is it not brave to be a king, Techelles,
Usumcasane and Theridamas,
Is it not passing brave to be a king
And ride in triumph through Persepolis?
(*She glares at a statuette of a boy cherub.*)
So you're going to be a man . . .

BELLE: Yes, I've stopped saving myself. I've decided to spend myself, get drunk, pick up bronzed young men on the Earls Court Road, lure them back to my nest, and ravage them—lovely . . . Oh, that's put you off as well, has it?

CARLYLE: Listen: 1963, this was: since World War II, US imperialism has been carrying on aggressive wars or armed interventions in various parts of the world.
We hold that to defend world peace it is necessary to arouse and organize the people against the imperialists, and to place reliance on the growth of the strength of the socialist camp, on the revolutionary struggles of the working people of all countries, on the liberation struggles of the oppressed nations, and on the broad united front against US imperialism and its lackeys.

AURELIA: Men. Big men.
Me heap big man, me fell squaw many many papooses—
Many many papooses make squaw very old
Me take away papoose-boys, teachem fight,
teachem hunt,
Teachem kill—

BELLE: You want to make your mind up exactly what you require your women to conform to, young man . . . I'm not giving myself to you and you alone, that's for bloody certain, and I'm not even going to pretend to—what for the price of two spaghetti bologneses and a bottle of Tunisian rouge.

AURELIA: —teachem rule squaw,
Makem heap big man again.
Fill up papoose-girls, make many many papooses.
Me heap big grand-dad—
My son, heap big warrior—
My grandson, soon finish papoose-games.
Soon. Teachem kill.

CARLYLE: With this line, it is possible constantly to expand the people's revolutions and manacle imperialism.
With this line, it is possible to turn to account all the contradictions between the US and the other imperialist powers, and to isolate US imperialism.
This is the line for the people of all countries to win both victory in revolution and world peace.

BELLE: No, no, it's a short lease on your *body* I'm interested in, if I've got to be blunt—you've got a mind like a limp wrist, it's appalling—claggy—Here, don't start crying, you're too big for that, Denton . . . Well, do you or don't you—want to squire me around the world's most exciting city tomorrow night?

AURELIA: And who keeps the great wheel turning?
Women.
Nice, passive, accepting, 'cultivated', polite, dignified, subdued, dependent, scared, mindless, insecure, approval-seeking women—who can't cope with the unknown, who want to feel safe with the apes, who want a Big Daddy in the

background and a big strong man to snuggle up to—and yet
more men to *rule* them from on high. Men's women.

BELLE: (*Listens, groans to herself*) Here, I tell you what—why don't
we not: I mean, just *not*—forget I ever phoned, go back to your
embroidery . . . (*Wearily*) no, I didn't mean that, forget I spoke,
I take it all back, everything, every word, the lot, I take it as far
back as you can get it. Good-bye, Denton. GOOD-BYE.

CARLYLE: (*Throws book on bed, picks up another—the Mao Papers*)
Listen: 1967–(*Reads*) 'The peoples of the world must have
courage, dare to fight, and fear no hardships. When the ones in
front fall, the others behind must follow up. In this way, the
world will belong to the people and all the demons will be
eliminated.' Mao Tse bloody Tung. And now, in South America,
in Palestine, the same young comrades are fighting the same
bloody war-lords that the Shanghai comrades were fighting, and
they want help, support, money: and what do they get?

AURELIA: Soothers, ego-boosters, relaxers, breeders. (*Turns back to
statuette*) The kind you're going to want when you grow up . . .
And all the other men in the world—and most of the women—
are busy making sure you get one.

CARLYLE: Pandas for Edward Heath. Banquets for Nixon.

BELLE: (*Puts phone down, makes a face at it, sees her other letter,
realises what it is, instantly cheers up*) Oh—I know what that
is—The Grapefruit Diet. (*She tears it open and starts to study
it.*) Now for the young beauties . . . (*Total dismay*) What does
it mean, eat steaks, pheasants, roast beef or lamb, at least once
daily? I can't afford any of that lot once weekly—what a drag .
. . Perhaps if I found a rich lover he'd pay for me to get thin
eating bloody great steaks—I'd like that.

JOE: On the train I met this bloke from the PRP. He talked all the
way. Took me home, fed me: I'd told him I had no money, so
he got me a job—and he kept on talking. By the time he'd
finished I was a Maoist—or what we call a Marxist-Leninist.
Screwing girls, smashing in faces, burgling the suburbs—slowly
they all fell into a perspective—they were all fumblings towards
a proper, organised fight against that over-whelming feeling of
helplessness we'd all felt under the walls of Strangeways: that
feeling that we might as well be inside it as outside, for all the
chance we had of a decent life. And you're forced to admit,
there was no keener comrade, nobody harder-working, more
unstinting of their time and energy, more dedicated in the fight
against capitalism than I was.
(CARLYLE *turns on* JOE)

CARLYLE: So what happened? Have you decided it's all wrong? Have you
decided people *should* live like you lived, that poverty is good
for you—is the class war suddenly over?

JOE: No. It's not that. It's just that—I suddenly felt, when I had the
urge to turn this idea down, that I'd be moving into some
political fantasy-land, I'd be deliberately turning down a small

fortune, just to prove that capitalism makes people poor—it seemed mad, if anything can safely be called mad. And it wasn't just *me* involved—Christ, no, I mean, if it was *just* a question of me making money, that would be different. But I'm going to bring work to at least half-a-dozen of my best mates. Their families can't live on revolutionary fervour and the Social Security money—they want to work: for money, for the going rate.

CARLYLE: There's people like you and me getting shot up against the wall every day in Chile, and Chou-En-Lai's friend Henry Kissinger voted 9 million dollars to help the CIA overthrow Allende. Does Chou protest? He invites Kissinger to dinner.

JOE: But that's how history moves, you see. And you're battering your head up against a wall trying to fight it. That's what I mean. People like you, you're mad. You're outside reality, you think it's tragic: I'm inside it, and I know it's logical.

CARLYLE: 60 years after the old man died picking beech leaves.
44 years after the Shanghai massacre.
21 years after the revolution.
8 years after the great Polemic against the Russians.
5 years after the Cultural Revolution.
Normalisation.
Who is the enemy now? Not ITT—Confucius.
(BELLE, *who has been growing happier and happier, bursts through to* CARLYLE'S *room.*)

BELLE: Hey, look at me, look at me, I'm *free*. I've decided, that's it, forget him, give him the elbow, alright you sod, you go off then.

JOE: Good, great, right on, that's what I like to hear.

BELLE: She was only a Republican's daughter, but she knew how to keep her Nix-on—hoi.

CARLYLE: About time you blew that creep down your nose.

BELLE: Marry her, in the White House, in a lighthouse, in a shite-house, who cares, you miserable moaning weasel, you stoat, ferret, egg-sucker: get out of my nest, I want to fly.

JOE: The world's your oyster baby—crack it.

BELLE: I have decided to capture the heart of Gunther Sachs. I love him. I dedicate my life to him.

JOE: Ya-hay! (*Swings her round*) Won't I do? (*Strikes a pose*) Brigitte Bardot would *swoon*—she wouldn't know what to do with that even if she was lucky enough to get it: where's your Gunther Sachs the noo?

BELLE: You're no good, comrade, you're just a hairy aggressive fella, with spots and armpits, I want *perfection*!
I dedicate my life to Gunther, to Mister Perfection.
To his lean good looks, like in the Austin Reed ad, to his brown skin like in the Silver Wing Holiday brochure, to his gleaming teeth as seen in Kolynos, Macleans, Signal, Colgate, and new PermaDent ads,

to his crinkly smile, as seen on Christianity ads, for Jesus
Christ, Saint Francis of Assisi, Billy Graham and His Holiness
Pope Paul;
to his serious brow, the hallmark of a thinker, as seen on
philosopher-type ads, such as for Erinmore Flake Pipe
Tobacco, for the complete Encyclopaedia Britannica delivered
to your door, and for Transcendental Meditation Twelve
Lectures;

AURELIA: All men have the Midas touch. Everything they touch turns to
shit.

BELLE: to his shining black healthy hair as worn in the shampoo ads,
Silverkin, Palmolive, Boots Three Hundred and Sixty-five,
Breck . . . for dry hair, and Vosene for dandruff;
to his jaw, strong and odiferous, as lotioned by countless manly
lotions after countless manly shaves;
to his flat but muscular body, as rolled into shape by a million
Health Clubs;

AURELIA: A few examples of the most obnoxious and harmful types of
men: Rapists, politicians—and all who are in their service;
popular pop-singers; Chairmen of Boards; Breadwinners;
landlords—

CARLYLE: The basis for men's domination over women has already been
undermined. The women in many places have now begun to
organize. The opportunity has come for them to lift up their
heads, and the authority of the husband is getting shakier every
day. The whole feudal-patriarchal ideological system is
tottering.

BELLE: to his tapering legs, as worn by Superman, travellers on BOAC,
and wearers of Dacri-Nylon swimwear;
to his genitals: never seen, anywhere, because they are *not* what
is to be sold, except to me:

AURELIA: Owners of greasy spoons and restaurants that play Musak;
'Great Artists'; Policemen; soldiers, scientists working on death
and destruction programmes, scientists working on industry's
earth-rape project.

CARLYLE: In order to build a great socialist society, it is of the utmost
importance to arouse the broad masses of women to join in
productive activity. Men and women must receive equal pay for
equal work in production. Genuine equality between the sexes
can only be realized in the process of the socialist
transformation of society as a whole.

BELLE: to his yacht;
to his helicopter—
to his twin-engined jet Executive Cessna;
to his Mercedes, his Lamborghini, his white Cadillac and his
Mini;

AURELIA: Liars and phoneys; disc jockeys, men who touch you in the
street, men who talk to you in the street. Men who look at you
in the street.

BELLE: To his schloss in Bavaria, his penthouse in Paris, his chateau outside St Tropez, his apartment in New York, and his mews flat in Belgravia;

CARLYLE: All culture, all literature and art belong to definite classes. There is no such thing as art for art's sake, art that stands above classes, art that is detached from politics.

AURELIA: Double-dealers; plagiarizers—
All men in the advertising industry,
Critics—including lady critics.

BELLE: to his innumerable boutiques selling trim little knickers to trim little chicks at an unbelievable profit;
to his bank-accounts, with Credit Lyonnais, Chase Manhattan, First Chemical bank of Philadelphia, a small clearing-house in Geneva, the Deutsches Bank and Barclays, DC & 0;

AURELIA: Bankers; censors; public and private,
And bringers of court cases—
All members of the death Army, death Navy,
death Air force, particularly, US Air Force Pilots . . .

CARLYLE: I hold that it is bad as far as we are concerned if we are not attacked by the enemy; in that case it would mean that we have sunk to the level of the enemy. It is good to be attacked by the enemy. It proves we have drawn a line between the enemy and ourselves. It is still better if the enemy attacks us wildly and paints us as utterly black and without a single virtue; it demonstrates that we have not only drawn a line between the enemy and ourselves but achieved a great deal in our work.

BELLE: to his factories in Germany, where all the workmen, you will notice, are always smiling, and there has never been a strike since 1954;
to his Spanish workmen, his Turkish workmen, his Arabs, his Portuguese, his Greeks, his Italians, his Yugoslavs and his German supervisors;
Men who seek power,
Men who fight for power,
Men who kill for power,
Men who lie for power,
Men who die for power,
Men who win power,
Men who use power,
Men who invent power,
Men who believe in power,
Men who force women to believe in power,
Men who kill, crush, maim, butcher, massacre,
destroy, devastate, desolate, and desecrate the women, the children and the earth in the name of power.
Off, off, off, off—off the face of the earth. It will not be enough to achieve equality with power-mad men in their man's stinking system.

CARLYLE: We are advocates of the abolition of war, we do not want war; but war can only be abolished through war, and in order to get rid of the gun it is necessary to take up the gun.

AURELIA: We shall never be free until man's whole stinking power money-shit system is over, over and out.

BELLE: to you, Gunther Sachs, I dedicate myself: I want to know what it means to LIVE.

CARLYLE: 'Be resolute, fear no sacrifice and surmount every difficulty to win victory.' (*Then*)
(*Repeat, all together*)

AURELIA: I thought I might go out and get some oven-ready pizzas—anybody want one?

CARLYLE: Lovely, just the thing—

BELLE: Yes. I'll come with you, in case you lose your way.

JOE: Er—shall I go down the off-license for a couple of bottles of wine—(*to* CARLYLE) Shall I?

CARLYLE: (*Shrugs*) O.K.

JOE: Coming?

CARLYLE: No.
(*The others have gone.* JOE *turns to* CARLYLE)

JOE: Carlyle—listen: don't just kick me in the balls, lovely. I need you.
(*He goes.* CARLYLE *sits back, holds her head in her hands.*)

CARLYLE: 'Wind will not cease, even if trees want to rest.'. (*She laughs*)

END OF ACT 1

ACT 2

As the house lights go down, the actors come back on to the centre stage and sit. Stage lights come up as house lights are out. A silence. AURELIA, BELLE, CARLYLE *and* JOE *have finished their pizzas in the sitting room. They are halfway through the second bottle of wine. The awkward silence is broken by* AURELIA.

AURELIA: In Italy, they make red wine from ox-blood, salt and a dash of pure sulphur. (*Pause*) They poured away half a million litres of it.

BELLE: Wonder where they got all that blood from.

JOE: Imported it from Germany—

CARLYLE: Through neutral Switzerland?

AURELIA: Would it come on trains, in tankers, or on the hoof as it were?

JOE: Probably got a load cheap from Biafra for the 1970 vintage, and Bangladesh for '71. They'll not run short of blood.

AURELIA: I'm amazed there's enough sulphur. To keep up with the blood.

JOE: (*Raising his glass*) Cheers—Moroccan, this, isn't it? (*Drinks; the others don't*)

CARLYLE: Where did you get the money for this?

JOE: Why?

CARLYLE: I want to know—last Friday you were penniless. Tonight you buy two bottles of wine: and you haven't worked since last Friday, have you?

JOE: Only in a manner of speaking.

CARLYLE: Did you steal this money?

JOE: Only in a manner of speaking.

CARLYLE: Where did it come from?

JOE: I got a cash advance: on my first contract. I'm so happy it's with you I'm celebrating it.

CARLYLE: So it's profit—

JOE: Yes, out of my two West Indian mates, George and Eddie, slaving away down in Lambeth all day, while I've been tucking my thumbs in my braces and smoking a fat cigar. (*Jumps up*) Here you are, ladies, (*Pouring wine into their glasses*) you're not drinking Biafran blood, my darlings, you're not quaffing Bengali plasma, or vintage 1942 concentration camp Chateau Eichman—no, that's good old West Indian sweat, that is, garnered in good old England, this very day. Ladies—(*Sniffs*) grab that bouquet—a trifle young, one might almost say coltish, but lively and unpretentious for all that. Won't you join me in a toast, to us, the fortunate employers.
(*A hostile silence.* JOE *grins*)

BELLE: What have you *really* come here for? Do you know?

JOE: (*Turning nasty*) Who are you? Eh? Who *are* you? What do *you* do for your living?

BELLE: I'm a psychiatric caseworker: I spend time with people when they're going mad, try to find out why. I deal mostly with young people—late adolescent boys, young married women with too many kids, lonely wives in tower blocks, put-upon schizoid 15-year-old daughters. There's a team of us just started up in Leytonstone.

JOE: So you're papering over the cracks in capitalism, are you?

BELLE: I'm what she calls a reformist.

JOE: (*Calmer*) Oh yes?

BELLE: I'm not bothered about overthrowing the system as much as her lot are—it's inefficient and unjust and totally loathsome, of course.

JOE: Of course.

BELLE: But I let those who are interested in power get on with the politics, while I get on with the people.

JOE: Heroically bandaging the wounded in the field-hospitals of the class war—

BELLE: Yes. You could say that. And you're just sharpening your sword, as it were. Not often I clap eyes on the enemy: makes a change. But enough's enough. I'm off to bed now. (*She goes through to her room.*)

AURELIA: And I'm going to wash up. (*Goes*)

CARLYLE: Would you like some coffee before you go?

JOE: No thank you. I'm quite happy. (*She goes. He laughs wickedly, then goes into* BELLE'S *room.*)

(*Standing in door*) You don't like what you see, do you?

BELLE: What?

JOE: Naked greed, aggression undisguised, lust for power over others, you don't like that, do you?

BELLE: (*Shrugs*) Everything that lives is holy, or whatever the man said.

JOE: You wouldn't fuck me, would you?

BELLE: I don't see what that's got to do with it . . .

JOE: Come on, say it—

BELLE: Well you're not exactly Gunther Sachs—

JOE: (*Goes over to her, aggressively*) Say it, or I will.

BELLE: I loathe you.

JOE: Good.

BELLE: I despise your every twist and turn—

JOE: Excellent, glad you've been noticing them—

BELLE: I'd rather fuck a syphilitic rattlesnake.

JOE: (*Jubilant*) Great! Now you're talking, wonderful, wonderful— why?

BELLE: (*Pause. Turns away*) You've upset me. I don't enjoy talking to people that way—

JOE: (*Suddenly jumps onto centre stage, into RED SPOT—all other lighting off*) Down with The Demon King, Liberate Little Devils. (*Turns to audience*) Ladies and Gentlemen, in this half I take the part of the Demon King. Willingly, fiendishly, I thrust it upon myself:
I am the savage Alsatian, lusting for blood: Are you a man?— I'll go for your balls: Are you a woman?—I'll jump up at your throat, with my great big doggy cock thrusting away for you down below. Are you a child?—I'll tear the hot flesh off your bones.
   Why?
   Because I want to know something: why don't we shoot all killer-dogs?
   Down with the Demon King! Liberate little devils!
(*He goes back to* BELLE'S *room. Lights to normal*)
Do you know who I am?

BELLE: You're a left-wing cat burglar with sweaty feet. I'm going to bed now, do you mind getting out?

JOE: No. Don't avoid me.

BELLE: Doesn't seem to be much chance of that—

JOE: You insulted me just now. I want to hear, from your own lips, why.

BELLE: If you want to know the God's honest truth, I couldn't care less about you; I've spent my whole life avoiding building contractors, and I don't want to start tangling with them now. I don't want to know—thank you very much.

JOE: But you've *got* to know, haven't you?

BELLE: Have I? Why?

JOE: Because of the objective condition of the class war: wind will not cease even though trees want rest.

BELLE: Gerroff . . . (*pause*)

JOE: In about twenty years' time, when I'm Managing-Director and Chairman of Chuckemup Building Contractors Ltd., Chairman of the GLC Housing Allocations Committee, the most right-wing Tory Mayor even Kensington and Chelsea have ever produced, with a dynamically controlling interest in seventeen subsidiary companies, and an ornament to the boards of twenty-two others—and just plain Sir Joseph, as yet—you will come to me, cap in hand, for help.

BELLE: Oh I will, will I?

JOE: Oh Sir Joseph, nice kind Sir Joseph, we are organising a nice lovely sweet little straitjacket and pethadine service for the thousands and thousands of psychotic wrecks now roaming in hordes through the streets of London, Birmingham, Liverpool, Edinburgh, Glasgow, Manchester and Leeds—will you spare us a pound from your untold millions? Do you know what I'll say? PISS OFF. I'll abuse you personally, almost certainly strike you, press a button for my ex-policeman—Gary, I think I'll call him—and have him chuck you off the penthouse roof of Stanion House. At the inquest, Gary will swear you defenestrated yourself out of unconsummated love for *me*. I shall wear black at the funeral, and walk very slowly indeed for about three weeks, to get sympathy. Do you know why I shall treat your appeal in this way?

BELLE: Because you'll be a capitalist pig.

JOE: Correct, but scarcely scientific. What all do-gooders, which means you, fail to understand about big business, which means me, is that, in the end, *you* are working for *me*. It will be in my interest to have you looking after the mentally mutilated, because I will be the one that will ultimately have driven them mad.

Listen: The Song of Driving Mad . . .

(AURELIA *and* CARLYLE *leap onto the centre stage.*)

AURELIA: The Song

CARLYLE: The Song

AURELIA: of Driving

CARLYLE: of Driving

AURELIA: Mad

CARLYLE: The Song of Driving Mad.

JOE: Take my wife: insanity begins at home.

AURELIA: (*Gushy, rich, young wife*) Oh darling, my poor tired worn-out darling. You do look so pale, so exhausted, you do work so hard—

JOE: (*Sir Joseph*) Never mind, my pet, so long as I can keep you in comfort, it will all be worth it . . . by the way—did a tea-stirring machine arrive this afternoon? Blenkinsop swore blind he'd deliver it before three . . .

AURELIA: Oh is *that* what it's for?

JOE: Yes, saves you all the bother of stirring your tea, my pet, my little honey-bun, my own little hamster . . .

AURELIA: Oh how lovely . . . Darling—

JOE: Mm?

AURELIA: I'd like to go out and see some people one evening

JOE: Out? See? People?

AURELIA: Well—yes, people—

JOE: Aren't the Gwatkin-Watts people? Aren't the Sebag-Montefiores people? Aren't the Chartered Accountants Association of Hemel Hempstead people?

AURELIA: I meant friends.

JOE: (*Hard look*) There's something funny about you lately, Geraldine—reminds me of that aunt of yours.

CARLYLE: (*Sings*)
> He's my man, an ordinary guy,
>   See him on the street you wouldn't notice him go by—
>   And yet to me, he's everything, he's just—my Bill.

JOE: (*Sir Joseph*) Some years later, at 4 o'clock in the morning . . . Lady Stanion is in bed . . . kipping (*He tiptoes upstairs, pushes open the door, mimes undressing quietly, guiltily. She stirs, sits up.*)

AURELIA: (*Lady Stanion—sleepy*) What time is it, darling?

JOE: (*Pretending it's quite usual*) Oh—about 3.30.

AURELIA: Where have you been?

JOE: Conference—you know how it is—

AURELIA: I never seem to see you these nights.

JOE: What on earth would you want to do that for?

AURELIA: Well—you know

JOE: No. I don't know. You've never yet given me any good reason for coming home early, as far as I can remember.

AURELIA: (*In floods of tears*) Oh, darling

JOE: It can't be sex—you haven't got any of that—

AURELIA: Oh, darling—

JOE: You're useless, you've got no go in you—it's like sleeping with a stunned kangaroo—the odd twitch, the odd hop and silence . . .

AURELIA: I really, really felt quite sexy tonight—

JOE: Aha! Been at the booze cupboard, have you—well I'm getting a lock put on it. There's something pretty unstable about you, you know.

CARLYLE: (*Sings*)
> Mr Wonderful, that's you

JOE: A few years later, over burnt porridge and menopausal toast—

AURELIA: Oh dear, oh sorry, darling, it's all dry, cracked, burnt-up—oh hell, (*Hysterical*) why can I never do anything in this flaming kitchen, why, why, why? What's the matter with me—oh, don't look at me like that—

JOE: Don't do anything *stupid* while I'm away, my dear. I shall be in Chicago for three weeks: I suggest you get yourself straightened out before I get back.

AURELIA: Straightened out?

JOE: Yes, straightened out. See somebody, a psychiatrist, a nut-tightener, and make sure he fixes you up—because do you know what you're heading for?

AURELIA: What?

JOE: (*Makes EC T noise*) Wheee!!

AURELIA: The Song

CARLYLE: The Song

AURELIA: of Driving

CARLYLE: of Driving

AURELIA: Mad

CARLYLE: The Song of Driving Mad.

AURELIA: The Song.

JOE: I'm very good to my employees, I'm a model employer, I have the Confederation of British Industry award for Benevolence to my Workers—nevertheless, I drive them *mad*:

CARLYLE: (*Is a ga-ga, goo-goo secretary to Sir J—on phone*) Oh dear—oh how frightful—yes, hang on a moment—(*to* JOE) Sir Joseph, young Charlie Ironside's fallen off his excavator, and they've had to chop his leg off—

JOE: (*Sir Joseph, in office*) Get on to the Legal Department, right away, tell them to sue him, in case he sues us.

CARLYLE: Nobody else will do that job, now young Charlie's lost his leg . . .

JOE: Get hold of that daft old bugger Williamson—he's cheap and he's willing.

CARLYLE: (*on phone*) You're to get Mr Williamson.
(AURELIA *comes in, cap in hand*)

JOE: Ah, Jenkinson—you've offended me, young man, I found your drunken comments most unseemly—I'm putting you on a three month trial, on half pay—if I get to know of even the slightest misdemeanour, Jenkinson—the boot.
(AURELIA *goes, crawling off.* JOE *mops his brow*)
Ah, time for you to leave me, Jennifer, off to your little flat in Barons Court. (*Bears down on her, as she covers up her typewriter*) I have many troubles, Jennifer. Many. I need—something nice to happen to me; like you.

CARLYLE: Oh, Sir Joseph

JOE: You're like a spring flower in my autumn garden . . .

CARLYLE: Oh, Sir Joseph.

JOE: (*Holding out a finger to her, which she boggles at*) You're like a hoover, over my dusty carpet—

CARLYLE: (*Taking hold of finger*) Oh, Sir Joseph—

JOE: She beats, as she sweeps, as she cleans . . .
(CARLYLE *kneels down and sucks his finger,* JOE *becomes triumphant*)
Hahaha—I hear old Johnson's gone under, right under, six feet under, and that leaves only Leveson—and he's looking a bit blue round the ears—Poor Mrs Johnson, taken it rather

badly—must have been fond of him, can't imagine why.
Jenkinson too, hahaha, poor young Jenkinson, he went down—
down for three years for exposing himself to little girls—
hahaha.

AURELIA: (*Says*) Ring, ring.
(CARLYLE *answers it.*)

CARLYLE: Poor old Mr Williamson did *what*? He drove the excavator up
Woodford High Street, tilting at the traffic lights—said he was
Sir Percival of Wales—

JOE: Have him PUT AWAY-
(CARLYLE *snivels in front of him.*)
Jennifer, woman, I thought you were on the pill: if you weren't,
you have only yourself to blame haven't you? Think you'd
better leave.—Yes right away. Here, here's two hundred—get it
seen to: now not another word. I don't ever want to hear from
you again. (*She goes, snivelling.*) She must be mad.

AURELIA: The Song

CARLYLE: The Song

AURELIA: of Driving

CARLYLE: of Driving

AURELIA: Mad

CARLYLE: The Song of Driving Mad.

JOE: And as for my tenants, my occupiers, of my tower-blocks, I just
stack 'em up, one on top of the other, coop 'em up, it keeps
'em happy 'cos it keeps the rain off their backs—fill 'em up
with kids, fill 'em up with pills.

AURELIA: Paulette Jones is 24 and lives with her husband and two year
old son on the top floor of a block of high rise council flats:
    'When John was first born he didn't sleep at all and going
    without sleep you just can't cope—with a new baby and
    housework and shopping and general things, it's just too
    much. And it does get very lonely at the top here—I mean
    when you're in a flat like this I suppose it is in a sense like a
    prison except you've got the key and you can let yourself in
    and out. So I found I was getting very tense and I was
    getting cross with John and that's when I went to my doctor
    and then she gave me these tranquillisers which helped
    tremendously but things didn't improve much with John so I
    had to watch him all the time. If I was hoovering I had to
    hold him under one arm and hold the hoover with the other,
    and that's just how things went on and it went from bad to
    worse. I'd never now be without a bottle of tablets in the
    house . . . I have to have them because you know there are
    days when things do get terrible and really my only
    communication with anybody is through the telephone.'

CARLYLE: Diane Meddows is 34. She has two daughters, one aged ten,
the other eight.
    'I became a housewife as soon as I left university and had
    the children straight away. I think you feel very trapped

with small children because just going out is a great expedition and I did get very lonely. I don't think I noticed how lonely I got until I look back on it and I see the very odd things I did, like one day I was walking home from shopping and a woman who was doing some market research stopped me and said would I give my opinion on some supermarket, and she said she'd call on me and I said "yes" immediately, it was absolutely lovely to talk to somebody, and she said she would call the next morning and when she called at 10 o'clock I had cake and coffee and everything ready for her. And really she was the last person I wanted to talk to, she wasn't interested in me, I didn't have anything to talk to her about, and yet just the fact that there was somebody sitting in my house and talking to me was good. After that I really got very frightened and very depressed, I couldn't bear people coming close to me and I was frightened to wake up and I couldn't sleep and—so I was very obviously depressed so I went to my doctor and he—I think originally he gave me tranquillisers which worked beautifully for 3 or 4 days for each pill—in fact suddenly no problems existed at all. But the effect lasted for a very short time and so within two months I was very depressed and unwilling to take any more tranquillisers because it was even worse coming down again from being buoyed up and feeling everything was alright to the depression I'd got into by that time. So my doctor put me on anti-depressants. I have been on a high dose of anti-depressants and tranquillisers for five years.'

(*At the end,* JOE *laughs uproariously*)

JOE: You see—MAD.

CARLYLE: And that is the Song of Driving Mad.

(*After* The Song of Driving Mad, JOE *goes back to* BELLE'S *room,* AURELIA *and* CARLYLE *go off. Lights go back to normal.*)

BELLE: (*Quietly*) I know all that.

JOE: Of course you did. I should think it was unavoidable, doing the job you're doing. And here am I, Sir Joseph Stanion, knowing full well that *that's* what you think of me. And here you are, in my office, cadging money to soothe my victims. What would *you* do? What would anybody do that was in their right minds? (*Makes chucking over parapet gesture*) Ta ta, try not to make too much of a mess when you land—

BELLE: Yes. Of course you would.

JOE: So?

BELLE: So what?

JOE: Do you know what you are?

BELLE: Frightened. Miserable. Lost. And on my own.

JOE: Wrong. I don't think you are on your own. I don't think you are lost, or miserable. There's thousands and thousands of you, and you're self-satisfied. Smug. Making merry as you pirouette like tipsy nurses round the beds of the grateful sick. You're not miserable—you're happy. Psychiatric social worker, caring only for people. Bollocks. If you really cared for people, you'd have to do something about me, wouldn't you? And you're not *frightened* to do it, you're not held back *by me*—you don't *want* to do something about me, you actually *want* me, don't you, you need me, because I'm the fella that builds your climbing frame, aren't I?

BELLE: I don't want you, and—

JOE: I'm going to fuck you . . .

BELLE: No you're not, Mister Cat Burglar—

JOE: (*Takes out flick knife and flicks it open*) Oh yes I am. You really *want* it, don't you?

BELLE: Get out of this room. I've never, in the whole of my life, come across a more loathsome reptilian nonentity. (*They move around the room.*) Fortunately for you, the whole of humanity does not operate on your level—not even all of your friends the bosses.

JOE: Oh we're pretty much all alike, underneath it all—we have to be you see—

BELLE: But you, you are the exception—

JOE: I said I'm *not* the exception, sweetheart, I am the Rule. Don't confuse yourself now—Hate me, hate my friends. Put up with my friends, put up with me. What's it to be?

BELLE: It's war, mister.

JOE: Fighting words, brave words—

BELLE: I mean them.

JOE: Right (*He suddenly hands her the knife, handle to her hand. She takes it. He rips open his shirt, offers her his chest.*) Do it. Now.
(*As they assume a classic pose, him kneeling, offering her his bare chest, her with the knife to it, the lights change—they are washed in purple, while a spot is the only other light, picking up* AURELIA *and* CARLYLE *when they come on to the centre stage.*)

AURELIA: In 1919 the soldiers coming home from the war and the workers in the factories had the knives at the throats of the British ruling class.

CARLYLE: Glasgow: tanks in the streets, sandbag emplacements on street corners, fixed bayonets, reinforcements: but one hundred thousand workers in George Square—ready to go:

AURELIA: A delegation from the TUC went to visit Lloyd George.

CARLYLE: (*Lloyd George*) 'Gentlemen, political power is in your hands.'

AURELIA: From that moment, I knew we were lost . . .

JOE: And they took the knife away.

AURELIA: Germany 1932. Hitler rising. The left divides.

CARLYLE: France 1937. The right wing on the run—the left divides.

AURELIA: Spain 1937. The Republic declared. The left divides.
And the knives were taken away.

Greece 1944. The revolutionary partisans come from the hills: power is theirs, but for a handful of British troops in a corner of Athens . . . The knife is at the throat of the Greek ruling class.

CARLYLE: Orders from Moscow: don't fight the British.

AURELIA: So the British get stronger, and the British fought them—

JOE: And the knife was taken away.

AURELIA: France 1968.

CARLYLE: France 1968. Ten million workers on strike, one million on the streets of Paris, the Army wavering, the Government no longer in control, the revolution finally about to succeed . . . .

The Song of Knives at Throats—

AURELIA: Orders from Moscow: Peaceful co-existence. Balance of Power.

CARLYLE: And the French Communist Party accepted a $12\frac{1}{2}$ per cent pay rise.

AURELIA: And a 15 per cent rise in the price of bread.

CARLYLE: And ordered the workers back to work.

JOE: And the knife was taken away.

CARLYLE: Glasgow 1971. Shipyards occupied. 36,000 workers solid: nearly the whole of Glasgow behind them . . .

AURELIA: And the workers are led by Wedgewood Benn.

JOE: And the knife was carefully taken away.

(*The lights change back.* CARLYLE *goes off.* AURELIA *stays on centre stage, reading.* JOE *reaches out, takes the knife from* BELLE, *folds it up, slips it in his pocket, gets up.*)

I'm not even going to rape you. You're my thing. From time to time, when I need to, I'll send for you. Don't ever tell me you care for people again, though. If you did, you wouldn't be standing there, and I wouldn't be walking out of that door, whistling.

BELLE: I care for people in the only way that I can.

(JOE *turns and walks out of the door. whistling. When he gets on to the centre stage, he turns to the audience.*)

JOE: Had her on the hip, as Shakespeare would have said—on the hype, as we have it down Notting Dale.

(*In* CARLYLE'S *room,* AURELIA *is sitting reading* Time *magazine. He says hello, she ignores him. He goes and pours himself some more wine, holds the bottle out to her. She ignores it. He shrugs, drinks. In her room,* BELLE *eventually gets out a blue overseas writing pad and begins to write her reply to stoat-head.* JOE *goes over and sits as near as he can to* AURELIA)

Where's Carlyle?

AURELIA: She was in the kitchen. Doing women's work. But I think she went out to get some coffee beans.

JOE: Oh. What are you reading?

AURELIA: The facts.

JOE: In *Time* magazine?

AURELIA: It makes a change. They make everything so beautifully coherent: Vietnam, the Philippines, Canadian lumberjacking, baseball, French rail strikes, Israeli politics—I can almost believe in its story of the world—at times I really wish I could.

JOE: Millions do.

AURELIA: Yes. Nostalgic, isn't it?
(*He reaches out a hand, puts it on her shoulder. She carries on reading as she shakes it off quietly and moves to another chair. A pause. He follows her.*)
I thought you came for Carlyle's body.

JOE: I did. But I find you—very poignant.

AURELIA: I hate men. If you tried to sleep with me I'd slice your cock off.

JOE: Would you?

AURELIA: If my razor-blade dispenser was handy, yes. Otherwise, I'd have to content myself with kicking you in the balls.

JOE: Sounds thrilling.

AURELIA: Contusion of the testicles is far from thrilling. I kicked one thieving lecher I used to work for in the balls, and he was in hospital for a week. Told his wife a policeman had done it to him.

JOE: Oh. Didn't you feel sorry for him?

AURELIA: Men are disgusting. You are disgusting. Go further away.

JOE: I want to talk to you.

AURELIA: Why?

JOE: I want to pry you open, like a barnacled oyster, and squeeze my lemon over your soft centre and watch you shrivel.
(*She stops reading, for once, looks into the middle distance for a second, then gets up.*)

AURELIA: I'm going to my room. (*She goes, stops*) I'm going to lock the door. Carlyle will be back in a minute.

JOE: Down with the Demon King. Liberate little devils.
(*He goes out of the door. A few seconds later he reappears as it were through the window of* AURELIA'*s room. She has been, meanwhile, reading some fresh evidence into her tape-recorder.*)

AURELIA: (*Reads into tape*) . . . You don't have to be a Raquel Welch to be a sex symbol. Melissa Yoke, the actress with the girl-next-door look has proved it.
'I couldn't believe it when critics hailed me as the new sex vamp', she said.
Melissa's blue eyes bubbled with laughter as she grabbed a sandwich with me in a Kensington coffee bar.
Just what is it about her that turns men on? 'Maybe it is because they get a feeling I am unspoilt and they read a look of innocence about me. At least that's one director's analysis. I can only go by what other people say . . .'
(JOE *appears in her room. She turns off the tape, puts it down, picks up her blade-dispenser.*)

JOE: Put it away, Mrs Crippen, I haven't come for your body.

AURELIA: What, then? The silver? My Barclaycard?

JOE:	We were having a chat, weren't we? I don't like being broken off in the middle of a chat: chattus interruptus, a primitive form of controlling conceptions, which leave the man pained and frustrated, and his partner jaded and listless.
AURELIA:	Did you walk along that crumbling cornice?
JOE:	How else?
AURELIA:	Thirty-odd feet above Mrs Corncrake's spiky railings? For a chat?
JOE:	It was unconsummated—
AURELIA:	(*Sniffs*) You'd have done better to spill your conversational seeds all over the sitting-room floor: you could have killed yourself on that ledge.
JOE:	You wouldn't even have pushed up the window to have a look—(*Shrugs, imitates her*) 'Ah well, one man less in the world, only three billion to go; not including the Chinese.' (*She laughs*) Can I sit down?
AURELIA:	(*Raising razor-blade dispenser*) Keep talking. Keep walking.
JOE:	Aggressive bitch, aren't you?
AURELIA:	I don't trust you.
JOE:	No. But it's a bit hard, chatting, with you waving that thing at my privates. Perhaps we could de-escalate a bit. I'll go further away, if you put that down.
AURELIA:	Alright.
JOE:	Alright.
	(*They do so. Pause*)
	What's the tape you're making up?
AURELIA:	Private.
JOE:	Oh.
AURELIA:	It's the evidence. The facts.
JOE:	Oh.
AURELIA:	It's what men do to each other. In the name of history. I've got twelve two-hour tapes. And what men do to the earth. In the name of improving it. Ten tapes. And what men do to women. In the name of love. Fifteen tapes: thirty hours.
JOE:	Bloody hell. Can I listen to some of it?
AURELIA:	I never play it back.
JOE:	How do you know it's recorded anything?
AURELIA:	There's an indicator.
JOE:	Oh.
AURELIA:	I remember.
JOE:	Everything?
AURELIA:	Once I've recorded it: it sticks.
	(*Pause*)
JOE:	Tell me something: would you kill for what you believe in—if you had to?
AURELIA:	I would kill men. I would not kill women.
JOE:	Why?
AURELIA:	Women are not responsible for history. Men are. Women don't believe in it. Men invented it.

JOE: What's wrong with history?

AURELIA: If you don't believe in history, you don't fight wars, you don't struggle for power, you don't compete: you work all together, to make the world fit to live in. You don't have leaders—only the people. You don't have nations, commonwealths, empires—men's games:
Is it not brave to be a king, Techelles,
Usumcasane and Theridamas,
Is it not passing brave to be a king
And ride in triumph through Persepolis—
I believe in the women of Persepolis. Women move among the realities: hunger, shelter, clothing, love, birth, death, children, shit, pain, anger, beauty. Men inhabit a world of destructive fantasy: wars, torture, cruelty, rat-races, boots in faces, stabs in the back, control, domination, rape, self-adoration: it's something to do with that thing between your legs. That's not a part of a human body for giving out love and beautiful babies any more: it's a gun, a napalm rocket, a moon-probe, a nail-bomb, an excoriating device for mastery over women and imposition of its will on other men. And for a few centuries lately you have forced your women to waste their unique and beautiful lives on you so you can get on with your fantasies. But the Age of Tamburlaine the Great is over. The pill and razor blade have cut him down, Mister Cat Burglar.

JOE: Oh.

AURELIA: Of course the women of Persepolis *might* one day let Tamburlaine back in—on foot, in plain clothes, filled with cowardice and humility, to take his place with the children; who will be playing among the ruins of the temples, palaces, fortresses, jails, supermarkets, customs sheds, rocket silos, and museums which will have fallen into decay, being no longer needed. But the second his fantasies begin again—and we'll recognise them, we know just what they're like—he will be taken away from all contact with the children, and made to serve the old and the dying for the rest of his days: not to punish him—to remind him.

JOE: Do you think that would do it?

AURELIA: The women will decide.

JOE: (*Gets up and walks around*) And the earth will be a better place?

AURELIA: It might even survive.

JOE: Ha. A likely story.

AURELIA: Have you looked at it lately? Have you been outside your own little metropolitan skull and *seen* it? Fields, hills, mountains, forests—raped; the face of the earth, weeping; weeping moon. Now there is nowhere left on earth where man has not killed, mutilated, ravaged, destroyed; for his fantasy of power.

JOE: Profit.

AURELIA: Power. A place in history. A scar on the body of time. A crystallization of vanishing flesh. An emblem of one man's presence. A lie.

JOE: Profit.

AURELIA: Profit can only be an excuse, or a by-product.

JOE: Not a very Marxist sentiment.

AURELIA: Marx was a man. A Victorian patriarch: He had to believe in history because he wanted his place in it. That's what drove *him*: certainly not profit. Power is greater, and more evil, and diffused throughout mankind: only women—and only *some* women, have learnt to live without wanting it. They are humanity's last hope, before night, of one kind or other, covers the earth. Have you got a cigarette?

JOE: What about Golda Meir?

AURELIA: She *is* a man.
(*He gives her a cigarette and lights it. In her room,* BELLE *finishes her letter with a flourish. She picks it up and reads it aloud. During this,* CARLYLE *comes in with a tin of coffee and a tin opener. She is surprised, intrigued, to find nobody there. She pierces the seal of the coffee tin, sniffs it, finishes opening it and goes back into the kitchen.*)

BELLE: (*Reading*) 'Dear Martin, Yes. Alright then. It's a bit of a relief, actually. We did seem to be drifting quite a long way apart.' I'm very tempted to—no, it's unladylike. 'No hard feelings, of course—though I must say you do have the strangest way of communicating these things . . .' Why can't I ever write what I want to write—something witty, acid and unforgettable, something to tingle in his ears through the long nights of his boring marriage, something scorching so he'd realise what he missed—'So here's to your marriage, may it be long and fruitful. I shall not throw myself under a train—' Not unless you change your mind, I won't—'So it's good-bye. Yours, Belle.' Hm. Pathetic. (*As she seals envelope*) PS How does she like your athlete's foot? (*Laughs*) PPS You may be interested to know that I've had more sexual thrills from re-reading The Tales of Beatrix Potter than I accumulated in the whole of our relationship, so I hope she's imaginative. Bye-bye, Prissy, Prissy Bang Bang. Keep it clean—(*Goes off to post it*) That's better. Hee, hee, I'm beginning to see life in a whole new perspective.

AURELIA: That's the end of our conversation.

JOE: Is it?

AURELIA: Yes. You can go—Carlyle's back, I can smell the coffee.

JOE: Do I have to go back that way? (*Indicates window*)

AURELIA: (*Laughs*) Did you really come that way?

JOE: Can I ask you something, before I go?

AURELIA: What?

JOE: Your vision—your feminist utopia: how, er—how are you going to get it together? I mean, between you, now, and that happy land, somewhere in the future, there stands something called western civilisation, and something else called the capitalist state, and something else called American Imperialism with the most advanced methods of physical control and psychic repression ever known in the history of the world—I, er, just wanted to ask you, really, what you intended to do about them?

AURELIA: Cut them up.

JOE: All on your own?

AURELIA: There are more women in the world than there are men.

JOE: But you're the first one I've ever met with a razor blade actually in her actual hand . . .

AURELIA: All women know.

JOE: Do they?

AURELIA: They just need waking up. And courage. They *know*.

JOE: You're wrong. They don't know. And they never will know. (*music*) And this is the song of Why They Never Will Know. (*Lights change, 'show' lighting on centre stage—*CARLYLE *and* BELLE *prance like show girls.* JOE *jumps across to centre stage*)

BELLE: The Song

CARLYLE: The Song

BELLE: of Why

CARLYLE: of Why

BELLE: They'll never Know

CARLYLE: The Song of Why They'll Never Know.

JOE: (*Australian accent*) I'm going to make a contentious statement, with political implications.

BELLE: Be careful, be very careful . . .

JOE: Children . . . are interested . . . in sex.

CARLYLE: I think *I'd* like to sit on *that* case if nobody minds.

JOE: So I'm dragged up in front of a learned judge

BELLE: Is it a woman—

JOE: No.

BELLE: Is it a man—

JOE: Yes.

BELLE: Is it a poor man—

JOE: No.

BELLE: Is it a rich man—

JOE: Yes.

CARLYLE: Fifteen months, and if I had a mill-stone I'd tie it round your neck and cast you to the bottom of the briny sea—

BELLE: Oo—those awful people—raping schoolboys—they ought to be locked away.

JOE: (*Irish accent*) Some of my mates in Ireland get a bit stroppy, they were being mucked about, you see, so they sent the Army in, and this General, he mucked them about even more, so they get even more stroppy, so he threw them all in prison-camps—

BELLE: Was this General a woman?

CARLYLE: No—

BELLE: Was he a man?

CARLYLE: Yes.

BELLE: Was he a poor man?

CARLYLE: No.

BELLE: Was he a rich man?

CARLYLE: Yes.

JOE: (*General's voice*) There's some political extremists behind this frightful situation, and I'm just going to have to shoot them. (BELLE *does Heath laugh.* JOE *fires at her.* BELLE *drops dead.*)

CARLYLE: (*Man in street*) Hooligans. Disgusting. Horsewhipped.

JOE: (*Young idealist voice*) I had a wonderful socialist vision of how we could build Jerusalem in England's green and pleasant land. I took it to the newspapers—

BELLE: (*Editor's voice—ripping it up*) Longhaired idealistic claptrap . . . that won't sell any advertising space—

CARLYLE: (*Editor's voice—another editor, who also rips it up*) Love to publish it, truly, but—you know, we do have a board of directors . . .

BELLE: Are they poor men?

JOE: No.

BELLE: Are they rich men?

JOE: Of course they are—so I went to the telly—I said: I want to tell *my* version of the news, for a change

CARLYLE: (*BBC voice*) Look here, old boy, we need balance and diplomacy, balance and diplomacy . . .

BELLE: (*ITV voice*) *Your* version of the news—that's not going to sell any advertising space . . .

JOE: So they'll never know my version of the news—the telly-men had spoken.

BELLE: And were they speaking for poor men?

CARLYLE: No.

BELLE: And were they speaking for rich men?

CARLYLE: Yes.

JOE: So I felt aggrieved. And I went to see the bishops

BELLE: Who spoke up for the rich men . . .

JOE: And I went to see the Professors in their Universities.

CARLYLE: Who spoke up for the rich men . . .

JOE: And I went to see the Chief Constable—

BELLE: Who spoke up for the rich men—

JOE: And I went to see the top Civil Servants—

CARLYLE: Who spoke up for the rich men—

JOE: So I thought I'd interest the leaders of the Labour Movement, my natural allies.

BELLE: But they *were* in the rich man's pockets.

JOE: (*Harold Wilson's voice*) I'm not actually a company director, but if I *were* a company director, I think I can safely say I'd vote for me.

BELLE: Were any of them women?

CARLYLE: No.

BELLE: Were all of them men?

CARLYLE: Yes.

BELLE: Were any of them poor men?

CARLYLE: No.

BELLE: Were all of them rich men?

CARLYLE: Yes.

JOE: So I went to complain to the Government. To tell them that everything that was published, and radioed, and televised, and poured into the minds of the millions of people, was always *their* story of the world, and nothing else was to be spoken. And the government said:

BELLE: (*Roy Jenkins' voice*) We really must be moderate. (*Heath laugh*) Hoist the spinnaker.

JOE: And they got everybody to believe we were a lot of perverts and fanatics, and ought to be locked away—and they're doing that, slowly, one by one: and everybody thought the New Jerusalem was a strip club, and the Socialist vision a dose of VD, and nobody knew, nobody ever knew . . .

CARLYLE: And that is the Song.

BELLE: of Why They'll Never Know.

(BELLE *and* CARLYLE *go off.* JOE *goes back into* AURELIA'S *room*)

JOE: So it's not much bloody good, is it? As long as all that lot are sitting on us, they're never going to know, and if they don't know, they're not going to do anything about it, and if they're not going to *do* anything about it, you might as well whistle up your arse—in fact, you'd do yourself a lot more good doing just that, because at the moment all you're doing with your heroic knife-waving and your adventurist man-hunting is diverting your own and other people's energies from your main enemy. That suits me, of course, because I've just joined them; but in the end, you'll be helping them far more than I will.

AURELIA: I don't care.

JOE: No, I thought you wouldn't.

AURELIA: We're getting stronger and stronger . . .

JOE: Yes, and very soon you'll be allowed to wear trouser-suits in the Savoy. And that will be that.

AURELIA: We *must* win.

JOE: Fantasyland. You're not really interested in winning in the first place, are you? You're getting your kicks from sitting here feeling bitter, fingering your guilt as if it was a turbulent glitoria, pulling yourself off with sentiment, purity, and a militant posture, chattering on about a utopia for all, but underneath it all you're panting—me, me, me, me, me, me

AURELIA: Get out—

JOE: You'll grow hairs on the palm of your hand, you'll grow bald, if you do that . . .

AURELIA: Get out.

JOE: You'll have to wear glasses like me. You'll end up in a looney bin, you'll chuck yourself in the river

AURELIA: GET OUT!

JOE: The door's locked.
(AURELIA *glares at him.*)

AURELIA: When you win. When you change the world. When you build your new state, your new system. You will never understand why it will be so like the old one. (*He goes to speak.*) Now get out. (*He goes through.* BELLE *has, at some stage, gone through into her own room.* CARLYLE *now comes in with four mugs of coffee on a tray. She looks at* JOE *in his disarray, smiles, and puts the tray down.*)

CARLYLE: You won't get much there, Joey.

JOE: I noticed that. Is she a Lesbian?

CARLYLE: She's more a sort of twentieth-century nun. A contemplative. Feeling it all, on our behalf, suffering.

JOE: She's not without a certain amount of aggression.

CARLYLE: Aimless. Pointless.

JOE: I tried to lead up to getting her to join the party, the PRP: She could have had my card.

CARLYLE: Hopeless. I've spent months at it. Here, take her some coffee. I'll give Belle a mugful . . .

JOE: Will I be safe?

CARLYLE: Quite safe.
(*They pick up a mug each and go off in different directions, arrive at the same time, and play the following scenes at the same time.*)
Coffee?

BELLE: Ta.

JOE: Some coffee.

AURELIA: Thank you. (*Takes it*)

BELLE: Has your friend gone yet? (CARLYLE *shakes her head.*)

AURELIA: Er, what you were trying to tell me. About doing things. I do *know* that. I *do* know.

JOE: Obvious, really, I suppose.

CARLYLE: Aurelia's been having a go at him, apparently.

BELLE: As far as I'm concerned she can chop him up into small pieces.

CARLYLE: Probably will.

JOE: Do you believe in heaven? In getting your rewards in the next world?

AURELIA: It sometimes feels like it.

CARLYLE: Do you feel like walking round the block, later.

BELLE: I might just go to bed.

JOE: That's what you're going to end up as, you know, if you don't watch it.

BELLE: Except old buggerlugs has really woken me up again. Got me going . . .

AURELIA: Either that or in the Thames. Westminster Bridge it would have to be. When the River Police find you, they grapple your bloated body on to their launch with boat hooks. It's the boat hooks I don't fancy.

JOE: Me, I wouldn't fancy the River Police.

AURELIA: Oh, they're quite nice.

BELLE: You haven't got any more strong, silent and sexy friends, have you?

CARLYLE: Only David.

AURELIA: Different sort of men, really, from your Metropolitan bullyboys.

CARLYLE: And you can't have him.

BELLE: Greedy.

AURELIA: I wouldn't mind them at all.

JOE: Just the boat hooks.

CARLYLE: Well, not till later.

AURELIA: (*Laughs*) Vanity, vanity.

CARLYLE: Sleep well. (*Goes*)

BELLE: As if I could . . . (*Switches on telly*)
   (*Pause*)

AURELIA: Why are you pretending to be a capitalist?

JOE: Because I am. I really *have* got two blokes working down Lambeth, and an office and a typist. I really am about to become the demon king.

AURELIA: I have no sympathy for the devil.

JOE: No. Nor have I. (*Quietly*) Down with the Demon King.

AURELIA: Liberate little devils. Shut the door behind you, Captain Oates.
   (*He goes. She plunges back into* Le Monde *weekly.* CARLYLE *has gone back to her room to drink her coffee. When* JOE *emerges from* AURELIA'S *room, she nods at him.*)

CARLYLE: Your coffee'll be cold.

JOE: Good. I'll finish off the Moroccan.
   (*Swigs it out of the bottle.* CARLYLE *studies him closely*)

CARLYLE: So, you want your money back?

JOE: Yes.

CARLYLE: And you want to resign from the PRP?

JOE: Yes.

CARLYLE: And you fancy a bash at my body?

JOE: Yes.
   (*She gets up and goes to her handbag, picks out a pound note and some change, hands them to him.*)

CARLYLE: That's your money back. The body part's out of the question: I don't fancy you. About the resignation: it's up to you.

JOE: Aren't you going to castigate me?

CARLYLE: I've told you how I feel at the moment—helpless. I'm going through a bad patch.

JOE: Aren't I "betraying the revolution'?

CARLYLE: The Russians are more disgusting than they ever were, even under Stalin. Now they've even got Castro torturing poets and suppressing the opposition.

JOE: We knew that was coming.

CARLYLE: As for People's China, our guiding star in the east (*Makes gesture*) only the Vietnamese are surviving as heroes—and now there's peace there for how long, I wonder, will they keep their

	heads up. It's the wrong moment to expect me to re-charge your batteries with revolutionary fervour.
JOE:	You don't need Russia. You don't need China.
CARLYLE:	No. All we need is the English working-class to stop making social contracts and seize the time. But will they? They don't care. And *why* don't they care?
JOE:	Don't be like that—
CARLYLE:	Because of their bungalows and their rose-trees and their Vauxhall Vivas. Because of their flats and their fridges and their Majorcan fortnights. Because of their desperate greed for trivial objects, and their hysterical clutching at the little they've got. Consume, consume the billboards are screaming, Hello Big Spender shouts the Daily Express—and down the rabbit-hole they go, like Alice—Drink me, You'll get Smaller, Eat me, You'll get Bigger, through the little door into the garden of delights and forgetfulness, puff, puff. Through the little door into Young Married Cosi-homes, Shangri-la, Shalimar, Windermere Driver on the old HP, through the little door into prep school for Julian, and municipal golf, and the Young Conservatives—what would dad have said?—never mind—through the little door into Burn Vietcong Babies. And do the Trades Unions teach them to fight it? Have the Labour Party, the Communist Party, the swinging Left or the industrial militants *told* them what's going on? They've told them to grab for more, more of the same consumable crap, more of the same eye-gum, ear-stoppers, gags, lobotomisers. Have they told them to get together and destroy these trivialising fools? Have they? They've been pushing them on for bigger and better bribes, bigger and better compromises, more total penetration by that corrupt ideology: they've gathered them in from the hill, driven them in to the fold, and now they watch, open-mouthed, as they are dipped, and fleeced and branded: and turned back onto the hill, naked, clean and happy.
JOE:	Bloody hell.
CARLYLE:	You've come to the wrong shop for cheering up. I'm feeling very Marcusean—which is the Marxist for depressed. And you, you just teeter on the brink of total capitulation to the enemy, body, soul and bank-balance, and tell me you represent the reality principle. I've had enough of the bloody reality principle: I'm in a state of permanent demonstration against it. Why, because I want to know if anyone is listening.
JOE:	So you're just another little Walt Disney, are you, animator of fantasies, defender of the status quo . . . ? Abandon hope all ye who enter here, the left-wing has lost the working class.
CARLYLE:	Not altogether. I don't believe that.
JOE:	Do you think they're still listening to you? Do you think that anybody's still listening to you?
CARLYLE:	Not you. Chairman of General Motors, Chairman of ITT, Chairman of United Fruit, Chairman of Gulf Petroleum,

whatever your names are: nor one of your democratically-voting, peace-loving, money-grabbing, dividend-lusting, skull-cracking boss-men, would hear me, if I cried out, amongst the angels. Nor you with your pragmatism, Harold. Nor you chief greaser of the party machine, your own slippery mind a machine, well-oiled wedgie: you too are deaf, hear only the teller's tally, the polite applause, the click of the apparatus, the hollow echo of the dubious deal.

No. It's hard to hear with your ears full of flannel.

(AURELIA *and* BELLE *have come towards the centre stage, one on each side. They now speak*)

AURELIA: The cries of the rice-merchant, petrol-jelly burning on the bone.

BELLE: The despair of the mad young woman, slashing her wrists in the meaningless flat on the seventeenth floor.

AURELIA: The blind babies, the crippled little boys, the exploded virgins of Indo-China.

BELLE: The screams of Mrs Fitzgerald, in her paranoid basement.

AURELIA: Fields, hills, mountains, forests, raped; the face of the earth, weeping blood; the weeping moon.

BELLE: The schizoid panic tearing breasts asunder; the lovely plunge, the body into the river, the needle into the vein.

AURELIA: The screams of humanity's mutilated body.

BELLE: The screams of humanity's mutilated mind.

CARLYLE: They rise to your ears, but you do not hear.

JOE: Who *does*? That's what you must tell me. Does anybody?

CARLYLE: To whom then, do they cry out?

AURELIA: To the young. To the dreams. To the painters.

BELLE: To the wives. To the irresponsible adolescents.

AURELIA: To the burning young women in countless bed-sitters.

BELLE: To the pale young men putting sixpences in milk-machines.

AURELIA: To the partially mad.

BELLE: To the totally happy.

AURELIA: To the dying, who can see.

BELLE: To the newborn, who can hear.

AURELIA: To the children of England, of Scotland, of Europe, the world.

CARLYLE: And to a handful of working men and women. Who still feel what they are, still touch their humanity, who one day will fight for it.

AURELIA: Fight for it.

BELLE: Fight for it.

CARLYLE: WE SHALL NOT BECOME MACHINES.

AURELIA: WE SHALL NEVER BE MANIPULATED.

CARLYLE: WE DESPISE YOUR REASONS FOR LIVING.

BELLE: WE HAVE OUR OWN.

CARLYLE: WE SHALL FIGHT FOR THEM.

From a million cradles, endlessly rocking.

JOE: (*Sneering*) To the workers? You're going to cry out to the bloody workers—listen, I *am* a worker—don't give me that.

CARLYLE: Yes. They have been led by the nose.
Blinkered. Deafened.
And they have been rolled in butter and fried,
And they have been given promises, promises,
And wooed, and won, and seduced, and garrotted,
And they have been atomised, their power
Sprayed into the air in a fine mist, invisible,
And they have been refrigerated, pressure-cooked,
automobilised,
And they have been tellyfied and radioed and techni-coloured,
And they have been taught to love trinkets more than freedom,

AURELIA: Coloured beads more than green fields,

BELLE: Plastic ducks more than mallard at dawn,

CARLYLE: Photographs more than fucking.
And to eliminate all armpit odour
And still they have survived.
And still they can hear the cries, and understand—
Without simultaneous translation, without sub-titles.
And the cries mount up, like sand below the sea,
A ridge,

AURELIA: A bar,

BELLE: A barrier

CARLYLE: A mountain.

AURELIA: Throwing up a ripple.

BELLE: Then a wave.

CARLYLE: Then a whole incredible tide of breakers racing steaming for the shore. The crack and spit as they bellow at the land and leap and whirl and spire and jet. With energy energy energy bounding. And the shore awaits.
(AURELIA *and* BELLE *go to where they were.* CARLYLE *sits,* JOE *jumps up, starts pacing up and down.*)

JOE: So why don't you chop me in two?

CARLYLE: You are already chopped in two.

JOE: (*Stops walking*) Ha. (*Starts again*)

CARLYLE: You wouldn't be here if you weren't.

JOE: (*Stops again*) I fancy you, that's all. I want to lay my hands ravenously all over your middle-class body. I want to put my working-class chopper in your middle-class minge. I want to make you.

CARLYLE: You're lying. You're posing.

JOE: Shall I show you?

CARLYLE: You'd still be lying. Still posing. You're chopped in two, Joey, and I can't join you together, because I am too. I'm going to bed now. I'm selling the paper down at the docks tomorrow morning, I need some sleep.
(*Pause*)

JOE: If I stayed, I could come with you.

CARLYLE: Don't be silly. I've told you, I don't fancy you. (*Grabs a book*) Here—read that, page 86. Bring it back within three days.

JOE: (*Opens it—finds page 86*) That bit?
CARLYLE: (*Looking*) No, that bit.
(*He starts to read.*)
No, on the bus, on your way home.
(JOE, *still reading, turns and goes out.* CARLYLE *gets her bed ready for sleeping in, goes off with her pyjamas to the bathroom.* BELLE *comes out, in her dressing gown, goes and sits on her bed, switches off the telly.* AURELIA *has been reading as before.*)

AURELIA: When I was eight, before we moved into the town, I used to run through the fields and woods of the lowlands with a beautiful little boy called Alistair. We used to dam up the streams and build houses in trees and stare at the farmer's wife as she milked the cows. One day I chased Alistair in a mad wild giggle at uproarious speed along a tiny wee path through our most mysterious forest. But the farmer our friend was having a border battle with the next farmer, and so he'd stretched barbed wire across the path, at the height of the face of an eight-year-old boy. Alistair was stuck to it, too pierced to scream. (*Shakes her head*) All my life. All his life. He lost an eye. Not so beautiful, any more. A barrister now. Safe enough he must feel.

BELLE: If I were to tackle the Fortescue Road block tomorrow, Number Seven and Number Two-Zero-Four, I might get Balls Road and Norton Land *and* Wuthering Heights or whatever it calls itself all done on Friday and I *might* just get away for a dirty week-end. But who with? That's one of the problems of being free, I suppose—free to frustrate.
(JOE *appears and wanders from place to place, reading from the Mao Papers*)

JOE: To be complacent and conceited—to refuse to apply the method of splitting one into two; to like flattering but dislike critical words; these are the faults common to all our comrades. A comrade must have at his disposal the method of 'splitting one into two': achievements and shortcomings, truth and mistakes. However, there is a formal logic deeply planted in the minds of some of our comrades which they cannot uproot. Formal logic denies the unification of the opposites of things, and under given conditions the transformation of one pair of opposites into another. Therefore, these comrades become complacent, conceited, capable of hearing only favourable words, unwilling to criticise themselves (i.e. splitting into two), and afraid of other people's criticism.
(CARLYLE *has come back in pyjamas. She brushes her hair.*)

CARLYLE: Shall I ever go grey? Or will it all fall out? (*Smiles*) Joey, Joey— fancy *you*, of all people, lusting for me. A cat burglar . . . Tomcat obviously. Out on the tiles. When a tomcat puts its thing in, it has barbs that shoot out and grapple on inside the poor lady-cat. So she can't get away, I suppose. No wonder they howl.

AURELIA: This bloody room's a drag. (*Stares around at it. Abruptly starts to read again*)

CARLYLE: Cunt-hooks. I wonder is that how the expression arose . . .

BELLE: (*Getting into bed*) Well, goodnight world. (*Pause*) Oops, mustn't forget my pill. What's a blood clot compared with the wild-uninhibited lascivious thrashings of two bodies in spine-corroding ecstasy? (*Swallows it*) What indeed . . . ?
(*During this,* CARLYLE *sits down on her bed.* AURELIA *sits thinking*)

JOE: Essentially, conceit is derived from individualism and nurses the growth of individualism. It is individualistic. Speaking from a class analytical point of view, conceit comes first from the ideology of the exploiting class and then from that of small producers. As workers, small producers have many good qualities. They are industrious, thrifty, not afraid of hardships, cautious, and realistic. But as small owners, they are individualistic and, what is more important, limited by their working conditions and methods and their use of out-dated means of production, they are scattered, narrow-minded, and ill-informed. They are often blind to the strength of the collective—they see only that of the individual. The history of social development is not the history of big men, but of the labouring masses. Nonetheless, conceited people always exaggerate the role of the individual, take undue credit, and become proud of themselves.
    In fact, the more one overrates oneself, the worse the result is likely to be. Leo Tolstoy, the great Russian writer, put it humorously: 'A man is like a mathematical fraction, whose actual talent can be compared to a numerator and his own estimate of it to a denominator. The bigger the denominator, the smaller the fraction.'

AURELIA: Even the moon. Pierced with tubes. Core-cutters. Rammed into her crust. Another historical event. They were jubilant in Texas as the rod was rammed home. Two scientists were told to say it was of vital significance. So it was.
(*During this* AURELIA *also lies back on her bed, reading*)

JOE: When people see only what is under their feet, not what lies above the mountains and beyond the seas, they are likely to be as boastful as 'the frog at the bottom of a well'. But when they raise their heads to see the immensity of the world, the kaleidoscope of man's affairs, the splendour and magnificence of the cause of humanity, the richness of man's talents, and the breadth of knowledge, they become modest. What we are dedicated to is a world-shaking task. We must focus not just on the work and happiness in front of our eyes, but also on the work and happiness of all of us in the distant future.

CARLYLE: I get so bloody *tired*. Why do I get so tired? All I want is for people to live and eat and sleep and love each other everywhere, everywhere, everywhere, with no fighting, no repressing each other, or ourselves, and no more politics. I can't *stand* any more boring bloody *politics*: the only reason I'm a Socialist is to eliminate politics. The single most attractive concept in Marx is the withering away of the State. Wither. Wither.

JOE: 'Wind will not cease, even though trees want rest.'

BELLE: (*Folded in with next two speeches. In bed*) Could have had Joey, I suppose. God knows how that would have turned out. Hard to tell, hard to tell.

CARLYLE: Getting quite flabby . . . get hold of a handful just . . . period on the way I suppose

AURELIA: Don't let me dream tonight. Please, don't let me dream.

CARLYLE: Always bloats me . . . the monthly bloater . . . A bloater a month keeps the doctor in bunth.

BELLE: I could just do with a good . . . (*Picks up letter, crumples it*)

AURELIA: I can't afford to dream. And not to grind my teeth.

CARLYLE: I wonder if Joey has barbs . . . David has a thing that looks like a wart.

BELLE: He wasn't much use anyway—not in that direction. Worse than useless in Washington.

AURELIA: And not dream. Don't let me dream.

CARLYLE: Yourself you touch, but not too much, because you've been told it's degrading . . . Donovan . . . Come, gypsy. (*Turns over*)

BELLE: Still, the future awaits. And so do I.
(JOE *is still quietly reading.*)

THE END

FISH IN THE SEA

Presented at the Everyman Theatre, Liverpool in 1972 and by the 7:84 England Company in 1975 with the following casts:

	Liverpool Everyman	7:84 England
Mr Maconochie	Brian Young	Shay Gorman
Mrs Maconochie	Jean Hastings	Patricia Kane
Mary Maconochie	Angela Philips	Vari Sylvester
Sandra Maconochie	Alison Steadman	Caroline Hutchinson
Fiona Maconochie	Pauline Moran	Sharman Macdonald
Derek Maconochie	Philip Joseph	Colum Meaney
Yorry	Anthony Sher	Shane Connaughton
Rev Griffiths	Barry Woolgar	(cut)
Dafydd Griffiths	Robert Putt	Howell Evans
Andy	Jonathan Pryce	Will Knightley
Willy	Terence Durrant	John Judd
Vince	Les Deegan	Colum Meaney
Roman Candle	Robert Putt	Colum Meaney
Mr Hackett	Barry Woolgar	Howell Evans

ACT 1, SCENE 1

The action of the play takes place in Liverpool in the early 1970s. The style is neither 'epic' nor naturalistic. The actors must create real characters, but be prepared to express that reality in a variety of ways, sustaining throughout the play a relationship between their characters and the audience by way of their own personal stage personae. Similarly, the settings for the scenes, while varying in degrees of verisimilitude, should maintain consistency through the quality of their wit and perception. It is important that the whole production creates a level of contact and communication with the audience over and above the realities of any one character, or group of characters. As the play begins, three of the characters come on to speak to the audience about the events of the play. They are looking back on them, inviting the audience to join with them in making sense of what happened.

(MR MACONOCHIE, YORRY *and* WILLY *come on together.*)

MR MACHONOCHIE: Life, and exploring, goes on.

WILLY: How to make sense of it.

YORRY: How to save anything useful from it. That's what we want to know.

MR MACONOCHIE: It all goes on, you see, life, as before, without any connections. Exploring, the same country, without a map or even a memory.

YORRY: Not making any maps, for those who come after us— scattering bits and pieces of our skin and bone down the back-alleys of our minds, leaving them to rot, for the dogs to wrangle over.

WILLY: Dogs ourselves, wrangling over our own bones, snapping at each other, greedy for the scattered remains of our own loves, struggles, victories, defeats.

MR MACONOCHE: How to make sense of it.

WILLY: Go back to where it all began.

YORRY: To eighteen forty-eight?

MR MACONOCHE: Well, you start wherever you like. As far as I'm concerned, it all began in the far-off year of nineteen sixty-eight, in a field covered with molehills near a place called Tyn-y-Gongl. And that all happened, because our Derek wanted to go to the Tuebrook Ebenezer Baptist Chapel Goronwy Rowlands Mondays and Wednesdays Boys Only Thursdays Girls only Federation Please Ring Bottom Bell Annual Camp.

(*Enter* DEREK *in sports kit. Some others, including* WILLY, *in jeans and plimsolls.*)

Our Derek was Braw: a sort of cross between brash and raw. Braw but not very bricht, if you see what I mean, not much moonlicht penetrated his nicht. We never got on. He was no more than five days old when he shat in my hand: his mother was getting the nappy organised so I had to hold him. The second I got hold of him, I got a handful of shit. And that's about all I've had from him ever since. The girls? Ah, well, the girls have been problems as well, but I've never had to wash my hands of them. What am I saying? Derek seemed determined to go to Tyn-y-Gongl. He said he'd never had a proper holiday and he was seventeen and a half. The Rev Teifian Griffiths seemed determined to take him, as well; not that any of us ever went to the Tuebrook Ebenezer Baptist Chapel, it was just that it was on the corner at the end of our street, and they conned all the lads in the neighbourhood into playing ping-pong for God. Rev Griffiths thought he saw a fresh way to their salvation by driving them out in two vans and a lorry to a wet field half way up a hill in Wales and letting them get on with it. He was wrong.

(*The lads are playing football. Enter* REV TEIFIAN GRIFFITHS *beating a dinner gong. They take no notice. He batters it in each of their ears. The main contestants are* WILLY, SAM, VINNY *and* DEREK.)

WILLY: Here, Vincent, can you hear something?

VINNY: Sounds like thunder.

WILLY: I've got a funny kind of ringing in my ears . . .

REV GRIFFITHS: Derek! Can't you hear? Have your friends all gone deaf?

DEREK: Aw, come on, lads, don't be like that—give him a chance.

WILLY: (*Sings*) Give me one more chance, etc.

REV GRIFFITHS: I've got something of the utmost importance to announce, and you won't get any food until I've announced it.

CHORUS: No food!

REV GRIFFITHS: Line up, then, line up—let's be having you.
(*They line up in a shambles.*)

REV GRIFFITHS: Right, first we'll say a short prayer to the Lord for all this wealth of natural beauty that he has bestowed on us.
(*He takes a deep breath, holds it, waiting for divine inspiration. In the silence a cheery voice from within,* DAFYDD AP GWILYM GRIFFITHS, REV GRIFFITH'S *brother, preparing the meal*)

DAFYDD: (*Chants*) Wart of toad and hair of dog,
Drips from the wall of an underground bog,
Ten used Kleenex, drop them in,
Scrape one Lime Street litterbin,
Add some wino's rancid spew,
Stir it up, it's Irish Stew.
(*Shouts*) Stew's ready! Come and get it! Irish stew today, lads!
(*He comes out battering a pan-lid with a ladle, sees what he's disturbing, in confusion tries to join in the praying, fails, backs out.*)

REV GRIFFITHS: Oh Christ. Thou who cometh down from heaven to open up for us the road out of eternal darkness and damnation, to snip open for us the ribbon across the golden highway to Thy Father's Kingdom, let me be Thy dogged bulldozer and these innocent children Thine Irish navvies to force through that tiny little link-road between our dark lane and Thy Golden Motorway that will see us right through to Eternal Gladness. Amen.

DEREK: Amen.

CHORUS: Beep-beep.

REV GRIFFITHS: Now before I get on to the main news item, I want to introduce you all to a newcomer. (*Shouts*) Iorwerth! (*To them*) Iorwerth has just come to join us, and I'm proud to say he is my only son, in whom, as it were, I am well pleased.
(*Enter* YORRY, *an innocent boy of sixteen and a half. Talks to audience*)

YORRY: I lived in the next street. I didn't know any of them. I went to school somewhere else, and I wasn't allowed out. I'd seen one or two of them out of the window. None of them in chapel.

WILLY: (*To audience*) We'd all seen *him* though. We thought he must be a bit soft in the head, or spastic or something. His dad never even let him go to the shop for the messages on his own. Soft Yorry, we called him.

REV GRIFFITHS: Iorwerth will be in Tent three—take your place Iorwerth. (YORRY *joins the lads.*)

And now to the main events of the day. I have arranged that this afternoon shall be Sports Day. There will be running races, high jumps, long jumps, and a football match. And, as a little surprise to you all, I have arranged for special transport to bring all your parents and relatives who are so inclined to come out to see you, and admire your sporting prowess.

(*A groan from the lads*)

We don't know how many of your families will be able to come, it has been a bit of a last-minute idea, but even if there should be only one person, let's put on a wonderful show. Now. A prayer before meat—er—Iorwerth, would you care to lead us?

YORRY: O God in heaven, give us strength to eat the stew my Uncle Dafydd has cooked. Thy will be done. Amen.

(REV GRIFFITHS *pauses, looks at* YORRY's *bland face, and decides he's not taking the mickey.*)

REV GRIFFITHS: In you go, boys.

(*They rush into the tent,* REV GRIFFITHS *protesting behind them.* WILLY *stays.*)

WILLY: Gorges heaved and epiglottises quivered. Mr Dafydd ap Gwilym Griffiths was a strange man. Storyteller, bard, Sanitary Inspector for Bootle Corporation, amateur golfer and Druid, but no cook. He lived rent-free at his brother's house; in return, he had to give up his summer holidays to help run the camp, lay off the booze, and pretend to be a Christian.

(*Enter* DAFYDD)

DAFYDD: Not eating, Willy?

WILLY: No.

DAFYDD: You got something against my cooking, then?

WILLY: No. I'm full.

DAFYDD: Full? What of?

WILLY: Er—you won't tell?

DAFYDD: Me? Of course not—who would I tell, anyway? What?

WILLY: Cold roast pheasant.

DAFYDD: Say no more.

WILLY: Do you fancy a leg? We've got seventeen all ready for roasting, it's no trouble, if you fancy a leg.

DAFYDD: I'd better not. You're surviving, then, out in the wilds. Nature's no problem, then?

WILLY: No problem. The scuffers round here's a bit thick as well.

DAFYDD: I gather Woolworth's shares have taken a pounding since you lot moved out here.

WILLY: Yeh. Not much left, really, except toothpaste and crocus bulbs.

DAFYDD: Once upon a time, you know, the Welsh used to descend from the hills and maraud the English plains, for fat beef, and pretty women.

WILLY: Getting our own back, aren't we? Don't fancy the women bit though. I'll settle for Liverpool tarts any day.

DAFYDD: A thousand Welsh fathers heave sighs of relief. But don't underestimate the women of Wales. They're dark, boy, deep, and mysterious . . .

WILLY: You can say that again.

DAFYDD: The glory of Wales, its women.

WILLY: Do you fancy a leg, then?

DAFYDD: Sweet, pure proper, sugared mouth; I
know a snug grip for lip-locking.
My pretty one of the shining brow,
your lips are like clear honey.
Like honey the grip of her lip, sweet,
pure, loving jewel,
Loveliest girl of all islands,
whitest skin under flour-white shift.
Sweet is her lip and her grip with her
teeth, she would tempt any angel.
She is most sweetly vocal
and best at the low harmony.
Yes, I fancy a bit of leg.

WILLY: You're on, then. Hey up, they've finished.
(*The others come out, looking sick.*)
(*To audience*) All afternoon, we did training. Running on the spot. Arm-swinging. Loosening up. Cycling movements lying on our backs. Jumping up and down. Short bursts of sprinting. Wheelbarrow races. Skipping. Shadowboxing. By the time they came, we were exhausted. When we saw what did come, what little strength we had left just ebbed away.
(*Music in*)

Enter The Maconochies

Totties, judies,
Jumbo-jumpered beauties
Fancy, Fruity
Rooty-tooty-tooty,
Sexy, Firey,
Flaming-with-desirey

A giggle, a wiggle
A something makes you wriggle.
Strange young girls
Strange young girls
They'd keep Shelley from his poet-ry
They'd keep Nelson from the war at sea,
They'd keep Longford from pornography
That's a definition of a Maconochie.

Totties, judies
Jumbo-jumpered beauties, etc.
(*Enter the* MACONOCHIES, *in a line;* FIONA, MARY *and*
SANDRA, *done up to kill, followed by* MRS MACONOCHIE,
and then MR MACONOCHIE. *They line up impassive, to
watch the sports.* DEREK *goes up to* MR MACONOCHIE.)

DEREK: Hello, Dad.
MR MACONOCHIE: Hello, son. Having a good holiday?
DEREK: Great, thanks, Dad.
MRS MACONOCHIE: Behaving yourself, are you?
DEREK: Aw, eh, Ma.
(REV GRIFFITHS *appears.*)
REV GRIFFITHS: Boys, I think we all ought to welcome Derek's parents, Mr
and Mrs Maconochie, and, er, his sisters, er . . .
FIONA: Fiona.
MARY: Mary.
SANDRA: Sandra. (*Giggles*)
REV GRIFFITHS: Fiona, Mary and Sandra. (*The boys are all boggling at the
three girls.*) Right, lads, line up for the hundred yards'
sprint, remember, we want a good show.
(*He organises them at one end of the stage.*)
On your marks, get set. GO
(DEREK *streaks ahead, the others are all boggling at the
girls.*)
YORRY: (*To audience*) For the rest of the afternoon, Derek streaked
ahead to victory. The rest of us had never seen such
wondrous visions all assembled ready for action in a
Welsh pasture. Derek won everything except the
wheelbarrow race—for which two of his sisters had agreed
to hold the tape. If my dad had thought of that earlier, I
imagine several Olympic records could well have been
smashed that afternoon. As it was, Derek was proclaimed
Victor Ludorum, and remained totally unaware that it was
not entirely because of his individual sporting prowess;
and our visitors were served with Uncle Dafydd's idea of
what you get at a Buckingham Palace Garden Party.
Like the others, I had fallen totally in love with all three of
them, each one to the exclusion of all others.
Since my mother had died, when I was seven, my father
had taken it upon himself to bring me up to be a credit to

her. This meant that I wasn't allowed to do anything I wanted to do, or anything anyone else did, or anything at all except go to a special school with no girls and sit in the front row at chapel. My main sources of contact with the outside world were ancient visiting preachers, and the lady who came to scrub the floor. Uncle Dafydd was strictly forbidden to have any influence over me whatsoever. Little wonder that on this, my first day of freedom, I was completely and helplessly in the thrall of Fiona Maconochie, Sandra Maconochie and Mary Maconochie. The damage had been done.

(*The* MACONOCHIES *leave.*)

WILLY: The damage had been done to me, too. That Sandra—cor flip. I'll tell you one thing. Not only was Derek Victor Ludorum. He was, suddenly, my very best mate, and for the rest of his stay in Tyn-y-Gongl, he lived like a king on cold roast pheasant.

That night, when we were lying in our bell-tent, all toes pointing to the pole, Mr Dafydd ap Gwilym Griffiths told us a story.

(*The lads are all lying in sleeping bags. The lights dim, as* DAFYDD *starts to weave his spell.*)

DAFYDD: Now, lads, as far as I'm concerned, Christianity was just one big mistake. You've heard how in Wales, we were all pagans, heathens, what have you. They probably didn't explain how all these miserable pagans wrote poetry of astounding beauty, how all the land was common land, and all the people worked together for the good of the whole tribe. The leaders, the kings, were poets as well as warriors, they led the defence of their land, and gave spiritual strength and depth of feeling to the whole people.

WILLY: We didn't really know what he was talking about. We'd all started thinking about those girls again. Only Yorry spoke up.

YORRY: But I thought that Christianity brought civilisation.

DAFYDD: I'll tell you a story. In ancient Ireland there was a king, called Sweeney, who was also a poet, and a high priest of the old religion. When St Ronan came to bring civilisation to him and his people—with a bloody great army— Sweeney slung a half a brick at Ronan, but bloody Ronan was wearing a huge iron cross on his chest, and the brick hit that, and bounced off. And Sweeney was defeated, and the old religion obliterated without trace. And Sweeney was afflicted with the flying madness—he grew feathers, and his arms turned into wings, and he flew through the wastes and bogs of Ireland, from crag to crag to crag, from tree-top to tree-top, eating only watercress from the ponds, and drinking the mountain streams. He flew over to Wales, right over the Irish Sea—and he landed, somewhere not very far from here. But Wales had been conquered by the Christians as well, and all trace of the old ways that would bring Sweeney back to his senses had been ruthlessly wiped out. All except for one ancient old crone, who lived at a mill. She spied Sweeney eating up the grain she had thrown out to her hens, and knew he was a poet, and she went out and talked to him in the old language, and hid him in the hen house, and fed him, and slowly the poor man began to recover his wits and to feel human again. But one day, the miller discovered him. He didn't say anything, he just sent for some other Christians, and together they surrounded the hen house, flushed out the poet-King, and stoned him to death, there and then. And that was the last of the old kings. But they do say that on dark nights, in this particular part of the world, a huge, feathered, flying ghost can often be seen, bleeding horribly, silently screaming, completely out of its mind with fear and madness.

(*A silence*)

Good night, lads. Sleep tight.

VINCE: Will you tell us a story tomorrow night, Mr Griffiths?

DAFYDD: Oh yes. There's plenty of stories. (*He goes.*)

WILLY: And after he'd gone, there was the silence of a load of lads, their imaginations stirred, their minds a-tingle with the legs and buttocks and bosoms of all three Maconochie girls all rolled up into one mammoth, seductive dream of a ripe and willing beauty, concentrating, breathing a bit heavy, trying not to groan. (*Lies down*)

YORRY: (*Sits up*) What were they all doing? Nobody wanted to talk. I got up, and, risking a visitation from Sweeney's mad, flying ghost, told my love to the hills from whence I had sprung, a love more pure, more lyrical, more passionate and more confusing than anything I had ever experienced before in the whole of my sheltered little life . . .

(*Sings*)

    I've found out love
    My life has just begun
    I've found out what I'm living for
    I've found love.
    Until today
    I was a little child
    Now I can't play I can't pretend
    I've found love.

LADS: (*counter-melody,* YORRY *continues*)
    Totties, judies
    Jumbo-jumpered beauties

Fancy, Fruity
Rooty-tooty-tooty,
Sexy, Firey,
Flaming-with-desirey
A giggle, a wiggle,
A something makes you wriggle.

YORRY: I've found out love. (*Repeat*)
(*The distant singing of a Welsh hymn by* YORRY'S
FATHER *can be heard, as* YORRY *sings on.* DAFYDD
appears, says over the singing)

DAFYDD: The great warmth of a maiden's love
has me captive night and day;
loving a girl with a long bright mane
and keeping it a secret.
From her lips I get wine,
her smile enfeebles me.
If they took all time to name her,
yet no man would know her.
Annes first will I name;
I'll make a pact in gems
with a fine girl in colour and form;
yes, she is gems indeed.
Sweet pensive Guinevere,
Gwladus of the sugared lip,
Catherine, Gwellian I'll greet,
Cari, Mallt, the properest girl,
Lleucu of hill primrose hue,
Lowri under green branches.
Soft is Myfanwy's kiss;
I'm at death's door for Gweirful;
Margaret's faith is mine,
she brings far-brought red gold.
I beat my cheek and keep my faith,
I love kissing my Janet;
wild and low is my look,
lying with Tegwedd has charmed me.
I'm weak, there's a spear in my skull,
my pain for Angharad grows greater.
There's an arrow in her deep bosom
which won't be drawn in a meteor's life.
A star under gold rushes of hair,
I spy out Alison for the wood.
In the woods there is white trefoil,
a green birch tree and Morfudd.
Alis, Isabel, Helen,
Eva or Nest is my bright girl.
And now she has been named,
for one of these is the girl.
(*Repeat of 'I've found out love' ends the scene.*)

SCENE II

(*The* MACONOCHIES' *living room.* MRS MACONOCHIE *ironing.* FIONA *doing her homework.* MARY *and* SANDRA *having a flaming row over a pair of tights, each heaving an end, the tug-of-war careering across the room, crashing into* MRS MACONOCHIE *on one side and* FIONA *on the other, who both protest loudly and push them away.*)

SANDRA: Gimme me tights, you cross-eyed faggot!

MARY: I told you they're mine, stop pulling or you'll rip them in two!

SANDRA: I bloody will, too, if you don't let go!

MARY: You've never had a pair of tights without holes in them since you stopped wearing nappies—STOP PULLING AT THEM!

SANDRA: If you don't believe they're mine you go and ask the girl in Lewis's—I bought three for the price of two, last Saturday.

MARY: They aren't bloody Lewis's tights, they're Marks and bloody Spencer's and they're mine and if you don't let go of them I'll pull your wig off!

SANDRA: You touch my hair, you jealous cow—just you touch it and I'll give you such a swipe across the ear hole you won't be able to stop the ringing for a fortnight!

MRS MACONOCHIE: Will you two shut your horrible noise, you're like a pair of kids!

FIONA: (*Pushing them away*) Gerroff, can't you, I've got to finish this before I go.

MARY: (*Still holding on—to* FIONA) And as for you, if you think we're hanging about here waiting for you to finish your daft sums you can think again—the dance was half over by the time we got there last week—all the bloody drunks were pouring in looking for somebody to carry them home before we'd got on the floor.

FIONA: I'll be there.

MARY: (*To* SANDRA) Let go!
(*She heaves,* SANDRA *lets go,* MARY *falls,* SANDRA *jumps on her,* FIONA *tries to separate them.*)

MRS MACONOCHIE: (*Advances with the iron poised*) You'll get this bloody iron on your arses, the lot of you, if you can't behave yourselves! (*Enter* MR MACONOCHIE. *He blows a whistle. They stop and look at him.*)

MR MACONOCHIE: Glasgow Rangers seven, Rio do Janeiro Young Convicts twenty-three. The only game they allow a sub for the referee.

MRS MACONOCHIE: Will you separate those two squalling cats before I send for the police.
(SANDRA *and* MARY *both start to appeal to him together. He blows his whistle again.*)

MR MACONOCHIE: Give us the tights. Come on, hand them over. (*They do.*) Right now, I'm going to chuck them in the fire. (*Screams of protest*) Unless you agree to abide by what I say. Ref's decision is final, right?

MARY: Listen, Dad, I bought those tights three weeks ago, and I've looked after them. Just because hers have got holes in, she fancies she can grab mine—well she can't.

SANDRA: I bought three pairs last Saturday.

MR MACONOCHIE: Well where are the other two?

SANDRA: Got holes in.

MARY: See!

SANDRA: But those ones are the only ones I've got left.

MR MACONOCHIE: I think your mother should have them.

MARY: For God's sake, Dad, we're going to a dance.

MR MACONOCHIE: Right, I'll ask you one question: if you lose, would you go, all the same, with holes in your tights? Think carefully, because one of you's got to lose. Sandra?

SANDRA: No, definitely not, I'm not going without those tights.

MR MACONOCHIE: Mary?

MARY: (*Carefully*) Well, if I have to, I will.

MR MACONOCHIE: Right, Mary. You get the tights. Sandra, as you're not going you can put my tea on, I've been working since eight this morning, and I don't see why your mother should have to do everything round here.
(MARY *goes off with tights*)

SANDRA: (*Suddenly all soft*) Oh Dad, I've got to go. I really have to. I'm meeting Willy.

MR MACONOCHIE: Are you? Well he won't be looking at the holes in your stockings, get up and get dressed.

SANDRA: Finished ironing my blouse, Ma?

MRS MACONOCHIE: Here you are—and next time you can iron it yourself.

SANDRA: Eh, Dad.

MR MACONOCHIE: Hello. Speaking.

SANDRA: If you lent us a few bob, I could go down to the shop and get a pair.

MR MACONOCHIE: I thought you worked for your living. I thought they paid you.

SANDRA: Yeh, but it's all gone.

MR MACONOCHIE: Then borrow some off Willy. He's going to be getting the benefit, not me.

SANDRA: Do you know what? You're real mean.

MR MACONOCHIE: On thirty-six quid a week basic I need to be.
(SANDRA *goes.*)

MRS MACONOCHIE: She's a bad loser that one, always was.

MR MACONOCHIE: (*to* FIONA) Aren't you going jigging?

FIONA: In a minute. We dissected a rat's left back leg today, and I've got to write up my notes for tomorrow first lesson. Can I have a pound?

MR MACONOCHIE: What?

FIONA: Well it's sixty pee to get in, and I've got to get there and back, and what with one thing and another it'll have to be a very small bottle of champagne I get with what's left over. I'm not earning my living, Dad. I'm still at school.

MR MACONOCHIE: The price of having a genius in the family.

FIONA: I'll give up school if you like, Dad.

MR MACONOCHIE: What, for the odd quid to go dancing? Here—keep the change. Bloody hell.

(FIONA *takes it and carries on working.*)

FIONA: Thanks, Dad.

MRS MACONOCHIE: Any of that for me?

MR MACONOCHIE: Oh Christ, here we go—anybody else care to strip me of my final quid? (*To woman in audience*) What about you, madam, I'm sure you've got as good a reason as any of this lot for taking away the last of my beer money, come on, don't be shy, it's only worth ten bob anyway, here you are, love. Spend it quick, before we start getting the full benefits of the Common Market—we'll be using them for blowing our noses on then—cheaper than buying Kleenex. (*To audience*) Daughters. When she produced three little baby girls, I had this beautiful fantasy, of getting looked after in my old age; love, adulation from tender, vibrant young women; respect . . .

(DEREK, *who has been cowering, lost in the* Echo, *unseen in an armchair, peers out.*)

DEREK: Eh, Dad, have you forgotten you had me?

MR MACONOCHIE: No, son. Every time I can't find the *Echo* of an evening, I think of you upstairs in the lavvy.

DEREK: Sometimes I think I was a mistake.

MR MACONOCHIE: You were all mistakes, son, but I didn't tell you that in case it undermined your self-confidence.

DEREK: What do you mean by that?

MR MACONOCHIE: Well, I'm not a Catholic, you know, and you weren't exactly planned.

DEREK: Is that a fact?

MR MACONOCHIE: I don't want you to feel unwanted, son, but if your mother wasn't so bloody unscientific, I'd be finding it easier to get a sit-down these evenings.

DEREK: Here you are then. Sit.

MR MACONOCHIE: Don't be touchy, now, Derek. I was only joking.

DEREK: Doesn't sound much of a joke to me.

MR MACONOCHIE: Oh come on, take it easy. You'll be away soon enough, and I'll be missing you along with the rest of them. Isn't it about time you started getting yourself sorted out with a job, talking about that. You *are* leaving school this summer, aren't you?

DEREK: Might as well, they said I wasn't bright enough for university.

MR MACONOCHIE: Ah well, that'll come from your mother's side. So what do you reckon on doing?

DEREK: I'm not going to slave my life away down at Robertson's
Engineering Works for thirty-six quid a week just for the
pleasure of complaining about it, and coming out on strike
every time the weather looks good.

MR MACONOCHIE: Are you trying to bring me down, son?

DEREK: Why not? You've spent the last seventeen years trying to
make me feel I was useless.

MR MACONOCHIE: No look, lad, if you want to knock me, you can do it easy
enough in a hundred ways, but don't ever knock me for
being a working man, or for the way I'm being exploited.

DEREK: Why not?

MR MACONOCHIE: Because I'll knock your teeth down the back of your
throat for it, that's why not.

DEREK: Yeh, but all the same, look, Dad, I know you never had the
opportunities we're getting: you mustn't blame us for taking
one or two of them. You probably would have yourself.

MR MACONOCHIE: Would I? I wonder if I would.

DEREK: I don't really want to talk about it. I've made my mind up,
and there's no more to be said.
(*He gets up and heads for the door, with the* Echo.)

MR MACONOCHIE: Eh, Derek.

DEREK: (*Flaring up*) Now don't start having a go at me, giving me
bloody rotten advice I don't need, trying to drag me down
to what you're stuck with—I know what I'm doing,
though it may surprise you to hear it, so keep your nose
out of my business.

MR MACONOCHIE: I wasn't going to say any of that, son.

DEREK: Oh. What were you going to say?

MR MACONOCHIE: Can I have the *Echo*?
(DEREK *gives it to him and goes.* MR MACONOCHIE *stands
looking after him.*)
Any chance of something to eat, love?

MRS MACONOCHIE: If that's all you're interested in, you can wait till I've
finished this lot. (*Pause*) Haven't you got any more to say
than 'Food, woman'?

MR MACONOCHIE: No.

MRS MACONOCHIE: Amazing.

MR MACONOCHIE: I'll just settle down to a nice quiet unbiased bit of a read.
Straightforward, the *Echo*, that's what I like about it. No
messing. Every worker's a hooligan until he's done fifty
years' loyal service, and every striker's out to wreck the
country's economy.

MRS MACONOCHIE: You're very bilious tonight. Care for some Andrews' Liver
Salts?

MR MACONOCHIE: Of course, they're bloody landowners and capitalists, so
who the hell else do you expect them to support? Honour
amongst thieves.
(*He swings back into the Scene as* MARY *and* SANDRA
groove in, stops aghast at the state of FIONA.)

SANDRA: Are you coming tonight?

FIONA: Yeh. Just ready now . . .

SANDRA: Ready? You haven't started . . .

FIONA: Won't I do?

SANDRA: You'll do for some.

FIONA: I'm not fussy. They can take me or leave me. Let's have a look in the mirror.
(*She has a quick look in the mirror, sings a burlesque number, does a few very sexy shakes and grinds, goes over to* MR MACONOCHIE, *kisses him.*)
Tata, Dad. (*She goes.*)

MR MACONOCHIE: And I thought she was the quiet one.

MARY: Tata, Dad, tata, Ma—see you later.

MRS MACONOCHIE: See you're back by twelve, all of you, and stick together. I worry about you.

SANDRA: We'll manage. If we're not in by morning, ring the morgue, and if we're not in the morgue, try the Adelphi.

MARY: Don't worry about us, Ma. Worry about the fellers.
(*They go. Silence.* MR MACONOCHIE *reading the paper*)

MRS MACONOCHIE: I'll get your tea in a minute.

MR MACONOCHIE: Don't worry, love. I didn't eat those sandwiches till five o'clock. (*Stands, shakes his pocket.*) I've still got a few coppers to my name. I'll wander down the club for a gill or two. Are you alright?

MRS MACONOCHIE: Me? I'll manage.

MR MACONOCHIE: I'll not be more than an hour.
(*He goes out.*)

MRS MACONOCHIE: Don't ask me, will you? I've just been stuck in here all day, having a wonderful time . . .
(DEREK'S *voice from outside the door.*)

DEREK: Ma?

MRS MACONOCHIE: Yes? Come in, can't you?

DEREK: Was that Dad going out?

MRS MACONOCHIE: Couldn't you tell?

DEREK: Can I come in, then?

MRS MACONOCHIE: Of course you can come in, whether he's here or not, what's got into you?
(*Door opens and* DEREK *comes in wearing a police cadet uniform. He stands, torn between pride and fear, watching her face. She turns to the audience.*)

MRS MACONOCHIE: I'll have to give him confidence. He always lacked confidence, did Derek. (*To* DEREK) Very smart, isn't it? Turn round. (*He does so. We see her dismay.*) Borrowed it, have you?

DEREK: No. It's mine. I've joined. Don't tell my dad, will you?

MRS MACONOCHIE: Well, I suppose he must notice, sooner or later . . .

DEREK: No. I'm leaving home. I go off on this course on Monday, then I can get posted anywhere, live in the station house.

MRS MACONOCHIE: But why?

DEREK: Do you think I shouldn't?

MRS MACONOCHIE: No, love, no. You've done the right thing.

DEREK: I'm worried, Ma.

MRS MACONOCHIE: Come here, you silly boy. It's lovely.

(*He goes over to her and she hugs him. Enter* MR
MACONOCHIE. *He does a take in the doorway.*)

MR MACONOCHIE: Hey, take your hands off her!

(DEREK *turns round. He sees who it is.*)

Jesus Christ Almighty!

(*His horror is all over his face.* DEREK *walks out, past him.*)

DEREK: That's it. I'm off. And I'll not be back.

MR MACONOCHIE: Lend us two pounds, love.

(*She nods to her purse. He goes and takes two pounds.*)
I've failed.

(*He turns and goes.*)

(*The scene changes to a dance hall, with a band playing
music.*)

(*The girls dance round a pile of handbags to the song.*
WILLY *and the lads come in and sing their own verses,
taking the mickey. Song ends with them all dancing
together. During the song,* ANDY *has appeared, with a
whisky bottle, clocking* MARY.)

Dance the Up and Down

GIRLS: Point a finger
Point a finger
Shake a shoulder
Shake a shoulder
Marching up and down
Marching up and down
And you'll be feeling fine
And you'll be feeling fine.

Knees up
Knees up
Toe point
Toe point
Marching up and down
Marching up and down
And you'll be feeling fine
And you'll be feeling fine.

Jerk an elbow
Jerk an elbow
Wag a hip
Wag a hip
Take a walk around
Take a walk around
And you'll be feeling fine
And you'll be feeling fine.

LADS:	Take a spanner
	Take a spanner
	Turn a sprocket
	Turn a sprocket
	Feel you're mucked around
	Wish you were under found
	It's the production line
	It's the production line.

Drill a little
Drill a little
Bore a hole
Bore a hole
Feel you're mucked around
Wish you were under found
It's the production line
It's the production line.

Hit your missus
Hit your missus
Watch the telly
Watch the telly
Feel you're gonna die
And you don't know why
It's the production line
It's the production line.

(*As the song ends,* SANDRA *and* WILLY *break off together.*)

SANDRA: So you got here then.

WILLY: Yeh.

SANDRA: One of these days you're going to meet me outside and take me in. That'll be the day.

WILLY: Couldn't do that, love.

SANDRA: Why not?

WILLY: Well, if I saw you outside looking like that, we might never get here.

SANDRA: Do you reckon?

WILLY: I might get all carried away.

SANDRA: Mm—passionate.

WILLY: Couldn't help myself.

SANDRA: Don't you like dancing?

WILLY: Quite like watching you dancing.

SANDRA: Quite like watching me drinking Babycham?

WILLY: Definitely.

SANDRA: Come on, then. Who's that feller with our Mary?

WILLY: Dunno.

(*At that moment* ANDY *bursts out in a drunken cackle.*)

ANDY: Is that a fact—eh? Mary, is that what your name is?

MARY: Look, shove off, can't you, you're drunk out of your head.

(*She starts to move away, but he grips her arm.*)

ANDY: Don't you bloody walk away from me, Miss Hairy Mary.

MARY: Lay off, can't you?

ANDY: Oh no. Oh no. I like the looks of you, chicken. You and me's going to do some dancing.

MARY: Well that's where you're wrong.

ANDY: (*To* BAND) Hey. Music! Come on, I'm wanting dancing . . . (*But* BAND *are sorting out their gear and chatting and anyway too far away.*)

ANDY: Ach, musicians.
(MARY *bites his hand. He doesn't let go. He stands and watches her biting, as hard as she can, laughing.*)
You bite till the blood runs, chicken. I'll give you my blood and if you want me to cry, I'll give you my tears: if you want to hear me scream, I'll scream for you like you've never heard a man scream, I'm not afraid to. (*She stops biting and is holding his hand.*) You and me, we have the same bad dreams, I can see them rising in your eyes.

MARY: Don't know what you're talking about.

ANDY: (*Laughs*) What's a nightmare, if you've nobody to share it with. Jesus, when I was a wee skelf living three stair up in the Gallowgate, me and my brothers used to have competitions.

MARY: At telling nightmares?

ANDY: Aye. But they're tearing down the Gallowgate. Dreams are not so easy to come by in Drumchapel.

MARY: I've never told anybody my dreams.

My Love is Like

ANDY: Then I'll sing you a song:
My love is like a red red rose
That's newly sprung in June:
My love is like the melodie
That's sweetly play'd in tune.

So fair art thou, my bonnie lass,
So deep in love am I:
And I will love thee still, my dear,
Till a' the seas gang dry.

Till a' the seas gang dry, my dear,
And the rocks melt wi' the sun:
And I will love thee still, my dear,
While the sands o' life shall run.

And fare thee weel, my only love,
And fare thee weel awhile!
And I will come again, my love,
Tho' it were ten thousand mile.
(*A MAN in a white jacket comes quietly up to* ANDY *and taps him on the shoulder.*)

Huh? What do you want, Jimmy? You tapping me, are
you?

MAN: Come on, Jock—outside.

(*He pushes the man violently away. The lighting changes.*
FOUR MORE MEN *in white jackets appear noiselessly,
wearing masks of Bosch animals.* ANDY *freaks, grabs*
MARY, *slides down on to the floor.* BAND *begins to play.*
They too have masks of humanoids. The music is ANDY's
horrors. It builds as the FIVE MEN *advance on them.* MARY
tries to look after ANDY, *tries to keep them off him. They
drag him away, knock him down, kick him, then kick him
out. They vanish, the lights change, music cuts. The first*
MAN *in white coat comes back to* MARY, *who is scared out
of her wits.*)

Keep away from that one, love—he's a nutter.

(*He goes.* BAND, *without masks, breaks into the number at
the beginning of the Scene.* SANDRA *and* WILLY, FIONA *and*
VINCE, *dance with mechanical movements.* MARY *doesn't
know what's going on, watches them. She walks around
looking at them; they seem completely inexplicable to her.
They move back, the* MUSIC *fades with the* LIGHTS—*she is
alone, outside the dance hall.*)

MARY: Was that me or him? I don't know. I don't know whose
nightmare I'm having. Horrible nightmares. The girls
complain about me screaming and thrashing around all
night, they should try living with it, every time my eyes
close, even during the day now, at work, when I'm not
concentrating. I keep seeing things, old women hammering
nails into their eyes, children peeling open like bananas,
empty drums dropping from the sky, people with
shopping-bags running for cover into crumbling shops,
rafters with rats clinging to them tumbling on their heads,
heads with plastic rain-hats and when you look from the
top it's bags of blood, and these tin-drums shattering all
around like it was bombs in the war, only who was
dropping them, and me, where was I? Doctor said I should
stop reading the newspapers, but I never read the
newspapers, only *Honey* and *Nineteen*. I sometimes think
I'm going mad. I think they're going to come and get me,
but they can't be bothered, at least so far not, but then I
think why should they, I'm just a boring ordinary person,
of no interest to such as them, they want something more
interesting than tin-drums falling from the sky, and I think
my brain is sort of boring and if I'm going to have
nightmares, I wish I could have interesting ones. I try to
make them more interesting, but it's like writing essays in
English at school, the writing just goes on and all the best
ideas just fly away, slip out, can't fit in. I keep having this
great idea for a nightmare about getting sliced up from the

top into rashers and walking about in different directions through fir-trees. But I can't get it. They just come out all uptight and frightening and boring. And that's why they won't come and get me.

(ANDY *comes on, sees her.*)

ANDY: Hey, chicken.

MARY: Let's have a look at you.

ANDY: No bother, no bother at all. Let's have a look at you, chicken . . .

MARY: Oh come on, you ought to get a doctor to that nose, it looks broken to me.

ANDY: Bust? (*Blows down it*) Nah. He had studs in his clogs, ah? See? Can you see 'em?

MARY: You want to see a doctor.

ANDY: I want to see you, you know. (*He looks at her.*)

MARY: Feller in there said you was a nutter.

ANDY: Aye. That's how they treat nutters round here, ah? (*Fingers his nose*) Some psychiatrist.

MARY: What do you do it for? All that mad stuff. You're not mad, are you? You know just what you're doing, don't you?

ANDY: (*Howls, crouching on all fours. She stares at him, not taken in. He points up.*) See? Full moon. (*Changes tack; sits*) Nah, chicken. (*Pounds his head*) Can't keep it all there, ha? (*Taps the side of his nose, knowingly*) Does you no good. Fight 'em. Make 'em take it, stick it on them. Spread it out, amongst the population, you know. Population gives it you, right? Give it back, yeh?

MARY: But they just battered you bloody near dead.

ANDY: (*Getting up*) Ah, what good does that do? Hah? (*Laughs*)

MARY: Well it didn't do you any good?

ANDY: (*Holds out his arms, showing himself.*) Look, look. (*Shows face.*) What's that, chicken, what do you see, go on, say it, what do you see?

MARY: Well, you're alive.

ANDY: (*Triumphant*) Ah!

MARY: But you're all bashed up.

ANDY: Nose. Busted, or not?

MARY: Bloody great stud-marks all over it.

ANDY: Bruises, few rips, few—scratches . . . Where are they, bird, outside or inside? Brain or body? Ah?

MARY: What are you talking about?

(*He goes to her, holds her face, looks in her eyes.*)

ANDY: You know fine what I'm talking about. You and me, hey, Liverpool biter?

MARY: Don't. You're frightening me.

ANDY: Bring out your dead, chicken.

MARY: Bury them for me . . .

ANDY: Leave them in the middle of the street for you, let the punters walk round them: let them crawl with maggots up the front doors and smell: fill all the little houses with the smell of plague. (*He leaps around ringing an imaginary bell.*) Bring out your dead! Bring out your dead! Lepers to the right! Bubonic to the left! Pile up your carcases, stack up your dead men.

(SANDRA *and* WILLY *come on, on their way home.* SANDRA *nudges* WILLY *to do something.*)

WILLY: (*Being a man*) Eh, Mary, do you want to come home with us?

(ANDY *stops, turns away, stricken, waiting for his fate.* MARY *looks at his back. Decides*)

MARY: I'll be alright, Willy. Won't be long.

SANDRA: See you outside, then?

MARY: Yeh. In a minute.

(*MUSIC in*)

Yeh. Don't worry.

(SANDRA *and* WILLY *go off, worried about* MARY. MUSIC *up.*)

Loving is Dangerous

Walk a rope without a net
A long way from the ground
The crowd looks up, they draw their breath

Will she
Won't she
Tumble down?

Take your life into your hands
Hope that he understands
All the danger that you're in
When you love a man.

Falling free above the clouds
In one long beautiful dive.
Will you, won't you, pull the cord,
Will you
Won't you
Soon arrive?

Take your life into your hands
Hope that he understands
All the danger that you're in
When you love a man.

The one you love
Is someone else
You've got to give them all you have
And they can tear
Your life apart
If love is safe, it isn't love.

So treat me gently don't destroy
My love, my hope, my trust in you,
If I must live my life in danger
Show me you care and I'll come through.

Take your life into your hands
Hope that he understands
All the danger that you're in
When you love a man.

ANDY: Hey, Snow White—come here.

MARY: What?

ANDY: For seven little years
I was seven little men.
You came and kissed them all.
Now I am one again.

MARY: You don't really know me, do you?

ANDY: Oh yes I do, chicken . . .

MARY: (*As they move off*) Don't keep calling me that.

ANDY: What's wrong with it?

MARY: I keep thinking I might grow up to be a hen . . .
(*They go together. As the Scene changes,* WILLY *comes on, talks to the audience.*)

WILLY: We reckoned that looked a bit complicated, that little scene. What we hadn't reckoned with was that Yorry—who by now was a student studying French and German at university—had fallen, from afar, romantically in love with his memory of Mary, and had chosen that particular night to stand under the hedge outside their council-house, clutching his guitar, and was slowly being driven into a state bordering on fine frenzy by the full moon and the thought of Mary. He fondly imagined she was kipping upstairs: it was round about half past midnight that he discovered his big mistake.
(WILLY *goes. The next set, a high hedge with three gateways cut in it, runs across the stage.* YORRY *sits under the middle of it, gazing at the moon.*)

Poem to the Moon

YORRY: The purest love a soul can know
Is known beneath the moon
The purest seed a man can sow
Is sown beneath the moon.

Of all the orbs that circle round
The universe of love
There's none can frenzy none astound
Quite like the moon above.

Except my love, my Mary, who
Consumes me with pale fire,
Outshines the stars, the pure moon too,
The universe entire.

(At the end of the poem FIONA *comes in wrapped round* VINNY. *There follows a short, sharp farcical sequence involving the three gateways and the hedge.* YORRY *dashes into Gateway 1, to hide.* FIONA *and* VINNY *drift into it.* YORRY *emerges, bedraggled, having crawled across two gardens, from Gateway 2. As he does so* SANDRA *and* WILLY *come on from the other side—he dashes back in.)*

SANDRA: What do you think we should do?

WILLY: What about?

SANDRA: Our Mary.

WILLY: Wait. See if she comes.

(A terrible giggle comes from Gateway 1. FIONA *puts her head out.)*

FIONA: Eh—he said he couldn't get my brazier undone.

VINNY: Come here!

SANDRA: Keep your eye on that one, Fiona, he's like a bloody octopus.

WILLY: How do you know?

SANDRA: I've heard.

WILLY: I'm getting serious about you, Sandra.

SANDRA: Are you?

WILLY: Yeh—I'm thinking of taking you for a walk on Sunday afternoon.

SANDRA: What, and missing the football on the telly?

WILLY: Er—well, after the Big Match. I'm not engaged to you or anything . . .

SANDRA: No. You're not.

WILLY: Would you like us to be—not now, you know. But sooner or later?

SANDRA: What kind of a proposition's that?

WILLY: Well—would you?

SANDRA: You'd better get a job first. My dad says he might be able to fix you up at his place.

WILLY: Have you been asking him? You sly little schemer.

SANDRA: Eh—come in here . . .

WILLY: *(Over his shoulder, to audience)* Said the spider to the fly.

(He vanishes into Gateway 2. A rustling sound. YORRY *emerges, covered in garden manure, from Gateway 3.)*

YORRY: Oh heavenly body holier than
            The goddess of the night,
            My Mary make this mortal man
            Immortal with your light.

(He is interrupted by the arrival of MARY *and* ANDY.*)*

YORRY: Oh no! Oh God! Oh Mary Maconochie!

(He dashes back into Gateway 3. MARY *goes into Gateway 1.)*

MARY: Ooops! Sorry, love.

(They walk along, she goes into Gateway 2.)

MARY: Bloody hell! You two.

(They walk towards Gateway 3.)

ANDY: I don't want no gateway with you, chicken.

MARY: Well you'll have to save up to buy a van.

ANDY: Come here Mary.

MARY: You might be mad, but you've got to be practical. There's about three hundred pairs of eyes peering out from behind them sleepy curtains—it's dark in here.

ANDY: I'm afraid of the dark, I always have been.

MARY: Not with me you won't be.

(They go in. The whole hedge begins to shake, whimper, giggle and moan. YORRY crawls out somewhere near the middle, scratched, torn and covered in shit. Song.)

Lonely as the Dark Side of the Moon

Lonely as the dark side of the moon
Hoping that the sun will reach me soon
But the sun moves around
The moon keeps turning, too
Until the end of time
The light will not shine through . . .
Lonely as the dark side of the moon
Hoping that the sun will reach me soon
I watch the universe
Whirling round my head
A million other worlds
The one I'm on is dead.

Blast off through the darkest night,
Rockets trailing fires in flight,
Light-years spin by in a day
Ripping through the Milky Way.
Spaceman,
Spaceman fly,
Fly out through
The black black sky
Burning past the far-off stars
Bending where the space bends
Turning round the edge of time
And through the time the world ends.
Spaceman,
Spaceman fly,
Fly out through
The black black sky.

Lonely as the dark side of the moon.
(Repeat first verse to 'will not shine through'.)
(This takes off into space fantasy and builds very big, then crashes down back to YORRY, lonely. As it ends he hears one of them getting ready to emerge. He crawls back under the hedge.)

(FIONA *comes out, calls to* SANDRA.)

FIONA: Sandra! Eh, Sandra, do you know what time it is?
   (*A muffled voice comes from inside Gateway 2.*)

FIONA: But it's quarter to one—Dad'll skin us alive.

WILLY: (*From inside*) Tell him times is changing.

FIONA: I told him that . . . he said he wasn't.

WILLY: Antiquated old bugger.

FIONA: Aw, come on, Sandra.

SANDRA: You go in—leave the door open a bit.

FIONA: I haven't got the key.

SANDRA: Haven't you? Oh hell.

FIONA: Haven't you got it?

SANDRA: No. (*Coming out, doing herself up*) Mary must have it.

WILLY: Oh, don't wander off looking for the bloody key, love.

SANDRA: But we'd better get it.

WILLY: You've got no soul.
   (SANDRA *and* FIONA *go to Gateway 3.*)

SANDRA: Mary! (*Silence*) Mary!

FIONA: Is she there? (SANDRA *nods*) Who with?

SANDRA: Sh! Mary, will you bloody speak!

MARY: Oh bugger off, can't you?

FIONA: (*Urgent*) Have you got the key?

MARY: You've got the key.

SANDRA AND FIONA: (*Together*) We haven't . . . !

ANDY: Jump in through the bloody window, can't you? Your sister's busy . . .
   (SANDRA *and* FIONA *look at each other.*)

FIONA: If you don't come out, I'm going to ring the bell.

MARY: You do that and I'll wring your bloody neck.

SANDRA: Well give her the key, then.
   (*A handbag flies out.* SANDRA *and* FIONA *look in it. It's not there.*)

FIONA: Mary!

MARY: What?

FIONA: It's not in it.

MARY: Well *do* something.

SANDRA: Do what?

MARY: (*Groans*) Hang on.

ANDY: What're you doing—where are you going.

MARY: How the hell can I concentrate with all that going on— have a bit of sense. (*Comes out*) Why can't you climb in through the kitchen window?

SANDRA: The kitchen window hasn't been unstuck since the last time the Corporation painted the place and that was about ten years ago—and my dad's gone round the inside with Evo-Seal, terrified in case some fresh air might seep in the place.

FIONA: We'll have to ring the bell—and if we do that, we'll all have to do it together, you know what Dad's like.

MARY: Boring bugger, why doesn't he go out and have a good time.
SANDRA: That'll be the day.
MARY: Sitting at home all night, watching the telly, creeping
                round the club for two light ales.
SANDRA: 'Never a drop more . . . '
MARY: What they call steady. A boring bloody slave.
                (*Sound of* MR MACONOCHIE *singing with gay abandon—he
                comes reeling up the street, arms flung wide, head back,
                pissed out of his mind. At the end of the song, he turns to
                go in, stops, looks at the house—which is through
                Gateway 2—makes a gesture of dismissal and turns away.
                As he does so, he sees the three girls.*)
MR MACONOCHIE: Hello there—what are you lot doing out at this hour?
SANDRA: Could ask you that.
MR MACONOCHIE: I've been getting drunk—any objections? At least I've been
                trying to . . .
MARY: Didn't manage, did you?
MR MACONOCHIE: I drank brown ales till the stuff was pouring out my ears,
                topped up with half a bottle of whisky, followed by four
                miniatures of rum. All I've ended up with is a bellyache,
                and a vague feeling I ought to be singing. Cost me three
                pounds seventy-five pee.
FIONA: What you getting drunk for?
MARY: Is something up?
SANDRA: Have we finally driven you to it?
MR MACONOCHIE: All my life I've hated three things: bosses, onions and
                policemen. My own dad was a policeman—once. Did you
                ever hear about the Liverpool policemen's strike? They didn't
                fancy some of the things they were supposed to be getting up
                to—helping the bosses keep the men down amongst other
                things. One or two of them had consciences in those days.
                There was a meeting outside St George's Hall, and they sent
                the military along to break it up. They drove all the
                Liverpool policemen back to the Walker Art Gallery, then up
                the steps and in—to that hallowed temple of the arts. Waiting
                for them, truncheons at the ready, was the Birmingham
                police. They fell on them, their brothers, and smashed them.
                They said men were killed in there that day, but who knows
                for certain? All I know is, my old feller came out with a
                couple of broken ribs and a cracked collarbone, and he didn't
                get them looking at the pictures. Serves him right for joining,
                some said. He ended up on the bins, not even that, burning
                the rubbish at the tip, came home stinking night after night,
                living with the rats and the garbage. He was never bitter:
                them Birmingham lads was just doing their duty, he used to
                say, when I could get him to talk about it. He blamed it all
                on a few shit-stirrers in Liverpool, leading the others astray.
                But I saw him broken. My own dad. By his own mates. And
                I've watched them since. Never. Never.

MARY:	Never what, Dad?
MR MACONOCHIE:	Our Derek—oh God, I can't bring myself.
SANDRA:	He's not—
MR MACONOCHIE:	He bloody is. He's got the uniform, trying it out, all proud of his little self.
SANDRA:	Well they're not *all* bad, you know.
MR MACONOCHIE:	No. I must try to be rational. Some people like onions.
MARY:	So it's shame on the house of Maconochie.
MR MACONOCHIE:	Don't take the mickey out of me, girl. The time's fast coming when the Liverpool police will have to do some more dirty work for the bosses—if it hasn't come already. And our Derek won't be going up the steps backwards. He'll be waiting inside with his truncheon.
MARY:	Come on in, Dad, it's past your bedtime.
MR MACONOCHIE:	He's my son. I've gone through my whole life, struggling and learning: and what have I passed on to him? What could I pass on to him? What's the point of all that struggle? We haven't won much—we're still in exactly the same position—and now I'm getting old; and nothing's been handed on to the next lot. Nothing. That's how it works—sweet forgetfulness. (*He looks at them, swaying slightly.*) Doesn't mean a thing. Doesn't mean that. Your heads are full of fellers, and your fellers don't want to know any more than you do.
WILLY:	(*Emerging*) You're wrong there, Mr Maconochie.
MR MACONOCHIE:	Hello, Willy—where did you spring from?
WILLY:	Just seeing Sandra safe home.
MR MACONOCHIE:	Any more of you lurking in the shrubbery?
WILLY:	Er—(*calls*)—Vince—come out. (*Enter* VINCE)
MR MACONOCHIE:	Bugger me—whose safety are you responsible for?
FIONA:	Mine—in a manner of speaking.
MR MACONOCHIE:	Don't tell me you came home unprotected. Did you? Come on, I'm not going to eat him.
MARY:	Can't we go in?
MR MACONOCHIE:	I thought we might have a party, in actual point of fact. Right here, wake up the neighbours. What's his name?
MARY:	Oh come on, Dad, lay off it can't you?
MR MACONOCHIE:	(*Suddenly determined*) Where is he? (*Goes looking*) Come on out, I'm not all that horrible. Not here—(*goes to Gateway 3*)—I only want to have a look at you, I'm quite a decent feller, underneath. (ANDY *steps out as he approaches, still battered.*) Bloody suffering tugboats—(*to* MARY)—is this him then?
MARY:	I asked you to keep out, Dad.
ANDY:	What do you want, mister?
MR MACONOCHIE:	I want to know what's going on round here, that's all.
ANDY:	Why?
MR MACONOCHIE:	Ah?

ANDY: I said—why?

MR MACONOCHIE: Where are you from then?

ANDY: Aw, come on, man.

MR MACONOCHIE: What are you doing round these parts? Working?

ANDY: I work in Coatbridge. I came down here to find my wife. She's run off with some bloke from Liverpool, I just want to lay my hands on them, just for a wee bittie, him first, then her. Then they can get on with it. I'm not wanting her back to Coatbridge or anywhere else. I'm wanting maybe a word in her ear. (*Silence*)

SANDRA: What you doing with our Mary then?

MARY: Keep out of this, Sandra.

SANDRA: Listen, I'm only—

ANDY: I'm not a married man any more, am I?

MR MACONOCHIE: Aren't you?

ANDY: (*Gestures that's all over*) Come away, now, Mary, I'm wanting to talk to you.

MR MACONOCHIE: She's coming in to bed now, mate. So are they all.

ANDY: (*Decides not to make an issue of it*) Right. She's going to bed. Right. Goodnight, Mary. I'll fetch you tomorrow. Seven. OK?

MARY: OK. (ANDY *goes. A silence.*)

MR MACONOCHIE: Any more in there?

SANDRA: One each is normal, Dad.

MR MACONOCHIE: Right then. Party's over. Goodnight, lads.

VINCE: (*Glad to be off the hook*) Goodnight, Mr Maconochie. (*Turns to go*)

FIONA: Eh—you.

VINCE: Yeh?

FIONA: Don't bother.

VINCE: Oh—er—see you, Fiona. (*Goes fast*)

FIONA: Not if I see you first—give us the key, Dad. (*Goes with key*)

MR MACONOCHIE: Come on then.

WILLY: Do you fancy a drink down the 'Legs of Man' tomorrow night, eh, Mr Maconochie?

MR MACONOCHE: I'll be in the club between eight and nine. I'll be drinking two brown ales—one after the other—then going home.

WILLY: I might see you there then?

MR MACONOCHIE: If you come in, you will. Can't help it.

WILLY: Right then, the club, tomorrow night. Tara, Sandra.

SANDRA: Eh, come here . . . (*Takes him on one side*) What are you going to say to him? We're not, fixed up, or anything. Are we?

WILLY: (*Innocent*) No. I was going to ask him about this job.

SANDRA: (*Agape*) You what?

WILLY: (*Still having her on*) First things first, Sandra.

SANDRA:	I thought you said—(*He laughs. She cottons.*) Get off home, you tormenting bugger you.
WILLY:	Tara. (*To others*) Tara.
	(*He goes.* SANDRA *watches him go.*)
SANDRA:	Do you like him, Dad?
MR MACONOCHIE:	I've scarcely met the feller. Seemed very friendly with our Derek a year or so back.
MARY:	(*Sniffs*) Cupboard love.
MR MACONOCHIE:	What's our Derek got in his cupboard?
SANDRA:	(*Giggles*) Me.
MR MACONOCHIE:	(*To* SANDRA) Goodnight, girl.
SANDRA:	Goodnight, Dad. (*Kisses him. Goes*)
MR MACONOCHIE:	(*Surprised*) She must be in love.
	(*Silence*)
MARY:	I'm in trouble, Dad.
MR MACONOCHIE:	Eh?
MARY:	No, not that. Him. Andy.
MR MACONOCHIE:	When did you meet him?
MARY:	Tonight.
MR MACONOCHIE:	Well if you don't fancy him, don't see him again.
MARY:	But I do.
MR MACONOCHIE:	Don't land yourself with that, love.
MARY:	He's mad.
MR MACONOCHIE:	Jack him in.
MARY:	He's dangerous, ought to be locked up.
MR MACONOCHIE:	What hit him?
MARY:	Five bouncers at the dance.
MR MACONOCHIE:	Fighter, is he?
MARY:	Desperate. He was only singing a song.
MR MACONOCHIE:	Drunk?
MARY:	Out of his head.
MR MACONOCHIE:	(*Shakes his head*) Best forgotten.
MARY:	Yes.
MR MACONOCHIE:	You're still young, love. You're a good girl. You deserve better.
MARY:	Couldn't do much worse.
MR MACONOCHIE:	I want you to have a happy life, Mary. I want all of you to, you know, but you were the first: I've never told anyone how much I wanted you to be happy; or how hard I worked for a better world for you to grow up into: all those bloody meetings, getting nowhere, organising, nobody there to organise—feeling older, a bit older every week: thinking, to keep me going, about you.
MARY:	(*Hugs him*) Don't say things like that.
MR MACONOCHIE:	I suppose I am a bit pissed tonight, else I wouldn't be talking like this. Perhaps I haven't wasted my three pounds seventy-five pee after all. (*Looks at her*) I put a big burden on you, Mary, don't I?

MARY: I don't mind that, Dad. I'd like to—you know—pay you back, in some way.

MR MACONOCHIE: For what? I failed. I never gave you a decent world to grow up into. I never changed a thing, in fact it's got worse. You ought to be giving me hell, child. Pay me back. Huh.

MARY: For trying.

MR MACONOCHIE: Just be happy. Learn from our mistakes, that's all I ask. (*Pause*)

MARY: Let's go in, Dad.

MR MACONOCHIE: Mary—if that feller comes tomorrow night. (*She hangs her head, looks away.*) Take care of yourself, love.
(*He goes in.* MARY *thinks a minute, sees her future, turns, goes in.*)
(Yorry crawls out from under the hedge.)

YORRY: I'm going to stop being stupid now. Well—stupid in that way. I couldn't go on much longer, being as daft as that. I had a few experiences with a few girls with varying degrees of success. But I never stopped being in love with Mary. All three of them really. But Mary. And all the girls I went with, I began to realise, I was using; not for themselves, but to prepare myself, somehow, to be good enough for her. That was how my privileged, protected fantasy operated. In reality: I didn't know what was going on.
(MR MACONOCHIE *comes on.*)

MR MACONOCHIE: In reality, Willy started going steady with Sandra, Mary got visited every month or so by this lunatic from Coatbridge, and Fiona devastated every lad in Liverpool who crossed her path. And I got Willy his job at Robertson's.
(*A large machine appears, to represent Robertson's Works. It has slots in it for two heads to poke through and four arms to work through.* MR MACONOCHIE *and* WILLY *fit into it.*)

WILLY: Do you know that a darts team from the sergeants' mess in some regiment in Germany played a game of a million and one . . . ?

MR MACONOCHIE: They'd have sod all else to do, I suppose.

WILLY: They hold the world record time for scoring a million and one.

MR MACONOCHIE: Can't think they'd have many challengers.

WILLY: Nine hours, forty-eight minutes, thirty-one seconds— Royal Hussars, they were.

MR MACONOCHIE: Did they make any money out of it?

WILLY: Don't think so. If there was money in it, I'd have a go, single-handed. How can you make ten thousand, fast?

MR MACONOCHIE: Get bought by Ipswich. It's the only way.

WILLY: Yeh, but they don't transfer spectators. Eh, do you think Everton would buy me off Liverpool—I've got a good yell, and I live nearer Goodison?

MR MACONOCHIE:	You'd have to pay them to have you. You keep putting Toshack off, every time he's about to miss an open goal. Your bloody yell put him off so much the other Saturday he nearly scored.
WILLY:	I do need the money though. I mean, me and Sandra's got to get somewhere, haven't we?
MR MACONOCHIE:	It's normal, if you're getting married, but it's not essential.
WILLY:	We're nowhere on the Corporation waiting list, and they've knocked down all the little houses, and flats cost a bomb.
MR MACONOCHIE:	Don't get downhearted, young love will see you through.
WILLY:	The money at this place is ridiculous.
MR MACONOCHIE:	Yeh, Robertson's only paying himself forty thousand this year.
WILLY:	Is that right? The fellers were saying he's going to sell up, plant, trade, order-books, even us.
MR MACONOCHIE:	Who said that?
WILLY:	Jacky.
MR MACONOCHIE:	He's right. Consolidated Metals of America are buying us out for over a quarter of a million.
WILLY:	Do we get a slice, like on a transfer fee?
MR MACONOCHIE:	We get bugger all. In fact, less than bugger all: Consolidated Metals owns tin-mines in Bolivia, steel-works in Venezuela. Compared with what they pay out there, they'll reckon we're on the gravy train. And if we cause trouble, bang, closed, like Courtaulds. I wonder whether George Brown still reckons he's a socialist?
WILLY:	What we going to do, then?
MR MACONOCHIE:	Threaten to come out on strike, now, for more money.
WILLY:	Now?
MR MACONOCHIE:	Yeh, just when he's selling. He'll be so scared of frightening off the Yanks, he'll give us anything. After all, he won't be paying it.
WILLY:	They must have thought of that one.
MR MACONOCHIE:	They can think again, there's nothing they can do about it. Jacky and me spent last night drawing up the demand.
WILLY:	What's in it for me?
MR MACONOCHIE:	A guaranteed minimum of thirty-seven pounds per week, plus overtime, plus three weeks' paid holiday.
WILLY:	Great. And you reckon we'll get it?
MR MACONOCHIE:	Something like it. We might have to come out for a couple of weeks, just to show willing.
WILLY:	Sandra's getting sixteen a week at the hairdressers, plus thirty-seven is fifty-three plus overtime—hey, we might be able to live.
MR MACONOCHIE:	Don't count your chickens. Would you come out, then, son? No strike money, no National Assistance . . .
WILLY:	Of course I'll come out—Christ, what do you take me for? You've got us lads wrong, Mr Maconochie.

MR MACONOCHIE: Have I?
                  (*Lights change.* YORRY *comes on dressed as young student militant.*)
          YORRY: (*To imaginary group of students*) Comrades! The time has come for the working-class of this country to hurl off the yoke of centuries of oppression and degradation. But how can they, seduced as they are by the momentary improvements in their standard of living, blinded as they are by the dubious joys of television and the lies of the bourgeois press, unless we, the student vanguard, go down and open their eyes and turn their struggles for wages into struggles that raise the ultimate question—the question of political power? They must rise up, force the sleepy heads of the TUC into calling a General Strike, now, and bring down this shameful, corrupt government of money-lenders and march into Whitehall tomorrow holding the reigns of the power-machine, grabbing capitalism by the throat and demanding Power for the People!
                  (*To audience*) After a childhood and youth spent in mortal terror of a worker so much as knocking on the door, I had suddenly clutched their cause to my bosom with all the fervour of Hercules holding up the sky on his back while Atlas went off to do the dirty work for him. Meanwhile, in reality . . .
                  (WILLY *on his own at the machine. Enter* MR MACONOCHIE)
MR MACONOCHIE: Right. That's it, then.
          WILLY: What?
MR MACONOCHIE: Robertson's refused point blank. Not a minute off the day, not a penny on the pay.
          WILLY: I've heard that before somewhere.
MR MACONOCHIE: Well stop working, can't you?
          WILLY: What for?
MR MACONOCHIE: We're coming out on strike, you daft git.
          WILLY: Great. Can't I just put this rod into the works before we go?
MR MACONOCHIE: We need those machines for when we come back. Come on.
                  (*They go off.* YORRY, *looking even tougher and more intransigent, comes on, mounts imaginary rostrum.*)
          YORRY: Comrades, the hour draws near. As the historical crisis of British imperialism matures to the point of irresistible conflict, every so-called debate in parliament becomes in fact a dialogue between the Tory and Labour bankrupts on how to meet the resistance of the working class most effectively. There is no doubt, there can be no doubt at all that the Don Quixotes of Toryism would long ago have impaled themselves on the windmills of working-class militancy if it weren't for the Sancho Panzas of reformism.

(*To audience*) The language was getting a bit more fancy every time I opened my mouth. The funny thing was, the more I said, the more powerful I became as a champion of the workers, the further I got away from them. Christ, even behind the locked doors of my childhood at least I had a relationship with the working class: pure terror. At this time in my life the working class was no longer a lot of people I lived in the middle of and inescapably knew: it was an object of pure fantasy. It came to replace the moon of my teenage poetry. And like the moon, it was a long way off. And like the moon, the distant contemplation of it drove men mad.

(WILLY *and* MR MACONOCHIE *come back to machine, start work.*)

WILLY: Ah, well, twenty-nine pounds fifty then.

MR MACONOCHIE: It's a step in the right direction. We have not been defeated. And there'll be plenty of overtime this week.

(ANDY *comes on in full Rangers supporters' gear, with* MARY: *he sings 'The Blue Billy Boys', the Rangers supporters' version of the song:*)

> We are the people
> Who sing of victory
> And tell of football glory from Kilmarnock to Dundee
> We follow Glasgow Rangers
> Our hearts are strong and true
> We are the people who cheer the boys in blue.
> A goal
> A goal
> We're ready to acclaim
> A goal
> A goal
> To win another game
> We follow Glasgow Rangers
> Our hearts are strong and true
> We are the people who cheer the boys in blue.

(*At the end of the song:*)

MARY: You do know it's Liverpool playing Chelsea, I suppose.

ANDY: Ach. Jesus, I'm wasting my time coming down here weekends.

MARY: Are you?

ANDY: Liverpool playing Chelsea: I tell you what, sweetheart, next Saturday, right, you come up to Glasgow.

MARY: What for?

ANDY: Rangers playing Celtic. The Battle of the Boyne all over again. Do you know every Orangeman in Ulster will be praying for Rangers' supporters—to kick the Papists' heads in.

MARY: You kicking for Rangers, then?

ANDY: Ever since I was strong enough to break a bottle.

MARY: It's a long way to go to watch a football match—besides, I can't afford it.

ANDY: Hitchhike.

MARY: Look, if you want to see me, you come down here. If you don't, stop in Glasgow. (*She starts to go.*)

ANDY: Mary, come here. (*Grabs her*) You and me, we've got to have each other.

MARY: Have we? You seem more interested in bloody football, and beating up your wife's boyfriend. Not to mention getting drunk and getting your head kicked in. Why can't you calm down a bit?

ANDY: Hey, this mate of mine I'm staying with: he's away out to the match. There'll be nobody in his room, and I've got the key.

MARY: So?

ANDY: (*Sings*)
 Will ye go, lassie, go,
 And we'll all go together,
 To pull wild mountain thyme,
 All among the blooming heather.
 Will ye go, lassie, go?

MARY: Couldn't we just go for a walk?

ANDY: Come ben the hoose, girl. In from the cold. Kindle our own fires.

MARY: Andy, I don't know you. And I don't trust you.

ANDY: You and me, girl, we know each other.

MARY: You keep on saying that, but it's not true—you don't even know what I work at, do you?

ANDY: What do you work at?

MARY: You're kidding yourself.

ANDY: Tell me, and I'll know.

MARY: No. You wouldn't know anything.

ANDY: Ach, Jesus, let's get to the match then.

MARY: I'm going home.

ANDY: Don't do that, Mary.

MARY: (*Suddenly savage*) Why not? You're mad. Completely mad. And if I stick around with you much longer, they'll be carting *me* off, not you. You can manage, can't you, you can get away with it—well I can't.

ANDY: If you go, chicken, I'm done for. You're my only hope.

MARY: Do you think I want to spend the rest of my life dragging you home pissed and battered? Do you think I'd have any hope left, after a year of you? I can't take it, Andy, I'm not strong enough. Every Saturday night for the last three months I've had to carry you out of some bloody back alley covered in blood—who do you think you're fighting? Why do you always pick big fellers, with half a dozen mates to help them? What the bloody hell's the matter with you? Are you trying to get yourself killed or what?

ANDY: I don't mind, killed, what difference does that make, to me, to you, to anybody? OK, chicken. Cheerio. Off you go, keep the change. I'll manage fine. Just fine. I've got one or two ideas that'll keep my mind occupied. My brother's got a job he needs me for, over in Belfast, and by Christ, he's pretty keen to have me—don't worry, you go off and find some feller that's nice and calm. You marry him, and lock him up, and you take him apart, because that's what you'll do, no bother. I'll go off and do what I've got to do—go where I'm needed.
(*She hesitates, worried, now not wanting to go.*)
Away you go, and don't ever forget: you can't tell lies to your own self and get away with it.
(*The band plays a quiet Scottish tune.* MARY *goes.*)
(*During the first verse of the tune,* ANDY *strips off all the Rangers' stuff he's wearing. The song is about a man going for a soldier. He ends up wearing the UDA-type combat-jacket he had on underneath. Then he gets out the peaked cap and dark glasses, tucks his trousers into his boots, and another six or seven men dressed the same way come on, a regular UDA contingent. The music has now become big and militarist. The UDA men break into the chorus of the Rangers song 'A Goal, A Goal' etc. At the end of the song, one of the others gives* ANDY *a gun.*)
Right, lads, what's doing?
(*They all go off.*)
(MR MACONOCHIE, WILLY *and* YORRY *come on.*)

MR MACONOCHIE: Bits and pieces of what was happening to us.

WILLY: We'd got no idea where they were going, where we were going. We weren't going anywhere. Nothing, actually, was happening.

MR MACONOCHIE: My lad joining the police. Mary's feller getting the push, going to Ireland to support the Rangers.

YORRY: Me, zooming off into a student's fantasyland.

WILLY: Me, supposed to be settling down. Preparing to be a dutiful husband.

YORRY: Then, one day, I decided quite suddenly to stop having fantasies, and do something. (*The other TWO go off.*) In the middle of last year I got overpoweringly sick of the endless abstractions and rubbishy rhetoric of a university full of middle-class kids training to inherit the reins, and the whip of society—there I go again, I really must stop it—and to piss off out of it and do an honest day's work. I never was going to benefit greatly from the further study of French and German, anyway. I went home to tell my dad.
(*The* REV TEIFIAN GRIFFITHS *enters in a towering rage.* DAFYDD *watches with interest. They are in the* REV'S *study.*)

REV GRIFFITHS: Work? A day's work?

YORRY: That's right. Get a job.

REV GRIFFITHS: I've never had the misfortune to come across anything so blind stupid in the whole of my experience.

YORRY: What's wrong with work, Dad?

REV GRIFFITHS: What exact description of work do you imagine yourself to be suitable for?

YORRY: There's factories in Kirkby. Docks. Warehouses. There's the new motorway.

REV GRIFFITHS: And for that you throw up the university, you hurl to the winds the gift of intelligence and application that the Lord God has given you, you cancel out the years of doing without, that your Uncle Dafydd and I myself have endured to see you through to a comfortable future and your rightful place in society?

YORRY: I haven't got a rightful place in society.

REV GRIFFITHS: I swore to your mother as she lay dying that you, boy, would have every advantage in life that my hard work, sacrifice and diligence could afford, and now you jettison, you have jettisoned, all that hope, all that struggle. Those were your mother's dying wishes, Iorwerth: are you, in all solemnity, prepared to defile them?

YORRY: I've had the opportunities, Dad. You've held your side of the bargain. I've learnt a great deal. All of it is telling me to get out and work and live like the ordinary people.

REV GRIFFITHS: So that's what these modern universities have taught you, is it?

YORRY: No. That's what I've learnt. They're supposed to teach you to be curious about life and involved in it: that's what I want.

REV GRIFFITHS: Building motorways? In factories? Never.

YORRY: That's what I'm going to do, Dad.

REV GRIFFITHS: Never.
                (*They stand staring at each other, with violence very near.*)
                I had rather die than see my wife's son turn into no better than a low-class navvy.

YORRY: The future of this country belongs to the working class. They cannot remain forever the object of the exploiting forces of society. They must take their destiny, and the country's future into their own hands. I commit myself to that future, and to their place in it.

REV GRIFFITHS: You spit on your mother's grave. You will suffer for it.
                (*He turns and goes.* YORRY *turns to* DAFYDD.)

YORRY: You were right about Christians, Dafydd.

DAFYDD: Greatest catastrophe to reach these shores, Yorry. Followed a long way behind, by the bubonic plague, and American moneymen.

YORRY: Was my mother as bigoted as that?

DAFYDD: He's using her. All those promises, he made them. She never asked him to. And she was too sick to argue. All her

life he crushed her, even on her deathbed. She never
argued.

YORRY: I wish I'd known her.

DAFYDD: Her life wasn't entirely black. You gave her great joy. And
before that—I shouldn't be telling you this.

YORRY: Tell me.

DAFYDD: Well, you know: she and I, had some moments of pleasure,
together. I like to think they made her life worth living. For
twenty years, on and off. He never knew her. She was small,
and dark, and secretive. A passionate, romantic woman,
brought up to religion, stunted by fear of a wrathful God
the Father. But nothing could totally destroy her. Nothing
can totally destroy any woman. Their being is inside them,
they can protect it. Ours hangs out, and is easier to snip off.
She would have understood you, don't let that twisted old
misery use her against you. Besides—ah well.

YORRY: What?

DAFYDD: Nothing. I'm a romantic old man, full of a Wales that is
dead and long gone. You want the future. Take it.
(YORRY *looks at him.*)
The future. The struggle. Young women. Music. Poetry.
Achievements. I envy you. (*Laughs*) I've never envied
anybody ever before. I always thought I had all the secrets
locked inside me, warm and flourishing, like passion fruit
in a greenhouse. But the roots are dry, the branches are
withering, and nobody ever picked the fruit.
(*Silence. The doorbell rings.*)
Oh God, not another visiting preacher.
(*He gets up and goes.* YORRY *looks after him.*)

YORRY: I wondered why he was living with us.
(*Enter* DAFYDD *with* WILLY *and* SANDRA, *her all smart and
sober.*)
Hello, Willy—don't say you've forgotten Tyn-y-Gongl?

WILLY: Yorry, is it? This is Sandra—er, Yorry.

SANDRA: Hello.

YORRY: I remember Sandra.

SANDRA: Do you?

YORRY: And Fiona. And Mary.

DAFYDD: What brings you into the house of God—looking for
salvation?

WILLY: No. We—we're thinking of getting married.

DAFYDD: Thinking about it?

WILLY: Well, we are, actually: we've come to see Mr Griffiths.
Sandra wants to get married in church, and this is the
nearest.

DAFYDD: The nearest to God?

WILLY: No, the nearest to their house.

SANDRA: I'm coming in a car, though, Willy—don't think I'm walking
to my own wedding just because it's at the top of the street.

DAFYDD: Have you broached the subject with Mr Griffiths yet?

WILLY: No. We had an appointment. Tonight.

DAFYDD: Oh. I see. Well, Teifian's been given cause to rush off into the black night. But—have you ever been in that miserable dump?

WILLY: The chapel? No.

DAFYDD: Well first of all, if you haven't so much as been inside the chapel in the whole of your life, I very much doubt whether Teifian won't think it virtual desecration to let you use it just as a background for your fancy-dress wedding, cars, or no cars—he's pretty strict Baptist, you know.

WILLY: Well I did go to the camp with the Youth Club.

DAFYDD: Worse and worse. The second thing is that if I were you I'd go and have a look at it quick, in case he says yes. I wouldn't want to celebrate anything in that barren hovel except a screech owl's funeral. But don't let me put you off.

SANDRA: But I thought churches were *for* weddings.

DAFYDD: Churches? Weddings? No—a sacred grove of ash trees on a grassy hillside in spring, with the pale-green leaves hallowing the sunlight, there, a flat-topped stone must be dressed with buds and blossoms and all the wild flowers of May, and the young branches of those trees which are special for constancy and fruitfulness; all around you, your people, solemn but smiling, anxious and glad, and above you and all around you, the small birds singing. At night, music, dancing, and the thin moon. That's what's for weddings.

WILLY: It'll have to be the Registry Office, then.

DAFYDD: Next best thing to an ash grove, Willy.

SANDRA: I'm not getting married in the Registry Office.

WILLY: Why not?

SANDRA: Because I've promised all the girls in the salon a bloody rotten church, that's why not—can't you organise *anything*, Willy? Oh God, what am I doing getting married to you?

WILLY: Not much option, have we, love?

SANDRA: Do you *have* to bring that up right now? I was hoping to get away with a white wedding, too, if we got a move on.

DAFYDD: You could try the Unitarians, they're not fussy. But you don't get any trimmings.

WILLY: Are you sure he won't do us here?

DAFYDD: Strictly Baptist is strictly Baptist. I tell no lies.

SANDRA: I've gone off it. The whole thing. Come on, Willy, before he comes back.

WILLY: What do you mean, gone off it?

SANDRA: Come on, let's get out quick.

WILLY: (*To* YORRY *and* DAFYDD) Looks as if we're going . . .

YORRY: Willy, I'd like to have a chat with you one of these days.

WILLY: Sure. How's the university?

YORRY: I've left. Couldn't stand it. I want to come back here, get a job, and do a bit of living.

SANDRA: Get a job? How you going to manage that, then?

YORRY: That's what I want to talk to Willy about.

SANDRA: Him? If it hadn't been for my dad he'd still be waiting for the snow to fall so he cold get a job sweeping it up.

WILLY: It's a bad time, Yorry, but if you're determined, anyway. You've got qualifications, you could get teaching jobs, office jobs.

YORRY: Don't want them. I've decided to join the working class.

WILLY: That's easy, the difficult bit's getting the work.

YORRY: Perhaps I could come round and see your father. I'd like to—er, see the rest of your family, some time, if possible.

SANDRA: Really? Perhaps you'd better come round then.

YORRY: Thanks.

SANDRA: Do you know where we live?

YORRY: Er—yes.

SANDRA: Oh.

YORRY: Can I come round tomorrow night?

SANDRA: Alright. (*Smiling*) See you there.

YORRY: Yes. See you, Willy.

WILLY: (*Astounded*) Yeh. Take it easy, then, son.
(*They go.*)

DAFYDD: (*Sighs*) Nobody wants trees anymore. Chop 'em all down. Cover the hills with spruce and larch and quick-growing evergreens from Norway. Plant them close together so they won't grow branches, a forest of telegraph poles, and industrial hillside. There's nothing magical about spruce, no groves: just row after row of invested capital. But the old trees *will* come back: the earth turns, and will go on turning.

YORRY: Do you fancy going out for a drink?

DAFYDD: A drink?

YORRY: You know—a pint.

DAFYDD: Well now, Yorry—that would be a revolution. I'm not sure Teifian would survive the fumes. Hee hee. A drink.

YORRY: Come on then.

DAFYDD: (*Capers about like a schoolboy, then stops.*) Here, I've got a packet of peppermints in my best suit pocket—I think I'd best nip up and get them.

YORRY: Leave them, Uncle Dafydd.

DAFYDD: Yes?

YORRY: Come on, only half an hour to closing time.
(DAFYDD *capers off with* YORRY, *but a bit apprehensive.*)
(MARY *and* FIONA *coming from work cross the front of the stage.* VINCE *comes the other way.*)

VINCE: Hello, girls.

MARY: Hello, Vince.
           (*He goes on. Stops*)
VINCE: Hey, Fiona.
FIONA: What?
VINCE: Not saying hello?
FIONA: Aw, creep off, Vince.
VINCE: Here.
FIONA: What?
VINCE: I want a word with you.
           (FIONA *sighs and goes over, leaving* MARY *alone.*)
FIONA: What word do you want to have, then? As if I couldn't
           guess.
VINCE: It begins with a Y.
FIONA: Yeh, why am I bothering . . .
VINCE: No, why have you gone off me?
FIONA: I've gone off men, the whole creeping lot of you.
VINCE: That's unnatural.
FIONA: Do you think?
VINCE: But.
FIONA: But what?
VINCE: You know—I'm quite keen.
FIONA: I know what you're keen on, and it's not my fantastic
           intellect, either.
VINCE: No. I'm serious about you. I'm dead choked you won't see
           me any more
MARY: Eh, Fiona, I'm freezing here.
FIONA: I'm getting colder and colder myself. Tata, Vince.
VINCE: Aw, don't go off, let me tell you . . .
           (*He puts his arm round her and starts to whisper urgently.*
           MARY *paces up and down.*)
MARY: Men. Think all they've got to do is put their arm round
           you, breathe their stinking breath up your nose, whisper a
           few corny phrases, fumble for your tits, and bingo, you'll
           satisfy their every whim. Once that's all over, and you're
           lumbered with them for life, all you've got is cooking and
           washing and ironing—you're supposed to be a lovely,
           warm, kind person that everybody loves—mum. Mum's
           the word.
           (*On the centre of the stage, the* MACONOCHIES' *living room
           is set up. Enter* MRS MACONOCHIE *mashing potatoes,
           looking at the clock.*)
MRS MACONOCHIE: Mash, you buggers, mash. If I'd put you on ten minutes
           earlier you'd just melt, wouldn't you? I ought to give 'em
           that powder potato, they'd never notice the difference
           except some nosey parker'd find the packet in the bin and
           suddenly scream they'd been poisoned. One thing about
           having babies inside you, at least you stuff down yourself
           what *you* fancy, and they can't complain: but once they cut
           that cord—oh mother, they never stop letting you know.

FIONA: (*On front of stage*) Tata, Vince.

VINCE: Alright, then?

FIONA: Well, I'll think about it. Tata.

MARY: Conned again?

FIONA: Yeh, conned again.

(*They go off.* MRS MACONOCHIE *scrutinises the potatoes.*)

MRS MACONOCHIE: You take a person. You peel her off. You cook her till she's all soft. You drain her off. (*Viciously*) Then you mash her. (*Enter* MARY *and* FIONA. FIONA *goes straight to a chair and starts reading, says 'hello, Ma', as she slides her eye over the table.* MARY *takes the pot.*)

MARY: Here, give us that. The way you mash potatoes, you'll do yourself an injury.

MRS MACONOCHIE: I've mashed more potatoes—

MARY: Than I've had hot dinners, I know. No sign of Dad then?

MRS MACONOCHIE: No, thank the Lord, he's late.

MARY: Sandra's just gone to the paper shop to see if *Young Married* magazine's arrived. She just can't wait that girl.

FIONA: You can say that again.

MRS MACONOCHIE: (*To* FIONA) You shift your bum, there's half-a-dozen hamburger steaks on the pan, turn them over.

FIONA: Not that muck again.

MRS MACONOCHIE: Can't afford meat, love. Not now. The animals have changed their diet.

MARY: What?

MRS MACONOCHIE: Well the price of grass hasn't gone up, has it—they must be feeding them on five pound notes. (*Enter* SANDRA. *Exit* FIONA)

SANDRA: What a little hive of industry.

MARY: Here, they're done.

SANDRA: Good, I'm starving.

MRS MACONOCHIE: Well you can butter some bread for everybody. (MRS MACONOCHIE *goes.*)

SANDRA: (*To audience*) I'm getting married in two or three weeks.

MARY: I don't want any of this. I'm trained for it. I'd be good at it. But I want something violent, short-lived and dangerous. (FIONA *comes in with knives and forks, sits at table and stares at them.*)

FIONA: Conned again. I thought I'd demolished that Vince. He must be impervious. I'm getting colder and colder. I feel like I'm on a bus going the wrong way, and I keep ringing the bell, and it won't stop—and I'm too scared to jump off.

SANDRA: Here, a woman came in today, and started doing yoga under the drier.

MARY: Must have gone to her head—ha ha.

SANDRA: She crossed her legs up under her armpits and went into a trance. We were scared to disturb her in case she jumped on to the wrong psychic plane: that's what Leonard said, anyway.

MARY: So what did you do?

SANDRA: We turned the drier off and left her.

MARY: Did she come round?

SANDRA: No. She's still there, locked in the shop. Leonard said we must leave her at that depth until the spirits aroused her or it might be fatal. And he left her a note with his phone number on, in case she comes round before tomorrow morning. And a couple of biscuits.

(*Music comes in: the girls sing:*)
> Drifting
> Drifting
>
> Anyway
> The wind blows
>
> Any way
> The tide runs
>
> Drifting
> Drifting on the breeze . . .
>
> Storms come
> Storms go
>
> Wild waves
> Calm seas
>
> Drifting
> Drifting.

SANDRA: (*Speaks*) I'm getting married in two or three weeks.

FIONA AND MARY: (*Sing together*)
> Any way
> The wind blows
>
> Any way
> The tide runs
>
> Drifting
> Drifting.

MARY: I want something violent, short-lived and dangerous. A clash, a batter, a hard bit of loving, and away. But where to?

FIONA AND SANDRA: (*Sing together*)
> Storms come
> Storms go
> Wild waves
> Calm seas.

FIONA: I'm on a bus going the wrong way, and I keep ringing the bell, and it won't stop—and I'm scared to jump off.

ALL:
> Drifting
> Drifting

FIONA: I'm shrivelling up inside, and I shouldn't be. I feel I've got a limp and a broken arm, and a steel corset on. I'm going to keep quite still, and see if I melt away.

ALL: Drifting
            Drifting . . .

MARY: No man's going to run my life. I'm travelling on my
            own—but where am I going?

ALL: Drifting
            Drifting
            Anyway
            The wind blows
            Any way
            The tide flows.
            (*Enter* MRS MACONOCHIE)

MRS MACONOCHIE: Trouble with you lot is you don't know what you want.
            You spend half your life chasing fellers, and the other half
            moaning 'cos you caught one. Where's your independence?
            Where's your dignity? (*Jumps*) Oh hell—here's your dad.
            (*She rushes into the kitchen.*)

FIONA: Somebody with him.
            (MR MACONOCHIE *and* WILLY *come in from work, nod at
            the girls, and sit.* MRS MACONOCHIE *comes in with one
            plate.*)

MRS MACONOCHIE: Now isn't that funny, Willy, something told me to get six.
            (*Looks at them and at the girls looking at them.*) What's
            up with you two then?
            (*MUSIC ends*)

MR MACONOCHIE: We're out on strike again.

SANDRA: Oh no.

WILLY: Yes, love. Nothing else to be done.

MR MACONOCHIE: We were due to get the pay rise today, the one we had the
            last strike over. Pay packets exactly the same as last week.
            Except they had a little note in them, saying: Dear
            Employee, As from yesterday this enterprise is under the
            control of Consolidated Metals of America, Inc, whom I
            am sure you will serve with the same loyalty and devotion
            as you have served me. For the moment they find
            themselves unable to ratify our most recent pay
            agreements, so for the time being they would ask you
            to accept wages at their normal rate. I wish you all
            much happiness under the new management, Yours
            F. Robertson.

MARY: They can't do that.

MR MACONOCHIE: They've done it.

WILLY: (*To* SANDRA) We had to come out, love. I'm sorry.

MR MACONOCHIE: And it looks like being a long one.
            (SANDRA *looks horrified, her wedding plans all
            overthrown, she rushes out of the room in tears.*)

WILLY: We can still get married, Sand.
            (*But she's gone.*)
            We could just have a longer honeymoon.

MRS MACONOCHIE: What, down the Sally Army hostel?

MR MACONOCHIE: You'd better go and talk to her, Willy. She's a good girl, just a bit disappointed, that's all.

MRS MACONOCHIE: Oh, leave her and have some dinner—it's been waiting hours.

WILLY: I'll just go up for a minute then—if you don't mind.

MRS MACONOCHIE: Suit yourself. Your dinner'll go cold before she will, though.

(WILLY *goes.*)

(*Music in:*)

Fish in the Sea

Little sharks
In the sea
Live on fish
Like you and me
As we glide
All around
And we hear
Not a sound
Through the strange
Green light
We move left
We move right
The Fish in the Sea
The Fish in the Sea.

MRS MACONOCHIE: Will you eat this, then?

MR MACONOCHIE: I'm sorry, love, I don't feel like anything.

MRS MACONOCHIE: It can't be that bad.

MR MACONOCHIE: You don't understand, love. We could squeeze old Robertson in a couple of weeks. He had nothing behind him, nothing coming in anywhere else. This lot have got billions of dollars, factories all over the country, all over the world. It could take months. If we push too hard they could close us down altogether. Don't tell her—(SANDRA)—that. She'd have hysterics. But it's on the cards.

(*Song part two:*)

Bigger sharks
In the night
Swallow up
With one bite
The little sharks
In the sea
That live on fish
Like you and me
In the strange green light
We move left
We move right
The Fish in the Sea
The Fish in the Sea.

MRS MACONOCHIE: So what are you going to do?

MR MACONOCHIE: We've done it. Had a mass meeting, tonight after work.
Strike now, talk later. But I've got a terrible feeling they've
got us by the short and curlies.
(Song picks up, stronger)
> We're gonna get together
> Get a harpoon gun
> We're gonna find a shoal of sharks
> And make them run.
>
> Don't wanna mess around
> With a baited line,
> Too late to stand and wait
> Till the weather looks fine.
> We're gonna drive them from the sea
> We're gonna live a life that's free.
> For all the, all the, all the fish in the sea.
> That's you and me
> That's you and me.

(The others come on, join in.)

MR MACONOCHIE
AND FIONA: We're gonna hunt the killers
Till they run away
We'll drive them all together
To Montego Bay.

> We'll light a stick of dynamite
> And throw it in
> BANG BANG brothers,
> What a beautiful din.

ALL: We're gonna drive them from the sea
We're gonna live a life that's free.
For all the, all the, all the fish in the sea,
That's you and me.
That's you and me.
The Fish in the Sea.

GIRLS: Little sharks
In the sea
Live on fish
Like you and me

MEN: We're gonna get together
Get a harpoon gun
We're gonna find a shoal of sharks
And make them run

GIRLS: Bigger sharks
In the night
Swallow up
With one bite

MEN: We're gonna hunt the killers
Till they run away
We'll drive them all together
To Montego Bay

GIRLS: As we glide
All around
And we hear
Not a sound
The Fish in the Sea

ALL: We're gonna drive them from the sea
We're gonna live a life that's free
For all the, all the, all the fish in the sea
That's you and me,
That's you and me.

(*Enter* YORRY, *all keen.*)

YORRY: I hear you're coming out on strike: is it official?

MR MACONOCHIE: It will be.

WILLY: It better had be.

YORRY: Do you stand a chance of winning? I mean, Consolidated Metals of America turns out to be wholly owned by the American Steel Corporation, the most powerful organisation in the world.

MR MACONOCHIE: Bigger sharks
Without fail
Are just food
For a whale
In the far-off
Arctic Seas
They eat sharks
When they please
And the sharks
Had for tea
Little fish
Like you and me
The Fish in the Sea
The Fish in the Sea

ALL: We'd better get together
And destroy those whales
Get a lot of little fish
And twist their tails
Rip them up the middle,
Peel off all the fat,
Slice them up in pieces
Throw the pieces to the cat
We're gonna drive them from the sea
We're gonna live a life that's free
For all the, all the, all the fish in the sea
That's you and me
That's you and me.

We're gonna hunt the killers
Till they run away
We'll drive them all together

To Montego Bay
We'll light a stick of dynamite
And throw it in
BANG BANG brothers
What a beautiful din
We're gonna drive them from the sea
We're gonna live a life that's free
For all the, all the, all the fish in the sea
That's you and me
That's you and me.

END OF ACT 1

ACT *2*

(As *the audience come in from the interval, the band*
play a number.)

We're Only the Band

Seen them come, seen them go,
We know more than they think we know,
We watch them dance too fast, too slow,
We wouldn't mind being at a picture-show,
'Cos we're only the Band
Yes, we're only The Band
Some of us are happy and the rest of us are canned,
'Cos we're only the Band.
We slide a look, corner of the eye,
Catch a little laugh, catch a little cry,
See a little spider, catch a little fly,
Feel a little sad but we don't know why
'Cos we're only the Band
Yes, we're only the Band
Some of us are happy and the rest of us are canned,
'Cos we're only the Band.
We're supposed to be the show,
But you don't know Oh no no,
You see us, but we see you,
In the end, the show is you—
Take your partner by the hand
Dance to the music of the band,
Treat her nice, good and true,
All the time we're watching you—
'Cos we're only the Band
Yes, we're only the Band
Some of us are happy and the rest of us are canned,
'Cos we're only the Band.

(*The* MACONOCHIE *living room. The same as end of Act 1.*
YORRY *steps out to audience.*)

YORRY: Suddenly I found myself in the presence of a real, live
strike: sitting in the heart of a family of strikers. The great
names of the past resounded in my ears, Lenin, Trotsky,
Rosa Luxemburg, Gramsci, the Petrograd Workers'
Councils, Connolly, the Wobblies, Joe Hill; the events of
Paris in sixty-eight seemed about to blossom into a
genuinely worker-based uprising on my very doorstep. The
theoretical outpourings of my university days, all,
suddenly, seemed about to move into vital living
relationship with a real struggle. The point of praxis had
been reached. Unfortunately nobody else seemed very
excited about it.
(*He turns back into the Scene.*)

SANDRA: It's all very well you going on about overthrowing
capitalism, Yorry, but I've got to get married.

WILLY: That's no reason for calling off the strike, love.

MR MACONOCHIE: She wants a posh wedding: I've just been on strike for four
weeks, and now we're out for God knows how long: I
can't afford a pair of shoes, let alone a posh wedding.

YORRY: Surely the strike is to work towards a happier married
life.

SANDRA: I don't want a married life, I want a wedding. And not in
any trees, neither. In a church, with cars, and a reception.

MARY: And presents.

MR MACONOCHIE: (*To* SANDRA) Why can't you just have a quiet splice in the
Registry Office and come back here for a bit of a do—
what's wrong with that?

SANDRA: Are you serious?

MRS MACONOCHIE: Listen, miss, when I married him it was a toss-up between
a fish-supper for all or ham sandwiches. And we went to
church by tram.

SANDRA: That was bloody wartime.

MRS MACONOCHIE: It worked, though, didn't it?

WILLY: I don't mind, Sandra.

SANDRA: Well I do.

MR MACONOCHIE: But you don't *need* cars and receptions—you've been
reading too many daft magazines.

SANDRA: We *need* somewhere to live.

MRS MACONOCHIE: You can live here till you get sorted out.

SANDRA: How can we?

MRS MACONOCHIE: Mary can sleep down here, there's a perfectly good settee.
And it won't be for long.

MARY: Oh no, just when I was going to get a room to myself.
What if I go on strike?

WILLY: And I move in? That should be interesting.

SANDRA: Parents. You give up the best years of your life for them,
and what do you get at the end of it?

MR MACONOCHIE: Well what else can we do?
                 (*Silence.* YORRY *steps out again.*)
      YORRY: It all seemed so far from the spirit of nineteen hundred
               and five, and nineteen seventeen. I thought about Ché
               Guevara in the Bolivian jungle, of the Chinese of the Long
               March, of Gramsci dying in prison: it didn't seem to be
               the same universe. At one point it looked as if they were
               going to go back to work and suffer defeat at the hands of
               the American imperialists, so their Sandra could have a
               white wedding.

Sandra's Song

She wants her white wedding and
She wants her white wedding ring
And all of the nuptial joy she can get
Bridesmaids and wedding-cars
Honeymoons with cocktail-bars
And a set of wedding-photographs so she won't forget.

She wants tea sets and tablemats
She wants saucepans and tablecloths
And all of the candlesticks that money can buy
Alarm clocks and pillowslips
Telegrams and taxi-trips
And a set of wedding-photographs so they can't deny

That one day she was a bride
Radiant, and beautiful, and trim
And once he stood by her side
No other man as handsome as him.

For since she was a girl in pigtails
They told her that this was her day:
Her magazines, her picture-shows, her horoscopes
All told her: They can't take this away . . .

And she knows very well that as time goes by,
She'll need to have something to remember:
For May's not important in June or July—
But it shines very bright in November—

So she wants her white wedding and
She wants her right wedding ring
And all of the nuptial joy she can get
Bridesmaids and wedding-cars
Honeymoons and cocktail-bars,
And a set of wedding-photographs so she won't forget:
And a set of wedding photographs
So she
Won't
Forget.

WILLY: (*Moving out of scene*) But we didn't go back to work. And Sandra compromised: she wore an off-white satin suit, and went to the Registry Office by taxi, and we got the back room at the 'Legs of Man', where you could buy your own beer and they let Mrs Maconochie bring her own sandwiches and trifles in paper cases, and the lads had a whip-round for us and somehow scraped up forty quid, and it brought tears to my eyes. If anything made me determined, that was it. Even Sandra felt a bit different after that.

MR MACONOCHIE: I cut the grass three times a week, trimmed the hedge till there was nothing left to trim, cleaned the windows, swept the chimney. I got so demoralised I even started doing the cooking, only bacon and eggs, mind, nothing fancy: didn't want to make the wife redundant or anything. And that Yorry kept coming round for a chat. He'd certainly read a few books.

(YORRY, MARY, WILLY, SANDRA *and* MR *and* MRS MACONOCHIE *in living room. Evening.*)

YORRY: Basically Bernstein thought he could revive Marx: I suppose for two reasons: one, because obviously capitalism had started operating with a bit more subtlety, and was giving far more concessions to the organised working class in the way of wages and fringe benefits, and secondly, because it looked as if the whole working class was getting the vote at elections. On a simple numerical calculation, Bernstein reckoned that there were more workers than bosses, so the revolution would immediately come at the next General Election. But Marx knew all about those developments, of course. As Rosa Luxemburg clearly pointed out, better wages don't alter the basic structure of capitalist society, with one class exploiting the labour of another, accumulating more and more capital from the profit. Equally, as Gramsci showed time and time again, the bourgeois state would never open its institutions, like parliament, to the masses, unless it had already converted those institutions into means of repressing the masses. Bernstein was fundamentally using devious, and wrong, arguments to re-write Marx because he was terrified of revolution. And from his fear and that of the corrupt Second International, sprang all the Western social democratic parties that have divided the working class of Europe, bolstered up the power of capital, and screwed up revolution ever since: from Ebert in Germany, who allowed Rosa Luxemburg to be clubbed to death with a rifle-butt, to Harold Wilson and the Labour Party: who are capable of far, far worse.

MR MACONOCHIE: So you think revolution's the only way, Yorry?

YORRY: It doesn't have to be violent: but the capitalists won't let go of power without killing a few people, so a few of them will probably have to get killed before they stop. Of course, at the moment they can talk about moderation, and peace, and respect for law and order because it's their laws and their order, and they're winning. Just let us begin to get organised and really worry them: they'll show teeth like crocodiles and get up to every evil trick in the book.

WILLY: It's nineteen seventy-four now, Yorry, things have changed.

YORRY: Yes, now Bernstein's dead, and we've got Wedgwood Benn: all he's doing is buying stocks and shares, keeping the same old bosses, and trying to turn socialism into a capitalist enterprise.
(*A knock on the door.* MR MACONOCHIE *looks at his watch and goes to see who it is.*)

MARY: Who's going to do all this revolution then, Yorry—my dad?

YORRY: Why not? And you, and me, and Willy.

SANDRA: And me. I feel like having a go at somebody these days. Why can't they just pay the extra and get these fellers back to work?

MRS MACONOCHIE: Hear, hear. They're driving me mad, the pair of them. Useless. That one—(WILLY)—spent two hours today peeling three pounds of potatoes. And when I looked in the pot, there was three tiny little round things, like lentil beans, nestling away at the bottom. And two and a half pounds of peelings in the sink.

WILLY: I can't stand spuds with eyes in them.

MRS MACONOCHIE: Well, you blinded these alright.
(*Re-enter* MR MACONOCHIE)
Who was it?

MR MACONOCHIE: Arthur, the convenor.

MRS MACONOCHIE: Wouldn't he come in?

MR MACONOCHIE: No. He was dashing around everybody. Willy, we're to go in at half past seven in the morning. Meet quietly in Jackson Street.

SANDRA: Going back—thank God for that.

MR MACONOCHIE: No. Well not exactly.

MRS MACONOCHIE: What then?

MR MACONOCHIE: It's supposed to be kept dark.

MRS MACONOCHIE: Well I'm not going to telephone New York—what?

MR MACONOCHIE: Apparently one of the lads was playing football on that patch at the back of the works. He saw some blokes going in.

MRS MACONOCHIE: Scabs?

MR MACONOCHIE: He went and had a squint in. They were dismantling the machinery, getting it ready for moving out.

WILLY: Jesus.

MR MACONOCHIE: They already had that big press on rollers, all set to load on a trailer.

WILLY: They can't do that.

MR MACONOCHIE: They're doing it. Or they think they are. We're meeting round the corner, all two hundred of us. Then a couple of lads'll knock on the door, and when they open it, we'll all be just behind them and move in. Sling out the manager, and put fresh padlocks on the doors. Then if they want to move the plant, they'll have to move us. The days when those bastards could treat us like idiots are over.

SANDRA: Won't the police come and arrest you? That's private property, that factory.

MR MACONOCHIE: The Upper Clyde blokes took over their works and the rozzers wouldn't go near them.

WILLY: Yeh, but it *is* their property.

YORRY: That factory is your property, Willy. They may have coughed up the capital, but that's been paid back time and time again, by *you*. The profit they've made out of you over the years could have bought half a dozen factories.

SANDRA: Some of them work there, too, you know.

MR MACONOCHIE: Right, so they can come and join us—and stop mucking us about—tomorrow morning, at eight o'clock, when Fancy pants Hackett puts his brown nose through the crack in that front door, he's going to get the biggest shock he's ever had in the whole of his life—BANG! In we come.

Don't Muck Us About

Don't muck us about
You'll get the back of my hand
Don't muck us about
It's more than we can stand
Don't muck us about
Or you won't know what hit you
Don't muck us about
Or we'll come out and get you.

In days gone by
We used to do
Exactly what
You told us to
You went too far
We found you out
We've had enough
So now we shout:

Don't muck us about
You'll get the back of my hand
Don't muck us about
It's more than we can stand
Don't muck us about
Or you won't know what hit you
Don't muck us about
Or we'll come out and get you.

MR MACONOCHIE: Right then, tomorrow morning, for the first time in my life, I do not intend to be late. I'm going to bed.
(*He goes, humming.* MRS MACONOCHIE *is watching him. Several of them turn and look at her. She is quite pleased with this turn of events. She puts down her knitting.*)

MRS MACONOCHIE: Well, I'm off too.
(*They all look at her. She rolls up the knitting, pretending not to notice. She goes over to the door. They're still watching. She stops in the doorway, her back to them, and waggles her bum. Then goes.*)

WILLY: We're all going to bed now, Yorry.

YORRY: Oh. Yes. (*Doesn't move*)

WILLY: Goodnight. Don't keep Mary up too late.

MARY: Gerroff, Willy.
(WILLY *and* SANDRA *go. Instrumental reprise: 'I've found out Love'.*)

YORRY: Can I just stay and talk for a bit, Mary?

MARY: Go off home, Yorry. I don't need outside agitators. I've got enough inside.
(YORRY *goes.* MARY *gets into bed. Music in, song*)
It's no good running from a nightmare,
It's no good trying not to scream
You can't get away from the love inside you,
It's no good running from a dream.
(*Repeat*)
(ANDY *comes in, in fantasy, in uniform, with a gun. Shoots her. Goes. She lies on the bed. Half tempo.*)
It's no good running from a nightmare,
It's no good trying not to scream
You can't get away from the love inside you,
It's no good running from a dream.
(*A knock on the door. She gets up. Goes to see who it is. Comes in with* ANDY *in reality, in scruffy old clothes, a plaster on his head, drunk, with a bottle of whisky.*)

ANDY: Are you on your own down here, Mary?

MARY: At the moment.

ANDY: Good. (*Takes his boots off*) I've got to have somewhere to stay, chicken.

MARY: Well you're not stopping here.

ANDY: I'm serious. One or two best-laid plans gone a wee bit sick on me, you know.

MARY: So you come round here, expect me to open both arms, fling back the bedclothes, and cherish you for ever. We broke up, you know, or have you forgotten that? And I've heard not a word from you for six months.

ANDY: I sent you my cuttings, didn't I?

MARY: They didn't give me much consolation.

ANDY: Ach, this uncle of mine kept sending word for me; I'd been in the army, you see: marksman on SLR: trained to kill: he said there was money in it. So there was, too.

MARY: Did you enjoy it?

ANDY: For a time. Until I realised what I was doing.

MARY: You might have stopped to think a bit earlier.

ANDY: The last bomb job, I put one in this little pub, then phoned
        them up to tell them to get out. A lot of our lads wouldn't
        do that, they really get a kick out of killing Catholics: I
        always did it, I got my kicks out of the risk of being
        caught. Well this time I rang, and the bloody stupid phone
        was out of order. There was a mother and two kids in the
        room above the bar, and ten blokes drinking. I drove up to
        the door and shouted to the fellers, and by Christ they
        sprinted and it was just as well they did. But the barman
        went up to get his wife and kids, you know . . .

MARY: You didn't send me that cutting.

ANDY: I asked could I go, but they said no. As soon as I walked
        out of the door, they telephoned the Army with my full
        description, and my address. I had to shoot my way out,
        and I'm not going back.

MARY: You know our Derek?

ANDY: I never met him.

MARY: He volunteered for Ireland, straight out of Police Training
        College. He's been there a year. Lucky you missed him.

ANDY: I'm not going back, Mary. I promise you, never.

MARY: Well you can't stay here. Dad would have a fit. And besides,
        I don't want you to. You can have a cup of tea, and go.

ANDY: I don't want a cup of tea.

MARY: Then you can just go.

ANDY: I can't go home, Mary. They'll be looking for me. I've no
        money, no job—nothing except what you see me in. Can I
        not just sleep on the settee?

MARY: I'm sleeping on the settee. On my own. I'm not being
        hard, I'm being practical.

ANDY: Well be a bit more practical and tell me where to go?

MARY: What about this mate of yours you used to stay with,
        when you were hunting down your wife?

ANDY: They've put him down for a year or two—assault with
        violence.

MARY: Well his room'll be empty, won't it?

ANDY: Don't talk rubbish: it'll be full of Irish construction men.
        Just what I need.

MARY: What you deserve. What did you go killing people for?

ANDY: I didn't think. That's the truth. I wanted to do something
        dangerous. I think I wanted to get myself killed. That
        would have been the best thing, bang—finito. I'm not fit to
        live with ordinary people: I'm not fit.

MARY: God, men.

ANDY: Have you no pity?

MARY: Of course not. Because you're not trying to do something
        about it. You don't *have* to be a murdering, drunken, nut

case, do you? Well, shift your arse and change your ways, before you start coming round here for sympathy.

ANDY: Christ, you're a great woman, Mary—come here, chicken, give us a hug.

MARY: (*Hits him*) Get out! (*Hits him again*) Get out, and don't come back!

ANDY: (*Shrugs*) OK. A friend in need. I'll fly away. I just want you to know—if I get picked up, I'll be down for ten years, maybe life.

MARY: You can look after yourself.

ANDY: I think I'm going mad, you know. You're the only one who's ever kept me together.

MARY: There's madness and madness. Yours was a kind I know about. Now it's gone evil. Come back when you're just a normal lunatic, and I'll take you in and protect you. I can't love a cold-blooded killer. Andy, get out and look after yourself.

ANDY: I'll be around.

MARY: Go on. It's not easy. Go on.
(*She turns away. Music in, lightly. He goes to her, touches her shoulder.*)

ANDY: Will you come with me, Mary? I'm that afraid. (*She shakes her head.*) I think I am mad. I've got so much to tell you. I've got to talk to you. If you think I'm worth rescuing—rescue me. (*No reaction*) See me tomorrow night, ah? I'll be outside. At eight o'clock?
(*Big drum in. She turns to him and nods. He goes.*)
Song (*Reprise*):
    It's no good running from a nightmare, etc.
(*Scene changes to inside factory. Sliding doors at the back are padlocked. The machine is covered over with a dustsheet.* MR MACONOCHIE *is sitting on a box reading a paper, smoking. A knock on the door.* MR MACONOCHIE *goes over to it, shouts.*)

MR MACONOCHIE: Hello? Who is it?

WILLY: (*Outside*) Willy. Open up.

MR MACONOCHIE: Anybody around.

WILLY: No. Only Yorry.
(MR MACONOCHIE *opens the padlock, slides back the door a fraction.* WILLY *puts his head in.*)

WILLY: Can I bring Yorry in? He's got the newsletters.

MR MACONOCHIE: Oh Christ, alright, bring him in.
(WILLY, *followed by* YORRY *with camera and pile of sheets, comes in.*)

WILLY: Couldn't get anywhere near the front entrance—bloody newspaper reporters snooping around in droves. I've got to go to the office. (WILLY *goes.*)

MR MACONOCHIE: They've sent enough reporters out here, why don't they print more than five lines about it?

YORRY: It's wonderful living in a country with a Free Press. Still, there's always *Robertson's Newsletter*.

MR MACONOCHIE: What have you got in there, Yorry?

YORRY: Arthur's speech last night, full text. The press handout that nobody printed. A few paragraphs from Gramsci on workers' control. All the messages of support we've been getting from all over. An interview with one of the canteen women about what she wants out of it: turns out she wants to operate a lathe. Reckons she could do it better than half the blokes.

MR MACONOCHIE: They're not going to like that.

YORRY: A lot of things are going to be stirred up by this occupation.

MR MACONOCHIE: Let's have one, then.
(YORRY *gives him a copy.*)
How do you get this printed, then?

YORRY: On the Ebenezer Baptist duplicating machine. About time it did something useful.

MR MACONOCHIE: What's your dad got to say?

YORRY: He's in hospital.

MR MACONOCHIE: What's up with him?

YORRY: They don't know. Or they won't say. It's bad, whatever it is—I'm thinking of bringing the paper out daily, now I'm getting organised.

MR MACONOCHIE: You'll kill yourself.

YORRY: I'm hoping Mary might come and do some typing—that's what holds me up. I can get the stuff together during the day, go through it with Arthur at six, get Mary to type it in the evening, run it off and collate it during the night and have it in here for eight in the morning.

MR MACONOCHIE: When do you sleep? (YORRY *shrugs.*) Is it worth it? I mean—we all know what's going on, don't we?

YORRY: It gives everybody something to read when they're sitting around. Something to think about a bit, as well. I want to do stories about some of the blokes—you know, interviews, what they think should happen, talk about their lives, families, interests.

MR MACONOCHIE: There's a feller in number three you want to get hold of, a lot of the lads'd like to know what he does with his money—never been known to buy a round in his life, Christmas, New Year or bank holiday. Crime, they call him, because he does not pay. Then there's the Broken Boomerang: he's always just going away for a minute and never comes back. Then there's the Shy Barrister—you can never get him up to the bar. And the Destroyer, up in number one—always chasing subs. They're the blokes you want to get in your paper.

YORRY: Would you like to write it?

MR MACONOCHIE: Write? Me? No—haven't got the imagination.

(WILLY *and* ROMAN CANDLE *come in.* ROMAN CANDLE *is another, older, worker.*)

WILLY: Eh, we're a public relations committee, you, me and Romer here—Arthur's going mad with the battering at the door, so he's sending all visitors round here to talk to us. We've got to decide who we talk to, who we don't, and who to shoot on the spot. And nobody, but nobody gets in further than here. Security gone mad, if you ask me, but Arthur's worried about stuff going missing—apparently there's quite a few bits and pieces going.

MR MACONOCHIE: Well it's not our lads, is it? That's what we let Hackett come in for, isn't it, to keep an eye on the stuff?

ROMAN CANDLE: The following political groups are to be given press handouts ad told politely to bugger off: IS, WRP, IMG, CPB (ML), YS, Spartacus League, Big Flame, Situationists, Anarchists, IRA, AIL, Clann na h'Eireann, the Fazakerley Rupamaros and all students.

YORRY: All of them?

ROMAN CANDLE: Who are you?

WILLY: This is the lad that turns out the newssheet, he's doing a good job, Rome.

ROMAN CANDLE: Let's have a look at your paper.

YORRY: (*Giving him one*) Arthur reads the copy before I set it up, you know.

ROMAN CANDLE: Oh yeah? Well that'll be down to this committee too, now—lighten his burden. So you can submit it to us.

YORRY: Would you consider writing something for it?

ROMAN CANDLE: No, I wouldn't. Right, let's get on with the committee meeting. All television and film cameras, outside. Interviews can be with Arthur, Bill or, if they insist on somebody who's not a shop steward, you, Willy.

WILLY: Me?

ROMAN CANDLE: That's the decision.

WILLY: We haven't discussed it yet.

ROMAN CANDLE: Right, let's take a vote. Mr Mac—yes, me—yes—you're outvoted. Don't worry, lad, we'll tell you what to say. Them groups—handout and tara. No interviews. Ordinary papers—talk to Arthur if we reckon they're going to do anything good. Left-wing press, in here, talk to us, cup of tea, no photographs. Delegates from other factories in the area, in here, cup of tea, shown round, chat to the lads, out. If they're bringing messages, take them to Arthur to read out. If they've collected money, call in Bill and he'll give them a receipt for the Strike Fund committee.

MR MACONOCHIE: Why can't we let the papers have a look round? We've got nothing to hide, might even do us a bit of good?

ROMAN CANDLE: They'll be stamping round all over, and what'd they be looking for? Stories about sabotage, equipment going to rust, trying to find somebody to say they're against the

	sit-in—and if they couldn't find anybody, inventing somebody. They're not on our side, Mac. Their owners are shitting themselves in case their own workers cotton on—think we should all be in prison for upsetting the national economy, which always means profits. Anything else?
WILLY:	There's that letter from the Gay Liberation Front.
MR MACONOCHIE:	What's that?
ROMAN CANDLE:	Fucking fairies' union.
MR MACONOCHIE:	Nancy boys? That's all we need.
WILLY:	Shall I read the letter out? 'Comrades—'
ROMAN CANDLE:	(*Laughs*) Sisters, they mean—
WILLY:	'Comrades, we support your stand—'
ROMAN CANDLE:	Support our stand—that's what they're after, is it?
WILLY:	'—for better wages. It is a blow against the entire wage system of this country, to which the whole of the state apparatus, the government, the press, TV, education, legal and judicial power and every other national institution is dedicated. It is a blow against the rule of capital, and the economic structure from which springs all the financial, social, political and sexual repression that we are all subject to every day of our lives. We, like you, wish every individual born in this country to fulfil their every potential for happiness. The powers that oppose us are great, but not unbeatable, because we are the people, and with strong enough organisation and courageous enough struggle, we must one day take charge of our own destinies. We enclose a cheque for twenty-seven pounds for your Strike Fund. Greetings.' I can't read the signature. Gay Liberation Front. (*Pause*)
MR MACONOCHIE:	You get some strange allies.
WILLY:	I like that.
ROMAN CANDLE:	Yeh, well . . .
WILLY:	Arthur better read it out at the next big meeting.
ROMAN CANDLE:	Oh, come on, fucking pansies. (*They look at him.*) Well, we'd look soft.
WILLY:	We'll take a vote on it, Mr Mac—yes. Me—yes. You're outvoted, Rome.
YORRY:	Can I print it?
WILLY:	Yeh—here—give's it back later. (*Enter* MR HACKETT *in a large overcoat, smiling.*)
MR HACKETT:	Can I disturb your slumbers for a moment, you lot? I'd like to go home for my tea.
WILLY:	You're off home early, Mr Hackett.
ROMAN CANDLE:	Is the deputy manager going to be staying in, or are you going to trust us not to smash the place up?
MR HACKETT:	I'll be back in tomorrow to make sure everything's alright.
MR MACONOCHIE:	Of course everything's going to be alright, we need these bloody machines to keep us working—that's why we're in here, remember.

MR HACKETT: Yes of course, of course. I don't know how much longer Consolidated Metals are going to stand for it, though, boys.

ROMAN CANDLE: Got no option, have they?

MR HACKETT: They didn't pay a lot for it, in their money. They could always write the whole thing off, forget about it. Then where would you be?

WILLY: We'd start up on our own. Run the place ourselves.

MR HACKETT: That'll be the day.

WILLY: Do you reckon we couldn't?

MR HACKETT: There's not one firm in the country would give you an order. You'd look a bit silly, I can tell you. Anyway, I don't want to start an argument. I want to get home—would you mind opening the cage?

MR MACONOCHIE: It's a pleasure.
                (*He goes over and unlocks the door.* WILLY *has been eyeing* MR HACKETT *suspiciously. He goes over to him.*)

WILLY: Excuse me, Mr Hackett, could we just—
                (*Goes to frisk him*)

MR HACKETT: Get away from me.

WILLY: He's got something in his pockets.

MR HACKETT: I'm off, good day to you.
                (MR MACONOCHIE *slides the door shut.*)

MR MACONOCHIE: Let's have a look.

MR HACKETT: What are you implying?

WILLY: (*Going over to him*) If you've got nothing to hide, you won't mind opening your coat, will you?

MR HACKETT: Don't be stupid.

ROMAN CANDLE: Open your coat, Hackett, or I'll open it for you.
                (MR HACKETT *is cornered.*)

MR HACKETT: Look, I'm taking a couple of things down to the station to put them on the train to some valuable customers. They're only small spares, but they're putting whole machines out of action. Be reasonable.

ROMAN CANDLE: Let's be having them.

MR HACKETT: I'm not trying to steal anything.

ROMAN CANDLE: I said, let's be having them.

MR HACKETT: You mean you won't allow me even to send off a couple of spare parts to firms who've brought us thousands of pounds worth of business? Regular customers that we look to for business in the future?

WILLY: We're getting the blame for those missing bits and pieces, Mr Hackett—and it's you been half-inching them all along.

MR MACONOCHIE: We let you in here as a sign of good faith, to show you we weren't bloody vandals.

ROMAN CANDLE: Drop those whatever you've got, and get out, and don't come back.

MR HACKETT: You're going to regret this.

ROMAN CANDLE: Open his coat, Willy.

MR HACKET: All right, all right—here.
(*Unloads half a dozen metal parts from inside his coat.*)

ROMAN CANDLE: That the lot?

MR HACKETT: Yes.

ROMAN CANDLE: We'll have a meeting to decide your fate. I don't fancy you'll be seeing the inside of here for a little while. Let him out, Mac.
(MR MACONOCHIE *opens the door.*)

MR HACKETT: (*To* YORRY) And as for you, whoever you are, you're just what we need.
(*He goes. Door closes*)
(*They sit, brooding. Quietly* WILLY *starts humming to himself. Picks out a few words—'Never, never, trust a boss . . . ', works out a verse, slowly the others start singing, find a chorus, and build up to a great, all-join-in, front-cloth number.*)

WILLY: (*Sings*)
A boss, a boss, who'd ever trust a boss?

MR MACONOCHIE: Eh? What? Who? Why?

WILLY: (*Sings*)
A boss, a boss, he's heading for a loss.

ROMAN CANDLE: Don't be nasty about the bosses, they're our friends.
(*Laughs*)

WILLY: (*Sings*)
Financiers and managers don't tell us what to do.

MR MACONOCHIE: They've got our best interests at heart, lad—how could you say such a thing?

WILLY: (*Sings*)
We are the people, and we are telling you.

ROMAN CANDLE: That's not how it is, Willy—if we work very, very hard and don't damage the National Interest, we'll make them a whole lovely great pile of money. And when they've taken their slice off the top, and interest off the middle and paid out the shareholders off the bottom and scraped up a few bob to buy some new machines so more of us can be chucked on the dole—*then*, they might give us a bit of what's left over, if we ask nicely.

MR MACONOCHIE: Exactly what I said—they've got our best interest at heart.

WILLY: (*Sings*)
A boss, a boss, who'd ever trust a boss?

MR MACONOCHIE: He's just a troublemaker.

WILLY: (*Sings*)
A boss, a boss, he's heading for a loss.

ROMAN CANDLE: Political, probably.

MR MACONOCHIE: Bloody agitator.

WILLY: (*Sings*)
Financiers and managers, don't tell us what to do. We are the people, and we are telling you.

ROMAN CANDLE:	Bit mindless, isn't it? Can't you think of anything more illuminating?
WILLY:	(*Sings*)

> They own this rotten workshop but we earn them their dough,
> And when we want some for ourselves, they say we'll have to go.
> There's labour cheap and well-controlled, they say, in Franco's Spain:
> Why don't they go and have a look, and not come back again.

ALL:	A boss, a boss, who'd ever have a boss, etc.
WILLY:	Your multi-national dealers, can swing from state to state,

> If profit's bad in England, then they won't hesitate
> To chuck us on the dole-queue, and bugger off to France;
> Will Mr Wilson stop them?—there's not a bloody chance.

ALL:	A boss, a boss, who'd ever trust a boss, etc.
WILLY:	There's just one way to stop them, take over what they've got

> Not just the bits and pieces, but grab the whole damn lot,
> We don't need Wall Street fixers, or jet-set buccaneers—
> We'll manage fine all by ourselves, so goodbye profiteers.

ALL:	A boss, a boss, who'd ever trust a boss

> A boss, a boss, he's heading for a loss,
> Financiers and managers, don't tell us what to do.
> We are the people, and we are telling you.

(*At the end of the song, the scene changes to* REV GRIFFITHS'S *study.* MARY *is typing skins, while* YORRY *is writing in longhand.*)

MARY:	What number's this one?
YORRY:	Mm? Fifty-one. Three months, one week. I'm running out of ideas. I've done profiles of practically every worker in the factory, reprinted the whole of Marx and Engels, analysed every move that Consolidated Metals of America have ever made, dissected the national press and TV coverage, taken the union leadership apart, and turned Willy into a Marxist intellectual: now I'm going to have to start repeating myself.
MARY:	Well I can't help you, Yorry. I don't understand a blind word I'm typing.
YORRY:	Really?
MARY:	I do get a bit tired, you know. I'm typing all day in that office, all night here.
YORRY:	And staying out with that Scots bloke . . .

MARY: I can't get him out of my head. I hate him actually.
          (MARY *types*. YORRY *writes on. Pause.*)
YORRY: How can I, that girl standing there
              My attention fix
              On Roman or on Russian
              Or on Spanish politics?
              Yet here's a travelled man that knows
              What he talks about,
              And there's a politician
              That has read and thought,
              And maybe what they say is true
              Of war and war's alarms,
              But O that I were young again
              And held her in my arms!
          Yeats wrote that when he was an old, old man. Two years
          later, Hitler marched into Czechoslovakia—he'd already
          begun to murder six million Jews, and a quarter of a
          million gypsies: not to mention the millions in the war. But
          I know what Yeats meant. Do you remember when you
          came out to the camp, at Tyn-y-Gongl? I thought you were
          the most beautiful thing I'd ever seen.
MARY: Me?
YORRY: I used to stand outside your house for hours, night after
          night, hoping to catch a glimpse of you. I've written about
          two hundred poems about you.
MARY: About me?
YORRY: But you don't care about me?
MARY: I haven't had much chance to think about it, have I? I
          mean—you kept it all very quiet, Yorry.
YORRY: I was frightened of you—laughing at me. I'm nothing,
          really, know nothing, do nothing, am nothing. Just a hole
          in the air, looked at objectively.
MARY: Don't do that to yourself, Yorry. You're quite interesting,
          and you do know quite a lot.
YORRY: I'm going to do quite a lot, too. I don't know exactly what
          yet—but I'm ready for anything. I want the movement to
          spread, across the whole of Merseyside, the whole of the
          North of England, join up with what's going on in
          Scotland, and declare a Workers' Republic and cut off
          everything south of Nottingham 'till the reactionary forces
          of the South are so weakened by uprisings among the
          workers of Bristol, South Wales and London that they
          capitulate without a shot being fired, then we encircle
          Birmingham: the last bastion of reaction; take it, and the
          country becomes a federation of Soviet republics, Scotland,
          Wales, the North, the West, the Midlands, the South-East
          and the East, with the capital in Manchester; and
          individual parliaments in each republic. So the factory
          councils and the area councils and the local branches of the

political organisations can have their say, and really run the country. And the universities will only operate for six months in the year—they don't do much more anyway—the other six months, everybody in them, staff and all, will spread out and work, among the people. And those who are to go to university will be elected by the others at their workplace, or in their commune—just like in China after the Cultural Revolution—what do you think about that?

MARY: What happened to those poems you talked about?

YORRY: The ones I wrote for you? I'm not a real poet. I burnt them. No loss to literature.

MARY: Why didn't you ever give them to me?

YORRY: You were a woman, I was a child. I'd like to marry you.

MARY: But you don't know me.

YORRY: I could learn about you.

MARY: Listen, when this thing's all over, you'll be off to somewhere else, find lots of other people to get involved with. Girls who are more—you know—your type.

YORRY: I don't think so. But if you don't want me. (*He shrugs, looks bleak*)

MARY: It's not that. Just—be a bit realistic.

YORRY: I've never been more realistic in my life. But I can't argue you into it. I'll just get on with this.
(*He picks up his pencil, stares at the paper. She watches him. He looks as if he might cry. She goes over to him. He puts his arms round her waist and clings to her, crying. She feels very sad for him.*)

MARY: Don't. Don't do that. Stop it, Yorry, it's awful, it's not right, you shouldn't do it. Stop. Yorry—don't cry.
(*He stops, determined to suppress it.*)

YORRY: Please! Stop mothering me.

MARY: What's wrong with that?

YORRY: I don't want a mother. I want a wife. You've rejected that, so leave me on my own.

MARY: Well—

YORRY: (*Calmly*) Mary—piss off.
(*They glare at each other. Enter* DAFYDD)

DAFYDD: Yorry—it's bad news.

YORRY: What? My dad?

DAFYDD: Half an hour ago. Very quick, very painless. He asked for you, but there was no time. I was with him when he—I'm sorry, lad.

YORRY: My father is dead. Long live my father.

DAFYDD: It was very quick

YORRY: I'll go straight round. I want to look at him. Mary, you'll just have to do those pages. You must leave before eleven. I'll take over when I get back.
(*She puts her coat on.*)
Where are you going?

MARY: To the hospital.
YORRY: I want to go on my own.
MARY: Of course. I'll come with you.
           (YORRY *goes. She follows.* DAFYDD *looks after her.*)
DAFYDD: Oh God. Beautiful young women sprouting every day,
           every house, every school, thrusting them out, more and
           more, budding and eager. And I, an old man, watch them,
           but am not even seen. Oh God. I wish I was the dead one.
           (*He sings:*)

The Fire Burns Brightly

> Young men, you don't know, you don't know
> Young men, you don't know what I know,
> When your young girl turns away
> You can try another any day—
> But mine has gone for ever long ago—
>
> Oh the fire burns brightly
> But the chimney's fallen in,
> And the smoke gets in your eyes and makes you cry.
>
> Oh the fire burns brightly
> But the house is falling down
> And we could have a conflagration by and by.
>
> Young girls you can smile, you can smile
> Young girls you can smile but stay a while.
> I've this thing called burning passion
> Oh I know it's slightly out of fashion,
> Won't you teach me how to modernise my style?
>
> Oh the fire burns brightly
> But the gate is cracked and old
> And on the pan the ash is piling high
> Oh the fire burns brightly
> But the nights are getting cold
> And this property's condemned, and soon to die.
>
> Old men you must feel, you must feel,
> Old men you must know just what I feel.
> All that shameful secret pain
> You'll never hold a girl again
> Oh the longing that your heart just can't conceal.
>
> Oh the fire burns brightly
> But the roof lets in the light,
> And the walls are heaps of rubble on the floor
> Oh the fire burns brightly
> On this demolition site
> When it's burnt me up, I know I'll burn no more—
> When it's burnt me up, I know I'll burn no more.

(*He goes. Enter* WILLY *and* MR MACONOCHIE.)

WILLY: So the occupation wore on, month after month.

MR MACONOCHIE: The strike fund ran out. The unions wanted a settlement, because they were running out. The only people who didn't seem to give a bugger were Consolidated Metals of America. They never even showed up. Nobody.

WILLY: I went with some of the lads down to their other castings place, at Stourbridge outside Birmingham. We knew they didn't recognise any unions there, but we were a bit taken aback at what happened. We went along at dinner time, to get to talk to them, tried to call a meeting outside the gates—but the manager locked them in. Locked the bloody gates. We managed to talk to one or two of the lads through the wire—they told us we were woistin our toime—then a couple of older blokes came along and told us to bugger off. So we did. I tell you— Birmingham.

MR MACONOCHIE: It was getting a bit hard on some of our fellers though— them with young families, or big rents, or HP to keep up, or all three together. The local shops round us were fantastic—they had to send to Blaenau Ffestiniog for more slates. Slipped the wives packets of this, that and the other. But we'd vanished out of the news, nobody was interested. Things looked bad.

WILLY: I spent a lot of time talking to Yorry. He kept saying we should get the place rolling, start production under workers' control. But there was no chance. All the people who supplied the metal, all the buyers for what we produced, were all in the Employers' Federation, they wouldn't touch us with a barge-pole.

MR MACONOCHIE: Then, one day, salvation arrived, in the shape of three Labour MPs.

WILLY: We had a mass meeting, in the works. God knows where they'd been, but suddenly.
(*Music. Tinkling, seductive sounds. Enter* THREE LABOUR MPS *in suits. They sing:*)

Three Labour MPs

BAND: Three Labour MPs,
Looking for someone to please
If anyone's going to lose us a fight,
It's three Labour MPs.

THREE MPS: We will give you pie in the sky,
And you can watch it flying by—
If you'll votey, votey, votey, votey,
If you'll vote for us.

BAND: Three Labour MPs,
Oh what a disease—
If ever the bosses are shaking with fright,
Get three Labour MPs.

THREE MPS:	Don't rock the boat, be good now, boys, Go back to work and shut your noise, And we'll see Wedgey, Wedgey, Wedgey, We'll see Wedgwood Benn.
BAND:	Three Labour MPs, Looking for someone to please If anyone's going to lose us a fight, It's three Labour MPs.
THREE MPS:	Oh we will lead you in your fight, Then we'll drop you right in the shite, If you'll votey, votey, votey, votey— If you'll vote for us.

(They go off very importantly. MR MACONOCHIE *comes on and watches them go.)*

MR MACONOCHIE: *(To audience)* All joking towards one side, we knew we'd had it, the minute those Labour MPs burst in on the act. They told us how clever they were being at getting questions asked in the House of Commons, at sucking up to American lawyers and accountants, how wittily they parried the thrusts of the managing director over cocktails—but it was perfectly obvious they'd come to get us back to work at any price. But the lads were getting desperate, and prepared to fall for it. So negotiations began, led by our fearless head office negotio-crats. And life went on. I got worried about the missus, me being out nights so much. And the missus got worried about Mary— her being out nights so much.

(The MACONOCHIES'S *living-room,* MRS MACONOCHIE *sitting up late.* MARY *comes in.)*

MRS MACONOCHIE:	Here you are then.
MARY:	Hello, Ma.
MRS MACONOCHIE:	What time's this to come in. It's quarter to three.
MARY:	I'm alright.
MRS MACONOCHIE:	If your dad was here, you wouldn't be. What's going on, girl.
MARY:	Been typing.
MRS MACONOCHIE:	Till this hour? Pull the other one, it's got bells on. You look terrible.
MARY:	I'm alright.
MRS MACONOCHIE:	You're not though. Who is it? Where are you going?
MARY:	I've been typing at Yorry's, what do you mean?
MRS MACONOCHIE:	Fiona went for you at eleven o'clock. You'd been gone half an hour. *(Silence)* Come on then.
MARY:	Leave me alone, Ma. I don't know if I'm coming or going. I think I'm going off my rocker.
MRS MACONOCHIE:	It's that bloody Scotsman, isn't it? He's come back, hasn't he?
MARY:	*(Nods)* He won't leave me alone.
MRS MACONOCHIE:	What do you go on seeing him for?

MARY:	I can't help it. He's there, all the time.
MRS MACONOCHIE:	Let your dad deal with him.
MARY:	He's dangerous. He'd kill anybody who crossed him.
MRS MACONOCHIE:	Well get the police.
MARY:	I can't. He's got a record as long as your arm and he's wanted for some stuff over in Ireland. He'd get thirty years.
MRS MACONOCHIE:	Well that's his problem, isn't it?
MARY:	(*Shouts*) How can I send a feller to prison for thirty years just because he's pestering me—it's criminal.
MRS MACONOCHIE:	(*Shouts*) Well I don't know, girl. You've got yourself in a right mess.
	(*Enter* SANDRA, *pregnant, as* MARY *and* MRS MACONOCHIE *are screaming at each other. She yells at* MRS MACONOCHIE *for some peace in the house.*)
SANDRA:	Can't you have some consideration? It's bad enough trying to get to sleep with this bugger kicking hell out of me. (*Silence.* MRS MACONOCHIE *sings:*)

Mum's Song

When you've lived a lot of living
And you've seen it all before
Done your taking and your giving
Till you can give-and-take no more

And you see it again
And you know you can't explain—
You wonder just what you've been living for . . .

Kids—
Don't want
Your money
Don't want
Advice
Just think
You're funny
Never
Think twice—

For babies need love and protection
For better of worse that's it—
They're screaming for food and affection.
All you get is a nappy full of shit—

Now school kids need clothes and need guiding,
And pounds and pounds of spuds to keep them fed.
Demanding that you keep providing
Till you're mad, or damn nearly dead

And then they are grown up—or maybe—
And sooner than you think they'll turn
And tell you, you're driving them crazy—
Oh when will parents ever learn . . .

When you've lived a lot of living
And you've seen it all before—
Done your taking and your giving
Till you can give-and-take no more.

And you see it all again,
And you know you can't explain
You wonder just what you've been living for . . .

(*At end of song, a short silence*)

MARY: Sorry, Ma.

MRS MACONCOCHIE: God, fellers do get desperate.

MARY: I keep thinking something terrible's going to happen to him.

MRS MACONOCHIE: No reason to let it happen to you as well. They're geniuses at passing the burden on to some poor woman: that's what they think we're for, really: holding their heads, taking the blame for the world they've made such a mess of.
(SANDRA *flops down.* MARY *puts her hand on* SANDRA's *stomach, feels for a bit.*)

MRS MACONOCHIE: I'll make us a cup of tea. I can't sleep without him in the bed, after all these years. Funny to think of them all sleeping down in that draughty factory . . . The only other time he's been away was when he had his gallstone out. I couldn't sleep then either. (*Goes*)

MARY: Is he kicking? Can I feel?

SANDRA: You can have him: carry him round for a bit.

MARY: I can't feel anything . . .

SANDRA: He'll be saving it up for when I get back to bed.

MARY: He is warm, though.

SANDRA: Should be, he's well wrapped up.

MARY: Oops, there he goes.

SANDRA: Mm.

MARY: I'd like one.

SANDRA: Soon enough, eh? Who d'you fancy for a dad?

MARY: Don't want one. I'm off men.

SANDRA: Well you can't do it all on your own, can you?

MARY: That part's too bloody easy. I just don't want anybody hanging around. Me, and him, and a few bob a week— that's what I fancy. We'd manage better without some dozy galoot crashing in every night, crashing round the place, crashing out in the morning.

SANDRA: I miss Willy when he's not here. She misses Dad.

MARY: Not me. Eh, there he goes again, ooh, having quite a little romp—cheeky sod—is it nice?

SANDRA: Lets you know he's alive and kicking. That's nice. Ma says it must be a girl, girls kick the most. Our Derek could hardly bother himself. He just sort of stretched himself every now and again.

DEREK: Did I?

(DEREK *has quietly come into the room, in a blue coat, looking bigger and fitter.*)

SANDRA: Good God, Derek, you give me such a fright.

MARY: Where did you spring from?

SANDRA: Ma—one more for tea.

MRS MACONOCHIE: (*Off*) What?

DEREK: She in there?

(DEREK *goes over to the door.* MRS MACONOCHIE *screams, off, and drops a cup. He goes into her.*)

SANDRA: I nearly dropped this on the spot—fancy not knocking.

MARY: He's a detective. Wonder what he's doing back here?

SANDRA: Perhaps he's got some holidays.

MARY: Funny time of night to start your holidays—it's gone three. (MRS MACONOCHIE, *looking pleased, comes in with a tray, followed by* DEREK.)

MRS MACONOCHIE: Tea for four.

SANDRA: Here, what are you up to going round giving people frights in the middle of the night?

DEREK: Ha ha—it's a raid. Perfectly normal time for a raid—how's tricks?

SANDRA: Not so bouncy. My dad and Willy still on strike, sleeping in the factory in case the US cavalry comes in the middle of the night, I've had to stop work, Mary's got problems and Fiona's taken to sleeping-pills. Only one at a time so far.

DEREK: Still in that factory, are they? When will they ever learn?

MARY: Depends what you want them to learn. If it's what I think it is, never—with a bit of luck.

DEREK: Hello, gone pink on us?

MARY: Bright flaming red when I see you. Cracked any good skulls lately?

DEREK: Nearly had mine cracked a few times, before I got transferred.

MARY: To what, the execution squad?

DEREK: Plain clothes. Promotion's quick over there. Another six months I'll be sergeant in CID, given a few good arrests, and I'll move back here.

MRS MACONOCHIE: What are you doing now, then, Derek? On holidays?

DEREK: Special job in Liverpool, so I volunteered, thought I'd give you all a surprise.

SANDRA: You did that all right.

MRS MACONOCHIE: What's the job, it is dangerous?

DEREK: Can't talk about it. Just being around when Liverpool CID pick a bloke up. Nothing desperate.

MARY: What bloke?

DEREK: Some joker we want to interview. I've got to get him back over there in one piece.

MARY: What's his name?

DEREK: What are you doing with yourself these days, Mary?

MARY: Aren't you going to tell me?

DEREK: You're joking. Still in Collins, Collins and Kops?

MARY: Why won't you tell me?

DEREK: He doesn't know we're on to him, yet. Any more tea, Ma?

MRS MACONOCHIE: It's empty. It sounds a bit dangerous to me, Derek.

DEREK: No trouble at all.

SANDRA: What's the life like?

DEREK: Interesting. Good money. Long hours. Trouble with Ireland it's full of bloody Micks . . . (*A bit of a silence*) What we ought to do is get out and let them massacre each other. (*Another silence*)

MARY: So you're doing well out of it?

DEREK: Not my idea, was it? You having a go at me again, Mary?

MARY: I can see why they didn't freeze *your* pay rise—too bloody valuable.

DEREK: We don't exactly hang around all day.

MARY: Nor does your dad. He hasn't even got a pay rise to freeze, God help us. He'll be one of the first to land on the scrap-heap, even if they do save the works.

MRS MACONOCHIE: Of course he won't.

MARY: Haven't you thought of that? Too bloody active—shit-stirrers, him and Willy both.

SANDRA: Willy? Thrown out?

MARY: What do you think? Willy's been making speeches to the papers, organising reception committees—they daren't sack Arthur and Bill, but they won't be too choosy about those just below them: out.

SANDRA: How can they do that when I'm in this condition? Anyway, how will they know?

DEREK: Easy. They'll have company men in there informing on every move. I knew Dad would end up in trouble. When you're in his position, keep your head down. It always pays.

MARY: Yes, keep in time and do as you're told—that'd suit you, wouldn't it? Because now you're doing the telling.

DEREK: Me? I just carry out orders. I don't question them. If I carry them out to the best of my ability, I get looked after, that's the way it is in this life. I don't like the sound of what you're saying, Mary.

MARY: Oh?

DEREK: It's all a bit easy, immature, all too clever-clever, all this stand up and fight them stuff. Look at Ireland—look where it's got them there—piles of corpses, innocent people maimed for life. Kids blown up—and nothing to show for it, except what they could have had anyway if they'd just asked nicely. They're just micks out for kicks. They'd murder their own granny if they could write a good song about it.
(*Silence*)

MARY:	God help your wife, if you ever get one.
	(DEREK *looks pained, and sad.*)
MRS MACONOCHIE:	Here, look, Mary, there was no need for that.
DEREK:	No. That's all right. (*To* MARY) A mate of mine fancied a girl there, actually. Half Catholic. They shot her dad in the kneecaps for letting her come out with him. He doesn't see her any more, in case her dad gets worse.
MRS MACONOCHIE:	How terrible, what an awful thing.
MARY:	This feller you're after—is he a Protestant or a Catholic?
DEREK:	Let's just say I don't know.
	(*Silence*)
	Well, it is good to be back in the warm, relaxed atmosphere of home. Is there anywhere for me to sleep?
MRS MACONOCHIE:	Well, Fiona's in your room, Willy's in the girls' room with Sandra, Mary's down here. I know what—you go in our bed, and I'll slip in with Sandra.
SANDRA:	You'll be sorry.
MRS MACONOCHIE:	Come on, Derek, you must be dropping.
DEREK:	I am. Good-night, Mary.
MARY:	Sleep well.
	(MRS MACONOCHIE *and* DEREK *go off.*)
SANDRA:	Eh, Fiona slept through everything. Amazing them pills. See you in the morning if I get up in time.
MARY:	Yeh.
	(SANDRA *goes.* MARY *alone. She moves forward, putting on her coat, then goes off.* MARY *comes back on with* ANDY: *they go and sit underneath a statue in St George's Gardens. He takes a small box of bullets from his pocket, starts loading some magazine-clips for a pistol.*)
ANDY:	You've got to live the way you want to live. Otherwise shoot yourself. Or shoot a policeman.
MARY:	You're talking mad, Andy.
ANDY:	Aye, they call that mad. It's what everybody needs, and it's what everybody's afraid of. Why do they lock mad people away? Because it's their own madness they are locking away. You too. You've got more madness in you than a hundred nut-houses have inside them but you treat it so *badly* girl. The best part of your own self, you kick it to death.
MARY:	Well, I *am* afraid of it.
ANDY:	Aye, because you're told you've got to be afraid of it. They won't let you nourish it, water it, till it bursts out all over the world. No, they want to bloody suffer.
MARY:	We all have to suffer a little, don't we?
ANDY:	A minister at home told me all about Jesus Christ. I said, but why did he want to suffer so much? Ah, says the minister, before Christ there was suffering in the world; but *he* taught us how to suffer with a purpose. Ach, away. I want to live in this world, I've no time for the next. And

all your boyfriends in their factory, plotting, and planning
for something that's going to come this year, next year,
some time, never: Christ, by the time it comes, they'll have
forgotten what they wanted it for. Look at the Russians—
millions of them bloody slaughtered fighting for freedom
from the tsar or some bugger: by the time they'd won all
their battles, they'd no clue what it was all for—and the
one or two who tried some living were shot, or they shot
themselves. And they're still waiting for freedom to break
out.

MARY: It doesn't have to be like that everywhere—you haven't
been to Russia anyway.

ANDY: No, but I've been here. I see what goes on here. (*Slams
clip into pistol*) It's too frustrating, Mary. You can kick
your dreams to death and your body to death and piss on
your life—I'm shooting my way out of it.

MARY: They'll just put you in prison—then where's your life?

ANDY: I'm not afraid of prison—that's nothing, nothing at all—
like going out—nothing to worry about. Until you stop
worrying about things like that, you can't begin to live.
The most difficult thing we've got to do, is to get in
contact with what we really desire: that's difficult. You can
find yourself wanting to piss in the street—away you go,
piss in the street—but that's nothing more than wanting to
break the rules: you can get used to pissing in the street,
pissing in the parlour—there's no more to it than doing it.
You can get to want to take a few risks—getting yourself
killed, put into prison. So you take a few risks—shoot a
few soldiers, blow up a few pubs—but you get used to
taking those risks. Your whole life's a bloody risk. But at
least you're out of the risk of dying alive through sheer
bloody slavery. It's only when you don't mind dying, don't
mind getting put away for a lunatic or a criminal, you get
to feel what maybe you really want. And do you know
what it is I really want? Just one other person on the earth
to feel the same. Freedom. That's what it is. I can walk, I
can fly, I can play snowballs with fire, I can spit in the eye
of the sun and the moon, I can dig with my hands through
to Australia: but without one other person, I can't love.
Without you, how can I love? I want to know what loving
means.

MARY: I could never be mad, if that's what you're asking me. I
don't want to be. Maybe I am, but I'm fighting it.

ANDY: Stop fighting it.

MARY: I can see where you are. I know where you are, but I'm
not going there.

ANDY: How can anyone stay in the world of the sane? Just look
at it. Just look at the way you make yourself live.

MARY: What's wrong with it?

ANDY: It's a quiet path to a quiet grave: it's slow death by boredom and organised poisoning. Suffer, suffer for something in the future, and when you die, you wake up dead. You're being conned, girl. There's nothing happening to your life, it just goes on, it gets longer and more unbearable, until you don't mind going out any more, in fact you look forward to it. How can you let that happen to you?

MARY: At least we're all in it together.

ANDY: We could be. You and me, chicken: we could be really together: all they've got is the illusion of being together: in the sane world, you're as alone as a frog on the North Pole star. You're born on your own, and all you'll do all your life, is play at the game of you and the others.

MARY: Dad's not alone. Willy's not alone. Yorry's not alone.

ANDY: They play. But does nay one of them ever tell one other what he is, does anyone know them the way you know me? What goes on inside, stays inside: rule number one.

MARY: But they're happy.

ANDY: We can only work each one of us from our own desperation, and shout it out till we know it, and know each other's, and begin to feel free of it. Try and wrap loneliness and despair up in Santa Claus gift-wrapping, and call it happiness and that proves what I'm saying.

MARY: So you think we must shoot people, kill and get killed, to feel anything?

ANDY: If we're truthful, first we want to destroy the world that makes us want to destroy it.

MARY: And for that you shoot people, and blow up that pub, and that barman, and his wife, and their baby?

ANDY: I didn't mean to do that.

MARY: But you did. And you'd like me to go with you, daft as a brush, to come out the other side feeling honest and truthful.

ANDY: Feeling *something*. It must be better than nothing.

MARY: The last few weeks, for the frist time in my life, I've really wanted to have a baby. Really, really. I can do that. You can't. I want my body to go on long enough for him to grow in it until he wants to come out, I want the strength to get him into the world, and I want the world to go on long enough for my love and his efforts to make him stand up, and walk, and talk, and learn and sprout hairs under his arms, and take off.

ANDY: Another liar into a world of lies.

MARY: He'll have his chance, the same as you're having yours: to me, that's what matters. And he won't be alone. We'll all be taking our chances together, one of these days. I'll not join your madness, Andy. I'll suppress it and suffer and pass on suppression and suffering, but not if I can help it.

I won't be seeing you again. I've warned you about Derek.
If you shoot a policeman, make sure he's not my brother.

ANDY: The world will never change, and none of us in it will
change ourselves, without brothers getting shot and babies
blown to little bits.

MARY: If I believed that, I'd shoot myself.

ANDY: Here. (*Hands her the gun. She won't take it.*) Scared? Shall
I do it for you?

MARY: You probably would, too.

ANDY: The final good turn for a friend in need. I've done it once
before.

MARY: Don't bother. With good turns like that, I don't need bad
ones. Tara, Andy. I'm sorry to let you down.
(*She turns and goes. He looks at the gun, slips it in his
pocket, and pockets the other clips. He goes, the other
way.*)
(*The scene changes to inside a factory,* MR MACONOCHIE
enters, talks to audience).

MR MACONOCHIE: When I was born, it was the 'twenties. I don't remember
the first Labour government, or the General Strike . . . I
just got told, later, that something went wrong with both
of them: it seems the blokes that ran them just hadn't got
the determination to see them through.

When I was a lad, it was the 'thirties—At the beginning,
the workers put in the second Labour government—To
protect them in a time of crisis—What happened? Oh I
remember what happened all right—No work. Dole
money cut. Kids running round with no shoes on their feet
and the arse hanging out of their trousers, and sod all in
their bellies. Hunger marches—beggars, fifty thousand
able-bodied men all wandering the streets of Liverpool
looking for odd jobs. Charity.

When I was nineteen, it was the 'forties. And I was
fighting the Hun. In the West Derby Athletes Foot. For six
years, all over North Africa, Italy, Normandy, France, the
Rhine and Sefton Park. And all the time I kept thinking
what it was going to be like in civvy street—not like the
'thirties, I was sure of that—and we had this sergeant—I
think he must have been a communist, because he'd
managed to incorporate a hammer and sickle into his
second-best cap-badge.

He told me we were going to change everything when
we got back—me and him. And a few million others. Run
it ourselves, and chuck the profiteers and the bosses into
the Mersey. I learnt a lot from him, came back alive and
hopeful.

Then we put in the third Labour government—under
Colonel Attlee. To change everything. They didn't do too
bad—at one or two things. But somehow they didn't quite

have the determination to see the whole thing through.
Funny that, about them not having the determination.
When I got married, it was the 'fifties. I was very
optimistic—we had the Tories back in, of course, but they
got themselves in such a state, I thought they were done
for, for ever. But we kept voting them back in. We hadn't
quite got the determination to throw them out, I suppose.
When I was forty, it was the 'sixties, I was still optimistic.
When we put in another Labour government, I thought,
right lads—now let's be having you.

At first, they couldn't do much because they hadn't got
a majority. So they had another election, and it seems they
could do even less because they *had* got a majority.
I began to feel old, and tired, and cynical—I began to feel
I'd seen it all before, and I didn't want to see it again.
Come the 'seventies, I got myself an allotment, and grew
vegetables, and prize raspberries—I got really excited
about the raspberries.

As for the other—the new and beautiful land—Oh
Christ—I thought it was all done for. The Tories were
back again, business was booming, and the alternative to
international capitalism was Wedgwood Benn—and none
of them quite seemed to have the determination to really
change anything: not so it mattered.

Then bugger me: *this* happened. Action. Determination.
At last. Young Willy—a new generation—getting stuck in
there like a good 'un. Even Yorry, for all he's a bit damp
behind the ears—everybody was alive, and having a go.
It's *got* to work.

I think—I think, if it doesn't, come the 'eighties, I'll be
on the way out.

But it *will*. It must. Don't you think?
(*The scene changes to* DAFYDD's *house*)

DAFYDD: (*To audience*) After my late lamented brother went from
amongst us, things began to change down the Ebenezer
Baptist Chapel Youth Club. We got a spry young minister
who'd been to London, and with my ever-willing help, he
set up a bit of a disco, and we got a band in, and to
everybody's amazement we had what Teifian referred to as
Mixed Dancing. I even got a bar going—wondrous are the
ways of the Christian in search of a congregation. I
became something of a secret drinker, an alcoholic of the
Lord. The old myths, the old legends and poems bumbled
around my head, a tipsy Celtic twilight, filled with dreams
of God and heroes and beautiful women. But I never
became a Church man. Remember Sweeney, the poet-king
of Ireland: with the flying madness cursed on him by a
holy saint Ronan, growing feathers on his arms, down his
back, flitting from tree-top to tree-top, from crag to crag,

taken in by the miller's wife, and fed and known for the poet he was—until the Christians came and kicked him to death? I remembered that savagery, as the days wore on: how poets, and madmen, will always take on themselves the secret truth of the people, and be hated for it, kicked for it. St Ronan lives. I never became a Christian.
(*Enter* WILLY, SANDRA, *now largely pregnant, and* YORRY. *He has been showing them the house.*)
Oh, hello, seen over the house then? Help yourself to a can, Sandra—Guinness is good for him, he'll come out bending steel girders.

SANDRA: Thanks, Mr Griffiths.

DAFYDD: You could call me Dafydd if you don't think it's too dangerously familiar . . .

YORRY: What do you think, Willy? The whole place is mine now, and we only use one living-room and two bedrooms. There's four more, you could take your pick.

WILLY: (*To* SANDRA) What do you think, love?

SANDRA: Well I don't know, I mean, it's your house, Yorry, I mean—you don't know what upheavals a baby could cause.

WILLY: Neither do you, yet.

SANDRA: Well there's your uncle, er, Dafydd here.

DAFYDD: Don't you worry about me—ever since Teifian's gone—may I never speak evil of the dead—I've had a new lease of life. I've started writing poems again—in Welsh, of course, thank God nobody round here understands them, they're a bit what you call—fruity. Babies? Have dozens of them. Fill the house with nappies and let them howl all night long, I'm happy. It'll be good to get the smell of some good, honest baby-shit into this ecclesiastical charnel house. Me? Count me in.

YORRY: (*To* SANDRA) Do you want to think about it?

SANDRA: (*To* WILLY) I'm not sure I'd like living in somebody else's house, Willy.

WILLY: I'm not buying a new one—it's only temporary.

SANDRA: Well Mary wouldn't mind seeing the back of us. She's getting fed up with that settee after all these months.

YORRY: You could have the whole house, if you like. I'll sign it over to you. Then it wouldn't be somebody else's house, and we'd be the lodgers.

SANDRA: You couldn't do that.

WILLY: He could—you're serious, aren't you, Yorry?

YORRY: I don't want to own property, why should I, what does it mean?

WILLY: Told you—amazing. Yorry, you're amazing. A bit bloody half-baked as well.

YORRY: Typical. I've told you before, you're shot through and through with the corrupt values of the ruling class. What

kind of revolution are we going to make, if the most
progressive militants in the most militant city in England
can't shake off the evil attitudes of their masters. Not even
slaves in ancient Rome were forced to share their owner's
religious beliefs. But you worship exactly what
Consolidated Metals of America worships—property, and
money.

WILLY: Because I haven't got them.

YORRY: Not 'I'—we. We haven't got them—where's your class
solidarity?

WILLY: But you have got them.

YORRY: And I don't want them—I'm giving them to you.

WILLY: That's why I said you were half-baked.

YORRY: That's what I mean—typical.

SANDRA: Don't start all over again, you two. I've decided. We move
in tomorrow.

YORRY: Will you?

DAFYDD: Calls for a celebration. Where's my jacket, we'll crack
open a bottle of Bells and fifty Players.
(*A battering on the door.* YORRY *goes to open it, as more
knocking begins. Enter* FIONA, MRS MACONOCHIE, *followed
by* MR MACONOCHIE *with his arm around* MARY, *who is
white and shaking, then* YORRY.)

MR MACONOCHIE: Sorry to burst in on you like this. We're having a bit of an
upset at home.

WILLY: What's going on?

MRS MACONOCHIE: That fool of a Scotsman's come raving drunk chucking
bricks through the window and screaming for Mary. Our
Derek's gone to get some help.

WILLY: Shall we go and sort him out?

MRS MACONOCHIE: Mary says he's got a gun. And he's mad enough to use it.
He's smashed every window in the front of the house. We
crept out the back in case he broke the door down.
There'll be no danger of him coming round here.

MARY: Yes. He knows.

MRS MACONOCHIE: Does he? Well why didn't you say, you soft haporth of
tripe?

FIONA: Because she wants him to find us. Don't you?

MRS MACONOCHIE: Leave her alone.

MR MACONOCHIE: Poor lad. Poor lad.

FIONA: Poor? He ought to be exterminated.

MR MACONOCHIE: What's he done to you?

FIONA: Fine family of hooligans we're going to look, with
gangsters like that yelling around the place, and the
windows all smashed.

MR MACONOCHIE: If all you're worried about's the neighbours, you can stop
worrying. They can think what they want. That lad's in a
bad way, and he needs proper care and attention.

MRS MACONOCHIE: He's a nasty bit of work all the same.

WILLY: Will he come here, then, Mary?

MARY: (*Nods*) He used to wait for me outside.

WILLY: Sandra, get your coat on, love, we'll take a walk round to my mother's. You too, Fiona, Mrs Mac. Come on; Mary.

MARY: No. I'm not running away again.

FIONA: Then you're as mad as he is.

WILLY: Come on love.

SANDRA: Is it safe to go out?

WILLY: Safer than staying here. Mrs Mac?

MRS MACONOCHIE: I think I'll hang on with her.

WILLY: So it's you and Fiona for the lifeboats.
(*He goes out and opens the front door as* FIONA *helps* SANDRA *on with her coat. It bursts open, off stage, and* WILLY *is flung back in to the room, clutching his face. Enter* ANDY, *a half bottle of whisky in his hand.*)

ANDY: Oh no. Oh no. You stay in here, pal.

WILLY: I'll knock your teeth down your throat, you drunken git.

ANDY: Oh no. I don't think so. (*He looks around, smiling at them all.*) So here we all are, locked in the house of a minister of God. Our spiritual home. (*Sharply*) Mary, come away, we're leaving this place. It stinks of sanctified suffering. (*To* MR MACONOCHIE) Let go of her. She belongs with me.

MRS MACONOCHIE: You're digging your own grave doing it this way. I've told you before, you can't force the girl to love you.

ANDY: Christ! You don't know what you're talking about.

MRS MACONOCHIE: Oh, don't I?

MR MACONOCHIE: Listen, Andy, you've had a drop too much, and you're very upset. But don't think you'll get anywhere by terrorising people and talking to them like that.

ANDY: Stop being so reasonable, man. It won't do any good. I'm not drunk . . .

MR MACONOCHIE: I hope you are.

ANDY: No. I want to behave this way. I want to break into this house of God and terrorise people, because I'm sick of people being so bloody reasonable. If you want me, you'll have to take me, but I have a wee shooter. Looking at you lot, I don't think I'll be needing it, just yet awhile. Come away, Mary, I can't stand here gassing with the old folk. There's three hundred of them out looking for me with very big boots on, so I can't hang around here all night.

YORRY: She's not going with you.

ANDY: Who are you? Oh, aye—you'll be the minister's little boy—swapped God for Karl Marx, and Jesus Christ for the nearest shop steward. Well I'm telling you, laddie, you're wrong on two counts. First, you should have stuck with the Lord, because the other'll never stomach you. And second, she *is* coming with me, because I know her, and she knows me, and my hideous truth is better than your beautiful fantasies, any day of the week. You can change the whole world, but you'll never know what she's all about, not till the day you die.

YORRY: You're dangerous, and you're mistaken. As we change the world, so that will change us. When we're ready, we'll do both, together. And if you want to take Mary by force you're going to have to shoot me first; go right ahead. I've got nothing to lose.

ANDY: You stay where you are.

YORRY: (*To* OTHERS) Get away from behind me—he's probably a bad shot as well as a stupid anarchist. How many people do you have to kill, to prove you're a man, Andy?

ANDY: I'll shoot you dead.

YORRY: OK by me. But first I'm going to jump at you, knock you to the ground, and kick your head in—ready?
(*He does so. He jumps,* ANDY *does not even get the gun out, he knocks* ANDY *down, and he and* WILLY *start kicking him.* MR MACONOCHIE *rushes at them.*)

MR MACONOCHIE: Stop! (*Spits*) Leave him alone, or I'll kill you!
(MARY *screams and rushes to* ANDY, *holds him.* ANDY *kneels up, his face covered in blood. He pushes* MARY *away.*)

ANDY: Come on, then—you've got me down. Kick me. Come on, lock me away. (*Nobody moves.* ANDY *gets up.*) Scared of my gun, are you? Here—here: take it. (*Gives it to* YORRY) What are you going to do, lock me up or shoot me? There's the safety-catch, right. It'll fire now. I'm asking you: shoot—here I am.

MR MACONOCHIE: Don't be daft, lad.

ANDY: D' you know I would sooner die than spend my life in some cell? Here—(*takes the gun away from* YORRY, *gives it to* MR MACONOCHIE)—you do it. For Christ's sake, come on.
(MR MACONOCHIE *puts the gun in his pocket.*)
You people. You'll do nothing. Nothing.

MRS MACONOCHIE: And just what are you going to do—look at you.

ANDY: Aye. You keep them in line, missus. I'm away. (*To* MARY) Look after yourself, chicken. (*To* MR MACONOCHIE) Give me my shooter.

MR MACONOCHIE: To use on my own son? Have some sense.

ANDY: Never. No sense. Never.
(ANDY *goes over to* MARY *and draws a line of blood down her face, kisses her, runs out.*)

FIONA: What did you let him go for?

MR MACONOCHIE: Our Derek can do his own dirty work. I'm not doing it for him. (*He takes the gun out of his pocket. Looks at it.*) What shall we do with this, then?
(YORRY *puts his hand out for it.* MR MACONOCHIE *gives it to him.* YORRY *puts the safety-catch back on, unloads it, and examines it.*)

MRS MACONOCHIE: Come on, girls, let's get back and sweep up the mess.
(As they get together, DEREK *comes in.)*
WILLY: Have you caught him?
DEREK: We will. We're on to him.
FIONA: He's just gone. He hasn't got a gun any more.
DEREK: Where is it?
MR MACONOCHIE: He's thrown it away.
DEREK: He's still got something. He's cut up two of the Liverpool boys who went in for him. When the others catch him, they'll tear him apart.
*(*DEREK *goes.* MRS MACONOCHIE, FIONA *and* SANDRA *start to go.)*
YORRY: Mary. Stay a minute.
(She nods. The OTHERS *go.)*
DAFYDD: I'll just nip round to the 'Legs of Man', eh? Bottle of Bells and fifty Players. Come in handy.
(He goes)
YORRY: Mary.
(He takes her hand. She lets him.)
We'll be alright.
(She bites his hand. He watches her. After she stops.)
Stay with me. I can try to look after you.
MARY: I want a baby, and I want to go.
YORRY: Go?
MARY: On my own, with the baby.
YORRY: I want you to stay, with me.
MARY: I'd be just as much on my own.
YORRY: We can try.
MARY: *(Shrugs)* We can try.
(They go off together. MR MACONOCHIE *comes on, and* WILLY.)*
MR MACONOCHIE: They never did catch him. His sort always get away with it, they're always on the loose. We didn't know what to make of it. It all goes on, life, as before, without any connections. Exploring, the same country, without a map or even a memory.
WILLY: The union leaders and the new bosses came to some sort of agreement. An extra thirty bob on the pay, five pence an hour extra on the overtime, no extra holidays and the same hours. But they strung it out until the wages freeze, so nobody's getting it anyway. The one bit they didn't freeze was chucking me and Mr Mac on the dole. He got a bit of redundancy payment, I hadn't been there long enough: I got shown the door. It had been agreed at a high level: twenty per cent to go. And in six months, the lot of them will be out, the works will be knocked down, and the land sold for development.
MR MACONOCHIE: Not making any maps, for those who come after us: scattering bits and pieces of our skin and bone down the

back-alleys of our minds. Leaving them to rot, for the dogs to wrangle over.

(YORRY *comes on.*)

YORRY: After the settlement, I read in the *Wall Street Journal* that Consolidated Metals of America were planning to rationalise their European production. The work that Robertson's had been producing was going to be done in Germany, and transported in great big containers all over the Common Market. Capitalism was changing: the question was: were we going to change with it—fast enough, big enough and well enough organised to catch up with it?

WILLY: They'd worked a flanker on us again. They weren't going to win, in the end. But how were we going to learn from it? What were we going to remember ourselves from all that lot?

(SANDRA *comes on with her baby and* MRS MACONOCHIE.)

MR MACONOCHIE: Sandra had her baby. He didn't look like anybody we knew so she called him Alexander.

SANDRA: God knows what sort of a world we'd brought him into. All these buggers did was argue.

WILLY: It's always the same, love, when you've lost a match.

MRS MACONOCHIE: Then it's time you started winning, isn't it?

MR MACONOCHIE: Yes.

THE END

LAY OFF

Presented by 7:84 England in 1975 and 1976 with the following cast and band members:

Chas Ambler	drums, vocals
Mike Barton	violin, bass, vocals
Dennis Charles	Personnel Manager, Mr Brassneck, General Motors etc.
Chrissie Cotteril	Silkworker 1, Jenny etc.
Tony Henderson	guitar, banjo, vocals
Hilton McRae	Henry Ford, Labour Relations, IBM etc.
Colum Meaney	Fred Taylor, Arther, Arnie, ITT etc.
Mike O'Neill	Keyboard, vocals
Vari Sylvester	Silkworker 2, Annie Morris, narration etc.

All the performers enter the stage space.

COLUM: (*Directly to the audience*) Hello, and welcome to 7:84's new show—Lay Off. (*Insert local reference such as: it's nice to be here in the theoretical city of Milton Keynes/back in riot-torn Lancaster University/here beside the seaside in Fylde, etc.*)
The show tonight is a story—and it's the story of four strikes, that happened in, as near as, the new town of East Kilbride in Scotland. The first one happened in 1960 or 61—

DENNIS: Wait a minute, wait a minute—these people haven't come here tonight to listen to a load of rubbish about strikes and troublemakers and shop stewards and other such hooligans—have you?
(*Try a bit with all those who want strikes—Yes
All those who don't want strikes—No*)
What?

CHRISSIE: Oh well, don't pay any attention, we're going to start with a bit of a singsong—OK?

DENNIS: Good idea.

COLUM: OK—but a song about strikes—right?

CHRIS: Jesus, compromise already. (*to band*) Alright lads?

BAND: Right—

CHRIS: (*Directly to the audience*) Will you join in? Good God—you're all intellectuals—give yourselves a chance, now—anyway, here's a song—OK, lads?

Which Side Are You On?

> Come all of you good workers
> Good news to you I'll tell
> Of how that good old union
> Has come in here to dwell

Chorus

> Which side are you on?
> Which side are you on?
> Which side are you on?
> Which side are you on?

> My daddy was a miner
> And I'm miner's son
> And I'll sick with the union
> Till every battle's won

> Oh, workers can you stand it?
> Oh, tell me how you can
> Will you be a lousy scab
> Or will you be a man?

> Don't scab for the bosses
> Don't listen to their lies
> Us poor folks haven't got a chance
> Unless we organize

(*After the first attempt to get the audience to join in with the song*) Come on, with singing like that, you'll get cuts, never mind 10%—come on, one more time. And to make it easy, here's the words—(VARI *and* HILTON *bring on a song-sheet*) Play that bit again—right?

CHRIS: Great, that was wonderful—considering.

HILTON: Well now, that was all about the old days, when 10% meant something—nowadays, if you only get 10% you're taking a cut.

COLUM: Now about these four strikes.

VARI: Look—start at the beginning, work up to it. Start where it all began—in the good old days when the fight was one lot of workers in one factory, or one pit, or one sweatshop, against one man—the boss. Him with the big cigar living in the big house on top of the hill.

HILTON: That didn't last long—the bosses soon got teamed up into bosses' federations—so the lads wised up, and got themselves together—they started the unions—(*Music in*) all over Britain, all over Europe, all over America, the thing to do was to get the unions rolling: here's an American song about all that, and it'll give you a chance to sing a bit better.
(*The band and performers play and sing, encouraging the audience to join in with a song-sheet*)

Roll the Union On

If the boss gets in the way, we're gonna roll it over him
Gonna roll it over him, gonna roll it over him.
If the boss gets in the way, we're gonna roll it over him
We're gonna roll the union on.

We're gonna roll, we're gonna roll, we're gonna roll the
    union on.
We're gonna roll, we're gonna roll, we're gonna roll the
    union on.

If the scabs gets in the way, we're gonna roll it over them
Gonna roll it over them, gonna roll it over them.
If the scabs gets in the way, we're gonna roll it over them
We're gonna roll the union on.

We're gonna roll, we're gonna roll, we're gonna roll the
    union on.
We're gonna roll, we're gonna roll, we're gonna roll the
    union on.

CHRISSIE: Wonderful—you're making a great stab at putting the George
    Mitchell singers out of business.

DENNIS: Now, where were we? Yes—the unions rolled on, and slowly
    the workers got some strength up—they were even able to feel
    confident in their own power—listen to this:
    (*The band and performers play and sing, encouraging the
    audience to join in with a song-sheet.*)

Union Maid

There once was a union maid, she never was afraid
Of goons and ginks and company finks and the deputy
    sheriffs who made the raid.
She went to the union hall when a meeting it was called,
And when the Legion boys come 'round
She always stood her ground.

Oh, you can't scare me, I'm sticking to the union,
I'm sticking to the union, I'm sticking to the union.
Oh, you can't scare me, I'm sticking to the union,
I'm sticking to the union 'til the day I die.

This union maid was wise to the tricks of company spies,
She couldn't be fooled by a company stool, she'd always
    organize the guys.
She always got her way when she struck for better pay.
She'd show her card to the National Guard
And this is what she'd say:

Oh, you can't scare me, I'm sticking to the union,
I'm sticking to the union, I'm sticking to the union.
Oh, you can't scare me, I'm sticking to the union,
I'm sticking to the union 'til the day I die.

HILTON: Sixty years later a pop group in England made a fortune out of that one—and most of what they made went to the bosses and shareholders of EMI. Strong as they were, they didn't get rid of the bosses and shareholders, not by a long chalk.

COLUM: They had a go. In Russia they made it, but unfortunately some fool of a woman shot Lenin in the head, and Russia ended up with Joe Stalin, and from then on, the bosses had a great weapon. Any time anybody wanted to get rid of the bosses, they said he was a blood-thirsty, slaughtering megalomaniac like Stalin preparing to seize total power—in this way, they kept total power all to their blood-thirsty, slaughtering, megalomaniac selves.

VARI: In spite of this, here and there, people tried to get not just better wages, but a whole better way of doing things. In Italy, they had a go—(*MUSIC in*) the car-workers of Turin, the craftsmen of Milan, the organised working-class the length of the land united behind the Red Flag, the Bandiera Rossa—

Bandiera Rossa

The people's flag is deepest red
It shrouded oft our martyred dead;
And 'ere their limbs grew stiff and cold
Their hearts' blood dyed to every fold.
Then raise the scarlet standard high!
Beneath its folds we'll live and die.
Though cowards flinch and traitors sneer
We'll keep the red flag flying here.
Look 'round the Frenchman loves its blaze,
The sturdy German chants its praise,
In Moscow's vaults its hymns are sung
Chicago swells the surging throng.
It waved above our infant might
When all ahead seemed dark as night.
It witnessed many a deed and vow,
We will not change its colour now.
It well recalls the triumphs past
It gives the hope of peace at last
The banner brigh, the symbol plain
Of human right and human gain.
It suits today the meek and base,
Whose minds are fixed on pelf and place,
To cringe beneath the rich man's frown,
And haul that sacred emblem down.
With heads uncovered swear we all
To bear it onward till we fall;
Come dungeons dark or gallows grim,
This song shall be our parting hymn.

MILTON: But they failed. They were ruthlessly crushed, and in 1924, Mussolini came to power, and fascism rescued Italian moneymen, with brute force, from conceding an inch to the demands of the people.

VARI: Here in England, the workers in the 1920s got fed up with carrying the burden of the ups and downs of capitalism, and in 1926 they had a General Strike. We all know what happened to that, don't we? In spite of the valiant holding on of the miners, the strike crumbled—the TUC just didn't have the strength of will, the organisation, the determination, or the political conviction, to carry it through. We lost.

(A *caption appears on stage saying* 'Silkworkers 1933')

SILKWORKER 1: I am 43. My husband left me ten years ago, and I have not heard of him since. I have six children, some earning, but not enough.

I am now unemployed. I have no more furniture to sell, I have already parted with everything I could spare to the neighbours for whatever I could get, and now I have three chairs, a couch and the beds left.

I don't suppose I shall ever have more for I don't know on Fridays who to pay first. I get the food from the nearest shop on "STRAP" and I must pay that debt, or there's no more forthcoming for the rest of the week. The rent is 7/6 a week and I must not get far behind with that.

It's the children's clothes that worry me most. They want so much feeding, and they always want their shoes soled. I can't let them go without shoes in the bad weather, but that means they must go without food.

SILKWORKER 2: My husband lost his job two years ago. He is 62 years old and I am 66. He had to go to the Public Assistance Committee, 18 months ago. His unemployment money was reduced from 23/– to 10/– a week. Later it dropped to 7/6 then 5/– for three months now it has been 2/6 for the two of us.

All my children are married except my youngest son of 21 who lives with us and pays me 20/– a week. He gives it regularly and ungrudgingly, but he does not realize that it's only enough to keep him. I can barely find the rent and rates and coal and gas money out of what remains, when I have bought enough food for him for the week.

There is little food for us, for this reason we never have our meals together. I buy 1/– worth of meat a week for my son, half a pound of bacon and I make him a milk pudding sometimes.

If my son were to know that his father and I have bread and butter and tea for every meal, he would not eat what I put before him, and that would not do. He must eat if he is to work.

(*At the end of the readings, a moment's pause, then the band with song.*

Thank You, We've Never Had It So Good

Thank you—thank you—thank you.

Thanks—for the television set
With integrated circuits and vertical hold.
I'm integrated into the circuit
It has a vertical hold on me.

Thanks—for the family motor-car
With easy smooth running and power-glide ride.
I'm easy to run, I work smoothly
Glide on the power that rides on me.

Thanks—for the domestic appliances
The washing-up machines and tumbling dry.
I'm washed-up mechanically every night
I'm beaten as I'm swept and cleaned out.

Thanks—for the deep-freeze foods
For the fresh-picked frozen fruit and the cubical fish.
I'm picked and I'm frozen and I'm packaged
I'm cut to size and convenient shape—

For *we've* never had it so good—
And they've never had us so sweetly.
We've never had it so good—
And they've never had us so completely:

(*Reggae beat*)

Thank you, man for the nylon sheets
To wash up in the Hoovermatic.
Thank you, man, for detergent-soap:
The change in our lives is dramatic.

Thank you, man, for the motorways,
To drive up in the lovely motor—
Thank you, man, for the jumbo-jet,
I'm afloat, I'm a floating voter.

For we've never had it so good (*Chorus etc.*)

Thank you—thank you—thank you.

VARI: After the war, a remarkable discovery was made. John Maynard
Keynes reminded the bosses, that it was no good making a lot
of things, if you didn't pay your workers enough to buy a few
of them from you. So through the 1950s and the 1960s we had
the great Consumer Boom—and we had never had it so good.
There is no doubt that since 1945 capitalism—that is, the
system of private enterprise that we in the so-called Free World
live and work under—has made huge advances.

COLUM: So before we can tell you the story of the Four Strikes in East
Kilbride, which is what we're here to do, I suppose we'd better

try to tell something of the bigger story, the most dramatic story of our time, the story of how capitalism in the Western world emerged from a world war—with Europe in ruins, and stony broke—

VARI: With Japan defeated by the greatest single act of terrorism known in the history of mankind. With only the USA enjoying the fruits of victory.

COLUM: But in 30 years, three main things have happened: one, science and technology have transformed Western industry; two, the growth of huge corporations has changed the entire economic structure of the West; and three, political power has slowly but surely moved from elected national governments to strange, hidden international forces that are difficult to see, let alone control.

VARI: Capitalism has been busy. It's been dynamic—

HILTON: Yes—we've been pretty dynamic—amazingly dynamic really, considering. And we owe a good deal of it, yes, a great deal, to our boffins. Here we all are, for example—aren't we? Simple enough—you'd say—us chaps here, just chatting to you chaps there—but hold on a moment, hold hard—stop. And think about it. Examine the electrical socket, out of which comes the juice that drives the band—well, yes—anyway, the lights, the amplifiers, the heating—yes, examine the socket. What are we plugging into exactly? Yes—the mains. But what is the mains plugged into? Power. Electrical power. From the power station. The National Grid. Perhaps this bit was produced from coal. In the old days the collier-laddies used to go down with little pick-axes and chip away at the seam—what have you got now? Bloody great machines tearing away at the bowels of the earth, thundering out more coal per shift than a thousand men. Perhaps our electric supply came from oil. Look at the technology that's groping around the North Sea, prodding away thousands of feet below the sea-bed, pumping the stuff ashore, computer-controlled refineries breaking down the crude—all the skills of geology, physics, higher mathematics, chemistry, all developed to their peak, so we can plug in our little plugs.

Or perhaps this bit of our electricity comes from nuclear energy, the mighty new power stations humming away day and night using up the terrible energy of the nuclear fission, all to give us our 240 volts. Yes, power, that's what we're plugging into. The power of science, of technology, leaping forward every year, every month, every day, to make life better.

Look at this thing—an amplifier. Solid-state, and British made. What's gone into that? The transistor. The printed electrical circuit. Miniaturisation. All discoveries of the last 20 years. What else? Packaging—look at that—fancy dials, lovely turnable controls, that light up, satisfying clunk as you switch it on. The skills of the packaging man. Brushed alloy face. Plastic leather bodywork. A beautiful, sophisticated piece of equipment not even dreamt of 30 years ago. The boffins have been busy again.

And how did we all get here? Bus? Train? Van? Car? The technology poured into the production of one motorcar today is astonishing. Yes, more can, and will, be done. But we've come a long way from the Austin 7.

And what are we dressed in? Man-made fibres—plastic shoes with compound soles, bonded together. Nylon socks. Terylene trousers. Dacron shirts. We're all dressed in chemicals. Plastic macs? PVC underwear? You never know, do you? Ha ha ha. And what have we all been eating? Without the boffins beavering away to develop the chemicals to make the fertilisers to improve the soil to grow the food—we'd be starving. The back-room boys, slaving away over a hot test-tube, quivering every muscle in the lab, waiting for the great Eureka—another mighty motion—or phut—the damp squib. Our new houses, unit-built—quicker to throw up, cheaper. Our phones, to talk to each other, our cosmetics so we look nice and smell nice—our vitamins, our package holidays to keep us healthy, our telly, our Long-Playing records, our tape cassettes to keep us amused, our very lives—for how many of us have survived only because some boffin discovered antibiotics? All those wonderful things we have, all, *all* are the products of the dynamism, of *us*, the capitalists, the mighty powers of science, and technology for *your* benefit. You know, I think, we're pretty remarkable people. Don't you? This is how we like to think of all of you—enjoying to the full the Marvels of Modern Science.
(*A caption appears on stage saying 'The Marvels of Modern Science'.*)
(*Muzak version of Red Flag.*)

DENNIS: Well, here we are, dear, surrounded by all the marvels of modern science—what a wondrous array of things we have to choose from . . .

CHRISSIE: Well—yes. They're none of them paid for, though.

DENNIS: Are you feeling glum, dear, perhaps a bit despondent, hangdog or down-in-the-mouth?

CHRISSIE: Er—yes, I do believe I am. What can have come over me these days?

DENNIS: What you need, my pet, is a comfy sit-down on our new polyvinyl space-craft-shaped inflatable armchair, with your feet up on the brushed-nylon latex-foam filled beer-barrel-shaped pouf, and a good glare at the telly.

CHRISSIE: Wonderful!

DENNIS: I'll switch it on.
(*They sit and stare. Music stops*)

COLUM: My name is Samson Skukune. I work for Rio Tinto Zinc of London, your British mining company. I work in Palabora, in South Africa. I have a wife and three children. According to the South African government the bare minimum for us to exist is

£44 per month. Your Rio Tinto pays me £33.90 per month. We do not have the right to strike for higher wages, even though my children are undernourished, and one is suffering from kwaziokor. He is becoming a little hazy in the head from not enough food. His belly is swollen and his face is covered with sores. I cannot afford to take him to the doctor.

There are more than 2,000 of us working in the mine—we all live in a compound in Namakaale, five miles away. After one year working here, we are forced to leave and move on from these places, in case we get to know each other too well, get organised, and demand better wages, better conditions. We would not be so foolish—the police would shoot us. Palabora makes a profit for your RTZ of 96 million pounds per year, minimum—it is very successful. By the way, Palabora is a copper-mine. I dig out of the earth, the copper that is used in this television set, these people are watching. I expect to die before I am 45 years old.

(*Music back*)

DENNIS: Feeling better, dear?

CHRISSIE: There's nothing quite like a good goggle for giving you that certain zest for life.

DENNIS: What shall we do? How about a nice cup of tea?

CHRISSIE: No, no. I don't fancy a cup of tea. Not since that programme about Ceylon.

DENNIS: Well I'll rush off and make you a quick cup of coffee, before they do a programme about Brazil.

(*Goes to get coffee.*)

DENNIS: There you are, my old dutch, as we say, pure coffee blown up and frozen in the act into fluffy lumps, now reconstituted by me and some hot water.

CHRISSIE: Mm, lovely.

DENNIS: And so much more convenient—now dear, here we are enjoying our leisure-time, but not, I fancy, to the full.

CHRISSIE: Well I'm quite happy, just sitting here—

DENNIS: Of course you're not, the countryside is now, don't forget, ours at the ignition of a sparking plug—what say you to a jaunt in the economy-sized family motor-car, now within easy reach of our socio-economic grouping?

CHRISSIE: Well, I suppose the motorway does beckon . . .

DENNIS: We must energetically use up all the resources available to us—after all, we cannot simply turn our backs on the marvels of modern science—now then—the Cotswolds?

CHRISSIE: Oh not again.

DENNIS: Well the M4 is a finer feat of civil engineering than that bumpy old M1, and far worthier of our usage. Howsoever, be that as it may—what about Kent? See Britain's beer in its natural stage.

CHRISSIE: Oo, the hop-fields.

DENNIS: No dear, ICI Maidstone.

CHRISSIE: Couldn't we just go and see my mum?

DENNIS: That would be a quite proper use for the car, but not, I fancy, a fully satisfying one. No, I really do think it'll have to be the Cotswolds again. So off with your cosy quilted nylon slipperettes, and on with the composition driving-shoes—the rich tapestry of England shall unfold before us . . .
(They sit side by side as if in car.)

HILTON: I work at Ford's Halewood. I started off working on the
(*as* FORD   headlinings, and I never thought I'd survive. I used to come
WORKER)   home from work and fall asleep. My legs and arms used to be burning. I didn't have relations with my wife for months. I've seen men took ill, injured, at work. They couldn't stop that line. You could be dying and they wouldn't stop it.

    In fact one bloke, he was only about forty, did die. We were in the locker room before the shift had started, and he collapsed with a pain in his chest. He went an awful colour, but then he reckoned he was alright. We went down the stairs on to the shop floor, walked across to the line and he collapsed again, y'know—flat on the floor. His face was an awful grey colour. We all rushed around him and the buzzer went. The line started. The foreman came across shouting 'get to work, get on the line', and there we were sticking things on the cars, and he was lying there . . . dead . . . in front of us.

    We make the Ford car that these people are enjoying the countryside in.

DENNIS: What a superb experience—glide suspension, robust road-holding, finger tip controls, faultless acceleration, and I even got to use the emergency blinders—oh bliss it was this day to be alive.

CHRISSIE: Mm—and such a joy to be able to adjust the seat back to your own convenience.

DENNIS: And so to bed—er, have they had anything on telly yet about cocoa dear?

CHRISSIE: Not yet—but it'll be alright, it's Cadbury's Drinking Chocolate, and they're Quakers, the Cadburys.

DENNIS: Good—and so to bed with a comforting cup of cocoa, to sip as we rest our heads on the PVC head-board, before we drift off into slumber-land and dream sweet dreams.

VARI: My name is Annie Morris. My husband works at the BP plant at Baglan Bay, in South Wales, making PVC. They make it by filling these giant vats with vinyl-chloride gas, then heating it up under pressure till it condenses into sticky white powder. Allan, my husband, then goes in the vats and scrapes this stuff off the sides. There's still some of that gas in there, though, and they discovered it can give you a peculiar kind of liver cancer. This only came out when three blokes died of it within a few months of each other, they'd all been working on what Allan does. They checked up, and 38 more were discovered around the world. One in Runcorn, and a bloke Allan worked with in Baglan. Allan says they must have known about it all along, another firm, Dow Chemicals, owned up to it in 1961. Still, he might be alright. The only thing is, there's another disease off that gas, called AOL, reduces your circulation and makes your joints weld together. And it makes men impotent. They checked 40 at Derby, and 18 of them couldn't. They're supposed to be getting the gas out first now, before Allan goes in. But he's been working there for seven years. When I go to bed at night, I find it hard to sleep.

Science is a Wonder

Science is a wonder, science is sweet,
Science puts the nation right back on its feet,
Science is the hero of the man in the street.
Science makes a soybean taste like real live meat.
Yes, it's a marvel.

Poly-vinyl-chloride—PVC
Making lots of bread for ICI and BP.
And the petro-chemical industry,
Doing lots of nice things for you and me.
And we need it.

Science is a wonder, science is nice.
We need it and we feed it and we never think twice
But someone in the boardroom has been loading the dice
They're taking all the profit but who's paying the price?
It's not the chairman.

VARI: Yes, science is wonderful, and the new dynamic force of capitalism was there to make sure it kept on being wonderful.

COLUM: Nils Bohr split the atom, releasing immense amounts of energy. First came the Bomb. Then nuclear power stations, producing expensive electricity and lots of profit all over the world.

DENNIS: Whittle developed the jet engine, for warplanes. The aerospace industry is now a multi-billion dollar business.

HILTON: Electronic guidance and surveillance systems lead to the computer business, already booming. With the use of the microchip, smaller computers will soon be on sale: no decent home will be without one.

COLUM: Fleming discovered penicillin. The sale of antibiotics, antidepressants, contraceptive pills and sleeping pills has helped many people, saved many lives, and made more than a few very rich.

DENNIS: From the petro-chemical developments have come man-made fibres, cosmetics, synthetic smells, dyes, paints, fertilisers, LP records, deodorants, margarine, plastics of all descriptions, stockings, tights, photographic film, and billions of dollars profit.

COLUM: In agriculture, fertilisers, pesticides and now strains of wheat have pushed up production to feed the ever-growing population of the world. They are available together as package deals from Fisons and ICI.

HILTON: Lasers, radar, vertical take-off aeroplanes, stereo, magnetic tape, new building materials, colour television—all these and many more brought to you by science and the profit-motive, hand in hand.

> Science is a wonder, science is sweet,
> Science puts the nation right back on its feet,
> Science is the hero of the man in the street.
> Science makes a soybean taste like real live meat.
> Yes it's a marvel.

(*A caption appears on stage saying 'Science at Work'.*)

HILTON: But, of course, science wasn't just used to invent cheaper goodies. It was also used to invent cheaper ways of making goodies.

VARI: In the old days, labour was just inefficient. Too many men, doing too little work, making too little profit.
(*Sings*)

> A growing boy won't grow, won't grow
> If he's living underground
> For the sun doesn't shine, the wind doesn't blow
> And the birds don't fly around.
>
> A breathing man can't breathe, can't breathe
> After ten years underground
> For your lungs go hard and your breath won't leave
> And you make a rattling sound.
>
> Working, working in my way
> Working, working, for my pay,
> Working, working all my day
> Just to make some rich man richer.
>
> The factory fence grows high, grows high,
> And it locks you right inside
> If you can't go on, lay down and die
> Or the man will say you lied,
>
> For your lathe-belt wheels won't stop, won't stop
> Oh I know 'cos I have tried,
> And the man wants more till the day you drop,
> For he's never satisfied.
>
> Working, working etc.

(*Enter* TAYLOR)

COLUM: Well hello. Name's Taylor, Fred Taylor. I hail from Philadelphia and I can't abide inefficiency. Now my daddy was a rich man—I make no secret of that—but we well, dad had me lined up for Harvard, but I guess I just dropped out—you know the sort of thing. I got a job as a common labourer, Midvale Steel Works—boss was a family friend. You know what I discovered? Inefficiency. Slacking. Even on piecework. Not one third of the work we should have produced *was* produced. Why?

Inefficiency, slacking. Those men were my friends. But they did not work as hard as they could have worked in case the rate was cut. Well, pretty soon I got to be gang boss. I said to those men: 'I aim to get more work out of those lathes, men.' They were my friends, but they didn't like it, no sir. But I said to the management, I want your confidence, and they gave me that confidence. For three years I fought a long, lonely battle for what I know was true, and right, and honest: a fair day's work from each man. I retrained those men. I showed my friends it could be done. They threatened to have me over the fence. I brought in new, more willing men. They could do it, they did it—but these other guys put the finger on them—corrupt, despicable blackmail. But in the end, well, they were persuaded: the truth will always win. In the end. Over many years of scientific study of efficiency and what I call "fairness" at work, I have come to my three main principles of Scientific Management.

One: No work-task is so simple or so complex that management can't learn more about it than the worker who does that task. You see, ordinary management just did not observe their men systematically: the men ran rings around them, dishonest, lazy rings. Scientific management must know more than the men, must discover those speedier ways of doing things their workers *know* about, and *could* use, but which they conceal. Why? Self-interest. I know. I worked.

Second principle: All possible brainwork must be removed from the shop floor and centred in the planning or laying-out department. Now this one is *the key* to scientific management. It's so obvious it makes me laugh. Why, if a worker is allowed to decide how much work he'll do and how he'll do it, he simply won't do a fair day's work. So what do you do? Principle one: Study the job. Principle Two: Plan it out in your management office. Co-ordinate. No principle is easy: tell the guys what their job is, and how to do it, and how fast it can, and *must*, be done. This is science. This is management. Study. Plan. Instruct. The only thing that remains for your gang-bosses, or your foremen is to get those instructions carried out to the letter. This may be tricky, but it can be done. It must be done—or your whole pack of cards collapses. And you have no management. No science. No fairness. No efficiency. What do you have? Waste. Dishonesty, anarchy. Chaos. These workers are my friends. They don't want to see their works closed down. Do they? Of course not. They are, at heart, honest, respectable men who admire fairness, scientific progress, and efficiency.
(*Chorus—Working, working etc.*)

    Now this job I'm doing got to do it,
    Isn't making any sense to me
    And the more I'm working—got to do it, got to do it
    Well the less sense can I see.

Done a hundred jigs—must get through it, must get through it
Where I once did twenty-three
And the rate keeps falling—they can screw it, they can screw it
Someone's winning and it's just not me.
Working, working, etc.
(*Enter* HENRY FORD)

HILTON: My name's Henry Ford, and as far as I'm concerned history is bunk. I've just been down to the slaughterhouse in Chicago, and what did I see? Not bands of angels coming after me—no sir. I saw a chain travelling along overhead, and from that chain were hanging the carcasses of animals, and as that chain passed down the line of men, bang—one guy killed the beast, slice, another guy cut its head off, slit, another guy disembowelled it, snip snip, another guy skinned it, hack, hack, hack, hack, four guys cut the legs off, carve carve, out came the ribs, chop chop—chops. Wonderful. What went in a cow came out saleable cuts of beef. That, my friends, is science. And I thought; what cannot be achieved in industry with this wonderful method? A belt, a travelling belt, along which your product moves. A line of men, or teams of men. At every stage, along that line, your teams of men make their contributions to your finished product. What went in a load of bits of metal comes out—a motorcar. I think I am about to become rich and famous. And with the aid of the scientific management techniques of my friend Fred W. Taylor, I think I am about to become *very* rich, and very famous. I have invented the production line. History may not love me for this—but, as I have already observed, profits is profits, and history is bunk.
(*Turns in to scene*)
How many processes do I see there on my production line? Two—a mere two. And I am employing five people. Am I a charitable trust? Forget it. You three—you're fired.

Work Song

Working, working, chorus, etc.
Belt that tackle on the chassis frame
Belt that tackle on the chassis frame
Belt that tackle on the chassis frame
Belt that tackle on the chassis frame.
(*Enter* HUMAN RELATIONS ENGINEER)

DENNIS: Hello. I am a personnel manager, or psycho-technological human relations engineer. I don't have a name. In this plant, it would appear that our production-line techniques are a little old-fashioned. We are told that what we need is massive new investment in computerisation of the whole process, so we have reluctantly agreed to a merger—to being eaten up would be more accurate—with a larger firm, who have the capital to invest in this computer-control business. It means that most of the men won't have very much to do, so we can get rid of half of them—which makes my life a lot easier—but the work for the few who remain—even though they are dealing with immensely complicated devices—will in fact become more boring. However, boring work in my experience leads to a more docile sort of work force, on the whole, so I don't mind, there'll be less for me to worry about. (*To one guy*) Here's your cards, and your redundancy money. You're layed off. (*Guy goes*) Don't worry—you're not going to be laid off—the machine needs you. OK? (*Second does machine minding*) Why can't they get machines to mind the blasted machines? That'll be the day: all my troubles'll be over. Thank God that went quietly. Bodes well for the future.

Work Song

(*Song—Sweet at first, then bitter note in verse, followed by broken rhythms*)

SOLO: I work here all alone, alone,
         And the tape says what to do
         My mind is all I own, I own,
         Very soon they'll own that too.

         For my needs are all explained, explained,
         And what they dream comes true
         My desires are computed and I'm well maintained
         And the next in line is you.
         Working, working, chorus, etc.

LAID-OFF MEN: We're not necessary
                 What nobody needs:
                 We're not necessary
                 Thrown out—like the weeds.

         For everything in the garden is lovely,
         And the lupins and the pinks grow tall,
         So we're piled up with the compost in the corner,
         To be decomposed and sprinkled in the fall.

         We're not necessary, etc.

VARI: Yes. Capitalism has used science and technology to make great leaps, in making available countless consumer goods and services that your man on strike for ten per cent would not have dreamt of. In theory, this leap could have been highly beneficial to the whole of mankind, but such are the conflicts within this system, men and women all over the world are still in misery, children starving and workers' lives constantly in danger, to produce these wonderful things.

COLUM: And capitalism has used a different kind of science and technology to devise methods of manufacturing these things more efficiently, more cheaply and with less human sweat. In theory, this mechanisation and computerisation of manufacture could be liberating millions from the drudgery of work. In fact, such are the conflicts within this system, it liberates people only to throw them on the dole and cut them off from the benefits they have worked so hard to achieve.

VARI: But there is no doubt that scientific and technological advances in products and in ways of making those products can and do make many people's lives better, more interesting, even longer.

COLUM: To carry on expanding, researching and developing, however, the big corporations need to control the two great uncontrollables—the workers, and the market. And even here, great advances have been made. We've come a long way from the image of the bosses that the old pit-owners put around . . .

Mr Brassneck's Song

(*Half spoken*):   Now I'm a pretty down to earth man—
I don't mince words nor fool.
I've made myself what I am—
I'm a boss, of the good old school . . .

(*Sing*):   I've made my brass
In a world that's harsh and cruel,
As I've drove down life's broad highway,
I've learnt this golden rule.

(*Chorus*):   Go one smarter than your neighbour
Put on your old silk hat.
Get out your cane
And your gold watch-chain
And there's welcome on the mat.

Bu-u-ut
Take no pity on your neighbour
If he should come unstuck.
If you crack your whip
And never make a slip
You can grind his face in't muck.

(*Spoken*):   Heehee, that's it—you'll soon get the hang and soon we'll all be singing it—here we go—

Now I've just got one big fact'ry
But I fancy three or four.
I can see my way to victory
When I walk that factory floor.

I've sacked all t' men and got some lasses
If they squeak they're out the door.
If I can screw some work from t' working classes,
I'll have fact'ries by the score.

(*Chorus*):   For I say: Go one smarter than your neighbour etc.

(Spoken):   I rule these lasses with a rod of iron—and they love me for it—only the other day a feller came up to me and he said, Mr. Brassneck, you're a hero to me, you are, you're like John F. Kennedy—oh thank you very much I said. Can't remember what he said his name was—something something Oswald . . . Must have been one of the Oswaldtwistle Oswalds. Here, and I've got a few words to say about them damn Reds that come sneaking in under the gates, upsetting my girls—militants, left wing students like Mick McGahey and Dingle Foot, and the like.

You must have an arse, you've got an elbow
But you don't know which is which.
'Cos they're queering up my pitch
The whole darn lot can go to hell, though.

If you lot want to grow much older
Soak the poor don't soak the rich.
Don't go getting any bolder
Or you'll end up in the ditch.

(Spoken):   No, just you.

(Chorus):   Go one better than your neighbour,
Put on your old silk hat, etc.
(*Enter smooth,* PERRY COMO-STYLE TECHNOCRATIC LABOUR-RELATIONS EXPERT. *He watches end of 'old boss' performance with distaste. Claps politely as* BRASSNECK *goes.*)

PC: Those guys—those old, blundering incompetent—yes, fools. Oh, they worked well enough in their time, but to see them now. You know, they really upset me. It's so—distasteful: bullying, authoritarian, a walking challenge to any worker, an open invitation to *battle*. And battle, my friends, is what we in labour relations are here to eliminate. Our task is easily reduced to a basic proposition: to get the most production from the labour force for the least cost. Now that task has to be tackled in a cool, modern, scientific manner. Look at this, for example:
(OLD BOSS *in office, enter* JENNY, *a worker*)

JENNY: Mr Brassneck, we're working harder, making more cotton, we want a rise. Ten per cent minimum.

BRASSNECK: How dare you come storming in here, waving your arms? Damn cheek.

JENNY: I've been sent—I'm a delegate.

BRASSNECK: And who gave you permission to stop working. You're costing me money—get back to that machine, at once.

JENNY: Ten per cent.

BRASSNECK: Not one brass farthing. If you don't like it you can go.

JENNY: Right—we're on strike, the lot of us.

BRASSNECK: Do your worst—it'll hurt you more than it hurts me, and I'm telling you now—you're wasting your time.

JENNY: You bastard—we'll see who wins.
(*They go off.*)

PC: Now what mistakes did Mr. Brassneck make in that little interview? Let's analyse them. (*to* BRASSNECK) Well, your first mistake, if I may say so, was to see her yourself. You see, you are the embodiment of wealth and power, and flaunting yourself like that is like waving a red rag to a bull. You, sir, must remain discreetly in the background—a few meetings in the boardroom, a few gatherings with fellow directors at your modest country house, some international flights on important export-winning business—maintain what they call a low profile. And if you *have* to reveal yourself, it must be as protector of the lawful interests of the thousands of widows and pensioners living precariously on their shares in your company. I would suggest, sir, that for a modest outlay of, say, six thousand per annum, you can hire an expert in these matters, such as myself. You will not only be buying my expertise, however—you will also be acquiring your own discreet distance from conflict. What do you say?

BRASSNECK: Five thousand.

PC: Five thousand plus 100 Ordinary Shares per annum.

BRASSNECK: Jesus Christ, what have I done?

PC: Now then, Mr B, mistake number two—any ideas?

BRASSNECK: Listening to you.

PC: Come, come, Mr. B, no hard feelings, the labourer is worthy of his hire. No—mistake number two was: CLASS. You aroused her class instincts—hostility, distrust, worse still—*solidarity*. Now I'm sure you can perceive how much that mistake could cost you per annum—hundreds of thousands of pounds. No, no—the message must be—there is no class distinction in Britain any more, we're all equal now, and we're all workers together—and anybody who says any different is a Communist dividing the nation in the pay of the Kremlin—right?

BRASSNECK: So they are.

PC: Yes, you've got the general idea. But subtlety, please, Mr. Brassneck. A bit of finesse. Never raise class instincts. It's costly. First of all, never bluster at your fellow-workers—always sigh, and shake your head, speak with a trace of a common accent, and invoke national unity, the need to control inflation, and the demands of the lower-paid. It works a treat.

BRASSNECK: Not with this lot.

PC: Exactly. Mistake number three. Negotiating at shop floor level. Always go for your national union official, take it to the top— these men understand our problems, and the problems of Britain, they have a much broader perspective on life, are more amenable to discussion—much more sophisticated. Chop these local lot down to size, they're all union members, they'll understand.

BRASSNECK: They'll still want more money.

PC: Mistake number four: you said no. Never say no, always negotiate—you can increase your productivity, pull the rug from under your shop stewards, introduce new labour saving machinery so you can lay off your militants, you can close down whole shops if you just negotiate. It's a two-way thing, you know, give and take.

BRASSNECK: It sounds effeminate to me, the whole idea.

PC: It's scientific, it's beautiful, it's engineering human beings into a manageable shape, it's controlling your labour force so you can predict your rising output with confidence, plan your expansion, your capital investment, your lay-offs, your marketing programme for years and years ahead. If you've got to do something unpopular, you can programme when to do it—just before Christmas, or the summer holidays, so they won't go on strike—you can even programme how long they'll go on strike for, how much it'll cost you, and whether it's worth it or not. It's organisation, Mr B. It's bringing things under *your* control.

BRASSNECK: But you've still got your unions, your Red wreckers and your wildcat unofficials, they still want more money and they're still a mob of working-class hooligans.

PC: Mistake number five, Mr B. You must never, ever, lose your self-control, especially not in front of the television cameras. Now: you want to see some results for your money—right? Watch this.
(*Sits at desk. Enter* JENNY)

PC: Come in. Oh hello Jenny, love, how are you? How's the kids—liking their new school are they? Sit down, sit down, take the weight off your legs—always glad to see you. You must feel free to drop in any time for a chat—now, what's our problem? Oh, before you begin, I've got some progress to report—I've been pushing through this idea of regular, quarterly get-togethers between a few people from the shop-floor and a few management blokes so we can hear what management's plans are, in outline, and mull over any problems about conditions in the works—lav. Paper, canteen facilities, new shift proposals—a bit of a consultation, so you all can have a say in how the place is run, if you'd like that. I think I can get the board to agree if I keep pushing, though they are a bit, you know, reluctant. We can't discuss wages, or manning, or any of that, naturally—just ways of making our working lives more—fruitful. What do you think?

JENNY: Sounds a bit pathetic, but it'll do for a start.

PC: Good, I thought you'd like it. Now then, what's new?

JENNY: The girls on Number Two reckon they're being pushed since these new machines came in. Productivity's gone up 25%, that's with half of them laid off—they're clocking up 50% more per worker, and getting a 12% rise—we reckon that's not on.

PC: Yes, I can see their point of view. I know what management will say, of course—the machines have to be paid for, borrowed money paid back plus interest charges—and we did agree that 12% was acceptable.

JENNY: Well it's not any more.

PC: Yes. The cost of living is getting out of hand.

JENNY: Too right it is, it's ridiculous.

PC: So really we'll just have to wait for the fresh round of across-the-board national negotiations starting next month, I think.

JENNY: Oh no we don't—we want action, now.

PC: You *are* a union member, aren't you, Jenny?

JENNY: Of course I am.

PC: OK, I'll ring your head office, have a chat with them, fair enough?

JENNY: Oh no you don't—you're just trying to split us up—they're arguing for cost-of-living increases that everybody wants. I'm talking about that lot in Number Two doing half as much work again for a few bob a week extra.

PC: By God, Jenny, you're quick—if you're ever stuck for a job, you can have mine.

JENNY: No thanks.

PC: But seriously, love, look—we made an agreement, let's stick to it, eh?

JENNY: You stick it where you like—there'll be a mass meeting this afternoon, and if they feel this afternoon the way they feel this morning, they'll be out, the lot of them.

PC: Well before this gets too complicated, I'll get in your area organiser from the union. He's a paid official, and negotiating is his trade—one moment—Arthur, come in now, would you. (*Enter* ARTHUR) Thanks for dropping by Arthur—you know Jenny, of course.

ARTHUR: Oh yes, Sister Jenny and I meet from time to time.

JENNY: Listen Arthur, those girls in Number Two are going round the bend. They're fed up and they're coming out.

ARTHUR: Now that's one thing we must avoid.

JENNY: What?

ARTHUR: We can't negotiate two rises at the same time.

JENNY: That's what he said.

ARTHUR: He knows his business, that feller. Now go back and talk to them, Jenny, make them see reason, tell them to stay put.

JENNY: (*Looks out of window*) You're too late—they're out.

ARTHUR: What? Oh dear me.

BRASSNECK: And a right mess you made of that. There's only one way to deal with this situation—sack them, the lot of them. And first to get her cards is that one.

JENNY: Oh hello, Mr Brassneck, where've you crawled out from?

ARTHUR: Jenny, love, that will never do—personal abuse . . . don't let's descend to that level or negotiations won't even begin.

BRASSNECK: You're fired.

PC: No no no no, Mr Brassneck, please—you mustn't go back to those old methods—we're all workers together, remember.

JENNY: You fire me and your plant shuts down for as long as it takes to get me back again.

ARTHUR: Jenny, he's perfectly within his rights—you've brought this on yourself.

BRASSNECK: Threats, eh? Well I'll starve you out of here—you're not so bloody popular as you think.

PC: No no no no—oh God—class solidarity invoked, abuse, bullying a woman—Mr. Brassneck, let's just have a quiet word next door . . .

JENNY: Don't push your luck, Mr Brassneck.

ARTHUR: No no no, Jenny—you're being abusive, truculent—let's have a quiet word next door.

BRASSNECK: (*to* JENNY) Communist!

JENNY: Capitalist!

ARTHUR & PC: No no no no.

BRASSNECK: Rabble-rouser!

JENNY: Profiteer!

ARTHUR & PC: No no no no. (*Sing*) Please—lady and gentleman—please—I don't know how this all began, but: please, lady and gentleman—harmony is part of the national plan.

Industrial Harmony

COLUM AND HILTON:
Ladies and gentlemen—please
Please
We don't know how this all began
But—please

Lady and gentleman
Please, please
Let us do all we can
For—HARMONY
It's in the National Interest.

(COLUM & HILTON *continue harmonising on the words* 'Harmony' *and* 'National Interest' *as*)

CHRISSIE:
I won't be insulted
I won't be abused
I'm not consulted
I'm not amused

You rob us and cheat us
You take all we've won
You think that you've beat us
But we've not begun.

COLUM AND HILTON:
Please,
Lady and gentleman,
HARMONY

(*They continue as*)

DENNIS:
You won't get away with
Your Bolshevik bluster
Don't like it here
You can sod off to Russia

I'm richer and stronger
Without any doubt
And I can last longer
So you can stay out.

COLUM: (*to* CHRISSIE) Let's be reasonable people
No need to take on the boss.

HILTON: (*to* DENNIS) Let's be reasonable people
No need to make any loss.

DENNIS AND (*to* COLUM AND HILTON) You mealy-mouthed puppet
CHRISSIE: Get out of my way
There's one way to stop it
And today is the day.

COLUM AND (*Pompous, military-ish beat—Eric Coates March*)
HILTON: We are the guardians
Of law and order
We are the protectors
Of status quo.

COLUM: You guard the frontier

HILTON: And I'll guard the border
Or they'll get together and blow

COLUM: If the working class
Won't compromise

HILTON: And the ruling class
Won't modernise

COLUM AND
HILTON: They'll both have—to GO!

CHRISSIE: (*Spoken*) That man's making half a million a year out of us, and
there's girls down there being robbed. We're all being robbed.

HILTON: (*to* CHRISSIE, *spoken*) Not *him*, Jenny, the shareholders—
widows, orphans.

CHRISSIE: He is the shareholders.

COLUM: (*Sung*) Let's be reasonable people
No need to take on the boss.

DENNIS: (*Spoken*) That harridan is trying to ruin me, close down the
factory and start a revolution . . .

COLUM: (*to* DENNIS) As a spokesman for the union involved, Mr.
Brassneck, I can assure you we wish you a fair return on your
investment, your factory to remain open to provide
employment, and we certainly do not want a revolution.

DENNIS: I don't trust any of you—spare the rod and spoil the child.
We've spared the rod for too long, now look at you.

HILTON: (*Sung*) Let's be reasonable people
No need to make any loss

HILTON: (*to* DENNIS, *spoken*) Come on, Mr. B, leave this to the
           professionals—you'll win in the end.
           (DENNIS *goes off.*)

COLUM: (*to* CHRISSIE, *spoken*) Come on, Jenny, leave this to your paid
           officials—you'll win in the end.
           (CHRISSIE *goes off.*)

COLUM AND (*Sung together*) We are the guardians
HILTON: Of law and order
               We are the protectors
               Of status quo.

COLUM: You guard the frontier

HILTON: And I'll guard the border
               Or they'll get together and blow.

COLUM: If the working class
               Won't compromise

HILTON: And the ruling class
               Won't modernise . . .

COLUM AND
HILTON: They'll both have—to GO!

HILTON: There are many ways of controlling the work force. Western
           governments use whatever device seems appropriate to maintain
           industrial law and order. For example, the CIA, working on
           behalf of the American multinational corporations, actually
           goes to the length of paying their agents to found whole new
           unions in South America to bring the work force under their
           direct control.

COLUM: They also specialise in paying for CIA controlled International
           Trade Secretariats, like the International Federation of Working
           Newspapermen, the International Federation of Clerical and
           Technical Employees, and the International Federation of
           Petroleum and Chemical workers. The technique is to subvert a
           union official, with intimidation or bribes, then create a new,
           tame union, or a new, pro-American International Trade
           Secretariat, and put their man in at the top to subtly disrupt any
           action. In this way they can divide and confuse the working
           class and make them look foolish in the eyes of the world. This
           book, written by a man who did this job for the CIA, tells the
           whole story. Oddly enough, he's still alive.

VARI: Sometimes the unions don't need to be subverted. Some
           American unions, for example, are world-famous for the total
           corruption of their leadership.
              Tony Boyle, boss of the United Mine Workers in the 1960s,
           rode around Washington in a huge chauffeur-driven limousine
           with a cocktail bar in the back. Boyle's daughter was paid
           $43,809 a year for an extremely vague contribution to the
           miners' general well being, and Boyle had arranged that his own

$50,000 a year salary would continue even after he retired. All the time the mining towns of Pennsylvania were dying. From Pennsylvania came Joseph Yablousky, a forthright critic of Boyle and his steamroller tactics—and in 1969 he stood against Boyle in the union election. Boyle used millions of dollars of union money for a massive campaign, and defeated Yablousky—but he couldn't shut him up. On December 31st 1969, three hired assassins broke into Yablousky's home and murdered him, and his wife, and his daughter, in cold blood. They were paid by Boyle, out of Union subs. It took four years for the plot to be uncovered—but now Boyle is in prison for life, and a Yablousky man is the new president. But even he is not going to achieve very much. Above him is the President of the American Federation of Labour, their TUC, one George Meauy.

COLUM: According to this book, Meauy is a principal agent/collaborator of the CIA in the US and world Trade Union Movement.

The British Trade Union movement has a long history of heroism, martyrdom, life-long sacrifice and hard-won victory. But today, the TUC seems to have been subverted—not by the CIA—but by their own confused thinking. They accept government direction, not realising that any government, Tory or Labour, is working for the capitalist system, which is designed to exploit their members. So they accept the exploitation of their members—while at the same time helping to make inefficient British capitalism even more inefficient, and unable to exploit their members properly.

VARI: Only the constant pressure of the ordinary workers of Britain, their shop stewards, and some of the more dedicated union leaders is stopping the TUC from giving up completely. But the history is there, the exploitation is here with us, the working class know the realities, and the movement rolls on.

A Share in the Losses

> In days gone by
> When the trees grew high
> And the sun shone all day long
> When the boss got rough
> And we'd had enough
> You would hear us sing this song—

(*Chorus*):

> Oh they're not going to win
> No we'll never give in
> For *we* all *stand* side by side together
> They can scream and shout
> But we know what we're about
> Will they stop this movement—never—

> We were shot, we were hanged,
> Into prison we were banged,
> Our wives and kids have died.

With their company cops
And their company shops
They bleed us of our pride.

(*Chorus*):   But they're not going to win, etc.

We were hunted, we were sacked,
We were fired, we were blacked,
As they tried to break us down
They spied, they lied
Almost everything they tried
Just to drive us out of town.

(*Chorus*):   But they're not going to win, etc.

Now their latest way to win
Is corrupt us from within
Put the unions on the board with the bosses
But we won't participate
In a system that we hate
And we don't want a share in the losses.

(*Chorus*):   But they're not going to win, etc.

(*A caption appears on stage saying 'Bigger is Better'*)
(*Enter* BOSS ONE)

BOSS ONE: Hello, I'm a little boss—a nice, cosy, bumbling sort of boss—I
don't smoke cigars or any of that, though I do have a nice
house and a couple of modest motorcars. I employ two hundred
and ten blokes making electric irons—Mason's (that's me
Mason)—very solid, very safe, very reliable, but a bit up-
market—you know, good but pricey. I keep getting under-cut,
people seem to prefer rubbish these days—so I'm not making
enough money to expand, and the banks don't fancy lending me
much. I'm turning over though, just about—I keep trying.
(*Enter* BOSS TWO)

BOSS TWO: Hello, my granddad Hector MacWhirter started this firm sixty
years ago. When I took it over it was in a bit of a mess, but I
concentrated on good, cheap electrical appliances—kettles,
irons, that sort of thing. We've got 500 blokes working at
MacWhirter's now, and the profit margin is quite satisfactory.
The plant's getting a bit out of date, I suppose, I could do with
getting rid of some of the blokes and taking on a few women, if
I could afford the new machinery they're turning out these days.
We have new investment plans for the year after next . . .
(*Enter* BOSS THREE)

BOSS THREE: Aha. Ahaha. What do I see? An untidy, inefficient, sector of
industry. Must make a note. (*Does so*) (*To audience*) Hello,
Klopstock here, Arnold Klopstock—Arnie to my friends. My
mum and dad were ordinary, upper-working to lower-middle-
class people—they ran a shop. I myself made some progress,

became an accountant, went into industry, and I am the new managing director, after many a boardroom backstabbing session, of the third largest electrical engineering firm in Britain. This, however, is not good enough. I aim to head the only electrical engineering firm in Britain. At the moment we employ 50,000 men on a wide variety of products, including electric irons. I think I'll expand that line. (*On phone*) Hello, Mr. Mason—I've been looking at your last year's results—

BOSS ONE: Oh, have you?

BOSS THREE: Yes—I think we might be able to help you. How about dinner some evening this week—say tonight?

BOSS ONE: That's very kind of you—no harm in talking to you.

BOSS THREE: Mason's Irons are world famous for dependability and long life: a useful reputation. (*Goes to dinner*, BOSS ONE *looks shaken*)

BOSS ONE: So. I can choose—get driven out of business, or be taken over by you?

BOSS THREE: That's the logic of it. We would offer you shares, of course—worth rather more than your little plant, at current valuation.

BOSS ONE: How many?

BOSS THREE: Within six months, Mason's Irons were ours; we moved production from Bugsby to our new plant at Gainsville, and they became cheap, nasty and profitable. Of course, Mason's two hundred men had to be laid off—even so, we sold more irons, and made more money. Mason retired, on the income from his shares. Mr MacWhirter became uneasy.

BOSS TWO: (*On phone*) Look here, Arnie, you're under-cutting like a Hong Kong toy maker.

BOSS THREE: Perhaps we should have a chat? How about dinner some time this week—say tonight?

MacWhirter Irons were, for some reason, immensely popular in Australia. They also had a patent on a reostat and a machine for making it cheap.

(BOSS THREE *to dinner*)

BOSS TWO: I want a seat on the board and 25,000 ordinary voting shares, plus chairman of MacWhirter (Overseas) Ltd.

BOSS THREE: Fair enough—for a limited period.

BOSS TWO: And a travel allowance of £5,000 per year.

BOSS THREE: If you earn it, you can have it.

With government help we closed down all of MacWhirter's in Dundee, except the reostat plant, employing 25 men. 4,975 were laid off, and production of MacWhirter Irons moved to Gainsville. They began to look remarkably similar to Mason Irons, which, of course, were really our irons in a different box. By now, we were the second largest electrical engineering company in Britain. With government help, we merged with the largest and took over the third largest. I am now chairman of what is called a national monopoly. We control the home market, and undercut foreigners if they threaten us: we have rationalised production of electric irons with our other electrical devices, streamlined the work force, and make enormous profits for our ordinary shareholders—widows, orphans and the like.

VARI: Another great step forward for the system recently has been the take-over/merger boom—giant companies swallowing up all the competition into one mammoth monopoly. In two years, 1967 and 1968, 5,000 British firms were taken over or eaten alive by the bigger fish. The same process has gone on all over Europe, and has been going on in America since the 1890s.

Who are the new giant monopolies of Britain?

Here are the British top 20 for 1973:

ICI—top of the pops, with world sales of 17,000 million pounds in one year, followed closely by:

Unilever
Imperial Group (tobacco, food and drink)
British American Tobacco
British Leyland Motors
British Steel Corporation
and General Electric Company—all with sales over £1,000 million in one year.
Courtaulds
Dunlops
GKN
Reed International
Rank Hovis McDougall
and Thorn—all with sales over 500 million in one year.
Hawker-Siddeley
BICC Cables
Associated British Foods
Lucas Motor and Aircraft Accessories,
Coats Patons Textiles
and Cadbury-Schweppes, with annual sales of a mere 349 million pounds.

DENNIS: How do you join the trendy club? Let's take the smallest on our list—poor little Cadbury-Schweppes. Its chairman is Lord Watkinson, the hammer of the Labour government, who is threatening to use his mighty power to stop Wedgies Benn and Michael Foot taking any of his profits for the workers. How did Lord Watkinson and Cadbury-Schweppes get this power they are threatening to use against an elected government?

HILTON: Not, as you might think, from crossing a chocolate bar with a glass of tonic water. Apart from Schweppes the tonic Ltd the lovable old Quaker firm of Cadburys bridged that gap with:

Bournville Finance Ltd
Bournville Trust Company
The Bournville Works Benevolent Co. Ltd
JS Fry and Sons Ltd
United Cocoa Developments Ltd
Cadbury-Schweppes Specialities

Cadbury-Schweppes Overseas
Cadbury-Schweppes Vending Ltd
Kardomah Ltd
Kenco Coffee Ltd the Jamaica Coffee Co. Ltd, Meriden
    Tea Ltd
and Typhoo Tea Ltd star of TV documentaries and friend
    of the workers of Ceylon

CHRISSIE: That's just in the hot cuppa line. In harder drinks they own:
Connaught Wines Ltd
Andre Slion Wines Ltd
Courtney Wines International Ltd
George Idle Chapman Ltd
Silva & Cosers Ltd
RB Smith & Son Ltd
and Kia-Ora Ltd

DENNIS: None of this, we hope, is to be rationalised with another lot
they own:
The Parozone Co. Ltd
Jeyes Laboratories Ltd
Petrel Ammonia Ltd
Three Hands Ltd
Farm Fumigants Ltd
Freshbin Ltd
Brobat Industrial Ltd
Aerosol International Ltd
Armstrong Laboratories Ltd
and Whiz Products Ltd
not to mention Healthy Products Ltd

HILTON: Then there's jam. They own:
William F. Hartley Ltd
and Chivers & Sons Ltd
as well as Cinsel Fruit Products.

CHRISSIE: On the way, they have picked up:
The College of Hairdressing Ltd
The School of Selling Ltd
RS McColl (England) Ltd
Kew Transport Ltd
JB Smith Transport Ltd
Middleton Plastics Ltd
and Magic Moments Beauty Aids Ltd

DENNIS: And in case you should owe them any money ever, they also
own—
Accounts Recovery Services Ltd.

HILTON: And that is only *some* of what they own in Britain. Overseas, of
course, they own:
12 companies in Australia
3 companies in the Bahamas
5 companies in Canada
2 in India

2 in New Zealand
6 in Ireland
2 in Greece
2 in Spain and
2 in Rhodesia and of course
2 in South Africa—PLUS
one company each in:
Ghana, Jamaica, Kenya, Nigeria, Tanzania, Uganda, Zambia, Denmark, Sweden, Switzerland and Pakistan:

VARI: No wonder Lord Watkinson stamps his foot when he can't tell the government what to do.

We Are The Champions

You may think you voted for a gov'ment,
To tell us what to do.
But we are bigger than the gov'ment—
And we are telling you—
If they won't do
What we want them to
Then they'll come tumbling too-oo-oo
They'll come tumbling too.

Oh *we* run this country,
This country runs for us
For might is right
So don't bother with a fight,
You're beaten: no fuss.

(*Football chant*):   We are the Champions
We are the Champions.
You may *think* the judges are impartial
But they're on our side too
And *we* make the laws up anyway
So we are telling you:

If you won't do
What we want you to
You'll be locked up for a year or two-oo-oo
Locked up for a year or two.

Oh *we* run this country, etc.

You may *think* the cops are neutral
The good old boys in blue
But *we* choose well and train them carefully
So we are telling you:

If you won't do
What we want you to—
There's a big flat boot for you-oo-oo,
A big flat boot for you.

You may *think* the common private soldier's
A member of your crew
But we went to Eton with the general
And he tells them what to do:

So if you won't do
What we want you to,
There's a firing squad for you-oo-oo
A firing squad for you.

You may *think* that democratic Britain's
A country run by you—
But we pull the strings and give the orders—
In a British way, that's true—

And if you won't do
What we want you to,
Then there's not much hope for you-oo-oo
Not much hope for you.

We're getting bigger
Getting bigger
Getting bigger
And we're getting so much bigger all the time.

VARI: But *why* have these companies got to be so big? Because all
their new and wonderful products are out of date before they
hit the market. The Japanese or the Americans will have come
out with something newer and more desirable before they've
taken their profits. So they have to have vast amounts of money
to spend on centralised research, buying up scientists, buying up
new inventions—even if only to stop others using them—and
even more money to develop their amazing discoveries. And
they need vast amounts of money to invest in the new,
expensive machinery that will produce the goods quicker and in
the end more cheaply than now.
      So they've got to be big.
(*A caption appears on stage saying 'Biggest is Best'*)
(*Enter* ARNIE, *smiling*)

ARNIE: Thank you. But you see, size itself brings its own advantages.
You can *rationalise* production. Now, I'll explain. If three little
firms have fifty men each making bumpers for cars, they need
three bumper-making machines, and 150 men. If one big man,
like me, buys them all up, I can buy one bumper-making
machine, make more bumpers faster, and sack 120 men in the
process. Ha ha. Unless they're British Leyland, who sack the
men and still lose money. Or take sales: one salesman can sell
chocolates, cocoa, coffee, tea, jam, cosmetics, parazone, and
wine for one firm just as efficiently as 20 salesmen for 20 firms.
So we can sack 19 salesmen, and invest their wages in
computers. Rationalisation.

Now, we can rationalise another way too—what we call vertically. No good buying cocoa from a firm in Jamaica—who take a profit, then hire a ship from another firm which takes a profit, then hire a lorry from another firm that takes a profit, then manufacture it into Drinking Chocolate. No, no—buy up the cocoa firm, *and* the shipping line, *and* the road haulage firm, sack half the old management and take all the profit yourself. That's how it's done. Economy of scale. We giants get more gigantic, our profits get bigger, and though there may be fewer of us—we are in fact more profitable. And industry booms. That's what we *all* want, isn't it? A booming industry? Of course it is. That's why I am now *Sir* Arnold. Goodnight.

VARI: The price for this wonderful process is the Lay Off. Hundreds of thousands of men rationalised out of work, oh yes, the government helps with the dole, or redundancy money, or re-training schemes—footing the bill for the ruthless advance of private industry—but it is never enough, and it's no compensation for the unplanned, uncontrollable wrecking of people's lives, of whole towns and communities by the furious logic of private enterprise. To create GEC for example, this happened: (HILTON, CHRISSIE and DENNIS *read figures of men laid off in 1967–69 from Booklet.*)

Laid Off

Mucking about in the garden
Planting daffodils in July
Feeling upset
In the launderette
Watching my days spinning by—

The kids run around playing cowboys
And the Indians bite the dust,
Seeing them play
Feel like running away
I'm the loner you just can't trust—

Laid off, with no further prospects
Laid off, like a bad egg
Laid off, society's rejects
Left to borrow, steal or beg.

At the start life was quite magic
Saw the sun and the trees and the sky
A stroll in the park, not so tragic
Then this feeling as the weeks roll by:

The ducks swim around in the duck-pond
They stick up their tails and live
Even the cat
Can't just sleep and grow fat:
Must do something just to know you're alive.

Mucking about in the garden
Planting daffodils in July
Feeling upset
In the launderette
Watching the days spinning by.

VARI: The trouble with the big British firms is that they are just not
big *enough*. And not ruthless enough. Not throwing enough
men on the dole. When Lord Stokes told 600 shareholders in
British Leyland that the British Steel Corporation was going to
sack 20,000 men, they rose up in a frenzy, screaming so should
we. And they were right. To make British Capitalism work,
particularly now, in a time of crisis, the bosses have to be cold-
blooded, merciless men, ready to crush the unions, brain-wash
the workers it wants to employ into docile slaves, and throw the
others onto the dole, even if it means children starving and men
going quietly mad. If capitalism is what we want, then that's
what we'll get.

Because the British corporations are not just in competition
with each other—they are fighting a losing battle against
another of the great advances of the last 20 years—the multi-
national corporation: who are bigger, more ruthless, more cold-
blooded, more merciless, and more successful than any other
businesses in the history of private enterprise. And as long as we
remain within the so-called Free World, these multinational
corporations are going to be the pacesetters—the whip crackers.
And we *do* want to stay in the Free World, don't we? (*Audience
response*) Of course we do—it brings us so many good things—

COLUM: And that brings us to the four strikes in East Kilbride I hope—

VARI: No no no, it's time we had an interval, these people are getting
sore bums—so 15 minutes break—there's a bar/tea/etc.—so
we'll see you in a quarter of an hour.

INTERVAL

ACT 2

COLUMIN: Hello, welcome back to the second half of the show. We haven't
got on to the Four Strikes at East Kilbride yet, I'm sorry to say,
but we're getting nearer every minute.

VARI: Before we get there, we'd just like to tell you who the strikes
were against: they were against a grand old English firm called
Standard Telephones and Cables, which, in 1927, was taken
over and is now a wholly-owned subsidiary of that mighty
colossus that bestrides the world, your very own ITT, and
believe me, every day and in every way, the world is their
oyster—
(*Enter* THREE YOUNG AMERICAN EXECUTIVES *to defend the
Multinational Corporations*)

The world's our oyster hm mm mm
The world's our oyster
The world's our oyster going to eat it up

Going to shake on the bitter vinegar
Watch it shrivel watch it shrivel
And we will wine and dine

For we are the Multi National Men.

HILTON: Hi folks—nice to see you all: hope you're havin' yourselves a really cosy time. Now I get a strong impression that these guys in this here show just don't like the multi-national corporations.

DENNIS: These guys are politically motivated traitors, juvenile idealists who think they're gonna set the world to rights, and they're brainwashed slaves of the slit-eyed dictator, Mao Tse Tung.

HILTON: And they're talking SHIT.

DENNIS: And we should know, 'cos we're the junior assistants to the senior vice-presidents of the maxi-multinationals.

CHRISSIE: Capitalism is still greedy, still hoards its money, still splashes out on huge junketings, in yachts, estates, even starlets, and still contributes cash to the seats of learning, even imports ballet companies and buys paintings. But all of these functions are now performed not by one miserly, or flamboyant, or big-handed individual, but by the corporation.

VARI: Likewise, success in the capitalist system is not measured in terms of being the man with the biggest business—but how profitable a corporation you work for, and how high up its ladder you have managed to climb.

CHRISSIE: A new breed of capitalists has appeared, dedicated to making his company more profitable than the next man's, because that way, not only will his company be bigger and better, but also he'll climb a few rungs higher himself.

HILTON: Thank you. Now these fellow-travelling hippies here would have you believe our corporations were part of some huge conspiratorial machine, trying to rob and destroy.

DENNIS: But we're not. We're human beings, businessmen. Merchant adventurers, the pioneers and explorers of our time, just as sure as Christopher Columbus, Vasco da Gama and Mark O. Polo were of theirs.

COLUM: And we should honour these great men of our time, as we honour the great men of the past.

HILTON: Examine for one moment, that mighty man, Thomas J. Watson. As a young salesman for National Cash Registers in Rochester, New Jersey, just before the turn of this century, our hero, as he loved to recall, chanced to meet a friend who happened to be a salesman for someone else's cash registers. Hi, said his friend. They exchanged a few pleasantries, and then his friend let drop to Watson he was travelling 20 miles out of town the very next day to see a prospective customer. When this foolish man

arrived the next morning, it was to meet Watson driving away
with the order for *his* machine in pocket. 'Why, Thomas,' his
friend observed, 'you must have got up early'. 'Sure,' said
Watson 'I had a job to do'—and he laughed all the way home
to his breakfast. Now that man went on to create a certain
company called International Business Machines, IBM—with
one quarter of a million employees the world over—not one of
them in a trade union—with stock worldwide worth more than
all the gold ever hoarded in Fort Knox. Its activities govern
much of the world's advanced technology in space, on earth,
under the seas and in thousands of industries, hundreds of
governments. 'Think'—that was Watson's motto, and that's
what he did, and what we should praise him for. In the words
of the IBM corporation hymn:

> In the year of grace 1968, IBM made a profit—a profit of
> 365 million pounds—one million pounds per day.
> And I am part of that great organisation. I work for, I live
> for, I am—IBM. THINK: one day, I could grow up to be
> President of IBM: even though I am Danish.

COLUM: Well Sosthenes Benn had a Danish father.
DENNIS: Who?
COLUM: Sosthenes Benn.
HILTON: Is he related to W—
COLUM: No no no: Sosthenes Benn started in a small way, selling
telephones in Puerto Rico. Then he noticed an amazing fact:
there were far more telephones per head of population in
America than there were in the rest of the world. No salesman
could miss such an opportunity. The rest of the world needed
telephones. Mr Benn would get them made in the cheapest parts
of the world, and sell them in the most expensive parts of the
world. Did he look back? Never. Communications—let nation
speak unto nation—phones, whole new exchanges, undersea
cables, radio links, satellites, bankers.
HILTON: Bombers?
COLUM: Well he made so much money in Germany he had to invest in
something. And Hitler was being nice to ITT, so he was nice to
Hitler: he invested in Fokke-Wolf bombers. And sold equipment
to German submarines.
DENNIS: But he was an American.
COLUM: Oh sure, a patriotic one too. He didn't neglect America—why
he sold High Frequency Direction Finders to American
destroyers so they could knock out the German submarines.
Who were attacking convoys crossing the Atlantic full of ITT
radio equipment for our boys in Europe. But he wasn't biased.
He also ran the telephone system that connected Argentina to
Berlin along which the German spies told the German bombers
and submarines when the American convoys left to cross the
Atlantic.

HILTON: I thought you said he was patriotic.

COLUM: Listen Mr IBM, your Thomas J. Watson got an Iron Cross from Hitler, that wasn't for typewriter ribbon, friend.

HILTON: OK—but he sent it back, later.

COLUM: That's what I call *narrowly* patriotic. Sosthenes Benn was first and foremost a citizen of the world—a businessman. ITT serves people and nations everywhere.

HILTON: With these beginnings, ITT never looked back.

COLUM: Listen. I have it on good authority that IBM have opened an office in Moscow. So will you stop insulting us Germans.

HILTON: Oh. I'm sorry, partner.

COLUM: That's alright. Mr Benn built a great international business in communications—but it took the financial wizardry of Mr. Harold S. Geneen to make it into an empire—a global conglomerate, a multinational masterpiece. He bought businesses all over the world—now we sell everything: telephones, exchanges, cables, railway signal controls, teleprinters, taps, bath tubs, air-conditioning, disc brakes, Koni shock absorbers, car components, bumpers, electronics of every type, capacitors, resistors, TV tubes, loudspeakers, quartz oscillators, integrated circuits, space laboratories, aircraft landing systems, second hand radar, military radio equipment, Hi-Fi, refrigerators, toasters, pills, Maws baby care, Abbey Life Insurance, Rimmel cosmetics, frozen food, soup, and very good smoked ham. And we have four of the biggest advanced research laboratories in Europe. Mr. Harold S. Geneen, you're a genius, a benefactor to the entire human race, and I'm proud to belong to ITT, to serve people and nations everywhere, with you.

DENNIS: I belong to General Motors. We just sell motorcars. A lot of motorcars. You see, in the 1920s, Henry Ford was doing pretty good, and we were lagging behind. Everybody wanted a Ford motorcar. Then when they'd got a Ford motorcar, they were happy they had a Ford motorcar. Now that is not good business practice. It took a genius like Alfred Sloan, General Motors president at that time, to spot what was wrong. Once they had a motorcar they had no reason to buy another one. As Mr. Sloan remarked—the primary object of General Motors was to make money, not just to make motorcars. So he invented the idea of having a different looking motorcar every year. With different styling, different colours, slightly different engines, different comfort features. In this way, everybody in the street would soon figure out who had an old car. But he didn't want people to feel bad, or inferior. So the General Motors Acceptance Corporation would accept your old model as down payment on a new model. And he produced a whole price-range of cars every year, so maybe you could afford a slightly better line of model this year from last year. They all cost much the same to build, but everybody on the street knew which cost more to buy. And every year, the whole range got better, fancier, and more expensive.

And that was the model for variety selling of expensive consumer goods the world over from then on. And now General Motors, gentlemen, owns plant in every country of the Free World, including your little Vauxhall motors here in Britain, Opal in Germany, and of course, our own Chevrolet in America. That was Alfred Sloan's contribution to General Motors, gentlemen, and to mankind, and I am proud to walk in his shadow.

(*They all clap.*)

(*Reprise: THE WORLD'S OUR OYSTER*)

CHRISSIE: Who are these people who run the multinationals? They try desperately hard to avoid the limelight. But an English writer, Anthony Sampson, was invited to the annual ITT barbecue of managers from all over the world, in their Executive Mansion in a suburb of Brussels.

VARI: (*Reading*) It was not immediately easy to tell the Europeans from the Americans, except perhaps from the shoes and trousers; for the Europeans too—whether Swedish, Greek or even French—had a hail-fellow style and spoke fluent American, joking and reminiscing about old times in Copenhagen and Rio. After a good deal of backslapping, shoulder punching and story telling, the executives sat down to their meal at trestle tables in the marquee. There was no special seating plan; the atmosphere was determinedly democratic and unsnobbish. But in the middle a bald hearty man was pointed out to me, the young president of ITT Europe, Mike Bergerac; and next to him looking small by comparison, was the mastermind behind the whole corporation—Harold Sydney Geneen. Later in the evening I was taken to meet Geneen, who was standing talking in the now almost-empty marquee. I was introduced as an English writer, and he told me immediately how much he liked England, where he had been born, and how he loved coming back to London. Then he went on to explain how he had admired the British Empire, and was sorry it had been given up so hastily. Why didn't the British government support the White Rhodesians? Didn't they realise that four-fifths of the British people were behind Ian Smith? He went on to talk about America's difficulties with the rest of the world—how her oil supplies were in danger, and how eventually she might need to move into the Arab countries to protect them. As he warmed to his tirade, his whole frame came to life: he began gesturing, pointing, and laughing, his fingers darting around, touching his nose, his ear, his chin, as if weaving some private spell. His greeny-brown eyes twinkled, and he grinned and laughed like a gargoyle. He seemed no longer a dark-suited owlish accountant, but more like an imp or a genie: almost like Rumpelstiltskin, magically turning thread into gold. I noticed that a clutch of vice-presidents were standing round listening, watching him carefully: they laughed when he laughed, and nodded when he nodded.

Businessmen, he explained, are the only people who know
how to create jobs, and make work for people; he was
responsible for 400,000 employees, all over the world, and it
was his duty to lobby governments on their behalf, as effectively
as he could. What do governments know about providing jobs?
Why does the American government waste time with anti-trust
questions, when it should be supporting the big corporations
which are battling with the Japanese, and contributing to the
balance of payments?

We parted amicably, with mutual incomprehension. But in
this marquee, like a nomad's encampment, I had begun for a
moment to get the feel of being inside this amazing corporation,
to glimpse it through the eyes of the master and followers. From
their camp they looked out onto a world benighted with
prejudice and unreason: where governments were merely
obstructing the long march of production and profit; where
nations were like backward native tribes, to be placated,
converted, and overcome.

HILTON: The same logic that had led to the national monopolies—GEC,
ICI, Unilever—led on, inexorably, to the creation of the
multinationals:

CHRISSIE: 1968 to 69: General Motors, USA.

DENNIS: Profit 724 million pounds

CHRISSIE: Ford, USA.

DENNIS: Profit 262 million

CHRISSIE: Chrysler of USA.

DENNIS: Profit 122 million

CHRISSIE: Standard Oil, New Jersey.

DENNIS: Profit, 534 million

CHRISSIE: Texaco, USA.

DENNIS: Profit 350 million

CHRISSIE: Gulf Oil, USA.

DENNIS: Profit 262 million

CHRISSIE: IBM, USA.

DENNIS: Profit 365 million

CHRISSIE: General Electric, USA.

DENNIS: 149 million

CHRISSIE: US Steel.

DENNIS: Profit 106 million

CHRISSIE: ICI, Great Britain.

DENNIS: Profit 182 million

CHRISSIE: BP Great Britain.

DENNIS: Profit 371 million

CHRISSIE: And as for ITT, it would take a very clever computer to work
out *its* profits, or where they go to.

HILTON: But there is more to the multinationals than profits. There is
massive economic power. The world output of one company,
General Motors, is worth more than the total output of
Belgium, or Switzerland. That means power. And this power

can be used to make the big profits even bigger, which in turn
makes their power even greater. If you are a young man
interested in money and power, the multi-nationals are for you.

Going Steady with the Corporation

SHE: I had a young man
I loved him very well
He told me that he loved me
My heart began to swell
Then he met with another
More beautiful than me
A sexy multi-national
Now he loves his company.

Boyfriend's going steady
With a global profit
She's richer and more beautiful
And he'll not forsake her.
I love him very truly
But I am no competition for the
Fascinating beauty of that worldwide corporation.

HE: I visited every nation
In a private jet
I hustle and I bustle
And I make them sweat
I hire and I fire so they cannot forget
I am going steady with the company.

SHE: Boyfriend's going steady with a groovy company
She moves just like a panther and she stings just like a bee.
She turns him on each morning
She drives him through the night
No simple girl like me can ever hope to win that fight.

HE: I'm satisfied and gratified and quite replete
She's quite a girl
I'm in a whirl
Knocked off my feet
If I could only marry her
My life would be complete
I am going steady with the company.

CHRISSIE: How does the multinational use this power? They all deny, of
course, that they have any, let alone use it, but one or two
interesting facts have come to light, which *can* be seen as
isolated, uncharacteristic mistakes, but which almost certainly
are extraordinary only in that they have been uncovered.

DENNIS: The first, and perhaps the most devious device that they have is
to shift their money to where it is going to be worth most. They
have a lot of money and easy ways of moving it from country
to country.

CHRISSIE: With their massive amounts of ready money to shift around, the multinationals can, and do, cause the pound to be devalued, by starting a panic selling their pounds. They even had the dollar devalued, by selling dollars and buying German marks and Japanese yen.

DENNIS: Early in 1973 the multinationals moved six billion dollars from New York to Frankfurt or Zurich, so spreading American inflation over here, and indirectly making our higher prices pay some of the cost of the Vietnam War.

HILTON: Of course, they can also shift their profit from the country it is made in, to wherever tax is low. A Swiss multi-national, Hoffman La Roche, made £25 million from selling Valium and Librium to our National Health Service. But they only paid British tax on 3 million—the rest was switched to Switzerland.

VARI: But all these nasty little bits of speculating and transfer price-fixing are only the icing on their cake. They don't care if Britain devalues, or inflation spreads to Europe, or the dollar gets weaker. As the chairman of Ronson said:

COLUM: 'The multi-national executive must set aside any nationalistic attitudes, and appreciate that in the last resort his loyalty must be to the share-holders of his parent company, and he must protect their interests, even if it might appear that it is not perhaps in the national interest of the country in which he is operating.'

VARI: Or, as another expert put it:

HILTON: 'As an economic unit, the nation-state—like Britain, or France, or Spain—is just about through.'
(*Music in* to the *Victor Jara Song: Levante*)

VARI: Chile. In 1970, Salvador Allende was elected President to stop his country being exploited. This is what he said, in 1970:

DENNIS: 'We have been an exploited people: a people who do not exist for themselves but who exist to contribute to the prosperity of others. What is the reason for our backwardness? Who is responsible for this underdevelopment which weighs us down? Despite much misrepresentation and much deception the people have understood. We know well through our own experience that the real causes of our backwardness lie in the system—in this dependent capitalist system which, on the national plan, sets up needy majorities against rich minorities, and on the international plane, sets powerful nations against the weak, where the many pay the price for prosperity for the few. We inherit a society torn apart by social inequality; a society deeply divided into hostile classes of exploiters and exploited; a society where violence is built into the institutions themselves, condemning men to insatiable greed, to the most inhuman forms of cruelty and to indifference to the suffering of others. We inherit a society crucified by unemployment, which forces increasing numbers of its citizens into redundancy. We inherit an economy crippled by inflation. Month by month it continues to lower the miserable wages of the workers. When they reach the last years of their lives, it reduces them almost to nothing.

Such are the returns of a life full of privations. We inherit a dependent society whose basic sources of wealth were appropriated by the internal allies of great international enterprises. The forms of our dependence are economic, technological, cultural and political.

The Chilean people have risen up against this form of existence. Our victory was gained through the conviction that only a genuinely revolutionary government could confront the might of the ruling classes.'

(*End of music after speech*)

COLUM: (*As* ITT *man*) We simply can't have these guys making speeches like that—it's communism. We must keep this world free—besides, we in ITT have got a lot of capital and equipment in Chile, and the boys in Anaconda and Kennecott are going to have their copper-mines nationalised. What does the American Government think it's doing? The Nixon administration is not being firm or statesmanlike —who handles South America in the State Department?

HILTON: It's a man called Check Meyer, sir.

COLUM: Get the dope on him, send it to Kissinger, have him fired—I don't care how much it costs. Get our Ambassador in Chile— what's his name?

HILTON: Korry, sir.

COLUM: Get the dope on Korry, I want to speak to him. Write to Kissinger, tell him freedom's in danger.

HILTON: Pardon me, sir, who's in danger, sir?

COLUM: *Freedom*, Democracy, US Policy. Get onto the World Bank, stop aid—how can we cause an economic crisis in Chile?

HILTON: Why, sir?

COLUM: So the military will have to intervene you idiot, and blow Allende's brains out.

HILTON: I'll check that out sir.

COLUM: Check it out? Do it. Economic disaster in Chile, right—it should be child's play, it's a socialist government—ring rent-a-strike.

HILTON: Just had a call, sir, the Chilean situation is now being handled by Kissinger and the CIA.

COLUM: So what? We're being nationalised. Order me lunch at the White House. I have an eighteen-point plan for dealing with Allende— everything should be done subtly but effectively to see that Allende does not get through the crucial next six months. No aid, from us or *anybody*. Ruin them with inflation. Subsidise the right-wing newspapers. Stir up the Chilean generals, find a good one— pay him. Get Allende. Get Allende. Get Allende. Freedom is dying.

VARI: In September 1973, General Pinochet led a military coup in Chile. Allende was shot. Socialism was crushed. 40,000 people were murdered. Including Victor Jara a young man who wrote this song, which ends—

TONY: Stand up, look at your hands
        Take your brothers' hand so you can grow—
        We'll go together, united in blood,
        Now and at the hour of our death. Amen.

COLUM: ITT were exposed. Documents came to light revealing ITT's remorseless campaign to force the US government to intervene in Chile, including the offer of one million dollars to the CIA to cause a blood bath, which they did.

CHRISSIE: All the other companies deny they use this kind of pressure on their governments. But there are curious coincidences:

DENNIS: 1951. Persia threatens to nationalise its oil.

COLUM: The CIA finances a coup. Mosadeq thrown out.

DENNIS: 1954. Guatemalan governments want to nationalise the land. United Fruit of America's interests threatened.

COLUM: US Marines invade. Government thrown out.

DENNIS: 1960. Cuban Government nationalise United Fruit in Cuba.

COLUM: Bombs on Havana. CIA finance an invasion of Cuba. It was defeated.

DENNIS: 1964. Brazil. Some mild reforms put forward by the government.

COLUM: CIA back coup—mass arrests, no reforms.

CHRISSIE: And in case we think it's only American governments who slaughter at the request of their companies—

DENNIS: 1965. Oman and Dhofar. Dhofaris rise up against their feudal, slave-owning Sheik. Shell Oil's interests in danger.

COLUM: Our RAF and our SAS have been killing people there ever since.

CHRISSIE: They still are, today.

COLUM: The multinationals form such a large and important part of their home country's industry, that their wishes cannot be ignored by those countries—in capitalist countries, the government's main purpose is to serve them and protect them. Sometimes the connections become a little *too* obvious.

VARI: (*as* DITA BEARD) Well hello there—I'm Mother Beard, and I'm the lady who threw the shit that hit the fan. Oh oh oh—pardon me. I have the odd heart attack from time to time, but I just sprinkle a little nitro-glycerine in my gin, and I'm right as rain. I'm loved. I'm respected. By Senators, Congressmen and creepy-crawly newsmen all over America. That's why I was bought, body and soul, by ITT, to represent their interests with the government, and with the President himself. Now there's no point in waiting till a man gets elected and *then* doing him a favour. Especially if that man is Richard Nixon. No sir—you gotta help him *get* elected first, so he's grateful.

Now ITT had some problems in America. Interfering pinko lawyers said we were getting too big, operating unfair deals with our own companies, and getting too many companies altogether. So Hal Geneen, he's the man I think most about in the whole world—Hal had his idea of how we'd work that out, with a bit of help. Now that's nothing whatever to do with the fact we secretly paid a 400,000 bill for the Republican Party's Congress—we just helped Richard Nixon to make his mind up to have it in one of our hotels, and we gave him as much assistance as we could afford. Well what do you know? Nixon came out top man, and he was our old friend—indebted to us, you might say. Now that had

nothing whatever to do with the anti-trust hearing falling out the
way we wanted it to. Nothing at all. I'm just friendly, and
generous—I'll help anybody—any congressman who wants a car,
or a private jet—these boys can't depend on the commercial
airlines, they're too busy serving their electors to queue up at some
lousy airport. I've found my way to the heart of many of our
greatest legislators, on behalf of ITT. Just as Hal Geneen and I
found our way to the heart of Richard Nixon. Which is why,
when that stupid lawyer wanted to screw up the anti-trust case
against us, it was he, dear Richard, who just picked up the phone
and said to that lawyer: 'Listen you unprintable unprintable, don't
you understand the English language? Delay the appeal.' Poor
Richard. He bit the dust. Me too—one of my memos on the
subject was leaked to some horrible reporter, and I was suddenly
very very ill: just when the whole thing was being investigated—
just like poor Richard. Well, now I'm better, and he's better: but
there's none of us quite so flourishing as Hal Geneen and his
dinky little corporation. Bye now.

DENNIS: That's the direct way to influence a Government: bribe the top
man. The big multinational corporations do just that, when it is
necessary. But generally speaking, governments in the free world
exist mainly to protect what is called the national economy. And
these boys are taking over more and more of the national
economy—even helping the export drive—so they are what the
government is there to protect. American and British governments
will invade smaller countries, overthrow foreign governments with
paid agents, dirty tricks departments, economic pressures, even
hired assassins, when their multi-nationals are threatened overseas.

At home—well, in America, governments allow these people
to destroy the face of the country, to make millions
unemployed, to run private police forces, to use the universities
as training grounds for their scientists, to wipe out competition
in all kinds of criminal ways, to bribe the union chiefs, to fix
prices, to become a law unto themselves.

In Britain, we are more subtle, and less effective. If one of
our own multi-nationals, like British Leyland, is broke, through
management stupidity and through handing out too much profit
to shareholders, instead of investing in a new plant—our labour
government has to give it £2,000 million—because we can't
afford to lose it. During the 1960s, Labour governments
financed the GEC and hundreds of other mergers to create our
own multi-nationals. And they were right—their job was to
make capitalism work—and that is the job Wedgewood Benn is
busy doing now. It has very little to do with socialism.
Investment grants, regional development grants, huge loans,
tax-concessions involving millions of pounds, are spent trying to
attract the American, French, Swiss, even Japanese multi-
nationals to invest in Britain—that is, to come in and exploit
our workers. And the Americans are coming—in a big way. In
spite of Ford's threats about closing down, in spite of Chrysler's

talk of shifting production, they, IBM, ITT, General Motors and their friends, are still here, and expanding. They are pumping their massive funds, their technological know-how, into the key electrical and engineering sectors of industry, the sectors that are growing in importance and profitability every year.

The multi-nationals are becoming the most powerful economic force in Britain, and all our recent governments, Tory or Labour, have given them exactly what they want.

Harold Wilson, 1974:

'We must take these giant oil corporations into state ownership. Our North Sea oil is vital to the nation, and we cannot see the profits from our oil, and control over the production of it, going outside this country. We must nationalise it.'

North Sea Oilman's magazines, March 1975:

'Oilmen weren't exactly dancing in the streets after Mr. Bell's announcement of a 45% oil tax last month, but a number of hard-bitten Texan faces in plush London oil headquarters were seen to soften after the news broke. Many would privately admit that under a Tory government the rate might have been considerably higher. And certainly the taxation proposals of this Labour government seem a long way removed from their pre-election propaganda about outright nationalisation. Let no one be in any doubt that sanity has prevailed.'

That kind of sanity will go on prevailing while the multi-nationals are stronger than governments elected by the people.

Harold Wilson, 1973:

'The Common Market is a Magna Carta for the barons of the multi-national mega-corporations.'

Harold Wilson, May 1975:

'Vote yes.'

(*The song—'You'll Never Walk Alone' is followed by a reprise of the football chant 'We Are The Champions'*)

Britain is penetrated through and through with the economic and political power of our own, and American, multi-nationals, and it will continue to be run by them whether we are in the Common Market or out of it. The Common Market is largely irrelevant to our new masters. Most of them are in favour of it. They can easily fix the officials of a United States of Europe—as they did in the United States of America. The Common Market makes it easier for them to operate in Europe—and will give them exactly what they want.

What do they want?

They want:

Every country they operate in to protect their subsidiaries legally, to give grants and support from public money to their subsidiaries, to allow them to raise funds for their subsidiaries on the Stock Exchanges, if necessary.

They want:

All those countries to pay for education and training to give them pools of skilled and qualified labour at all levels, and to pay for scientific research, so they can use it.

They want:

All those countries to control prices and incomes, so they can control their costs and profits, and so those countries can afford to carry on consuming their goods.

They want:

All those countries to keep their working classes in order, obedient and disorganised.

And they want to move their money and their goods between these countries exactly as it suits their profits, with no interference.

By and large, they're getting all these demands now and will get all of them even more easily in the Common Market. It is a milestone on the highway to their utopia.

COLUM: Utopia for an international corporation would be world government. A world without frontiers. Absolute freedom of movement of people, goods, ideas, services, and money to and from anywhere. No armies, navies, or air forces, only local police. A single global system of patents and trademarks, of building and safety codes, of food and drug regulations. A single, global currency. A single central bank.

Nation states would have the same relationship to a world government that the states of the United States have toward Washington, or the cantons of Switzerland have toward Berne (in other words, they would cease to exist as nation states). Obviously the words "balance of payments" would be found only in history books concerning the savage days before humans learned to live peacefully on the same planet.

Utopia—ITT Style

(HEAVENLY CHOIR):

(*Spoken*): I have a dream.

(*Sung*):   A dream of freedom—oh-oh-oh
            A dream of splendour—oh-oh-oh
            A dream of prosperity—oh-oh-oh.

(*Spoken*): I have a dream.

(*Sung*):   A dream of peace—ah ah ah
            A dream of unity—ah ah ah
            A dream of (world wide) prosperity—ah ah ah.

(*Harmonies*): Utopia—Utopia—Utopia

            Where every man's a consumer
            Whether yellow, black or red
            Obedience, trust from each worker
            And nothing under the bed.

            A world without wars, without conflicts
            A world made of compromise
            A world of predictable profits
            A world that holds no surprise.

(*Chorus*):   (*Anthem*) And we'll march on to our final goal
               Through all calamity
               We want this world—body and soul,
               We're the end of history . . .
               And we'll have this world—body and soul
               For that's our destiny.

               Utopia—Utopia—Utopia

               A world full of free-floating voters
               A world with no real dissent
               A world made for General Motors,
               A world full of deep content.

               A world where we've no competition
               A world we manipulate
               The world of the corporation
               The multinational state.

(*Chorus*):   And we'll march on to our final goal
               Through all calamity
               We want this world—body and soul,
               We're the end of history . . .
               And we'll have this world—body and soul
               For that's our destiny.

VARI: The Utopia of the multi-national corporations: a world-wide state
         dominated by huge monopolies, with a brain-washed, slave-like
         working class, a middle class of managers and scientists, and an
         ever-diminishing elite of men like Thomas J. Watson, Sosthenes
         Benn, Henry Ford, Alfred Sloan and Harold S. Geneen, who will
         rule the world. This, as we have tried to show, is the way
         capitalism is going, and must go, by its own terrible logic. The
         logic of size and efficiency in the service of profit.
             Is this what we want?
             More important—have we ever been asked if this is what we
         want? Are we *allowed* to decide our own and our children's
         future, or must it just happen, behind our backs, beyond our
         control? No. We can decide. We can fight for the only
         alternative to the multi-national corporations—socialism. And
         the one great service the multi-nationals have performed for
         humanity, is that they have made the fight for socialism truly
         international, on a practical, day-to-day level. The workers of
         the world will have to unite.

COLUM: And that definitely brings us to the four strikes at East Kilbride.
         For the organised working-class to replace these multi-national
         profit-machines with an international system that will
         rationalise, mechanise, automate, increase production and make
         even greater scientific progress for the benefit of *all* of humanity,
         the organised working-class has two great weapons: the
         contradictions built into the capitalist system, and its own
         ability to learn from struggles.

(A drum plays as two banners are brought on, saying 'Strike One'.)

COLUM: Strike One is easy—in fact, there wasn't even a strike, just the possibility of one.

DENNIS: In the early 1960s, ITT's Standard Telephone and Cables opened a small plant employing about 200 workers in Carfinn, a small town near East Kilbride. They refused to recognise any trade unions. After nine or ten months, the 200 workers felt they were being robbed. They demanded union recognition.

COLUM: ITT simply closed the plant down, and went away. 200 on the dole.

(Drum again with two more banners saying 'Strike Two'.)

In 1963, they opened up again, in East Kilbride New Town, a bigger plant, with 500 workers, making wave-guide tubing and submerged repeater under-sea cable.

DENNIS: And this is the first contradiction in the capitalist way of doing things. In spite of the fact that workers are a nuisance to them, they sadly *have* to have them. ITT was expanding, it needed more output. It had to come back to where it could get the labour.

CHRISSIE: ITT immediately recognised the unions—the old AEU, and the Coppersmiths, and set up negotiating procedure. They laughed at the manager at Carfinn, and said he was a nutter. But they hadn't reckoned on the shop-floor activity, or on the strength of the shop stewards. In 1966, they decided to undermine the shop stewards. In 1966, ITT decided they'd set their own speed and bonus times—which up to then had been set in agreement with the shop stewards. There was a mass meeting. This meeting instructed the shop-stewards committee to uphold the principle of mutual agreement. The management refused. The committee called a strike. The Convenor, Ken Macmillan, was sacked. The workers refused to go back until he was reinstated—he was, after all, only doing what they'd told him to do.

COLUM: The strike went on for three weeks. ITT needed the equipment badly—they gave in: the principle was upheld. Ken Macmillan was reinstated.

(Drum again, two more banners, 'Strike Three'.)

By 1969, the work force was 800, and now they were making new telephone exchanges—ITT were making a fortune from the Labour Government supplying Subscriber Trunk Dialling equipment.

HILTON: One job involved wrapping wire round terminals with a high-speed revolving barrel gun—bzz—just like that. The girls at East Kilbride were not going fast enough for ITT, so they brought over two girls working in Bell Telephones Belgium—also owned by ITT, to show how fast it could be done. Unfortunately, none of the management spoke French. Ken Macmillan did. He discovered that one girl had seven years experience, and the other was so good she was made a supervisor. ITT were using pacesetters—and trying to set the workers of one country against those of another. They failed.

DENNIS: Contradiction number two: as technology becomes more
sophisticated, so the workers have to become more
sophisticated—this could lead to trouble.

HILTON: By this time, Ken Macmillan was working with others to form a
combine, uniting all ITT workers in the UK, of whatever union.
ITT did not like this. In 1969 he went to ITT Monkstown, in
the North of Ireland, to establish contacts with the 4000
workers there.

CHRISSIE: While he was away, the manager, a son-in-law of ITT's
European technical manager, and inclined to the irrational, had
provoked a walkout.

HILTON: When Ken Macmillan came back from Ireland, he was sacked.
Again. So the workers decided to stay out. But this time ITT
had made plans. The same telephone exchange equipment was
being made in ITT Portugal and ITT Belgium. The Labour
Government's Postmaster-General, one John Stonehouse, gave
them an import license.

COLUM: The strike went on for nine weeks—but they couldn't win. ITT
were laughing at them—they were getting the equipment, and
the profit anyway.

DENNIS: The strike ended in defeat. Macmillan was *not* reinstated.
Militants were made redundant. Many workers tore up their
union cards, in humiliated anger—till only 30% of the work
force was in a union. Within 15 months, there were four or five
convenors, two having to give up through mental breakdowns.
ITT put in a different manager every year. There were no strikes,
except one by TASS for recognition. Until February 1975.

COLUM: By this time, the factory was made up of 450 women, and 150
men, with 20 women shop stewards, and 5 men. For the last
four years, the convenor has been Kathy Dobbie. They learnt a
great deal from their previous defeat.

VARI: Strong links were built in an unofficial combine with other ITT-
STC plants, in Ireland, in England, and at Treforest in Wales. A
paper was started by a TASS member, spreading news of ITT's
activities in every factory to all the other factories. Links were
made with the Portuguese after the overthrow of the
dictatorship, contact was made with Belgium, the TEWU
International branch led to contacts with the illegal workers
commissions in Spain, contact was made with the International
section of the French Trades Unions, no opportunity was missed
at conferences, meetings, summer-schools, to make links with
workers in other European countries, particularly with people
who could join in any struggle against ITT.

DENNIS: Contradiction Number Four: Capitalist organisation has
become International. This has forced working-class
organisation to become international.

COLUM: In February 1975, a dispute broke out in East Kilbride over pay.
ITT refused to make a reasonable settlement. ITT East Kilbride
came out on strike.

VARI: Now they were not only making telephone exchanges themselves, but providing vital parts for the Northern Irish factory. If ITT could get those parts elsewhere in Europe, and keep Monkstown going, they could starve East Kilbride back to work. But the first thing Kathy Dobbie did was to contact Monkstown: the shop stewards there guaranteed that parts *not* made in East Kilbride would be blacked. Then every ITT plant in Britain was contacted. All expressed total solidarity. Then contact was made with the only two other factories that could supply the vital parts. First in Portugal. The Portuguese workers, in their newfound freedom, said they would not produce extra parts, or allow any to go to Monkstown. Second Belgium. The answer was the same.

COLUM: All this happened before the other ITT managers even knew East Kilbride was on strike.

CHRISSIE: The strike went on for seven weeks. In April, Monkstown was grinding to a halt. Three or four days before their production would have had to stop, ITT were defeated.

DENNIS: Now East Kilbride wages are slightly ahead of those in other plants in the U.K. and the others will be looking for parity. This time there will be no threats of closing down, and shifting production to another factory, or even another country. ITT are, for the time being, on the run.

(*More banners appear, saying, 'Strike Four'.*)

(*Beat with poles on the floor. Rhythm of poles, into piano and guitar intro to*)

A Share in the Losses

(*As song goes on, band go back to their instruments. Before the end of the song, break*)

VARI: But there's still a long way to go. The monopolies and the multi-nationals are still years ahead of the working-class, and most unions, and the TUC, simply accept them as realities, as they accept the whole evil, anti-human, corrupting capitalist system. But there is nothing pre-determined or fatalistic about it. We can decide, and must decide whether we want it, or not. And not be put off by fears of turning into another totalitarian state: if all of us want socialism, and fight for it, and get it, then all of us will learn from that struggle, and from the mistakes, and achievements, of other times and other countries, and decide for ourselves, how our country will be run, our industry organised and how our own lives will be lived.

(*Chorus*): Oh they're not going to win, etc.

THE END

On curtain on a good night: The Internationale.

REJOICE!

---

*Presented by the 7:84 England Company in 1982
with the following cast:*

Joyce: Angela Bruce
Leon: Frank Iwediebo
Jack: Nick Stringer
Molly: Bridget Thornborrow

The action of the play takes place in Liverpool in June and July 1982.

ACT *1*

Molly and Joyce's flat. It is on the first floor of a small two-storey terraced house, only sketchily converted, and looks out onto waste ground and oil-tanks, with a distant view of the Mersey and Birkenhead, aglow with a summer evening sky. It's about 6.30 and children are still out in the street. The room does not have a lot of furniture in it, and most of that is cheap second-hand. A few leftish and feminist posters may be stuck on a cupboard door. Children can be heard playing outside in the street, happy, energetic with skipping songs and military noises. Someone calling as they come upstairs—waiting for an answer—Joyce comes in from work, is disappointed to see no-one else is there, she gets rid of her bag etc.

Home in the Evening

JOYCE: Home in the evening
            Day's work done
            Wash the morning's dirty dishes
            Think about having a little, well, fun—

            Open the paper
            Wonder why
            This old world keeps spinning onwards
            Look out the window—how strange is the sky.

            There's a cloud in the West
            Like an old oak tree
            With branches that ripple and grow
            There's fire in the harbour
            Explosions at sea
            And words we all hear but don't know
            And the tides of the air have a strange undertow.

Shifting
>   There's a rift in the rock beneath my feet
Shifting
>   There's a shift in the rift makes your heart miss a beat
Sliding
>   And the layers of the earth all slide apart
Sliding
>   There's a crack in the core like a broken heart.

And the children laugh and play
Over the hills and far away
Yes, the children laugh and play
Over the mountains and a long, long way away.

Home in the evening
Day's work done
Need a friend, an arm around me
Shiver it's chilly now the sun has, well, gone.

Open the larder
Cupboard's bare
Sense there's someone watching waiting
Fingers touch when nobody's there.

There's a cloud in the West
Like an old oak tree
With branches that ripple and grow
There's fire in the harbour
Explosions at sea
And words we all hear but don't know
And the tides of the air have a strange undertow.

Breathing
>   Not a breath in the air just a taste in the mouth
Breathing
>   There's a death in the breath of the wind from the
>   south
Bleeding
>   From the ears and the eyes that are gaping open wide
Bleeding
>   And the poison in the chemistry is burning up inside.

And the children laugh and play
Over the hills and far away
Yes, the children laugh and play
Over the mountains and a long, long way away.

Home in the evening
Day's work done
Wash the morning's dirty dishes
Think about having a little, well, fun—

(*At the end of the song,* JOYCE *flops down on the sofa. Sound of children playing. She gets up, goes to the window and watches them play.* MOLLY *comes in quietly, depressed.* JOYCE *doesn't notice her until she has taken the shopping bag to the kitchen, come back and sat down.*)

JOYCE: (Quietly) *What's up?*

MOLLY: We won the war.

JOYCE: Tell your auntie Joyce . . . another suicide?

MOLLY: No. Murder—assassination—genocide.

JOYCE: Oh yeah—

MOLLY: The Leckie Street Centre is going to be closed down by order of the government spending cuts.

JOYCE: And what about you?

MOLLY: A redundant social worker is something to be—

JOYCE: Just like that?

MOLLY: Oh—soon—two or three months. We'll protest, but they're doing far worse and getting away with it. I hate this country.

JOYCE: Not Zimbabwe again!

MOLLY: Yes. I mean it this time.

JOYCE: Tell me something: do you want to go because of the government or because your family fortune is tied up there and you can't get it out?

MOLLY: It's my money, guilt-money from my rancid old dad who made it whipping black people to work his tobacco fields. If I go there I control what happens to it, and my mother will have to drink herself to death on her own money. And when I get my hands on it, I intend to use it in a way that the government will approve of.

JOYCE: Don't go there—

MOLLY: (*Laughing*) You can come with me. It's not Southern Rhodesia any more . . . This country is beginning to smell. If that centre closes, I leave.

JOYCE: We'll think of something.

MOLLY: Forty of our present projects will have to go—unless, of course, they can be funded from the private sector. Joyce, what are we going to do? We look after sixty human disaster areas at the centre, sixty alcoholic wrecks. Now, if we carry on, some of them will get better: if we don't carry on several, and I mean several, will die in a mess of blood and vomit inside three months.

JOYCE: I thought you said they were horrible—disgusting—violent—

MOLLY: They are. One of the men came into my office this morning, smiled sweetly at me, walked straight up to my desk and plonks his plonker on it.

JOYCE: What did you do?

MOLLY: I asked him to take it away again. He just stood there grinning like an idiot till I took a swat at it with a ruler. (*Pause*) He'll die that one, in some gutter. The women are the most worrying. Sleeping rough kills them off like flies—they've

mostly got TB and several varieties of pox. If they can't come
into the centre for treatment they won't go anywhere else.
They'll just rot away at various points inside their anatomies
till the snow comes and covers them forever. And why?
Because we must make the private sector strong . . . these
people are a drain on the average businessman, who has, by
the sweat of his brow and the cunning of his brain, earned
himself a load of cash. Why should he pay rates and taxes just
to keep some derelict out of the gutter? If they want to die in
squalor, who are we do-gooders to interfere? Perhaps we're
doing it more for ourselves than we are for them—eh?
Bastards!

JOYCE: Calm down a minute . . . are we going out to eat?
MOLLY: I've got fresh asparagus in that basket.
JOYCE: Oo, lovely. Anything to go with it?
MOLLY: It was too expensive to get anything else—
JOYCE: But we can't live on asparagus—we'll die: it's like trying to live
on grass.
MOLLY: If I just lay my neck before the axe and let that centre close,
then I'm killing them, just as much as that murdering Minister
is—
JOYCE: But you've no choice.
MOLLY: One of us has got to stand and fight.
JOYCE: Well, it won't be him.
MOLLY: Then it's got to be me.
(*Music in*)
MOLLY: When sweet Anne Boleyn fell from favour
    She compliantly laid her sweet neck on the block—
    Saint Filumena, both virgin and martyr
    Went smiling and peaceful to die on the rack
    For accepting your fate is a virtue
    That generates deep peace of mind
    But I don't eat shit
    Or go down on my knees
    So the Tories can kiss my behind.

    I'm going to fight, fight, fight against the Tories
    Don't want their ifs and buts—
    Don't believe a word of all their stories
    Going to fight, fight, fight against the cuts

    They can turn out the troops to the Falklands
    They can stockpile their nuclear death
    They can spend more and more on their war-plans—
    Till Thatcher has dreams just like Lady Macbeth:
    No, money's no object for slaughter
    The Treasury's spokesmen are dumb—

    But I can still speak—And my message tonight
    Is: the Tories can all kiss my bum—

> For there's old folk that need looking after,
> And there are those can't survive by themselves
> There's children and mums who need nurseries, and
> There are schools that need teachers, and books on their
>   shelves—
> But suddenly cash has stopped flowing—
> Should we laugh, should we cry at this farce?
> Well I'm not amused—and all I can say
> Is, the Tories can all kiss my arse—

(JOYCE *applauds, then stops—laughing at* MOLLY.)

JOYCE: Very good, great—Right On Molly!

MOLLY: Eh?

JOYCE: Well don't you think that's all a bit old-fashioned? All that seventies stuff about Fight, fight, fight—Maggie, Maggie, Maggie; Out, Out, Out . . . It's all a bit dated now.

MOLLY: What?

JOYCE: I've seen you social workers on your demos—'What do we want? The right to work. When do we want it? Now!' (*Looks at watch*) Oh bloody hell, I'm late for the office. (*Waves*)

MOLLY: I know I'm a bit pathetic from time to time, Joyce: but I do keep going.

JOYCE: Ah, don't be put down so easily—come here—(*Gives her a cuddle*). Now then, if you're going to do all this fighting, you'll need to stop crying all the time, like a good little Sister—

MOLLY: Right On Joyce—

JOYCE: Listen, if you're still in the 1970s in your job, I'm back in the 1870s in mine. Fifty invoice clerks slaving away in Brownings Tea and Coffee Merchants—it's like something out of Charles Dickens—we just get issued with felt tip quills.

MOLLY: That young lad followed me home again tonight.

JOYCE: Old, ancient Mr James Browning went and died still trying to run the company at 81.

MOLLY: I tried to lose him, and I thought I had but I didn't. I went all around the houses, then just as I turned in the gate, there he was, waiting, laughing at me. It's not very nice. Should I ring the police.

JOYCE: Didn't you say he was black?

MOLLY: I didn't mean to encourage him but he's got nothing to do all day but hang around the centre so I let him help me to keep him out of mischief. He's wonderful—chats up all the alchies, holds them down when they start screaming and freaking out, wipes up all the messes. It was fine until about a week ago, then he decided he'd fallen in love with me, like some knight of old . . . goes around quoting courtly love poems he found in the library and follows me everywhere like a pet lamb. He's not done anything dodgy—but I suppose he might.

JOYCE: If you ring the Merseyside Police you will merely arouse every dirty thought that ever lurked in their dirty minds and they'll go on the rampage again, castrating every black male in all directions. They'll be round here giving more aggro to you and me than a regiment of rapists; then they'll go away and there he'll be again—laughing at you.

MOLLY: Come here—

JOYCE: No, I'm thinking.

MOLLY: Still come here—

JOYCE: The son.

MOLLY: I don't want the son.

JOYCE: Jack Browning! The son and new chairperson of Brownings Tea and Coffee Merchants—44. (*Molly looks quizzical.*) Age— 44, vital statistics 44–44–44. Lives in a big, lonely, spooky house by the beach in Blundellsands.

MOLLY: What are you rambling on about?

JOYCE: The Jack Browning Centre for Disintegrating Alcoholics—the private sector to the rescue—can't you see? He's just come in to his uncle's slice of the action—must be worth about two or three million—and he's dying to do good for the underprivileged.

MOLLY: Oh, come off it, Joyce.

JOYCE: Get in there girl, or give up. Go and see him at his home and, don't wear a bra.

MOLLY: Sister!

JOYCE: Do you want to carry on with your valuable work? Do you wish to rehabilitate the plonker-plonker?

MOLLY: I'll have to think about it.

JOYCE: She'll have to—! About two hundred thousand pounds she'll have to think.

MOLLY: How about asparagus with melted butter?

JOYCE: Did we buy butter?

MOLLY: No.

JOYCE: Then we haven't got any. However, I have a craving for Italian salami so I'll go and get some . . .

LEON: (*Alone outside* MOLLY *and* JOYCE'S *house sings*)
Underneath this bush or tree
Down this sleepy, leafy road
I wait to see if she'll see me
Like some greasy slimy toad.

If only her golden ball
Would fall into the pond
I'd jump in, clothes and all
I'd place it in her hand.

She's a princess
I'm a frog
In all sincerity—what can I say—I can't say better than that
She's a princess
I'm an out-of-work frog
And any day now she'll pick up a brick and squash me flat—

If only she'd see it's me
No rapist Ripper or thug
She'd pour out cups of tea
And make us all feel snug.

But no, like the girl in the tale—
She'll turn her back and pout—
And I'm no Prince beneath my skin—
I'm a frog all the way to my long intestine—
She'll end up just picking me up and throwing me out—

She's a princess
I'm a frog
In all sincerity—what can I say—I can't say better than that
She's a princess
I'm an out-of-work frog
And any day now she'll pick up a brick and squash me flat—

So underneath this bush or tree
Down this sleepy, leafy road
I wait to see if she'll see me
Like some greasy slimy toad . . .

(Enter JOYCE *with the shopping. Music continues quietly under*)

JOYCE: Eh you! What's the game?

LEON: Oh—I'm lost . . . and far from home—

JOYCE: You're giving my friend bad dreams you are. Are you a rapist?

LEON: Well I would be but I left my rapier in the police station and they won't give it back.

JOYCE: Smart Alec, eh?

LEON: I'm suffering from terminal sarcasm.

JOYCE: Haven't you got anything better to do than follow women around?

LEON: Is she your friend?

JOYCE: Yes. She's not available.

LEON: What's her name?

JOYCE: I told you—leave off.

LEON: No, go on—tell us. I know it's Miss Evans, 'cos I work for her at Leckie Street. But what's her first name?

JOYCE: You're all she needs . . . Look, bugger off home like a good little lad before she gets the needle and rings the rozzers. If the scuffers pick you up for pestering a white girl you can wave ta-ta to your two front teeth . . . so shift.

LEON: But I'm not going to do her any harm! Don't you understand? I love her. And I'm enjoying it, it's a very rare sensation, and it's not doing her any damage—and it's doing me the power of good . . . (*Music up*).

JOYCE: I'm sorry, but you've picked the wrong Princess. You see—I'm her frog.

LEON: Oh!

JOYCE: And I'm not going to change into a prince either.

LEON: Oh!

JOYCE: Don't worry about it, just lay off.

LEON: What is her name?

JOYCE: Molly.

LEON: (*Disappointed*) Molly?

JOYCE: What did you expect—Guinevere? Now come on, Sir Galahad, bugger off back home. She's unobtainable.

LEON: (*Clutching his heart, enjoying it*) Oh—oh, that's what makes her all the more—desirable. I dedicate myself to her. Lady Molly of the Dingle.

JOYCE: Are you stark, staring, raving mad?
(MOLLY *comes on unseen. She carries an axe.*)

LEON: No. I shall wait for her. Tell her I shall be at her service in Leckie Street by day and here every night for the rest of my life.

JOYCE: Oh sod off can't you?

LEON: I've told you I won't do her any mischief—

JOYCE: Yes, but—can't you see? You're oppressing her . . .

LEON: Standing out here? In the rain? In the snow? Not asking for anything, not even a cup of tea? Or a match? Or a warm by the fire? Or a hot bath?

JOYCE: You are a menace to women.

LEON: What? What am I doing? There's thousands and thousands of youths roaming this city, robbing, thieving and cracking skulls, just for something to do. And me, that doesn't intend to lay a finger on her, you accuse *me* of being a menace. Listen you're lucky it wasn't my kid brother took a fancy to her—he's only fifteen but he's doing eighteen months for GBH.

JOYCE: Look she's not your sort, you'll just end up more bitter and frustrated than you are already. She won't see you—and if she did, you'd not like her. She went to a very expensive school for young ladies and her family own half of Rhodesia. She's dozy and do-goodie, and awfully decent. (*Molly reacts*) She'd probably patronise you—she'd be really kind to you and then turn away and leave you with nothing but the sight of her pretty little arse receding towards a comfortable chair.
(MOLLY *emerges, gripping the axe.*)

LEON: (*On one knee*) Molly!

MOLLY: She would, would she?

JOYCE: What are you doing here?

MOLLY: I came to rescue you! You'd been gone too long, I got worried—I can see you were quite safe!

LEON: Molly!

JOYCE: Yes, he's harmless enough, persistent though . . .

MOLLY: You seemed to be enjoying putting him off—patronise him will I? Do-goody?

LEON: (*Tries again*) Mo . . . Oh sod this—eh you! Miss Evans!

MOLLY: Oh Leon, get up. You look utterly ridiculous, now please go away.

LEON: Where in this wide world would be a place for me, if not by
        your side?

MOLLY: What?

LEON: Do you mind if I smoke?

JOYCE: That was tactics all that I was saying—you can't be upset about
        that.

MOLLY: Well I am. Very. (*To Leon*) What my friend was saying about
        me is very far from the truth. The only black person I patronise
        is her and I'm not do-goody, I'm do-baddy. But about one thing
        she is correct, I'm not for you Leon.

LEON: That doesn't matter—you don't seem to understand. I don't
        need you to be for me . . . what's giving me the charge is *me*
        being for *you*. You don't, in fact, have to do anything, except
        glow in the moonlight.

JOYCE: He's a nut-case. Bugger off, Leon, you're littering the footpath.

MOLLY: There's no reason to be rude, Joyce.

JOYCE: What? You're liking this aren't you? (*To Leon*) Glowing in the
        moonlight. Pathetic. (*To Molly*) And you're even more pathetic,
        lapping it all up . . .

MOLLY: Well, it is a bit unliberated Leon. All this fantasising you're
        going in for stems from those ancient times before the Pill,
        when extreme sexual frustration due to the high risk of
        conception if intercourse took place and the severe moral
        hypocrisy of those bygone ages, led to this amazing heightening
        of passion, unfulfilled desire running riot through the psyche,
        and consequent elaborate, erotic fantasies seizing the fevered
        mind of the adolescent, male or female—

LEON: You make it sound so—magical, Molly . . .

        (*Music in*)

            They say to be in love is painful—
            They say it's old-fashioned and sick—

MOLLY: They say it perpetuates stereotypes—

JOYCE: They say it's a confidence trick

LEON: But I must disagree profoundly

JOYCE: And I shan't apologise

LEON: This sensation I'm experiencing currently—
            Just won't be cut down to size.

            I'm daft
            About being in love
            I'm crazy
            For romance
            I'm soft
            About the stars up above
            And the moon in June just makes me swoon
            I want to hold her in my arms and dance.

JOYCE AND MOLLY:	You're just A typical male A woman's just an object Of your fantasy You've lost Your way on the nature trail You're also losing contact with reality.
LEON:	The Youth Opportunity Programme Was something we greatly enjoyed But at walks in the park and holding hands, We're still a bit under-employed . . . My mates all went into the Army Except those who went to jail But I want to fly like a bird in the sky I don't want the right to fail.
	I'm daft About being in love
MOLLY	You're just A typical male I'm crazy For Romance
JOYCE:	A Patriarchal fantasy I'm soft About the stars up above And the moon in June just makes me swoon I want to hold her in my arms and dance.
	I've just completed this experience Called the work experience scheme My mates all experienced racial abuse But I had this wonderful dream . . .
	I've chucked petrol bombs at the coppers It's Exocet missiles next time It's great sublimating that long-suppressed hate But I've found That love is sublime.
	I'm daft About being in love
MOLLY:	You're just A typical male I'm crazy For Romance
JOYCE:	A Patriarchal fantasy I'm soft About the stars up above And the moon in June just makes me swoon . . .
JOYCE:	He's a schizophrenic nut with dangerous delusions and over active glands . . .

MOLLY: (*Spoken*) I think he's in love . . .

LEON: I want to hold her in my arms—(*whirls* MOLLY *round*) and dance . . .

(*At the end of the song,* MOLLY *hands* JOYCE *the axe*)

MOLLY: Here, take this home with you . . . I'm off.

JOYCE: Where to?

MOLLY: A big, lonely, spooky house by the beach in Blundellsands . . . I looked Mr Jack Browning up in the book, and rang him. He was very intrigued and asked me over right away..

JOYCE: Here. (*Gives her the axe*).

MOLLY: Is he a plonker plonker?

JOYCE: You'll be quite safe with your chopper chopper—any bother— just fetch it down smart-ish in the general area of the groin . . . the medium is the message.

MOLLY: Mmm. I wonder if I could actually do that . . .

LEON: Don't worry about it. I'm coming with you.

JOYCE: Oh no you're not . . .

LEON: Who says so? I'm her protector, aren't I? If she is in peril—I'll be there—Crosby ho!

JOYCE: Bugger off, you, this is serious—

MOLLY: I'm trying to get a lot of money for the centre, for people who need it . . . it really is serious.

LEON: What does that make me? A joke? I don't think you quite understand. I've adopted you—for better or for worse, for richer or for poorer, in sickness and in health—till death us do part . . . See that? (*Produces a knife*) Any bother from what's his face—and—(*Gesture*). That's a very offensive weapon, that.

JOYCE: You are a bloody schizophrenic.

LEON: Isn't that just like life today? Come on, Miss Molly—you are a damsel! Sounds like you're going to be in distress! But fear not, for who comes pricking o'er the plain, but me—your Dark Knight of the Soul—

JOYCE: Are you going to let him come with you?

MOLLY: I've had an imaginative brain-input, or idea. Yes. (*To* LEON) You can come with me, but you must do exactly what I tell you, ok?

LEON: I am in your service, fair Moll. If I fail, may Charlton Heston split me in two.

MOLLY: (*To* JOYCE) If I'm not back by midnight, send out a search party.

JOYCE: Have you gone cuckoo?

MOLLY: Yes, but they'll never notice in Crosby . . . Come on, Lancelot.

JOYCE: If she thinks she's going to the seaside without me, she's mistaken. She may need Leon to protect her from Mr Browning, but she'll need be to protect her from Leon . . . Eh! Hang on . . . (JACK BROWNING'S *house. Enter* JACK BROWNING *with a pile of mail and a waste-paper bin. He is constantly looking out of the windows, anxiously waiting for what he hopes is a nubile young social worker to turn up out of the evening murk.*)

JACK: Do I want to join the all male sauna and massage club? (*Dirty laugh*) No, I don't think that's quite my scene. There was a thing in here about Install-your-own-jacuzzi, now that sounded fun . . . thin needles of steaming hot water drill into the flesh, causing indescribably pleasurable tingling feelings conducive to relief of tension, subsequent utter relaxation and sensations of the mystic renewal of life. For our Installation Consultant, phone Widnes 07077 . . . (*Tosses it away*) . . . Widnes? I could certainly do with some but—perhaps Miss—er, Ms—olly Evans . . . sounded, um, broad-minded, on the phone. Good golly, Ms Molly. She'll be too young to remember Little Richard, I imagine. (*Opens invitation*) Aha! The North-West of England Conservative Party Annual Garden Party! Councillor and Mrs Browning? . . . Garden Party! . . . Councillor and *Mrs Browning* . . . sixteenth of next month . . . Didsbury Grange Hotel . . . to meet the Prime Minister . . . Now there's a turn-up for the books, eh? They must have heard I've come into Uncle Sefton's dough, they've never invited me before. That will come in very handy, that do . . . if I'm ever going to get a decent constituency, I'm going to need all the contacts I can get in the higher reaches. All this grass-roots District Council stuff gets you nowhere in the Tory Party . . . they look down on you for it. No. Sod it . . . I think I'm ripe for Westminster. Pity there isn't a *Mrs* Browning—still, look at Norman St John Stevas: never did him any harm—celibacy. (*Looking out again*) Not that I intend to remain CEL-I-BATE! Not much longer, not with Uncle Sefton's two and a half million to live off. Mother can sod off to the Costa del Sol, all found, and this place can *hum* with *UN*-celibate activities: frisking fillies, jetting Jacuzzis, champagne breakfasts . . . (*Sad*) But I'm too *old*. And the wrong shape. And it would be very bad for the image at Westminster—poor old Profumo. (*Looks out again*) Yes—some modest advice to Miss Evans on fund-raising for her Alcoholics, a cup of Horlicks, and B.E.D. with a few Annual Reports and a copy of the Old School magazine . . .
(*Door bell rings. He leaps in the air in fright*)
Shit! (*Tidies himself up*) Coming . . . . (*Very anxious as he combs his hair etc.*) Oh. Oh. What could that ring signify? What change in my life? An offer of a safe Tory seat in the Home Counties? A hot-blooded, lusty young woman, eager for me? Or a mugger with a razor? Oh, the abyss! The terrors of taking steps, opening doors. (*Bell rings again.*) Coming! (*He goes, quite normal*) (*Off*) Sorry! Sorry to keep you—Yes?

MOLLY: (*Off*) Molly Evans—about the Centre—you said to—

JACK: Yes, yes—come in—are these people with you, bring them in too—I thought you'd be alone—go out onto the sun-lounge— Tea? Drink? I'll bring coffee, and I've a little bottle of wine open . . . Go on in—shan't be a sec.—
(*They, MOLLY, JOYCE and LEON, troop out onto his sun-lounge, not too sure about it all.*)

JOYCE: (*Loud whisper*) I told you—if he's got a bottle of wine open, it's your body he's after—

LEON: No chance—see that? (*Knife*)

MOLLY: Put it away, Leon, you're like a droopy old flasher—

LEON: Do you think I can't use it?

MOLLY: That's what all you flashers say—stop proving you're virile all the time. You're virile. OK? (*Leon sulks*) I came to get money—a lot of money, for people who are going to die if I don't: now you remember your part of the bargain: you'll do exactly what I tell you—but exactly!

LEON: Of course I will—

MOLLY: Then put your flashing blade in its scabbard, Zorro, and be a good little Uncle Tom for ten minutes.

JOYCE: If it meant you'd get the money, would you stay the night?

MOLLY: I don't think it will come to that—

JOYCE: But if it did?

MOLLY: (*Laughs nervously*) What a terrible imagination you've got. Would you stay with me?

JOYCE: You *would*!

MOLLY: Of course I wouldn't!

JOYCE: We'll see . . . .
(*Re-enter* JACK *with large tray with coffee, wine, glasses etc.*)

JACK: So sorry to keep you—are you making yourselves at home?

JOYCE: Absolutely. What a delightful residence you have, Mr Browning.
(MOLLY *gives* JOYCE *a dirty look.* JOYCE *suppresses a giggle.*)

JACK: Pity it's dark—you can see right across the Mersey to the Wirral and over to Wales on a clear day—and all the big boats sail in right past my front door—

JOYCE: Did you live here when you were a little boy?

JACK: Oh yes, wasn't I lucky? I've still got my railway-tracks laid out upstairs, and my old Meccano: (*To* LEON) did you play with Meccano?

LEON: What's Meccano?

JACK: No. (*Pause*) I take it *you* are Miss Evans? And *you* are . . . ? (*To* JOYCE)

JOYCE: I'm her flat-mate—Joyce—(*sticks out her hand*). Pleased to meet you. (*Shake*)

JACK: (*To* LEON) And you? (*To* JOYCE) Coffee? Wine?

JOYCE: Er—wine.
(JACK *pours a glass of wine. Looks at* LEON)
Well?

LEON: I came with them.

JACK: (*Hands wine to* JOYCE) There you are. (*To* LEON) Why? (*To* MOLLY) Glass of wine for you, Miss Evans?

MOLLY: Yes please—

JACK: (*Pouring. To* LEON) Why did you come with them to my house?

MOLLY: Leon helps at the Centre . . . a voluntary worker . . . there are a lot of dark streets.

JACK: (*To* LEON) Do you work at this Alcoholics place?

LEON: Yeh! . . .

JACK: (*Gives* MOLLY *glass*) Right, Miss Molly Evans—Let's get down to business—

LEON: Shall I just help myself—?

JACK: Oh (*Vague*) . . . yes—whatever you want—(*To* MOLLY) Now, my dear, I know you think I'm very rich, with money pouring out of the taps, but the reality is—I'm not. If you want to know the details, all Uncle Sefton's money was in stocks and shares—the income from these goes to my mother, who was his sister, until she dies. All I got was the responsibility for Brownings Tea and Coffee Merchants, which needs money putting *into* it, not taking out of it: so you see, rich I ain't.

JOYCE: But this place must be worth half a million?

JACK: Crumbling. Dry rot. Woodworm. Rising Damp. Worthless. And I've got to live somewhere. This is my childhood acre.

LEON: What?

JACK: Where I was brought up. (*To* MOLLY) But don't think your journey was all in vain, my dear. I am a businessman, and I do want to help you.

MOLLY: Mr Browning, this government has squeezed the local authorities till they daren't provide anything for anybody— they've done that to keep the rates and tax-level down so that private firms like yours could make a lot more profit—and so you are! But what are you doing with the money?

JACK: For the time being, ploughing it back in—modernisation. I'll give you an example: we've got two hundred and fifty invoice clerks handling our sales back-up very slowly and very inefficiently. As soon as we can save up enough to get a computer in, ten people will do the same work, fast and clever.

JOYCE: What? When?

JACK: In eight or nine months' time, actually—that's confidential, by the way—(JOYCE *almost collapses—covers up*) (*To* MOLLY) so you're quite correct my dear. Profits are rising—but they're being ploughed back into industry, to get this country back to work again—look what the Germans achieved between 1945 and 1960—total recovery, and *more*. That's how it's done— dedication, hard work, and ploughing back the profits.

MOLLY: So where does that leave my derelicts?

JOYCE: And where does it leave the other 240 clerks in Brownings?

JACK: It leaves them on re-training programmes, getting some A-Levels, making themselves more skilled, more up-to-the-minute, more *mobile*, more valuable to an employer. Do you know why wages in this country *cannot* rise? Because what the work-force has to sell, its labour, becomes worth less as the twentieth century rolls by. Already its price is artificially high, unreal, protected. They've *got* to be unemployed: to learn their lesson. Let them use their time out of work to make themselves worth *more*. Then you just watch their wages rise, bonuses go up, they'll end up working from home, with a couple of cars, two holidays a year, and a nice little cabin-cruiser on the Welsh coast for week-ends. That's what we're after: happiness. Human happiness.

MOLLY: And is that what you're offering my alcoholics?

JACK: It's up to them. They will have every opportunity to become useful members of society: if they reject that opportunity, then society may well reject *them*. Every great civilisation had its human dustbin: why should we succeed where Franklin D. Roosevelt failed? Of course, we must try. And we shall. You and I together, Miss Molly Evans, we shall try. But we have to get our priorities in order: for far too long this country has been ashamed of the one commodity that gives it strength, meaning, and the ability to do good: Profit. Thank God, at last, that crippling shame has been banished from our national psyche—we can stand up and demand Dividends: I feel like I imagine a homosexual must feel when he 'comes out'— liberated, relieved, a trifle giddy with the novelty of it. (*Music in*)
Not, or course, that I am, er, 'gay'—

Coming Out For Profits

I was a closet capitalist
A furtive secret boss—
Ashamed to smile without a twist
Reviled by every socialist—
I hid my little vice
Though I thought it very nice
Whenever I made a profit, instead of a loss . . . Sh!

I'm a big bad wolf come in out of the cold,
I no longer care who knows it, I've learnt to be bold:
I've come out of the board-room, before I'm too old—
I'm kinky for profits to have and to hold—
I stand up for dividends, I'm randy for gold—
I'm randy for gold
I'm randy for gold
That's what does it to me—
That's what does it to me!

(*At the end of the song,* MOLLY, JOYCE *and* LEON *don't know what to say.* JACK *is also a little shy.*)

JACK: There are, of course, other things in my life. Other pursuits— romantic, artistic, physical, spiritual: mostly unattainable, but I pursue them. The love of a young woman, for example. The gift of painting a beautiful picture. Knowledge—of the countries and the peoples of the world, of laws and constitutions, of music: even just to play the piano with a modicum of satisfaction. All these I pursue, I hope for, one day. There *is* more to my life than being a money-making machine: much, much more. And you three—well, you've caught my fancy. I want to help. Let's put it no higher than that.

MOLLY: Well—how much can you afford to donate? At the moment the Centre costs £120,000 per annum. Now I'm sure if you put in 50% of that in a covenant over the next seven years, we could get the Corporation to match you pound for pound, and the Jack Browning Centre would be born . . . (JACK *is laughing.*) Why are you laughing?

JACK: Stop, my dear, stop: don't get carried away. I've told you: my resources are very small, and required elsewhere.

MOLLY: Then how can you help? What can you give us?

JACK: Advice.

(LEON *goes for his knife.* JOYCE *stifles hysterical laughter.* MOLLY *looks around the room trying not to scream.* JACK *has sat back and looks thoughtful, solemn.*)

JACK: You may not think you need it—but you do. What you don't seem to realise is that you and your kind have been living in a dream-world for thirty-odd years: a fantasy-land of subsidy, of subventions and committees, boards and tribunals all dishing out what was never theirs to people who had done nothing for it. Where the non-productive section of the community was getting bigger and bigger by the hour, and the tiny wealth-making section was breaking its back trying to earn enough to support the others, and failing, miserably. We were sliding down the slippery slope into the Third World, weighed down by the burdens of welfare, the habit of not producing anything, and subsidy, hidden and open, to millions of people. Now that has all changed. (*To* MOLLY) More wine my dear? While you've been living in your land of Nod, we've been doing battle in the real world, and we do know a hawk from a handsaw.

(MOLLY *stands, her mouth opening and closing, not knowing where to start.*)

JOYCE: No wonder there's riots. Next time I'm joining in.

JACK: There will be no more riots. For years the British State has been blackmailed by demonstrations, sit-ins, work-ins, strikes, riots and all the other bullying paraphernalia of the left. That is over. When a handful of SAS men blasted their way into the Iranian Embassy in London and shot those gunmen dead, every terrorist, every holder of hostages, every occupier of somebody else's building, every red Brigade, Angry Brigade, heavy Brigade, was served notice that the British State no longer played games. And when our task force marched into Port Stanley, everybody realised that we were no longer heading for the Third World: we were heading for a place in the sun; a seat at the top table; and if our paras, commandoes and fighter-pilots could not be stopped by a military junta with an army, an air force, a navy and a hysterical population on their side— then your Socialist Revolutionary parties and your black anarchists are going to get nowhere. Nowhere. Any riot in future will be merely an expression of defeat—an eruption of weakness.

When Mrs Thatcher came out of 10 Downing Street that night and told us that the Task Force had gone into action, some moaning Minnie, probably from the *Guardian*, started quizzing her. She soon stopped him. 'You shouldn't be asking those questions', she said—'You should Rejoice at what our boys are doing!' She knew what she was saying: 'England is strong again! Rejoice!' The wonderland of welfare is over— Task Force England is sailing to Victory. And nothing is ever going to be the same again. That's why you need my advice.

MOLLY: Are you in the National Front?

JACK: (*Laughs*) Wouldn't that be convenient for you? No. I'm not racist. Nor am I a Nazi. I don't hate foreigners, nor do I believe in pure Anglo-Saxon blood: I'm a normal, Christian, enterprising, English person, with both eyes wide open.

MOLLY: Then why do you want to help?

JACK: Aha. But I don't want to help *you*: I want to help your customers, your derelicts. You seem to have designated yourselves their guardians for some reason I can't fathom— probably couldn't get a job anywhere else—so I suppose to help them I must treat with you. I wonder how Jesus Christ would have got on if every bloody leper he went to cure had a social worker beside him with his hand out for £8,000 a year plus luncheon vouchers. (*Laughs at his own joke*)

MOLLY: Mr Browning, I think we've made a terrible mistake. I think we ought to go.

JACK: (*Quietly, seriously*) Please don't. I'd be very upset if my somewhat callous sense of humour drove you away. Molly— may I call you Molly?—you told me on the telephone there were lives at stake; it's not often I get the chance to save lives, here, in my own native city. There are also minds to be rescued: theirs from decay and dementia; yours—which interests me greatly—from stagnating in a pool of welfare-state-induced self-pity . . . So we have got to make a bigger effort, you and I.

JOYCE: But you won't save anybody with *advice*, Mr Browning.

JACK: Do you think not?

JOYCE: Nor with abuse.

JACK: No. You are quite right. I must apologise if you thought I was abusing anybody. But my advice could come in handy— particularly if it lead to large quantities of cash . . .

JOYCE: Oh.

MOLLY: And do you think it could?

JACK: Oh it could.

(JOYCE, MOLLY *and* LEON *sing*)

ALL: Where does it come from?
       Who can tell?
       Where is it going to is what we need to know—

JOYCE: Pick up the pennies and
       Run like hell—

ALL: Charity is helpless till—
The cash begins to flow:

MOLLY: For what's produced by cunning and greed
Can serve to save a soul in its hour of need . . .

ALL: If the money by some trick
Was extorted out of you—

LEON: Although it makes you sick

ALL: It can make you better too . . .

MOLLY: What, er, is your advice, Mr Browning?

JACK: My father manufactured sewer-pipes. And grids, gratings and man hole covers. He was a very successful industrialist. But he was also passionate about Wordsworth: the poetry, of course, but above all the philosophy—and the beneficial effects of close contact with nature on the human psyche. (*Suddenly turns to* LEON) Were you involved in those street battles in Upper Parliament Street last year?

LEON: (*Hesitates, looks to* MOLLY *for what to say*) Er—no—

JACK: Of course you were—how could you not be?

LEON: Well only a bit—

JACK: Throw any petrol-bombs?

LEON: Only little ones . . . Babycham bottles, that sort of thing—

JACK: Set fire to anything?

LEON: Well—a Chief Constable or two—nothing that mattered—

JACK: Looting?

LEON: Eh, hold up! We've had the Court of Inquiry—the pigs didn't kill nobody, so we never nicked nothing, alright?

JACK: Now tell me: what kind of place do you live in?

LEON: A house! In a street!

JACK: Do you share the house?

LEON: We're on the top floor—there's other families, like, on the other floors, but it's a big house—what's all this about?

JACK: My father built this house by the sea, with space around it, trees, grass, wild places, rose-gardens, because he believed the environment we live in means *everything*: I grew up here, for example, and never wanted to throw a petrol-bomb at anybody—not even my worst enemy. My father would argue that if Leon spent, say, a month in this house, close to the sea, the gardens, the peace and quiet, he too would become a happy, well-integrated, peaceful member of society.

LEON: (*Alarmed*) I don't have to, do I? I'd go berserk—

JOYCE: What's this got to do with your father's money?

LEON: Do I? Eh?

JACK: It has this to do with it: under the terms of his will, the money has to be spent on a scheme for those in need of a cure from the effects of industrial society's pressures. The scheme would be to transplant them from their urban squalor to the heart of nature, and there watch them blossom. For example, if you took over a small country house in the heart of the Pennines—which the Trust would pay for—and *that* was your country rest-home, then we could support the centre in town as a sort of pick-up point. The only thing is, some of them would have to agree to a six-week trip to the hills every now and again. And you'd have to go with them.

MOLLY: And that's what we'd have to do to get money?

JACK: That, or something similar: private sector funds, you will find, won't just be thrown at you as the ratepayers' money has been in the past.

MOLLY: But these people don't *want* to be dragged into some damp nature-cure in the Pennines—their problems are what other people have done to them, how to summon up the will-power to walk down the street, where the next penny's coming from . . . They need help where they live, not up a mountain—that's ridiculous.

JACK: Clearly you don't want them to get better—

MOLLY: What?

JACK: You don't want them cured, you want them bandaged up so they can stagger on chronically sick, unable to leave the nest, permanently crippled—

MOLLY: I know that syndrome, Mr Browning, and it's not mine.

JACK: Then send them to the countryside. Hire a good doctor, a psychiatrist, nurses—give them good food, walks in the fields, work in the vegetable garden—watch them grow stronger and fitter . . .

MOLLY: Then send them back to die on St George's Plateau.

JACK: But they won't!

MOLLY: What else could they do? Look around this city you and your private sector have built for yourselves . . . So you can rationalise and make profit:
　　24% unemployed—
　　One violent crime every five minutes—
　　Kids without a chance, giving up.
　　Sniffing glue at 12, hard drugs at 15.
　　Education—pointless;
　　Looking after yourself—pointless;
　　Looking after your house—pointless;
　　Going on living—not too much to be said for it.
You want me to take men and women who can't cope with all that up to some Shangri-la in the hills, make them feel better, then dump them back in the same dung-heap they've just got away from? Is that it?

JACK: (*Standing up*) My father believed in it: it's his money . . . I personally think I could even make young Leon here into a young Tory, given a month in the right environment . . .

MOLLY: You can't be serious—

JACK: Never more serious in my life. What are you? Some sort of fatalist?

MOLLY: Of course not—

JACK: Then you must believe that people can change—and what changes them more profoundly than their environment—

MOLLY: But—this is crazy—

JACK: Not at all: let's put it this way: if this young man can change from being an out-of-work, aimless layabout, to being a determined, strong-minded contributor to the nation in four weeks, then your alcoholic wrecks can be dried out, cured, filled with the urge to go out into the world and *compete*, in six weeks in the Pennines.

MOLLY: It can't be done—

JACK: Let's have a wager. If Leon will agree to live here for four weeks, and listen to what I have to say, and stay away from his home environment, *completely*—then I guarantee I'll have him fit to take to the North-West of England Conservative Association Garden Party in Didsbury next month. If I fail you will have the satisfaction of being correct—but no money. If, however, my father's theory works, then you will organise the Harry L. Browning Country Home in a house in the Pennines which a friend of mine wishes to sell privately. And you will run it for a minimum of three years reporting monthly to me, as Chairman of the Trustees. Perhaps you'd like to talk it over, I'll be back in a moment.

(*He goes.* MOLLY, JOYCE *and* LEON *look at each other.*)

LEON: What's going on here?

JOYCE: Leon—it's your big chance to prove you love her!

LEON: That guy's crazy—

MOLLY: No. He's the New sanity. Social Darwinism—the Survival of the Fittest—

JOYCE: (*To* MOLLY) Do you want Leon to do it?

MOLLY: That's up to him. Do you want to save the lives of a few drunk old farts, Leon, a few rotting old, nasty old, evil old winos?

LEON: Do you?

MOLLY: Yes.

LEON: Do you want me to?

MOLLY: Yes. But they won't thank you for it—

LEON: Will you thank me for it?

MOLLY: In my own way—yes.

LEON: What's the deal again?

JOYCE: You stay here for four weeks, while he tries to turn you into a Tory—if he does, she gets her money, on his terms—

MOLLY: But if you don't—we get nothing . . .

JOYCE: Will you do it?

LEON: Er—well—

(*Enter* JACK *with a bottle of champagne and a tray of glasses, smiling.*)

JACK: Well? I brought this to seal our bargain—we have got a bargain?

(*They all look at* LEON.)

LEON: (*To* JACK) You bet you can turn me into a Tory?

JACK: Well—something drier than Prior—what do you say?

LEON: And I've got to stay here for four weeks—

JACK: Right. Soak up the environment and take in my advice.

LEON: Well—I'm not too busy this next few weeks. I'm on—

JACK: Bravo! (*Fires champagne cork*) Glasses? (*As he pours*) I'm really looking forward to this Leon: you'll be a challenge: but a few months ago you were burning and rioting: now you are about to become a useful, motivated member of society. What a challenge! But I tell you: if we in the Tory Party can't win the hearts and minds of you young black kids—we don't deserve to lead the country. However I know we *can*: if we go about it in the right spirit so (*Raises glass*)—let's Rejoice!
(*He and* LEON *drink.* LEON *smiles.*)

LEON: Mm. That's nice.

END OF ACT 1

ACT 2

JACK BROWNING'S *garden—early evening, summer.* LEON *alone, walking with a book.*

LEON: Me! Me! Me! (*He tries to throw his chest out.*)
I! I! I!—I want! I want! I want!
It's no good I'll go back and try that again—(*His exercises are not very convincing even to him.*) Me! Me! Me!
I want! I want! I want to buy! I want to buy!
I want to own! I want to possess! (*Steps*) It's no good—I'm never going to get it—
(*Tries again*) Me! Me! Me! I want to own things!
Ah sod it, I'm off home.
(JOYCE *appears from behind a bush—in commando gear followed by* MOLLY *who comes on behind him.*)

JOYCE: Oh no you don't, our Leon.
(LEON *turns to run but straight into* MOLLY.)

LEON: Hello Molly: I'm doing my best, honest—

MOLLY: Is it difficult?

LEON: Difficult? It's murder—

MOLLY: We appreciate it, Leon.

LEON: It's mad: I have to keep getting into a different lot of clothes every five minutes, and have baths twice a day and have shaves. I get elocution lessons and tennis lessons, and wine tasting and which knife and fork to use lessons, and I've got to listen to the story of the day's activities on the Stock Exchange, and the Commodity Market—and to understand about futures and debentures—and how to read the newspapers: not the cartoons and the jokes, but all the writing—

MOLLY: Are you any good at it?

LEON: Brilliant! But I can't stand it. I've had enough—you'll have to
get someone else—

JOYCE: No Leon—it's got to be *you*—

LEON: (*Feebly*) Me! Me! Me!—I'm suffering from a punctured ego—
he's given me exercises in ego-building—and aggression—and
possessiveness—but I'm deficient: I'm abnormal; that's how I
got into this in the first place—
(*Music in*)

I'm Happy With What I Stand Up In

LEON: When I was a little lad
I didn't long for toys
I didn't watch the telly,
I made very little noise—
I didn't want a football
I didn't bunk off school
They thought I was a cissie
Or at very best a fool—

But now I'm supposed to feel all those sensations
But I'm glad to report all I'm feeling is frustration . . .

Don't want to own a million pounds
Haven't got a bank to store it—
Don't want to drive a Rolls Royce round
Haven't got a garage,
        Wouldn't thank you for it—
I'm happy
        With what I stand up in
Nobody
        Can take it away
I'm happy
        With what I stand up in
I don't want your money
I don't want your mansion
I just want a dream world
With room for expansion—
I'm happy
        With what I stand up in
I'm happy—
        That's all I can say
I'm happy
To sing
I'm happy
To dance
I'm happy
To sing and to dance and to play—

Now I'm a wild young youth
They say I should run mad

Should burn and loot and riot
Be big and black and bad—
Should take what's been denied me
Should rob it, grab it, con it
But I won't nick a telly
Can't bear to watch what's on it.

But now I'm supposed to feel similar aggressions
And a burning desire for undesirable possessions.

But I don't want to own a million pounds
Haven't got a bank to store it—
Don't want to drive a Rolls Royce round
Haven't got a garage,
     Wouldn't thank you for it—
I'm happy
     With what I stand up in
Nobody
     Can take it away
I'm happy
     With what I stand up in
I don't want your money
I don't want your mansion
I just want a dream world
With room for expansion—
I'm happy
     With what I stand up in
I'm happy—
     That's all I can say
I'm happy
To sing
I'm happy
To dance
I'm happy
To sing and dance and to play!
(*At end of song*)

MOLLY: Poor Leon—never mind, you've obviously tried your best. I'm certainly quite glad you'll never be a Tory—

JOYCE: Don't talk sentimental horse-shit, Molly. OK so he's sweet and innocent, and you want to take him into your English upper-middle-class social worker bleeding heart: but you told me people will die if you don't get this rich man's money, and your centre will close, and maybe you'll go away back to live with your mother in Zimbabwe where all your daddy's money is—

MOLLY: Well I might have to—

JOYCE: Yes of course. And where does that leave *me*?

MOLLY: You can come with me—

JOYCE: Mummy would be charmed . . . Leon: you stay in this rich man's stinking house. You pass the Garden Party Test in Didsbury—and we'll make sure the rest of the bargain is kept to the nearest hundred thousand pounds. OK, little brother?

LEON: But it's really boring. These big houses—they're nothing but trouble. And you can't get people to clean the place, or cook your dinner, or cut the grass . . . and you lie awake all night wondering if you're being burgled, and you sleep all day 'cos there's nothing better to do . . . who needs to be rich?

MOLLY: Have you gone off me then, Leon?

LEON: No, but I could do with some token of your esteem—a favour to tie to my lance—a chiffon scarf, a kerchief, a used Kleenex—anything—

MOLLY: Here (*Gives him an ornamental badge*)—wear that—

LEON: Does it mean: do this for me, and I shall be yours, body and soul.

JOYCE: I've warned you, Leon, about that—

MOLLY: It means you have my esteem: more I cannot, at this moment, give—will you stay?

LEON: Your eyes . . . Yes. I will—

MOLLY: (*Gives him a gentle kiss*) Thank you, Leon. You *are* my hero— (*Noise of car approaching, which continues with a stop on gravel, door closing etc. during the following:*)

JOYCE: Here cometh William Wordsworth looking for his daffodils— let's blend into the landscape, superman—

LEON: Will you come back again soon though? I get really cheesed off—

MOLLY: Next Tuesday—same time—

JOYCE: One false move, Leon—you'll die—we'll be listening— (*They dive into the undergrowth.* LEON *gives a look of utter despair, hears* JACK *approaching, goes into his original routine.*)

LEON: Me! Me! Me! I want! I want to own! I want to own a shop full of Space Invader machines— (JACK *comes in, back from the office, with his briefcase etc. He watches* LEON *fondly, but critically—even painfully.*)

LEON: I want to possess something! I want to possess something!

JACK: What?

LEON: Oh—hello—had a good day at the office?

JACK: No—I had to fire Uncle Sefton's secretary. She thought now he's dead she runs the firm: not surprising after fifty-odd years, but wrong. *I* run the firm. The secret is never to let them forget that—

LEON: I couldn't do that—stick my neck out—

JACK: If you are to succeed, you must: the only other way is cowardice—a boss can't escape his responsibility, which is by and large, to be unpleasant. Leon, I'll tell you something for nothing—what's wrong with this country? It's this: it's run by hundreds of thousands of bosses who are so busy pretending they're really *not* bosses that nobody gives any orders—ergo nobody obeys any orders; get me a drink, will you?—nobody says which way our industry's going, so we've lost all sense of direction—we wander about in a maze of indecision, afraid to ask the workers to do any work in case we upset them. Afraid to modernise in case the unions don't like it, afraid to make a profit in case that looks like capitalism, ashamed of the very thought of success—because, you see, that's not very nice for those who've failed! Now how do you think this sorry state of affairs came about?

LEON: I don't know—perhaps they *are* ashamed. Perhaps they should be—

JACK: Exactly! Perhaps you are correct! *But*! Can the industry of a great nation run on shame, on being sorry, on worrying about others? No! It never has and it never will! (*Sips*) Perfect! Sit . . . Now, at the end of the last war, the electorate of this country saw fit to dismiss Winston Churchill—remember?—and to replace him with an assortment of semi-Communists. Those people—for whatever reason—set about a massive and systematic destruction of the nation's superego. Do you know what I mean? The Welfare State, amongst its many other crimes, has corroded the will to personal power—the strength of the organised masses has terrorised strong and capable men into quivering, apologetic weaklings. The serried ranks of junior management cling together in symposiums and conference-halls, grey, cautious and collective—their superegos faltering, wispy and wrapped in flannel—do you know what I'm talking about Leon?

LEON: Oh yeah. It's the same at school. They won't say: 'Do that one more time and I'll crack your skull'—they say: 'Leon has been caught robbing a container-lorry full of fags—so let's all sit down and talk about his family background.'

JACK: (*Delighted*) Exactly!

LEON: And if you don't pass your exam, they don't say: 'You're a thick idiot for not working hard enough.' They say: 'Don't be discouraged, there's room for all in our multi-achieving society.'

JACK: The glorification of Failure! You've hit the bull's-eye!

LEON: (*Sad*) But you still don't get a job . . . or get into college . . . . or get any money—

JACK: No. Because in the end, this philosophy is a lie: in the end, it's up to you: to get anywhere, you've got to decide where you want to go, and then, like the Royal Marine Commandos, you must read your compass correctly, load your pack on your back, and YOMP!

(*Music in*) Yomp! Yomp! Yomp! Yomp!

Believe In Yourself

As you stumble through life's forest
And you can't see wood for trees
If your days are vague and aimless
And you're sure you've caught some dreadful disease

If your head is full of fireworks
And your strength is sapped and gone—
Don't sniff cocaine to ease the pain:
Learn lesson Number One—

Believe
    In Yourself
Have faith
    In Yourself—
Build your ego up with every passing day
It's you that comes first, forget about the others—
Remember Cain, remember Abel—
Well they were brothers—
Alone you came into this world,
Alone you'll pass away—
You know that Number One is Number One
And Number One Rules OK!

If you're wandering far from life's fairway
And you're hacking about in the rough—
Then you bury your ball in a bunker
And you tear up your card 'cos enough is enough:

If your boat's in a storm with no anchor
And you find out the crew has all gone—
Don't jump in the sea—just yell Leave this to me!
With Lesson Number One!

Believe
    In yourself
Have faith
    In yourself
Build up your ego with every passing day!
It's you that comes first, forget about the others—
Remember Cain, remember Abel—
Well they were brothers—

Alone you came into this world
Alone you'll pass away—

You know that Number One is Number One
And Number One Rules OK!

If your friend is trusting and kind
If he's crippled, old or blind—
Rob him, cheat him, grab his dough
Because the Bible tells you so!

Don't be bashful, don't be coy!
Be a brave bold little boy!
If your friend's in a desperate plight . . .
Shit on him from a very great height—

Believe
    In Yourself
Have faith
    In Yourself
Build your ego up with every passing day!

It's you that comes first, forget about the others—
Remember Cain, remember Abel—
Well they were brothers—

Alone you came into this world
Alone you'll pass away—

So Number One is Number One
And Number One Rules OK!
(*At end of song*)

JACK: So that's why you must do your exercises—but I heard you just
then, Leon—(*Mimics*) me, me, me—pathetic! You must stride
around the garden, yelling your message to the passing
warships—Me! Me! Me!! Look over there at the mountains of
Wales! Look at the towering cliffs of the Great Orme! Feel
proud to be alive! Thrust yourself into the universe! Be active,
and positive, and assertive! Go on—

LEON: (*Trying*) Me! Me! Me! ME!!

JACK: Now you're getting somewhere—more, MORE!

LEON: ME!! ME!! I, Leon Jones, I exist—(*Treads on* JACK's *briefcase*)
Oh sorry—

JACK: No! Don't apologise! Be assertive!

LEON: Get your briefcase out of my way, you!

JACK: Great! Now—be possessive, demand!

LEON: I want! I want! I WANT MY TEA!

JACK: Haven't you had any?

LEON: (*Shy*) No. I'm starving—I haven't had anything all day.

JACK: What? Didn't Mrs. Edwards turn up?

LEON: Er. Yes: but, well—

JACK: But well what? I left a note telling her to cook you lunch—fillet
steak en croute, followed by raspberries and cream.

LEON: She said it must be a mistake. She said I'd written it. She said
she wasn't going to work here any more if I was here because
her husband wouldn't like her being here on her own with me.
(*Feebly, ironically*) me, me, me.

JACK: I see. Don't worry about it, Leon—you must learn to ride above
that sort of petty prejudice. (*Laughs*) If I paid any attention to
all the prejudice against capitalists, Tory councillors and
dwellers in large houses, I'd be a nervous wreck. But I don't pay
any attention to it. I shall speak to Mrs Edwards on the
telephone, severely: she'll cook for you tomorrow!

LEON: But I fancy some steak tonight.

JACK: You shall have some. What else happened today?

LEON: The cleaner came. And the gardener. And a lot of groceries in a
van. And the bin-men. But they wouldn't take any rubbish
because it wasn't laid out in green plastic bags—it was in black
plastic bags, so they wouldn't touch it—said you'd have terrible
trouble shifting black ones . . .

JACK: Didn't you tell them who I was? Didn't you explain I was
virtually their employer?

LEON: I said you were on the Corporation, and they said you should know better–

JACK: I'll privatise the bastards—

LEON: Sounds very painful—

JACK: I'll cook you a steak—

LEON: Great—medium rare, with garlic and peppers, eh? That idea of wrapping it up in pastry's last . . .

JACK: Au poivre it shall be—Claret or Burgundy?

LEON: 1968 Fleurie. Is that alright with steak au poivre, the Fleurie? I could go a splash on that—

JACK: Perfect—I'll open a bottle right now—

LEON: Great—let it breathe a bit—while you cook—

JACK: (*Sternly*) And while you have a bath and dress for dinner—

LEON: Dickie-bows again? Ah come off it, Mr Browning, I can't get those dickie-bows to stay done up—

JACK: All history is the story of humanity's struggle to rise above the beast: to dress for dinner is to strike a blow for mankind. Only horses eat in their working clothes . . .

LEON: OK, OK—but I wish you'd get me a made-up dickie-bow!

JACK: Leon: as you would say: no chance. (*As they go*) Vichyssoise?

LEON: Only if we've got chives—I've been reading TS Eliot . . .

JACK: Have you now? Leon—next week we might try you out in public. In a small way: how about dinner at the Adelphi?

LEON: That sounds nice. I'd be interested to know what you make of Sweeney Agonistes—

JACK: In Oxford in my day it was fashionable to sneer at TS Eliot. But given the present return to older values: England, the Church, the Queen—well I wouldn't be at all surprised if old Tom Eliot didn't make quite a come-back . . .
(JACK *and* LEON *exit.*)
(MOLLY *and* JOYCE *come out of the bushes open-mouthed*)

JOYCE: Well done Leon . . .

MOLLY: Yes it was very convincing . . .

JOYCE: Very convincing.

MOLLY: In fact.

JOYCE: Yes, me too.

MOLLY: Perhaps there really is a strong deep centre to Leon's personality, way down below, holding him all together . . .

JOYCE: No chance.

MOLLY: But a lot depends on Leon . . . my future.

JOYCE: Our future . . .

MOLLY: If he cops out, Mr Browning's money stays right where it is.

JOYCE: And you, sweet little sister, go a long way away.

MOLLY: Leon has got to keep at it . . .

JOYCE: Or die.

MOLLY: It's nice of you to say all that, Joyce, and I know you mean it. But you were getting along fine without me—

JOYCE: Was I?

MOLLY: You're very independent really. I'm sure I don't mean all that much to you—

JOYCE: Oh—I could put up with you a little longer; we've only had a year together—

MOLLY: It's me; how would I manage? I mean without you? What a strange place to be having this sort of conversation—shall we go home?

JOYCE: I'm easy—

MOLLY: Yes—you are—

JOYCE: Molly!

MOLLY: I just glow in the moonlight—

JOYCE: You are a trollop.

I Don't Need You

JOYCE: I don't need you but I like you—
Like you being around
I wouldn't die because I lost you
But I'd rather that you were found.
Don't want to give you the impression
I'm head over heels in love
Don't go feeling that you're more to me
Than a bucketful of diamonds or the stars up above.

But every time I see you I get a hungry feeling
That I really want to eat you 'cos I find you so appealing.

I don't need you but I like you—
So girl why don't you stick around.

MOLLY: Don't misunderstand me but I want you
Want you somewhere about—
But please don't think you're something vital
Just answer when I shout.
Don't want to give you the impression
You're all that I desire
My heart beats no faster than usual
And my lips don't burn don't burn like fire.

But every time I see you come walking through the door
I want to feel you close to me, then closer some more.

I don't need you but I want you
So girl why don't you stick around.

JOYCE: I never intended
To feel this way again.

MOLLY: I thought I ought to try it
As a gesture against patriarchal men—

JOYCE: I never wanted
The full domestic hype . . .

MOLLY: I thought we ought to
De-mystify the stereotype . . .

BOTH: I don't need you but I like you
        Like you being around
        I wouldn't die because I lost you
        But I'd rather that you were found.

JOYCE: Don't want to give you the impression
        I'm head over heels in love.

MOLLY: Don't go feeling that you're more to me

BOTH: Than a bucketful of diamonds—or the stars up above.

        But every time I see you come walking through the door
        I want to feel you close to me then closer some more 'cos

        I don't need you but I like you
        So girl why don't you stick around
        (At least till pay-day)
        So girl why don't you stick around . . . ..

        (*At end of song,* MOLLY *and* JOYCE *go off home together*)

        (JACK *and* LEON *come in tennis gear, hot from playing three sets.*
        LEON *is looking angry with himself, moody.* JACK *pours orange*
        squash from a flask, passes one to LEON.)

JACK: There you are—well played!
LEON: You beat me—again!
JACK: That first service of yours is quite wicked when it goes in—
LEON: Yeh—when. It's no good if it goes out nine times out of ten, is
        it?
JACK: Some very fine rallies, too—you're a natural—the right shape—
LEON: You beat me in straight sets—
JACK: It was hard work. Maybe next time—
LEON: Yeh. Next time I'll *smash* you—
        (*Pause*)
JACK: Ten out of ten for aggression, Leon, and ten out of ten for your
        will to win.
LEON: (*Sarcastic*) Thanks—
JACK: Let us examine that game of tennis—you fought to win out
        there as if your life depended on it. You really *hated* me every
        time I lobbed you, every time I dropped one short. But you had
        the deepest satisfaction whenever I failed: you laughed out loud
        when I fell on my back, you sniggered at my double faults—
        OK! Fine! Absolutely the correct emotions. And in the last set,
        when I offered you a fiver for every game you took off me, you
        were magnificent, a raging, desperate beast-
LEON: You owe me ten quid—
JACK: You shall have it. It was worth every penny to see you come to
        life like that. Now I want you to remember that feeling to the
        end of your days—because that's what is called being
        motivated. Without it, we all crumble away into hopelessness
        and the Dole Mentality—with it, we conquer the world. Are
        you with me?

LEON: Yeh. I'm with you.

JACK: But. And it is a big but. A motivated man without *gracefulness*, is not a pretty sight. If other people can see how desperate, determined and brutal you are—it can stand in your way: the thing is they won't like you. So what must you do?

LEON: Cover it up.

JACK: Precisely: don't lose it, weaken it, or dilute it—just learn how to cover it up. There are many ways to do this, and we'll study them all: together they add up to what's called a *social manner*: that, Leon, is what you have to acquire in the next six days. A tall order—but shall we try? Can you do it?

LEON: Of course I can do it! No problem!

JACK: Hm. Good. Well we can begin by studying how to *lose* gracefully—and still come out on top—a purely British facility which is much admired the world over, particularly by those who haven't got it: like the PLO and the Argentinean army . . .

LEON: and the Merseyside Police—

JACK: *Exactly.* Don't know how to lose, so they keep killing people. Really petulant, adolescent behaviour—not what I'd call New Tory at all: that's why we had to have Michael Heseltine up here—to apply a little social manner to the proceedings. Now if *you* are the loser, it's your job to make it appear that you didn't lose—you merely allowed the other person to win. If, for example, you had gone straight to the flask, and poured me a drink with apparent concern for my physical condition, *then* the boot would have been on the other foot. You would have achieved moral superiority and it would have cost you nothing—indeed it would have been at *my* expense . . . you would have done a remarkable Heseltine!

LEON: Do you mean to tell me that this is what you lot spend hours and hours working out?

JACK: Of course not. It comes as naturally as mother's milk if you go to the right school. It's people like you who have to spend hours working it out—and believe me, Leon, you're going to have to, and very quickly. (*Giving him paper from briefcase*) But let's move on a little. Now—how to *win* gracefully—when we came in from tennis I did something very significant, I poured the drinks. I didn't ask you to, or wait to see if you would—I went straight to the flask and poured, yours first. Kindness, concern, consideration for others: wonderful devices, essential ingredients of a social manner. (*Takes racket*) Immediately after pouring your drink, what did I say?

LEON: I wasn't listening, I was too depressed—

JACK: Generosity in defeat, that's one thing—which I'm afraid, Leon, you sadly lack. Well played, I said. Wonderful first service, excellent rallies—

LEON: Lies, all lies—I was dire—

JACK: Generosity in victory, Leon: it's how to distinguish the gentlemen from the players—and it need cost you nothing. If you thrash some poor fellow on the squash-court, all you have to do is slap him on the back, say well played, let's have a shower and I'll buy you a bottle of decent champagne. Of course, he doesn't allow it. He buys *you* a bottle of *excellent* champagne, and sends it round with his chauffeur because you've had to rush off to a fictitious board-room, so you get the whole bottle of bubbly to yourself! Are you with me?

LEON: Wouldn't work down our street—

JACK: No. But you, Leon, can learn. You *must* learn, fast. Now—let's assume you've lost, say at tennis.

LEON: I did.

JACK: You'll never achieve anything if you keep moaning on about losing! Generosity! If necessary, Counter-Generosity! Now—I, as winner, say: Well played—now, what's your comeback?

LEON: Er—listen, Jack, I'm not in your class: you're brilliant, pure brilliant—have you ever thought of going professional? Honest to God, if you weren't such a genius at making money in the Tea and Coffee business, I'd swear you could make your fortune on the Pro Circuit . . . let me buy you a ticket for the Centre Court—in fact, have mine, you'd appreciate it more than me—I only go for the strawberries—

JACK: Well—a bit over the top, but the right side to err on. Now: doesn't that make you feel better than grumbling and sulking?

LEON: It makes me feel as if I won—

JACK: Leon: you're a natural!

LEON: No no—it's the wisdom of my teacher; everything you say is so clear and on the ball—would you like some more fruit-juice?

JACK: Love some, thanks . . .
(LEON *laughs*—JACK *realises he's been taken.*)

JACK: Aha. Very good, very good: I'll need to keep an eye on you, young man.
(LEON *pours him a drink.*)

LEON: I do like these lessons, though—it's like swimming underwater with your eyes open—a green world, blurry, where everything's further away than it looks . . . tell me some more for my social manner—

JACK: Well the latest mannerism, and perhaps the most useful of all— is to appear to *care* about whoever you're talking to more than anything in the world—like Mrs. Thatcher visiting the wounded Commandos, or talking to the unemployed—she must have got it from Her Majesty The Queen.

LEON: I can't do that!

JACK: Not many can! Sir Keith Joseph failed dismally at it, and got demoted. Norman Tebbitt certainly can't manage to look caring, even on television. Willie Whitelaw's quite good, but a bit Deputy-Dawg. I think you should take as your model the *firmer* kind of caring of Mr John Nott—Mrs T. does overdo it a bit . . . it doesn't come naturally—probably grammar-school.

LEON: I thought you liked her?

JACK: Oh I do—but a prospective Tory Candidate can't afford to be completely uncritical: one must look to the future. How many

of us were caught licking the wrong boot when Ted Heath bit
the dust? No no: I'm loyal, don't fret, and so perhaps are you,
by now? Are you, Leon?

LEON: (*Looking very caring*) Well, you know, what concerns me most
deeply about this whole question, is: could one possibly betray
a friend? Take it from me, and I mean it, I am giving this whole
matter my most earnest attention, and I know, that by next
Saturday, a satisfactory outcome will emerge . . . I could never,
ever let you down.

JACK: I'm touched by your concern, Leon—

LEON: I'm a member of a caring society—

JACK: But I want your beliefs to spring from a clear vision of the
truth about our society, and from your own inner certainty and
strength—not from your concern for me—

LEON: Don't worry. I'll put on a good face for Didsbury—

JACK: Leon—that would be unreal, untrue—

LEON: Yes—but as Michael Heseltine said: what's wrong with cosmetics?
(JACK *looks at him, wondering what he has created. Phone
rings*)

JACK: OK, Leon. You win.

(*Jack goes and music in*)

LEON: No, I don't win. But here I am
An accident, freak, big mistake,
So what does it matter what I do or why:
No work no money no road to take:
For by nineteen eighty-three
The last thing in the world that's needed
Will be me—

(*Music continues quietly under*)

LEON: (*Speaks*) So if anybody wants to know why I'm doing it, well—
why not? If the whole of your life's pointless and everybody
keeps telling you you're the wrong age and the wrong school
and the wrong colour, and you've got no past, not much of a
present and no future, and a nice person comes and places her
beautiful big eyes right up to yours and says help me: well, you
do . . . even if you can't win . . .

(*Sings*) For I'm only trying to see
What it feels like to be someone like me—
(*At the end of song,* LEON *wanders off into the garden.* JACK
*comes in carrying the phone on a long lead, his hand over the
mouth-piece, checking to see if* LEON *is listening—he sees he's
gone, calls after him:*)

JACK: Have a quick shower, Leon, and into your smart casuals—we'll
go and watch an hour of cricket—(*Then speaks into phone—
conspiratorially*) I'm glad you called me back, Simon—it's about
the do at Didsbury. I think I've hit on rather a good thing, and I
hope you'll see the point of it—you know we Tories have a
dreadfully 'county' sort of image. Our Garden Parties may be
popular amongst the faithful, but they could lose us a few votes

among the green-eyed deserving poor—well, as my personal contribution to dispelling that image, I intend to bring along as my personal guest an unemployed seventeen year-old youth from Toxteth, fresh from the rioting, reeking of petrol-bombs— (*Listens*) I'm afraid so: not quite as the ace of spades, but pretty dusky—(*Listens, then testily*) But that is the whole point Simon: I think there'll be a great deal of mileage in it for the press— Black Rioter Wows Them At Tory Garden Party, or A Dream Come True, Leon the Looter at the Didsbury Do! He can publicly agree with Michael Heseltine that what Liverpool really needs is an ornamental garden, I tell you, he'll win us half-a-million votes! (*Listens, then grimly*) Simon, I was intending to make quite a sizeable contribution to party funds at Didsbury . . . thank you—I'm glad you've seen my point. Do not worry: I can vouch for this boy's behaviour, he will charm the knickers off the Marchioness—till Saturday next, Simon. (*He hangs up, does a little dance of glee*) Oh what fun! (*Then*) Watch out, Ms Evans—Task Force Browning has reached Ascension Island— (*He goes off looking for* LEON)

(*Mid-evening the following Saturday. It is dark. On the table, a few bottles of champagne.*)

MOLLY: (*Calls off*) Hello! Anyone at home?

(JOYCE *comes in, looks around, turns light on—*)

JOYCE: Nobody's back yet—

(MOLLY *comes in—sees champagne.*)

MOLLY: Well let's make ourselves at home—care for a sundowner?

JOYCE: I could do with a smoke—

MOLLY: Don't! He'd arrest you! (*She is opening a bottle of champagne.*)

JOYCE: Are you serious?

MOLLY: We could leave a stash in the tea-caddy and go home and ring the drug squad.

JOYCE: Why waste it on the drug squad? We'd only have to buy it back again. OK, OK—we'll stick to the posh lemonade—

MOLLY: If we can open it—in my previous existence, young men rushed forward at this point brandishing quips and banter, sweeping blond locks from well-bred brows and hooted with mirth as the cork hit the ceiling and the bubbly squirted down one's cleavage. (*It opens*) There! Not so romantic, but it will get us pissed just the same. (*Pours*)

JOYCE: How on earth did a decent, god-fearing girl like me fetch up with a harlot like you?

MOLLY: Drink that and shut up. I wonder what's happened to Leon and his Leon-trainer?

JOYCE: Mr Browning probably got his tongue stuck in the lace-holes of Willie Whitelaw's left boot—

MOLLY: They should be back—it's half past seven—I can't wait: Leon wouldn't have deserted, would he? Gone off home in a fit of nerves before the great moment arrived?

JOYCE: Could have—he's a law unto himself, our Leon—

MOLLY: I bet he has! I'll strangle him. I'll kill him! How could he let me

down like that. I don't know which of them is more
whimsical—Browning for setting up this ridiculous gamble, or
Leon for not going through with it.

JOYCE: Well—

MOLLY: If he hasn't gone through with it!

JOYCE: On the other hand, he may have gone further than we thought
possible—he was beginning to sound a little crisp at our last
rendezvous.

MOLLY: No! Surely not that! If I've been responsible for turning a
perfectly innocent, political bomb-thrower into a Young
Conservative—I'd rather lose the money . . . . .

JOYCE: That's why I'm here. To make sure you don't lose the money.
You would go, wouldn't you?

MOLLY: Yes.

JOYCE: And leave me behind?

MOLLY: Don't say that—
(*Sound off. Car arriving. Stops.* JOYCE *goes to window to see.*
MOLLY *sits in misery.*)

JOYCE: Hm. He's on his own.

MOLLY: He can't be—

JOYCE: Sit down and look normal. Prepare to do battle—just because
his environment failed with one nutty youth doesn't mean to
say you're going to fail with your alchies—
(JACK *goes across window*)

MOLLY: Sh! We've lost . . . accept it gracefully—

JOYCE: No.
(*They wait, feeling the worst.* JACK *comes in, enigmatic.*)

JACK: Ah good—you've made yourselves comfortable—so sorry I'm
late, one or two little things cropped up—(*Sits*) oh, my poor
feet—garden parties are hell on the old plates of meat

JOYCE: Take your shoes off—feel free—

JACK: Oh—I couldn't—

JOYCE: Go ahead. Drink?

JACK: No—well—a sip: (*Shoes off*) aah! Relief . . . (*takes drink*)
Cheers.

MOLLY: I'm sorry about Leon—

JACK: Are you?

MOLLY: That it didn't work. But it doesn't mean to say—

JACK: Didn't work—oh, it worked. He's a Tory through and through.
He spent forty minutes alone with Mrs T.—nobody else could
get near her: not even I. In fact, neither she nor anybody else
even acknowledged my existence, let alone all the work I'd put
in on him . . . they *all* wanted to *own* him. And he clearly went
to the highest bidder.

MOLLY: Then where is he?

JACK: He's recording his fourteenth interview, this time with Granada
upon the ruins of the Rialto. He can't go wrong. He's charging
two hundred pounds for TV interviews and forty for radios, he
even tried to get repeat clauses out of ITN—and the Daily
Express is making him into a serial for five thousand pounds—I

thought one could do worse than set up in business as his manager. Do you mind if I turn on the radio? He's due on Radio City any minute—

(*Turns on Transistor—White Reggae on—turns it down*)

JOYCE: Then your theory worked. You won. Shouldn't we be celebrating?

JACK: I'm not sure—ah—listen—

(*Record ends, the* DJ, *with a Mancunian mid-Atlantic merriness, rides over it*)

DJ: (*Recorded*) Yes, *Madness*, and from *Madness* on the turntable, let's turn to madness on the streets. Here's a young man with a message: Leon Jones, what do you, as a young black guy, have to say to the kids who've been causing all the trouble lately—

LEON: (*On tape*) Well I'm black, and I'd like to be proud of it, but how can I be when all this rioting and looting is wrecking our good name? Why can't they just stop it and show a bit of enterprise? Instead of hanging round the streets, we could be making things to sell, say leather belts, or beads or wooden animals for the tourists, raffia mats, painted CS canisters—we must get our aggression channelled into business instead of all this scrapping with the busies—I mean the police officers.

MOLLY: Christ!

DJ: Now I believe you have passed some time this afternoon at the big Conservative Garden Party in Didsbury—how did that come about?

LEON: Oh just some bloke I met thought Mrs Thatcher ought to hear the other side from Toxteth—the positive side.

DJ: And? Did you get to see Mrs Thatcher?

LEON: Oh she was all ears—she told me they were going to encourage us poor people to fend for ourselves—get private industry to give us free business advice—get us loans for that tricky first year—that sort of thing . . . she and Mr Heseltine really seemed to *care* about our problems, and I think we should be giving them a chance to help us, not throwing missiles at the police officers. They understand us: we should take advantage of their concern—I found it touching—

DJ: Leon—may your message ring loud and clear into the hearts and minds of Moss Side, Toxteth and Brixton—

LEON: Thank you—

DJ: Now from a message from Liverpool to a message from the Bronx, the Message, from Grandmaster Flash!

(*Music in. Jack turns it off. Silence*)

JACK: 'Some bloke I met'—self-centred young lout: it was I, it was I who was supposed to be making contacts, not him! It was I who was going to get nominated for a safe seat, not Mr Leon Jones.

JOYCE: Is he?

JACK: Very nearly, one fool from the Wirral—ha!—what a hope—Selwyn Lloyd would turn in his grave—if he was dead. Is he? Well he wasn't at the Garden Party—but nobody mentioned me, oh no. Not even Leon. 'Some bloke I met' indeed.

MOLLY: Nevertheless, it is what you wanted: you have won your bet, and the Harry L. Browning Centre for Environmental Rehabilitation is born—and—you have been proved correct!

JACK: Have I? (*Sound of car outside, door closing etc.*)

JOYCE: (*At window*) Oh yes: and your hour of triumph is at hand—our beautiful butterfly has emerged from the chrysalis—

JACK: Yes. He has changed since you last saw him. You won't be too hard on him will you?
(LEON *walks past the window looking incredibly elegant and cool in a traditional but beautifully cut suit which he has managed to make his own—carrying a small executive leather briefcase, and wearing large, non-shade specs. He doesn't look in, but goes past very seriously.*)

MOLLY: Oh Joyce, what have we done?

JACK: Good, isn't it? The specs were his idea . . . do you think they're a bit over the top?
(LEON *comes in, goes and shakes hands with the girls.*)

LEON: Hello Molly—hello Joyce. (*To* JACK) Sorry I'm late, we had trouble with the camera crew: the union shop-steward insisted on danger money for filming in Myrtle Gardens (*Laughs*)—fifty quid a head. Ah, champers! And the way they went on about black people, non-stop jokes about Sambo and Rastas and tea-cosy hats!

MOLLY: So you could hear?

LEON: Oh I joined in: I couldn't afford not to, if I wanted some decent shots of myself on the telly. We got on like a house on fire—as we say in Lewisham . . .

MOLLY: Don't make jokes like that Leon—

LEON: Why not? (*To* JACK) Did you record that interview on Radio City?

JACK: Er . . . no: came on us a bit suddenly—sorry—

LEON: I caught it in the car—did you like it?

JACK: It, er—made some very telling points—

LEON: Thirty quid—and it lasted sixty seconds: fifty pee a second. And I've got two German companies offering eighty quid each plus expenses but Ronnie reckoned they'd go to a hundred and fifty—

JACK: (*Alarmed*) Ronnie? Ronnie Banks?

LEON: That Ronnie at the Do—he's offering to handle all my public relations for a very low percentage, because of the importance of my attitudes—

JACK: A very low percentage? The man's a spiv!

LEON: He's going into Parliament at the next election—

JACK: Ha! Is he? Didn't say which constituency he thinks he's got? No, he wouldn't—too fly—handling your PR? Leon—you're making me very unhappy . . . you do realise the man is completely unprincipled?

LEON: I need good management. And I need it right now! Everybody at the Garden Party was really nice to me, really encouraging. 'Tell the world what you've told me, and the world will be a better place'—that's what Lord What's-his-name said . . . and suddenly they all started throwing money at me for interviews and articles—so I've got to make the most of it—just like you taught me, Jack . . . so far, over ten grand–

MOLLY: Leon—are you doing all this—I mean—do you still think it's all for me?

LEON: Oh yes. Funny that—it all started with me pretending to be crazy about you, didn't I?

MOLLY: Yes.

LEON: I wasn't really. I was bored out of my skull because I had no idea what to do with myself. (*To* JACK) Now I have, haven't I?

JACK: Oh yes—you're brimming with ideas—

LEON: Can I borrow an old suitcase? I'll send it back—

JACK: Yes—what? Where from? I mean from where will you send it back?

LEON: Well I can't stay here, can I? Four weeks was the deal—well I've stuck to my part of the bargain—four weeks and two days, in fact. I studied my lessons and did what I was told—now I'm off.

JACK: You don't have to move out—

LEON: I need to. I don't want to sound ungrateful, but it's a question of who you know—and Ronnie knows everybody—

JACK: I'm not without a few acquaintances myself—

LEON: Yes, but—oh never mind can I borrow an old suitcase to put my things in?

JACK: What you call your things were all bought for you by me.

LEON: Oh. If you want me to leave them, I will—

JACK: No no no no—let's not nit-pick—yes. A suitcase—under the stairs—take two. Or three.

LEON: Thanks. Don't go Molly—hang on a minute, and I'll give you two a lift into town—the driver from Granada's waiting outside—
(*He goes. Silence.* JOYCE *laughs.*)

JOYCE: I'm sorry.

MOLLY: Congratulations, Mr Browning, you made an excellent job of him—

JACK: My sympathies lie entirely with Dr Frankenstein—

MOLLY: He is everything you wanted him to be—your environment has created its own image—your theory has been proved one hundred per cent correct.

JACK: I hardly think that is fair, on Leon, or on my environment: he's just gone a little too far, taken my lessons too literally, been a bit over-enthusiastic—I'm embarrassed . . .

MOLLY: Nevertheless, you've won—your gamble came off—are you now going to contribute fifty thousand pounds per annum to the Leckie Street Centre?

JACK: Well—my father's trust—I shall need the consent of the other Trustees of course—

MOLLY: Who are they?

JACK: Business associates of my father—good friends—

MOLLY: They'll agree?

JACK: They should do: they'll have certain conditions of course—

MOLLY: Such as the house in the Pennines?

JACK: Well—don't let's be too specific about the house—however, I do know my fellow trustees. They will demand strict aversion

therapy, and no kid-glove softly-softly-catchee-monkee
rubbish—we'll contact this chap Sargent: get one of his men
along to put the frighteners on. Give 'em the pills. Give 'em the
booze, and watch them retch. I could probably persuade one of
the big drug companies to sponsor him—call him a Fellow or
Director of Research, Glaxo are cleaning up this year, they
might . . . yes: let them try out their latest wonder-drugs up
there, get right into the fore-front of medical science—yes yes
yes—one of the big drug firms will bite. Private Enterprise, my
dear, if once it is set free, will astonish you!
(*He goes.*)

JOYCE: You've got to decide whether you'll take his money or not—
MOLLY: There's no choice—I must.
JOYCE: To give him the chance to idle a few hundred thousand pounds
out of the Trust, buying properties in the Pennines? To provide
a regiment of guinea-pigs for Glaxo? To let some sadistic
psychiatrist turn off their booze and watch them suffer?
MOLLY: Joyce: this was your idea—remember? We're going through all
this lunacy to get the money—right? To save the Centre—right?
And we *have*!
JOYCE: Sure—Rejoice with the rest of them: I'm just an invoice clerk
about to be made redundant by a down payment on a microchip. Why should I care if the Welfare State has disintegrated—
I was paying for it, remember. And where was it going? On fat-
cat Directors of Social Services, or arty-farty pseuds more
interested in who's screwing who, and the next rung up the
ladder, than in people in need—
MOLLY: No—
JOYCE: I've seen them. I've met them, I've been groped by them.
Cynicism! That's what comes off your "colleagues"—like the
smell of rotten meat. Millions of rip-off artists picking up a
packet and millions of people who need it not getting half what
they need—oh what you were doing made sense—the city
fathers were worried about the growing hordes of alchies and
druggies, the human litter in the gutters: so they hired you to
keep the streets of Liverpool tidy in lieu of a dust-cart.
MOLLY: Joyce—you can't mean this: people are healthier, live longer, don't
have rickets, or TB, or die in childbirth, can read and write, go to
university, live in reasonable houses, keep going when they're out
of work, because of this thing-without-a-purpose.
JOYCE: Tell that to Leon—
(*Jack enters.*)
JACK: (*Applauding*) Hear! Hear! I think you'll find, my dear Molly,
that Joyce is quite right—that is why we must wield the axe on
the dead wood, hack a way through the tangle of quangos—
question every penny—and where there's a real need, look for
help from the private sector.
JOYCE: Mr Browning, when I said her friends were cynical—they
became naïve idealists beside your partners-in-crime. If she is
reduced to taking your money, it will be because you lot have

taken the money she should have had away from her, to spend on computers to put people like me out of work, so you'll still be riding on the pig's back in the year 2000.

JACK: (*Laughs*) Who'd put you out of work?

JOYCE: You would. You intend to. I am one of your slow, inefficient invoice clerks and you will replace me.

JACK: Are you really? I'd no idea.

JOYCE: Oh yes: and I know where your money and your father's money comes from: Brownings buy tea and coffee wherever it's cheapest in the world—wherever the natives are so hungry they'll work for nothing, wherever people *are* dying in the gutters, and not many live to be as old as you are now. That's where you buy. And you dye it and package it and sell it for twenty times what you paid for it, and you pay more to the ten people who make your adverts than to the twenty thousand women who picked your tea off the bushes in the first place—

JACK: My dear, you're talking about the nineteenth century—

JOYCE: Yes, but we're still living in it—you're keeping us there—we want to get out . . .

MOLLY: If your money comes from exploiting people in the third world, Mr. Browning, how can it hope to do any good here?

JACK: Are you rejecting it? I'm sure I shall think of something to do with it, if you are: but I *had* hoped—

MOLLY: Are you going to insist on aversion therapy?

JACK: I imagine the Trustees will—

MOLLY: And a research Director sponsored by a drug company?

JACK: If we are lucky enough to find one willing—yes . . .

MOLLY: And you would let them try out drugs on the patients?

JACK: If that is the price for getting their support, I see no reason why not—

MOLLY: And I report every month to you—

JACK: I shall look forward to it—

MOLLY: What other control will you have?

JACK: As Chairman of the Trust, I am responsible to my Trustees, and I would expect you to discuss all your proposals with me in depth, say—over dinner—

MOLLY: And if you didn't agree with them?

JACK: My dear, what makes you so certain that *your* ideas will always be correct? You are very dedicated, but you are also very young. You may have experience of Social Work Theory—but not a lot of experience of life—

MOLLY: Quite. Mr Browning, I can't accept your money. Thank you for offering to help, but I don't think it would work out.

JACK: Have I been unreasonable? Made any improper demands?

MOLLY: No.

JACK: You seemed most concerned to carry on your work—to save actual lives, you said. Have I offended your intellectual vanity, is that it? Is your intellectual vanity perhaps greater than your desire to save actual lives?

MOLLY: I can't take any money from you—thank you for being so patient—

(LEON *comes in, in his old jeans etc.*)

LEON: (*To* MOLLY) Are you fixed up now, then? Have you got the money all arranged?

MOLLY: I'm not taking it.

LEON: What?

MOLLY: I can't accept—

LEON: Fifty thousand pounds a year?

MOLLY: It's not on—I'm sorry.

LEON: Is he giving you aggro? (*Produces knife*) See that?

MOLLY: Oh not that old thing again, Leon—put it away.

LEON: I wouldn't mind, you know—

JACK: Leon! My star pupil—

LEON: Shut up and sign the cheque, or I'll do you.

JACK: I can't believe it—

LEON: I couldn't show my face at home if I was a real Tory. Everyone our way knows how much I'm getting for this—it was the only way *I* could win. Every other way, I lost.

MOLLY: You've still got my gratitude, Leon—

LEON: But you haven't got the money—shall I ask him nicely?

MOLLY: No. We'll think of some other way—but thanks.

LEON: Say that again—

MOLLY: Thanks—

LEON: Would you like a ride home in my Granada Granada? Come on—ta-ta, Mr Browning—thanks for all the steaks and the fine wines—and the two suitcases full of new clothes: my mum'll be proud of me in them-

MOLLY: Cheerio, Mr Browning—

LEON: OK—you and me can sit in the back, and Joyce can sit in the front with the driver—

MOLLY: Don't get flash, Leon, just because you're rich and famous—

LEON: No chance—

(*They go.* JOYCE *stops.*)

JOYCE: Mr Browning—I don't want to lose my job.

JACK: No. Quite. I'll make sure you don't. Joyce, do you think I'm such a dreadful person?

JOYCE: You are what you do.

JACK: I believe in what I'm doing: the alternative is too dreadful to contemplate—creeping totalitarianism, communism.

JOYCE: Don't worry about it, Mr. Browning. Just remember my job—Joyce Edmonds, Invoice Department—Number D305 . . .

JACK: D305—I'll remember—

JOYCE: Goodnight—sweet dreams.

(*She goes. Jack, very troubled, goes for a peppermint sweet, unwraps it.*)

JACK: I don't know what I'm worrying about. We're winning—
(*Swallows sweet*)

THE END

WATCHING FOR DOLPHINS

Presented by Freeway Stage during 1991–92 with
the following cast:

Reynalda Ripley: Elizabeth MacLennan

*The action takes place in late 1991, in a bungalow on the main
road through the mountains of North Wales to Holyhead.*

*The main room has a dining area, centre stage, with a dining
table, on which several dishes are being prepared for the oven
all at the same time—a leg of lamb, with potatoes peeled and
ready to roast; cannelloni in a flat tray, with a meat and tomato
sauce; a flan dish with pastry in it ready to be filled; a tray of
jam tarts and four artichokes. Also, various sizes of plant-pots,
some flowers in assorted stages of being re-potted, and some
bags of earth and peat, bottles of plant-food, anti-bug sprays, a
watering-can and lots of trowels, hand forks, etc.*

*There is also a small circle of easy chairs round a fireplace, a
television set and all the furniture is from the G-plan era.*

*An ironing board with an ambitious pile of ironing—sheets,
pillow-slips, table napkins, etc.*

*There are three exits—on one side to the veranda, upstage to
the kitchen, and on the other side to the rest of the house.*

REYNALDA *is beating a mixture in a large bowl with a small
wooden spoon. She is a beautiful woman in her 50s, sexy and
serious. She is about to open her bungalow as a Bed and
Breakfast place, if she can get it all ready. It is now 5.30 in the
afternoon, so she doesn't have long.*

REYNALDA *was brought up in one of the best English radical,
non-conforming intellectual families, but has gone through a
lot since then. She has played her part in most of the liberation
struggles and revolutionary movements of the 60s, 70s and 80s,
and through committing herself to them more completely than
most, has learnt from her experiences a great deal more than
her limited background might imply. But she has always
retained her girlish good nature and sense of fun, and has never
lost the physical and intellectual dynamism that she acquired in
childhood. She is a doer, and she makes things happen. Often
though, her sense of determination is greater than her ability to
cope with all the projects she sets herself, and she becomes
confused, scatty and sharp.*

*As she beats, she surveys the rest of the scene—ten jobs all in
the middle. She shrugs, dips her little finger in the mix and
tastes it quite sensually.*

REYNALDA: Mouth-watering! They've got to be drooling for it like Pavlov's
dogs . . . when I think of all the bodily functions the average B
& B has to absorb. Appalling to think what might go on in my
little bungalow . . . Mouth-watering will probably be the one to
encourage—B & B may be only ten pounds, but 'Evening meal'
at eight pounds 50—there's where I make serious money!
   The question is: will it be tonight?
   I mean, will anyone stop? Come in? Stay?
   (*She has been pouring the mix into pastry ready in a flan dish,
   but suddenly realises:*)
   Oh God, the jam—it's supposed to be underneath . . . I'll just
   have to scrape it in under.
   (*She is now pouring the mix back, anxiously, then gets the jam,
   dollops it in the dish, and repours the mix over it.*)
   I really should have ironed the sheets yesterday, but I've never
   known a place like North Wales for the rain—they've been out
   on the line for six days, getting wetter and wetter and smaller
   and smaller, now I'm sure the fitted ones won't fit any more,
   and the top sheets will be like nappies.
   (*She's done the pie.*)
   There—Empire cake! I shall have to explain that to my travel-
   weary Germans, my modest Americans. An opportunity for a
   little lesson in British history—Empire cake! You could go in
   the oven now! Yes—in!
   (*She carries it to the kitchen—a clatter of pans and trays as she
   pops it in the oven.*)
   Well, that's one in the oven as we used to say—
   Now—ironing—no, get rid of the plant-pots—
   Hm—how long will this
   (*She brandishes the leg of lamb.*)
   take to cook to a delicate pink? And (*Sings*)
   Where have all the garlics gone—Long time passing—
   (*She goes and sits at the piano, and plays a burst of Mozart.
   Suddenly remembers.*)
   Sheets.
   (*She carries on into the melody, then stops, gets up, picks up
   the ironing.*)
   Some B & B ladies only have the one set of sheets. I
   remember waking up one morning with a dreadful sick—
   vomiting-sick—headache in a B & B in Sheffield, where I'd
   been speaking at a conference, and the next morning after
   I've been speaking I always get a migraine—but she thought
   I'd been 'on't' batter'—and at eight o' clock she wanted her
   sheets because she only had the one set, and they had to be
   washed and dried in time for the next victims, so when she
   heard me retching my ring up in the two foot by two foot

loo, she nipped in and stripped the bed. I stumbled back like the last seconds of Giselle only to find my tomb was looted before I'd even died.
(*Folds another sheet, stops, stroking it lovingly*)
Fortunately I had my spray-cans with me, I managed to get AUSCHWITZ in pretty big letters all over the front wall before she spied me at it—I was on my Kawasaki and halfway to Leicester before she could get my number, and I gave a false name of course, I always do—And that's why I'm having two sets. Cotton. (smiles) it was good fun in them days: they don't seem to get up to much fun any more.
(*A minute pause as a smile crosses her face as she thinks of the 'fun' of the past, then she moves on.*)
Now! Sheets—into bedrooms—make beds—no, later.
(*She goes off to the rest of the house, busily. From there can be heard a chorus of Bandiera Rosa.*)

    Bandiera Rossa la triomphera—Room I
    Bandiera Rossa la triomphera—Room 2
    Bandiera Rossa la triomphera—Room 3
    Eviva la Comunista e la liberta!

(*She comes back in on the last three words.*)
Now—Plant pots.
    Geraniums! Add a splash of colour to the dullest veranda, greet the passing tourist with a beckoning blush—saying 'Come in, come in, here you will find a houseproud hausfrau, with dinky cakelets on the doyley and winking Welsh warmth (*She winks warmly*)—not to mention crisp Welsh-laundered linen laden with lavender on the lie-awake beds, dream sweet, sweet dreams (*She has lapsed into Dylan Thomasese*) oh boyo—here is the nooky nook to ingle in, the olde-worlde oakie-beamies to Tudor under, the kiss-me-quick canopied beds to four-poster in!
(*She pauses, then, with some grief*) Oh, oh, oh—what am I doing to myself?
(*She sweeps up the tray of pots.*)
Gerania! To the verandum!
(*She exits grandly to the veranda, a crash as two pots go.*)
Oh fuck!
(*She crosses to the kitchen.*)
Who can I possibly blame for that?
(*Emerges with brush and dustpan.*)
The trouble with living on your own is you can't blame anyone! Perhaps I should get a cat . . . Damn! I meant to put the jam-tarts in with the Empire cake—why are they so dim-looking, big round eyes gazing at the teeth that will crunch them like Christian martyrs bearing the breast to the Roman sword! Oh dear, now I've upset them—
(*She goes and puts the dustpan and broom by the veranda door . . .*)
Later, later—don't go away!
(*To tarts*) Sorry.

(. . . *and rushes the trays of tarts into the kitchen. More crashes, and curses, She emerges with a burnt forearm, nearly crying with pain. She goes straight to the sideboard and puts on Burn Cream.*)
I hope the mice stay quiet tonight; can't have all my Bed and Breakfasts tucked in and the mouse's version of a clog-dance going on all night, tell-tale turdlets on the bread-board and tiny teeth-marks in the corner of the butter-packet—
(*She has gone to the piano. She plays a piece of Beethoven, then stops, thinking.*)
Burnt flesh . . . . mass graves: the guilt of the human race— where we begin: Extermination camps. 1968 began in Dachau; ended with General Yazov.
    Who will be coming to my house?
(*She pretends to hear the doorbell, puts on her best smile, goes to greet them, brings them in—an elderly, rather distinguished German couple, who exist only in her mind. She makes a great fussy welcome.*)
Hello, hello, and a warm Welsh welcome to you—come in, let me take your bags—yes we have a double room—yes, one with twin beds, not one big one, yes, ten pounds fifty per person B & B, and evening meal you'll take yes? Good: eight pounds fifty—Welsh lamb, or cannelloni tonight, with artichoke for starters and home baking to finish—yes, the room, follow me please—(*Goes off*) there you are, Room Three—the bathroom's there, plenty of hot water—oh, I haven't made the beds up, won't take a second later on—You like it? Good—come through to the lounge, get a warm by the fire—when you're ready—can I have your names please? Oh, what a nice card, lovely, oh it's for me, I can keep it, thank you very much.
(*She comes in looking at a pretend card.*)
Judge Horst Schencker, Oldenburg. Ach so, mein freund—you are slumming it here in my house—he has the teeth of an assassin, and she has all the charm of a well-chewed bone!
(*She suddenly switches to reality via bone and the joint.*)
Oh Christ, the joint! If that goes in at six and the cakes come out in ten minutes—and the roast potatoes—in now, I think, and the mint, fresh from the garden! Chuck some on—now, aha, here are the garlics (*Sings*) under the potatoes everyone— when will I ever learn—when will I ever learn?
(*She strips the garlic and rams six cloves into the meat whenever there's a hole, or she cuts one.*)
There, that'll sort out the men from the boys—
(*Sniffs it*) Brings tears to the eyes.
(*She puts it all in a roasting tray, stacks the potatoes round it, then appalled:*)
I haven't got any fat! How could I? You can't roast without something—lard, dripping—I'll have to use the Italian olive oil, but then what'll I do for the salad—oh well—(*She pours the oil all over the roast and potatoes.*) Allora—to the ovens, Agnellito.

(*She bears it off, and after the usual clatter comes back, dejected.*)
I can't do this. I feel as if I am in the middle of a divorce. From the love of my life: Passion, Commitment, Action. It has been drawn out of me like an eye-tooth, leaving a void in my head, a hole in my stomach, an emptiness in my womb, in my heart—not a lot . . . I feel like a last year's bird's nest. I feel like a mother-cat watching an old woman drown her kittens—I feel . . .
(*She closes her eyes, forces herself to change gear.*)
I feel I must put away the ironing board.
(*She does so, busily, singing the* Housewives' Choice *signature tune, then heads straight for the piano; she plays a disturbing piece of Bartok.*)
Poor Bartok. Fancy being a Hungarian in 1939? Now: the sheets are done, the roast's in the oven, the gerania are on the verandum, the cakes are burning—no, not yet—soon. The question is: shall I put up the sign 'Ty Coed, Bed and Breakfast, Evening Meal' with the sweet little slider saying 'vacancies' one way, and 'No Vacancies' the other? Or shall I not bother? No, I must, I must—I must increase my bust.
(*She goes to the piano, plays* The Moldau. *Then turns to audience.*)
President Havel of Czechoslovakia has had his palace guard uniforms redesigned by a Hollywood movie costumier—and their drill sequences devised by the choreographer of The Sound of Music. True—or false ?
    Or half true ?? Or—Who Cares? Think 90s, Think Now, Think Twin Peaks, Think Post-Modern . . . You, my girl are part of the Post Modern Condition.
    Lights! Camera! Music! Action!
(*As a young, enthusiastic, half-trendy, half-commercial movie director*)
The thematic is . . . this dame! She's old, she's cookie, she is—alone. Glenn Close—no, too old, Michelle Pfeiffer!
    Give me some music!
    In olden times she would have been burned as a witch, but—nah, that was in days of yore. She runs a motel, a rooming house, among the hills of Kentucky . . . No, Wales, England.
    On the night in question she hangs out her customary sign. It creaks. Great. She sits with a sense of foreboding until the twilight hour, Then—she notices . . . what was it? The sheep had stopped bleating. The lambs too.
    Then she hears it—far, far away, but drawing ever closer the disquieting sound of a pride of Harley-Davidson motorcycles . . . Like a chain saw in the night.
    She sits, still and silent. She longs to shut out the mounting, mounting roar of the powerful throbbing, throbbing machines. In a magnificently, magnificently cheap, and I mean cheap, effect that sends shivers up the spine, she flicks on the TV. And what is she watching but a culturally significant heap of shit

showing the hideous gang rape of a lonely woman who keeps a rooming house.

Fantastic—do you like it?

She closes her eyes, but it is in her ears, that sound, that sound, mounting, mounting! She sits rigid with terror, her eyes fixed on the doorway—but they come through the back door, through the kitchen, through the empty veranda . . .

They got to be young, they got to be hard, their leather encrusted with steel and fake diamonds. One tall guy smiles—through er, silver teeth. He takes his video camera in his hand—Wow, wait a minute, I've got it we film them filming her! Terrific! Isn't Post-Modernism Unreal . . . ? So the team goes for what they have come for . . . They have come . . . to make a documentary for Channel 4.

(*Channel Four Music. Reynalda acts out being interviewed.*) Me? Here? Sit? OK? (*Clapper goes in front of her face*) Now? (*Finger cues*) Good God . . . Well—after I suppose ten years of supply teaching, I got a full-time job, at the Noam Chomsky Primary School in Deptford . . . I loved my kids and they loved me, but quite a few of the white kids' parents were National Front. They organised a petition to have me sacked, for teaching Marx, Engels, Stokely Carmichael, Black Power and the Koran . . . No, the children were very interested, they suggested it . . . What do you mean, wasn't that a bit reckless—do you realise what kind of caution you're advocating? Do you think the school curriculum should be dictated by the National Front . . . you do? You think parents should have more choice? What does that mean? Projecting the prejudices of one miserable generation onto the next, and the next—what role does that give to education, e-ducare, to lead out of- Latin . . . Where does that leave Socrates? No. I may not be Socrates, but I was offered the hemlock—CUT!

(*As NF parent*) I don't want my Richard having Karl Marx and Muslim prayers stuffed down his throat—he come home one night, he gets my little rug, he faces it to Mecca, he kneels on it and he starts wailing! His dad went ape! (*own voice*) They wanted to experience different religions, different ways of life—so they would understand each other, other people—they were wonderful children. They brought tears to my eyes—CUT!

(*Headmistress's voice*) Miss Ripley was popular with her class to some extent, but her methods were not satisfactory I'm afraid. Eventually the Governors—yes, we're opted out—well they agreed—she had to go—well, it's not the image we wanted for Noam Chomsky. And when she invited various oddbods in to chat to her class—well . . . Oh, er, various oddballs—old black men, grannies from Bangladesh, unemployed youths with drug problems no doubt, and of course homosexuals, men with earrings, women with Eton crops: that's where the Governors drew the line, I mean it is against the law! And they are the

responsible persons! As am I, of course! No. Oh dear me NO—
CUT!—Thank you very much.

(*Own voice*) No, I can't get teaching work anywhere . . . Am
I sorry? Only for our society, and for the children—What?
Repeat? Oh for sound—OK . . . No, I can't get teaching work
anywhere . . . Again? Must I? No, I can't get teaching work
anywhere.
(*C4 Music, loud. She walks away from the memory, back into
her real scene.*)
Right now hang your bloody sign up—turn your life into a
business; you may as well, everything else is a business—your
health, your teeth, your eyes, your children's education, your
old age, your funeral, why not open your doors and turn your
home into a profit-centre?

But am I ready? The cakes are cooked, the lamb's in the
oven, the flowers are in their pots, the sheets are ironed, the
carpets are hoovered, the bedrooms are dusted, the towels are
on the beds, the bathroom's spotless, there's bog-paper and
stuff to make it flush blue, and the cash-box lies open—But do
I lie open?

Living out an empty life in Dalston was killing me: no work,
no action, the old comrades making money in the media, no
AIR, no SPACE, no room to think! Why Wales? My gran was
Welsh. The bungalows were cheap. I forgot about the fucking
rain . . .

Demonstrations, rallies, meetings, car stealing, border-hops,
failed kidnappings, graffiti campaigns: I've gone through most
of them in my time—but this little gesture is the most obscene.
I'm afraid of it. I don't want to do it, But . . . (*Has a terrible
thought*)

Oh God—what if they're Americans?
(*She goes to veranda and comes back in as if linked arm-in-arm
with the 40-year-old American couple—whom only she can
see.*)
Well, Mr and Mrs Offaly, a warm Welsh welcome to my little
house: I hope you'll regard it as yours for as long as you
choose to stay—of course, just the one night—and by the way
will it be the Evening Meal for both? Welsh lamb tonight! It's
eight pounds fifty, now that's about twelve dollars, for three
courses—Good, now: double bed, or two singles? Ah, a couple
after my own heart, all in together, lovely snuggles—and it's
very romantic round this part of the world, so they say (*laughs
wickedly*)—and after we've all had dinner we sit around with
the port and the brandy and we all tell stories—or sing a
song—it's great fun in Ty Coed after dark.

Might I ask—what's your line of business Mr Offaly?

Really, Executive Vice President Finance—for a fruit
company—well well—I'd have thought you'd have been staying
in a five-star hotel in Chester, going round in a limo with a

driver, not a—Ford Escort . . . Are you the Accountant for the
firm?

No, you were one, you are one, but now you deal with
economic strategy—I see, like which countries to invest in,
where to buy your raw materials, that'll be fruit I suppose, no,
wrong again (*Slaps her own wrist*)—fruit yes, but it's land to
grow fruit on, as well, you'd be in charge of buying bits of
Central America, Latin America, South-East Asia on the
cheap—oh and labour—even cheaper, I suppose—ah, and
minerals under your land, like bauxite, titanium, lead, silver,
gold, uranium—well, now that's a long way from apricots: and
you take your profit out in boat-loads of copper and coffee-
beans—I seeee—what an interesting world, the Fruit World—
I'm really looking forward to our after-dinner chat, what with
you and Doctor Schencker, I'll be agog!
(*She jangles their room key provocatively.*)
Room Two, Mr and Mrs Offaly—it has all you need, if you
need anything, just pop in—yes, pop in, pop in, pop in!
(*She watches them off then turns away in disgust*)
Am I really going to have to go through with this? It's what
we're all doing now—all of us, all of us: grovelling, grovelling
to these people. Fifteen years ago we were trying to blow them
up! I was anyway . . .
(*She goes to piano, plays Scott Joplin—speaks over*)
Suddenly it turns out all the ones who went quiet and looked a
bit sickly whenever I opened my mouth, all the prune-lipped
ones who didn't know much about politics actually, all the
crafty careerists in the Labour Party, suddenly it turns out they
were all correct, all along . . .

They knew: Communism Kills! Well, we *all* know that
now—don't we? And socialism is dead—how convenient for
the New World Order . . .
(*She furiously plays the rest of the melody—then stops and
speaks very simply to the audience.*)
On the day I was born in Highgate, a few hundred miles away,
the concentration camps were full, the gas chambers working
flat out to process the Jews and the gypsies and the
Communists. Not much further away, Stalingrad and
Leningrad were under siege, and millions of Russians and
Georgians and Ukrainians were dying, because they were
Communists. And gallant little England was fighting wicked
Adolf Hitler, and when I was two I waved a Union Jack for
Winston, and Roosevelt, and good old Uncle Joe! And when I
was five, we won the war, and we danced in the streets, and my
uncle Harold who was with the partisans in the mountains of
Greece sent us photos of his boys hugging and kissing and
dancing with these Communist guerrillas who had been so
brave. So brave . . . and Mikos Theodorakis, the young Greek
composer, got out of the Nazi prison.
(*She plays Theodorakis piece.*)

By the time I was ten, they were bad, these Communists, evil, more wicked than Hitler, but my father who had fought all his life for Freedom for the Colonies said at least the Reds believed in the self-determination of nations, so I joined the Young Communists, but when I was 16 the Hungarians got a bit over-determined and the Russians invaded them and said who the government should be, and father sadly had to admit that all that was precisely what he'd been fighting against all his life. He found he suddenly had a lot more free evenings, and I took up tennis.

And Theodorakis was a Communist so he was put back in prison by the Greeks—but he did not give up . . .

(*Plays more Theodorakis* (*Z Theme*))

When I was seventeen I spent a year in Rhodesia on the copper belt, and found out a bit more about colonialism: that it hadn't died with the independence of India, nor would it die with the independence of the whole of Africa. It would only end with what we called the building of socialism—with heroic People's China as the guiding light, the red star in the East; and our revolutionary duty was to stand by the colonial peoples fighting their liberation struggles, and from Algeria the voice of Franz Fanon said the colonial peoples had to overthrow their imperial father-figures, before they could begin to grow towards maturity.

And this beautiful image of the boy-child David slaying father Goliath in order to make a proud nation where true liberty, true equality and the true psychic health of the human spirit could begin in what we still saw as the lands of the smiling brown children—that we understood . . . and the only people really interested in this vision were the Communists, so I joined the Party again. And I joined the CND.

While I was at Oxford I discovered the English working class: not I'm afraid, in Somerville, no, while I was selling the *Daily Worker* at eight in the morning outside Cowley Motors. I wanted those car-workers to see their prosperity was based on the exploitation of the Third World. They saw me as someone with even greater prosperity, which was based on exploiting *them*. And half of them voted Tory! At Somerville, we talked till late in the night . . . . Oh God!

Ignorance of the English working class, of course, was ridiculous—but I had that in common with most of the English intelligentsia, left, right and certainly centre. But were we really so wrong? Most people in the Third World would be dead before they reached forty. That was a fact. And in countries with rulers 'we' supported, torture, assassination, military rape and violent seizure of peasant land were commonplace.

At Oxford, all the smart, the smug and the rugger-buggers, the rah-rahs and the crinklies—the people who now govern Britain: we knew they were wrong then—but now we're to believe they couldn't possibly be wrong, ever . . .

By the mid-1960s, I was working as a researcher in the BBC, mostly on farming programmes. I joined the International Socialists: IS. At work I shut my mouth, did my job, I was quite good at it: but Monday and Thursday evenings, and Sunday all day, we planned the overthrow of . . . I think every government in the world—US, Soviet, Chinese, and, of course, the British. I can't remember what we did approve of—even the Cubans were ideologically dodgy.

And I got closer to the English working class—I moved in with a Trinidadian painter and decorator called Jim in a two-room flat in Oxford Gardens—turned out he had another, angrier, woman, and two kids, in Cambridge Gardens. We both kicked him out, but I stayed on in the flat, and made a lot of women friends. Including her.

When nice Mr Rachman who owned the street decided to clear us all out and make the area expensive and white, I began, slowly, to learn about politics: the politics of fighting for somewhere to live, for enough food for the children who lived on my stair, in the next room, the children who might have been mine. The children now sleeping in cardboard boxes, or shooting up to escape the aimlessness.

When I was twenty-eight, two things came along to change my life. The BBC discovered I was in the IS, and were very British—said nothing, did nothing—but they drew a few Christmas trees against my name, and didn't renew my contract. I was never interviewed, or told why. That was in March 1968. In May, Paris blew up, then the whole of France. I hadn't found a job, so I went.

There was joy in the streets, everywhere red flags and black flags flying together, there was excitement, imagination and a new revolutionary emotion—there was love. Power to the Imagination! Down with the Society of Spectacular Consumption! Nous irons jusqu'au bout—we go on to the end! (*Plays* The Internationale.)

And every night at the demos, on the barricades, the black spectral patriarchs with their rubber truncheons and CS guns were defied and wrestled with, and beaten. Every night became a purging nightmare, and every day the dawn of a liberated psyche. Then the wily old General, with his sober deep voice and his long probing nose, made fools of us, and bought the Communist Party out, and in three months was re-elected with even more fatherly authority, and all was lost.

One of the mildest of my comrades took an overdose and succeeded. Another who was training to be a singer joined the Red Army Faction: Baader Meinhofs: Lisa Jurgens.

And was that the end of the story? No—suddenly there was a huge network spreading across Europe into India, even across America, Cuba, Latin America, New Zealand, Australia—hundreds of thousands, even millions of young men and women whose conspiracy was to live in hope, to believe in the future, to trust the imagination and to want to dismantle the power-structures—ideas, fantasies, analyses, dreams, new constitutions, plots, plans, books, magazines, action programmes, all rattling to and fro across the network. The war crimes we are now on trial for—

And Theodorakis? He'd been thrown back in prison—by a Fascist junta: but in 1974, the Junta was overthrown by the courageous youth of Greece—and he was free again. Your tanks will rust, he said, our songs will live.

(*Plays* 'When Spring Smiles'.)

Our ideas were taken by those with the mental banality to become professional politicians—or should I say Pragmatism? They turned them into what they had never been. We were struggling to re-define the whole nineteenth century concept of work, of alienated labour: we ended up on marches against unemployment. We saw high technology as the way to set people free from the drudgery of mass production—to an explosion of creativity, to more interesting lives. Now it is a way to divide the whole world even more sharply, to take more power away from those with nothing, and give it to those who invest, and manage, and keep the knowledge to themselves.

We wanted an active, informed, pluralist democracy—now politics is about choosing a new Absolute Monarch every five years. Our confrontations with state power became ritualistic, the political solutions of the men so—laboured.

During the 70s, like millions of others, I joined my first women's group. Not radical feminists, I still liked men, in their place. In bed. Everywhere else they were useless, and most were pretty useless there too, but—well, we met, and we talked: about these things, and about the patriarchy that ruled the world for the good of its own psyche, its belly and of course its magnificent phallus.

We gave one another confidence, and the courage to be different. We got together with other groups now and again to make noises about abortion, which we won; about violence against women, rape and the images of women in the media, which we lost; about the right to be fat, which went away, and the right to look like yourself, and to grow old looking like yourself, without being cast as a witch. We're still fighting that one. And for the right to open our mouths to speak—and not be told we're ball-breakers. Somehow in the C.P. and the I.S. I was made to feel ever so slightly guilty about not being born into the working class. With the women, it didn't matter at all, we were all women, and together. And we changed the world. It may not feel like it, but we did. For a time.

Oh, the 1970s had their moments, but we could see what our hopes were being used for. Could anything have been further from Kate Millet, Marx and Marcuse than Uncle Jim Callaghan?

Oh yes—he was the beginning of the end, let's not blame it all on Maggie—PC Jim called us to order, put on the handcuffs

and threw us in the nick, and when Lord High Executioner
Thatcher came to try us, we found our lawyers were working
for the prosecution; they apologised on our behalf and changed
our plea to: Guilty.
(*She is brooding on this, when she remembers the cakes.*)
Oh Christ the cakes!
(*She runs into the kitchen, yelling:*)
He—e—elp!
(*Bang Crash. She emerges with a dark brown object.*)
There's nothing half-baked about my cooking—
(*Puts it on the table, cuts a bit, blows it, tries it—*)
Mm—it'll do. I'll tell them they're called King Alfred cakes.

Where was I? The 80s, I suppose. And the world turned
upside down. Tearing ourselves apart became our highest
political activity.

And in every part of our lives, we were crushed: by political
skill, or by brute force. Some people found their voice, of
course—Clause 28 united the Gay movement, some women,
like those in the mining communities, found some strength. But
on the whole, the Top People cracked the whip till we trotted
round the ring and jumped through the flaming hoops—if we
didn't we were put out to grass.

They were bitter years. And hard to endure. What was
coming at the end of the 1980s was something else.
(*Plays Shostakovitch No. 11*)
We knew the Soviet Union had nothing to do with socialism
any more, driven by power-greedy men, corrupt bureaucrats
and incompetent managers, all intent on exploiting the working
class more ruthlessly than any capitalist would ever dare. We
knew this antiquated, grinding model of state capitalism had
been imposed on every one of Russia's satellites, inside the
Soviet Union, in Eastern Europe, and all over the world. We
knew it was wrong, had failed and it had criminal tendencies.
As if this was not enough of a burden for socialism along
comes nice Mr Gorbachev to tell the world that this disaster
area, which he still called socialism, didn't work. Very
perceptive of him.

And who was looming up behind him? Boris, all ready to do
business! And what was Boris's alternative to the socialism that
never had been socialism? Capitalism, red only in tooth and
claw—and whose brand? Thatcher's brand, that was putting
millions out of work and creating a land of joyriders and
yuppies!

And one by one all the spivs and frustrated entrepreneurs of
Eastern Europe leapt onto the bandwagon of Freedom! And the
world believed that socialism in Poland meant repressing the
trades unions, and socialism in Hungary meant shooting the
workers, and socialism in Czechoslovakia meant the iron rule
of hated men who put playwrights in prison, and socialism in
East Germany meant the Stasi down every street, and socialism

in Rumania meant evil dictators who murder their opponents and starve disabled children—and then, in the name of Communism, the ancient grisly bears of the Kremlin, the throwbacks to Stalin and Beria, ordered the sad young men of the Soviet Army to roll their tanks into Estonia, Latvia, Georgia, anywhere where people hated them, ordered them to shoot their mums and dads on the streets of Moscow. And we thought of Hungary, of Prague in 68, and for two days—well—despair, I suppose. Then the miraculous—these young soldiers refused to shoot their brothers, and people would not give up the little bit of freedom they had won, and almost unbelievably away went the grizzlies to the Siberian wastes. And just as we had seen in Dresden, and Gdansk, and Prague and Tallin, and Bucharest and Timisoara and Berlin, suddenly people found they had power—and what were they using it against?

Socialism. And the very word socialism has become a foul word, anathema, another scar on history, like Nazism and the holocaust. We have become, in the eyes of the world, the very horror that we had set out to drive off the face of the earth. Saturday August 24th 1991:

President Landsbergis of Lithuania said: 'The time has come for Bolshevism's Nuremberg, a trial similar to the liquidation of Nazi influence 45 years ago.' And whether it is true or a brilliant archipelago of lies, we are defeated by it. For the moment. And it is best to admit it.

Theodorakis is now a Minister without Portfolio in Greece—in the right wing government.

(*Plays another phrase—of Dead March. Then Mozart 23, slow movement melody.*)

And now I am 52. I'm not allowed to teach children any more. My references are not satisfactory. So I have used the money my father left me when he died to buy a bungalow in Wales, and to turn it into a bed and breakfast place in the summertime, and a one-person convent in the winter, for silence, prayer and contemplation.

I went on a boat to Cyprus once, from Marseilles. As we rounded Sicily, there appeared a school of dolphins, playing with us, roving freely through the warm seas, frisking like kittens, having fun, moving as one . . .

Then, just as suddenly, they went away. I spent the rest of the voyage standing at the rail, hoping to catch another glimpse.

I feel like that now, every night I read the newspapers, watch my telly, phone my friends—'just to keep in touch'. But I stand here now, at the rail, at 52, watching for dolphins. I scan the sea, but it's polluted, empty. But they are there. They will come.

(*She looks down at the table, lifts two artichokes.*)

What am I going to do about the artichokes?

And *this* is the dining-table—for God's sake!

(*To the cannelloni*) And as for you—

(*Goes to the kitchen—re-enters, busily clears and lays the table*)
I once went to Japan, to see how they did things: it was while
they were trying to build a new airport on some old farmer's
land, and their revolutionary left decided to stop them. My
contact took me along supposedly to cover the event for
Socialist Worker. They were mostly university students, but
they came on like an army—not hundreds, but thousands of
them, in uniform, with red bands round their foreheads, and
they had these great bamboo poles. They formed up in military
order, wielding these bloody things, and stood there, guarding
the birth-right of this handful of puzzled old men, who didn't
want to cause trouble, so they backed off bowing a lot, smiling
nervously. The world's press and television were there to see
fair play. I thought we were on to a winner. Then I saw the
forces of law and order, massing on the half-made road. There
were millions of them.

When the man said the state was, in the last resort, a body of
armed men, he must have been thinking of the twenty thousand
Japanese policemen in awesome riot gear, and their mountains
of machinery, enough to take the whole of France in one day,
and the command systems—radio, closed-circuit TV, helicopters
hovering, spies, agents provocateurs, and the arsenal of gas-
guns, stun-guns, rubber-bullets; and behind them, real bullets, in
lightweight automatics; behind them an airborne division, a
navy, an air force—enough, you might think, but no, more. The
whole apparatus of press and television was part of their fire-
power, mobilising world opinion against these rabid dogs, these
kamikaze militants, these syphilitic rapists, who stood with
what suddenly appeared to be a pathetic show of heroism facing
the might of the state, the will of the city planners and their
partners, the airport's investors. They moved in on the students;
the cameras blinked with excitement. The forces of law and
order prevailed: there was a lot of blood. And I came as near as
I'm capable of to a kind of despair, not just because my friends
were being mauled and injured, which they were, but because I
found I could no longer believe in the rights of these
impoverished farmers. I could no longer see why Tokyo
shouldn't have its airport. Worse, I began to wonder whether
this particular act of revolt was not simply part of a psychic
need, projected into the headlines to give it credibility. And I
began to wonder how much of this was in all our actions, until
I found myself censoring these thoughts; and then censoring my
report, writing for the Socialist Worker readers what they
wanted to read, perpetuating the mythology, casting the students
as simply class-heroes, the police as demons, butchering in the
service of the millionaires. I tore it up, sent no report. But even
that was suppressing my doubts—I began behaving like one of
Graham Greene's whisky-priests, I was having a crisis of—of
what? of 'faith'? Once you think your beliefs are based on
'faith', not on reality, how do you keep going?

I came home to teach black kids in Dalston, and I knew we were right. I read my papers, saw Reagan supporting the murder-squads in Central America, saw Thatcher launch her merciless attack on the poor and the powerless, saw the wicked old men of China destroy the hopes of their own youth in Tienanmen Square—and I knew we were right. But . . .

That body of armed men: in Tokyo, Tienanmen, Guatemala, El Salvador; the British SAS, our lovable policemen, beating up the miners and the Poll Tax marchers: the British Army in the Malvinas, and their glorious apotheosis into guardians of peace; love and liberty in the Gulf War. To grow strong enough, violent enough to defeat them would turn us into what they are. To give in to them would leave me living with an incapacitating guilt, a sense of disgusting complicity—

But in the streets of Prague, against a dictatorship; in the streets of Bucharest, against a murderous dynasty; in the squares of Dresden and East Berlin against an armed secret police; and in the very heart of Moscow itself against the Red Army—people who know they are right have stood up together, and won.

And what they all want is what they think we have got—

Maybe, when they find out that it's not quite what it seems, maybe then—

Or something else—

An unexpected sighting, the water suddenly alive, teeming—

And here I am in Bwlchgoch—opening my B & B, trying to work out what I can do. And who I can do it with. I am not alone. And I have not given up.

(*Suddenly comes back to her reality, as it were, sees the German couple coming in:*)

Ah, Herr Doktor Professor Schenker, I hope you are feeling rested after your journey . . . you must be pleased to get a break from your hard work—Judging, isn't it? Trying people? How very trying. Listening to legal arguments all day, sending people off to prison, and all the time knowing you could be wrong? What a burden! Yes, yes, down you sit—how about a sherry before dinner? No—Frau Schenker? Never? Well I suppose you both need clear heads—Tell me, Professor, I seem to recall your name from some famous trial—no, not Nuremberg, I don't think . . . Quite, you weren't *important* enough in those days. No, in Cologne I think, wasn't it one of those terrorists, not Ulrike Meinhof, but another girl—Lisa something—that's right! Lisa Jurgens—the name sticks in my mind I don't know why—I did know somebody of the same name once, in Paris . . . You sent her to prison for eighteen years, I think. What a shame she hanged herself in her cell before she could begin her punishment.

Of course, of course, we realise the police took all possible precautions . . . silly girl. Shot a banker, didn't she? Or was he an arms-dealer? You didn't get round to hanging him—

(*Turns to door, to greet the imaginary Offalys*)

Ah, good evening Vice-President Offaly, good evening. Mrs Offaly—quite offally restored I trust. Meet Judge Schenker, Mrs Schenker—Judge, Joe Offaly works for the firm that once owned all the bananas in Nicaragua, what a lot of bananas, a lot of the copper in Chile and millions of acres of sugar-cane in Cuba! Isn't that wonderful! I'm sure you and he have a lot to talk about. So why don't you four just get together a while—dinner will be ready in half an hour, so if I could just take your orders: Arty-choke, judge, you'll enjoy tearing the leaves off one by one, dipping them in vinaigrette, biting off the good bits and throwing the rest in the rubbish bin. That sounds like your number. And you, Vice President Offaly? You'll just eat the hearts out. Now—for the main course there's a fricassee of chicken's gizzard in wine and cream, that's the throat bit, torn out, marinated in clam sauce, then scarified in brandy—or there's good old Welsh lamb, four months old, you can just see its dewy eyes looking up at you, hear its little bleat for its mother, see its tail twitch as the chopper cops it . . .

(*She backs off, nodding contentedly, smiling—Becomes the universal tourist hostess:*)

You like Welsh welcome?

You love warm Welsh winking?

Your woman not so sexy? We have ways of Welsh intercourse for the business visitor . . .

You want a warm bosom, a lovely green valley?

You'll want for nothing, in the Wales of the brochure . . .

'Where once ugly pits defiled the countryside, strong men bowl black bowls over close-cut crown greens: They could all be yours, for a very modest sum.'

Ah—so, good. We do things the Nissan way . . .

All the energy and imagination that went into global revolution—it can cook your cannelloni for eight-pounds fifty per night . . .

Ja—Bitteschon. Ve make New Europ, ja?

(*The lights have gone in on her. She looks again at the empty chairs:*)

Judge and Frau Schenker,

Vice President and Mrs Offaly:

I am your servant.

I am your assassin . . .?

(*Noise and lights outside of a car stopping. The doorbell rings. She knows what it means.*)

THE END